The
Yanagita Kunio Guide
to the
Japanese Folk Tale

Copublished with *Asian Folklore Studies*

YANAGITA KUNIO (1875–1962)

The
Yanagita Kunio Guide
to the
Japanese Folk Tale

Translated and Edited
by FANNY HAGIN MAYER

INDIANA UNIVERSITY PRESS
Bloomington

This volume is a translation of *Nihon mukashibanashi meii*, compiled under the supervision of Yanagita Kunio and edited by Nihon Hōsō Kyōkai. Tokyo: Nihon Hōsō Shuppan Kyōkai, 1948.

This book has been produced from camera-ready copy provided by ASIAN FOLKLORE STUDIES, Nanzan University, Nagoya, Japan.

Manufactured in the United States of America

Library of Congress Cataloging-in-Publication Data

Nihon mukashibanashi meii. English.
   The Yanagita Kunio guide to the Japanese folk tale.
   "Translation of Nihon mukashibanashi meii, compiled under the supervision of Yanagita Kunio and edited by Nihon Hōsō Kyōkai."—T.p. verso.
   "This book has been produced from camera-ready copy provided by Asian Folklore Studies, Nanzan University, Nagoya, Japan."—T.p. verso.
   Bibliography: p.
   Includes index.
   1. Tales—Japan—History and criticism.
I. Yanagita, Kunio, 1875–1962. II. Mayer, Fanny Hagin, 1899–
III. Nihon Hōsō Kyōkai. IV. Title.

GR340.N52213   1986   398.2'0952   85-45291
ISBN 0-253-36812-X

1 2 3 4 5 90 89 88 87 86

Contents

PART ONE

Folk Tales in Complete Form

PART TWO

Derived Tales

Preface

This work of Yanagita Kunio (1875-1962), who started the movement to collect folk tales in Japan and led it for more than fifty
years, has been delayed in coming to the attention of Japanologists
and folklore scholars. It is my purpose in bringing out this edition of
the Japanese sage's book, *The Yanagita Kunio Guide to the Japanese
Folk Tale*, to call attention to Yanagita's great work and leadership in
collecting Japanese folk tale treasures and in building up an apparatus
for the study of their priceless cultural legacy. By rendering *The
Yanagita Kunio Guide to the Japanese Folk Tale* into English and edit-
ing this imposing body of 347 folk tale-types and the distribution of
their variants in Japan, I have attempted to bring this corpus into con-
formity with Japanese folk tale scholarship for the use of scholars in
the West. It was called to the attention of Western scholars first by
Naoe Hiroji. In his translated article in 1949, he called it "the largest
accomplishment of Japanese Folklore Science after the war....This
scholarly work sums up the result of thirty years of fairy tale
research."[1]

Yanagita Kunio should be understood as a prominent figure in
modern Japanese intellectual circles in order to give a perspective to
his approach to the folk tales of Japan and the leadership he provided
for collecting and publishing them. Yanagita was born Matsuoka Kunio,
the fourth of seven sons of Matsuoka Misao, a physician and scholar of
Confucian classics. Due to his poor health, Kunio did not continue
beyond the local elementary school. He was sent to his older brother
who was a doctor and then to another who had literary friends. Kunio
read all he could get his hands on in the fields of history, literature,
and Japanese classics. He met prominent literary men and began to try
his hand at writing poetry in his early teens.

When Kunio was nineteen, he passed the entrance examinations to
First Higher School, Tokyo. When he completed his study there, his
brothers pooled their resources to send him to Tokyo Imperial University, from which he graduated in 1900 from the Department of Law,
Division of Political Science. In the following year, he was appointed
to a post in the Ministry of Commerce and Agriculture. In the same
year, he took the name Yanagita when he became engaged to Ko, the
youngest daughter of Yanagita Naohei, a Justice of the Supreme
Court.

Duties in the Ministry of Agriculture took Yanagita to outlying
regions where he could see at first hand the conditions of farmers—
their antiquated tools, their meager incomes, and the poor educational
opportunities for their sons. Although Yanagita belonged to the intellectual elite because of his education and because he was a govern-

ment official, he still had a way of meeting farmers man to man. He sat by their open hearths to exchange views on their problems, to sample their local foods with a relish, and to listen to their dialect and legends. Yanagita established the habit early in his work of taking down detailed notes on what he saw and heard and making entries in his diary. These notes provided the basis for his many lectures and articles.

The young official also had literary talent. He had begun to publish his poems when he was sixteen years old. He belonged to a group of young writers who were interested in current literature both at home and in Europe. He had a good reading command of English and French and could get along with German and Dutch. In 1907 Yanagita helped found the Ibsen Society of Japan. It was his interest in poetry which led him first to the folk tale. He had noticed some poems of Sasaki Kyoseki (later called Sasaki Kizen), who was a student at Waseda University. Yanagita arranged a meeting with him. Sasaki told Yanagita at that time some tales and legends that had been handed down in his family in Tōno. Yanagita was struck by the unmistakable traces of old Japanese beliefs in the tales. He resolved to investigate them further. He took the opportunity when he visited Tōno later to hear more tales. The result was *Tōno monogatari* (Tōno tales), which he published in 1910.[2] Yanagita then encouraged Sasaki to collect other folk tales in his area and made it possible for him to publish them.

Two of Yanagita's friends, Ishii Kendō and Takagi Toshio, then set out to gather tales. Ishii published his *Nippon zenkoku kokumin dōwa* (All-Japan stories for children)[3] in 1911, attributing each story to some old province in the country. Takagi, who was on the staff of the newspaper *Asahi Shinbun*, advertised in it for tales and took time to edit what came in. He published his *Nihon densetsu shū* (Japanese legends)[4] in 1913. Here we see the pattern of Yanagita's ability to enlist others to join his efforts.

Yanagita and Takagi started the journal *Kyōdo kenkyū* (Local studies) in 1912. This publication provided an outlet for information about life in all corners of Japan. Many men with whom Yanagita had made contacts earlier now provided information about folkloristic topics, including folk tales. The journal had to be suspended after four years because the work of the two young editors had changed, but during that interval it had received items from 200 contributors. They lived in Tokyo, Kyoto, Osaka or Hokkaido, and in thirty-eight prefectures, as well as in Korea, China and Formosa.

Yanagita was appointed Chief Secretary to the House of Peers in 1914 and held that position until 1919. He went to Geneva in 1921 with the official group of observers from Japan to the League of Nations, serving in that capacity for nearly two years. When he returned to Japan, he joined the editorial staff of *Asahi Shinbun*. In the meantime, his interest in folklore and folk tales grew. He invited a number of men, including Sasaki Kizen, to contribute to *Rohen sōsho* (Hearth-side series), some forty little books on folklore and folk tales from Hokkaido in the north to the Marianas in the south. By 1930 Yanagita was able to select a representative body of folk tales for publication. His *Nihon no mukashibanashi, jō* (Japanese Folk Tales, Vol.

I)[5] became the standard item in the field for many years, being listed in bibliographies to the present. It was not simplified for children. The second volume contained tales from Korea, the Ainu, the Ryūkyū Islands, and Formosa that had been selected by specialists in those areas.

Yanagita's work on the *Asahi Shinbun* involved extensive travel and lecturing. He finally resigned from it in 1932, at the age of fifty-seven, an age when most men would be looking forward to retirement, in order to devote his full time to his cultural studies in folklore. He raised money for young collectors to go into the field to look for tales, he started publishing houses and journals to publish their findings, wrote introductions for their books, and traveled and lectured to build up interest. Groups began to be formed at schools or in local centers to study their own material, frequently after Yanagita had given a lecture for them. At the *gun*, or county, level, books were compiled to record local industries, government, religious sites, and history, usually devoting space to folk tales and legends that were being preserved. Most of their publications were sent in either manuscript or printed form to Yanagita, and from these he built up his extensive files of notes on tales and legends. Because of his paternal interest, he was in touch with activities in all of his land.

If one examines the years to which source material in this reference work of Yanagita belongs, one can to some extent chart the spread of the movement to collect tales. Yanagita used only six items that had appeared before 1910. There are sixteen sources that appeared in the decade 1910-1919, and fifty-three in the following decade. He drew from 100 sources in the 1930's, after which restrictions and shortages due to World War II brought publishing to a virtual halt.

Sasaki Kizen died in 1933, leaving seven collections of tales and many articles. Among the young men whom Yanagita was encouraging was Seki Keigo, a teacher from Nagasaki. Yanagita had written an introduction for Seki's collection of tales from his native Shimabara. Since Seki showed promise, Yanagita opened opportunities in editorial work to him.

Yanagita was quite capable of writing his introduction to this present work, but a few comments by the translator may be helpful. His use of the chatty "mashita" endings for verbs was proof that he did not intend his essay "About Folk Tales" to be a scholarly presentation to this very important reference work.

Yanagita wrote of the difference between a legend and a folk tale and of Seki's original interest in the legend. When the present work on folk tales was being compiled, Yanagita invited Seki to take the main responsibility in compiling the companion work on Japanese legends.[6] By comparing the main division in that work with those in this work on folk tales, one can see clearly how Japanese regard legends. The titles for the legend's division are "Trees," "Stones and Cliffs," "Water," "Graves," "Hills and Passes," and "Shrines." Legends give brief accounts of what was said to have happened at named places and they are not stories of village life.

Yanagita's story of how he used the little handbook, *Mukashibanashi saishū techō*, when at the hearthside of a farmhouse shows how he was able to establish warm, personal contacts in his travels. Although he expressed doubts about the results of the little book, the titles with only a couple of exceptions have become standard names in new collections as well as in this reference work. The *Mukashibanashi kenkyū* was republished by Iwasaki Bijitsusha in 1980, which shows how highly that effort is regarded today. And Sanseidō republished the *Zenkoku* editions of folk tales in 1973-1974. One can conclude that the steps Yanagita took in guiding efforts to collect folk tales were wise ones.

Yanagita's comments upon approaches to the folk tale were based upon his background in reading and experience. He was aware of the Aarne-Thompson *Types*,[7] but it did not contain oriental material and its comparative approach was different from his. He treated tales as wholes and looked in them for old cultural and religious themes. That does not mean that he was not interested in the similarity between tales in other countries and those in Japan. He wrote before the modern innovations in methodology—the morphological work of Vladamir Propp, the categoriest of Lèvi-Strauss, the motifime-sequence of Alan Dundes. But he probably would not have been impressed had he heard of them.

Yanagita's speculation about the interchange of tales in the distant past now seems to have been warranted by recent etymological studies. The Japanese language is now regarded as a composite with strains from other composite languages. In a lecture to KBS Friends in 1953, Seki Keigo pointed to the similarity of a tale in Japan with that of one told by Altai tribes in the Baikal region of Mongolia, two regions with no historical contact. This is a tale about a bee and a dream of treasure. He said the version told in Niigata Prefecture was closer to the Altaian version than to versions told in other parts of Japan.

Yanagita's hope that his reference work would encourage others to report tales has been well fulfilled by the great volume of new collections which have been published since World War II.[8]

Yanagita received a number of honors for his efforts in the field of folklore in Japan. He received the Asahi Cultural Award in 1941, was made a member of Japan Art Academy in 1947, and he received the Order of Cultural Merit in 1951. Yanagita's authorized collection of writings, *Teihon Yanagita Kunio shū*, numbers thirty-one volumes and five supplemental volumes, each about five hundred pages long. It is estimated that this represents only about sixty percent of his total writings.

The only recognition by Westerners of the activity of collecting and publishing Japanese folk tales before World War II was when Eugen Diederichs sent Fritz Rumpf to Japan in the mid-1930's to make translations of folk tales.[9] Rumpf selected thirty-six items from Yanagita's collection of tales. Cultural exchange was becoming difficult in the West at that time, and scholars in the United States gave Rumpf's and Yanagita's work little attention.

Attempts by Seki Keigo and Hiròko Ikeda to index Japanese folk tales deserve comment. Seki had access to materials in Yanagita's hands, but from the start he was interested in the comparative approach to tales in Europe. He set up his own files according to Aarne-Thompson—"Animal Tales," "Ordinary Tales," and "Jokes," with subtopics which he felt fitted Japanese tradition. He was not hampered by paper shortages when he published his *Nihon mukashibanashi shū-sei*,[10] so he could give a complete rendition of a normative version of a tale for each tale-type. He followed it with entries according to geographical distribution, sources, notes and references as Yanagita had done in his *Guide*, but with more numerous entries.

The only difference, actually, between the presentations of Seki and Yanagita was that Seki numbered tale-types, thus placing it into the category of an index. He numbered tale-types to 671 in the text of his *Shūsei*, but at the end of Part Three, he presented a *kata* (type) index in which he reduced the number of tale-types and changed their order. This resulted in a new number for a tale-type. Seki's work "Types of Japanese Folktales,"[11] reduced the number of tale-types again and made changes in their order, hence a third number for a tale-type. Seki presented themes in this work in the Finnish method of handling variants, adding sources and distribution below. The English work has never been produced in Japanese, and cross-reference to Seki's work is by the numbers in the text of his *Shūsei*. Seki has retained that numbering in his *Nihon mukashibanashi taisei*,[12] but he gives new numbers to newly discovered tale-types. It remains to be seen how they will be utilized in subsequent cross-referencing.

Hiroko Ikeda, a research assistant on Yanagita's staff who could speak English, was sent to the United States to introduce the work of Japanese folklorists to academic circles there. She contributed entries to Stith Thompson, *Motif-Index of Folk Literature*,[13] as her first experience in indexing. Although she relied upon Yanagita's *Guide* and early volumes of Seki's *Shūsei*, she made no reference to them in her entries, and Thompson did not list them in his bibliography. Ikeda's *A Type and Motif Index of Japanese Folk-Literature*[14] was published in 1971. This was her adaptation of the Second Revision of Aarne-Thompson's work[15] to Japanese material. She also employed the Finnish method of treating variants, but with more detailed breakdowns and references to sources than Seki had done. Her work, vexingly enough, gave yet a fourth number to a Japanese tale-type. Her numbering is not used in cross-referencing in Japan.

I have omitted a translation of the official N.H.K. (Japan Broadcasting Association) preface to Yanagita's work because, as usual, such contributions have little scholarly value. Takanao Iwasaburo, whose name appears as the writer, was president of N.H.K. at the time Yanagita's *Guide* was published, but plans for the project had been set up in 1941 when the former president, Komori Shinichirō, was living. In spite of Takano's enthusiasm for the results, his Preface does not give a reliable account of the circumstances. N.H.K. provided a place to do work, furnished materials, and paid Yanagita's assistants who worked upon his files under his supervision. N.H.K. also stored the complete work outside of Tokyo to protect it from bombing and lent the support of its name to the project when restrictions upon publishing by individuals would have made it difficult for Yanagita to complete the undertaking alone.

The folk tale is now a recognized area for research at several universities in Japan. A major project in the field has been the publication of *Nihon mukashibanashi jiten*,[16] a dictionary-encyclopedia that explains terms concerning oral literature as well as titles to the folk tales and their distribution. It also includes names of scholars in the field in the several countries of Europe, Africa, Asia, and the Americas. More than 150 scholars and collectors have contributed to the volume. It shows the extent of interest among modern Japanese not only in their native folk tales, but in the work of scholars in the West.

Japanologists have overlooked the folk tales of Japan, perhaps because the scope of Japanese studies was established before folk tales were being collected in Japan. The entries of Ikeda in Thompson's *Motif-Index* failed to open to Western scholars the great work of Yanagita and deprived them of any idea of the great number of collectors and scholars in Japan and the folk tales which they had made available. Areas in Japanese studies have broadened considerably since World War II. In the last few years Japanese oral literature such as *otogizōshi* and *Nara-ehon*, partly illustrated and partly script, and ballads are being studied. This present volume will open the field of oral literature still further to Western scholars.

History is usually divided into periods of time marked off by records of certain events or great personalities, but cultural history is a continuously flowing stream of human concepts. The contents of tributaries never actually merge into the main trunks of great rivers. They retain their characteristic sediments. In the same way, the strong currents of culture seem to affect changes, but old outlooks and practices are preserved along the margins and in little eddies. These relics of the past, still identifiable in Japanese custom and thought, are what Yanagita looked for in the tales of his land. This handbook will point to such relics of Japan's cultural heritage in folk tales for scholars in the West.

Fanny Hagin Mayer

Footnotes

1. Naoe Hiroji, "Post-war Folklore Research Work in Japan," *Folklore Studies*, VIII (1950), p. 281. The use of the term "fairy tale" for "folk tale" by the translator was unfortunate.
2. Yanagita Kunio, *Tōno monogatari*, Shuseidō, 1910.
3. Ishii Kendō, *Nippon zenkoku kokumin dōwa*, Dōbunkan, 1911. I have retained the old reading "Nippon" for Ishii because it sounds like a challenge, which he intended it to be, to the sugary tales for children that Iwaya Sazanami had put out.
4. Takagi Toshio, *Nihon densetsu shū*. Musashino Shoin, 1913.
5. Yanagita Kunio, *Nihon no mukashibanashi, jō*. Ars, 1930.
6. Yanagita Kunio, supervision, Nihon Hōsō Kyōkai, ed., *Nihon densetsu meii*. Nihon Hōsō Shuppan Kyōkai, 1950.
7. Antti Aarne and Stith Thompson, *The Types of the Folktale*, FFC No. 70. Helsinki, 1928.

8. Fanny Hagin Mayer, "Japan's Folk tale Boom," *The Journal of Japanese Studies*, Vol. 4, No. 1 (Winter 1978), pp. 215-224.
9. Fritz Rumpf, *Japanische Volksmärchen*. Jena: Diederichs, 1938.
10. Seki Keigo, *Nihon mukashibanashi shūsei*. Kadokawa. Part One (one volume), 1950; Part Two (three volumes), 1955; Part Three (two volumes), 1958.
11. Seki Keigo, "Types of Japanese Folktales," *Asian Folklore Studies*, XXV (1966).
12. Seki Keigo, *Nihon mukashibanashi taisei*. Kadokawa, 12 volumes starting in 1978.
13. Stith Thompson, *Motif-Index of Folk Literature* (six volumes). Indiana University Press, 1958.
14. Hiroko Ikeda, *A Type and Motif Index of Japanese Folk-Literature*, FFC No. 209. Helsinki, 1971.
15. Antti Aarne and Stith Thompson, *The Types of the Folktale*, Second Revision, FFC 184. Helsinki, 1961.
16. *Nihon mukashibanashi jiten*. Kōbundō, 1977.

Translator's Notes

The *Yanagita Kunio Guide to the Japanese Folk Tale* may seem at first glance to one who is accustomed to well-defined, clearly presented reference material to be confusion compounded. The brief notes may prove frustrating to one who expects to find a digest of tales. The arrangement is primarily by the title of a tale-type. The geographical distribution of variants listed by prefecture, which follows, is according to Japanese order, from the northeast to the southwest. Most of the names of the prefectures may be readily recognized by those familiar with Japan, but the *gun* within them and frequently lesser units will doubtless be unfamiliar. Some prefectures list more than ten *gun* as having reported folk tales. A reader will get the idea from the geographical designations that he is probing into the corners of the whole of Japan.

What has been going on in those corners of Japan is of more importance. The abbreviated titles of more than two hundred sources of collected tales that follow the geographical designation attest to the fact that folks at those places have now recorded tales which have been handed down for generations among them. These abbreviated titles form the basis for the entries in the Bibliography of Sources (from p. 323), which will open a whole new area of research to Western scholars. The abbreviated title is then followed by the name of the tale as it appears in the source. The English version is not necessarily a literal translation. Titles have never been applied systematically to folk tales in Japan. A title may be one used by the storyteller, one supplied by the collector, or even by the editor of the published version. The diversity in titles confirms the fact that the folk tale is not a standardized product in Japan. It is a living, widely distributed form of oral literature. I have enclosed the Japanese version of titles in parentheses for those who may enjoy the dialect in which some are rendered.

The titles are then followed by notations, which are just that—notes. They were selected from the files of Yanagita Kunio, the great scholar, which had been built up over the years, and not made especially for the *Guide*. In other words, a student must knuckle down and read the source for the complete version of the entry. Many notes are no more than marginalia which can be seen in the books of Yanagita's library, which is now housed in Seijo University.

Some students may be inclined to consult the *Guide* in Japanese, directly, but by doing so they cannot make use of the work I offer as editor. Proof reading of the original work had to be kept to a minimum because of the shortage of paper in Japan when it was published. I was asked by Yanagita and members of his staff to make corrections in the text where I found errors. Because of the same shortage, many titles to stories had to be omitted. I have furnished over 1300 of them after consulting the source material, and at the same time I made uniform pagination, supplying it in many instances. The new Japanese edition of 1971 modernized some characters and brought place names up to date, but it made no corrections. I see no reason to alter administrative geographical names when they are still identifiable. The basis for my rendition of place names is Ikei Kasuka, *Saikin chōsa Nihon bunken chizu awasete chimei sōran* (Osaka, 1937). No period in particular is designated on the map of old provinces which I made. I simply include those mentioned in the text.

I have rounded out some of the notes into simple sentences, but left others alone to preserve the feeling of notes, which they are. I have edited some notes to give direction to those which Yanagita left as questions in light of the facts now available. It is possible that some selections of notes were not suitable and some appear more than once. Yanagita's comments point perhaps to an old version, to a version where episodes have been combined, where the work of a professional storyteller is apparent, or to one depending upon a translation from a foreign source. Yanagita even points to poor versions. A beginner can glean considerable information and sidelights on the tales from Yanagita's jottings. Nearly half of the tale-types have a condensed version of a normative example. Others can be guessed by their titles and notations. The scarcity of notes was due to the fact that only samplings could be used in order to keep the work within a single volume.

Items listed as "further reference" following the entries sometimes will be the least satisfactory to Western students. They are Yanagita's personal notations which he added, and there is no way now to be sure what he had in mind when he made them. It is enough for Japanese to see the notations of this famous scholar, and few would attempt to probe them. I edited a few, particularly the foreign entries. The references open the door to comparative studies within Japanese literature. Although the references, too, are highly selective, they may challenge some student in the West who is looking for a new approach to Japanese studies. Themes belonging to folk tales included in written literature can be recognized only by one who has had access to the folk tales.

My other contribution to this volume is the Bibliography of Sources. It gives the correct transcription of Japanese titles, names of authors, publishers, and the like. Yanagita's library was not cataloged at the time the *Guide* was compiled. His assistants who worked on the project decided to list relevant books which were on the shelves of the N.H.K. library where they did their work. Their list in the volume is not a complete representation of sources. I have noted in the Bibliography the items which have been republished recently and others which are scheduled to be revised and enlarged. The present efforts to make available sources which have been out of print shows how highly the early work of collectors is valued. I have also furnished several indexes and lists for students with specialized interests.

The arrangement of the folk tales was Yanagita's prerogative, of course, but there is some criticism in Japanese circles about his dividing the tales into only two main groups, "Folk Tales in Complete Form" and "Derived Tales." A few think that "Stories about Destiny" should be a separate group, and they are listed as such in many new collections. The question still remains as to what, exactly, Yanagita meant by "Derived Tales." In general, they are shorter and have fewer episodes than stories in the first group. Stories about the origin of animals may have been originally parts of a longer cycle. Yanagita placed the titles of most humorous stories in parentheses because he regarded them as closer to anecdotes than to folk tales in form.

A line placed to the right of titles which Yanagita considered to be important is in the original Table of Contents. They come close in number to the one hundred tales he mentions in "About Folk Tales." The current volume does not mark each such title in the Table of Contents, and I have thus set these titles in italics in the Alphabetical List of Titles as well as the list of Japanese titles in the last part of the volume. Other types are considered related to or close to the titles near them, or to be traces of tales which may yet be found in more complete form. This accounts for several tale-types which appear to be duplications.

Yanagita did not number his tale-types, a necessary step for an index, because he did not intend his work to be an index. He considered it too soon to number tales, for he anticipated that new tale-types would come to light. Cross-reference to the work of Yanagita is by the title of a tale-type. I have numbered his tale-types to facilitate cross-reference to the anthology of complete versions of them, *Ancient Tales in Modern Japan* (Indiana University Press, 1985), which is arranged according to the *Guide*. No significance beyond that should be attached to the numbers in this translation. Students may feel more comfortable with some sort of numbering, but Yanagita's judgment that it was too soon to number Japanese folk tales appears to have been sound in light of the several systems of numbers which have been presented by Seki Keigo and Hiroko Ikeda.

Western students who do research in Japan experience many frustrations. Information is not presented in the assertive style of academic disciplines to which they are accustomed. Open-ended statements which allow for uncertainty are the accepted way of presenting studies in Japan. Japanese scholars have bowed only recently to the Western ritual of footnotes. But foreign students learn to live with circumstances in Japan and to work with them. The notes of Yanagita presented in this work might be considered unique even in Japanese reference material, but the work is nonetheless valid and outstandingly useful. I have relied upon it for more than thirty years of research, translation and writing in the field of the Japanese folk tale. The 3000 items drawn from 200 and more sources will be useful to any scholar.

Acknowledgements

A translation and bibliography of this length could not have been accomplished without the interest and help of many individuals. I cannot express my gratitude now to each and every one to whom I have been indebted during the years since I first undertook this wearying project, but I have given the names below of those scholars who have been so helpful to me.

The first whom I must name is the late Yanagita Kunio, who put a copy of his *Nihon mukashibanashi meii* into my hands in 1952 with the advice that it would be helpful to me in my studies. At the same time, he welcomed me to visit his library to consult sources. Then I must mention Professor Hisamatsu Sen'ichi of Tokyo University, who encouraged me to concentrate upon Japanese folk tales in my study while enrolled in the Graduate Division of Japanese Literature (old system). My preliminary translation of *The Yanagita Guide to the Japanese Folk Tale* was accepted there as my second Progress Report in 1955. Professors Ikeda Kikan and Ichiko Teiji also showed interest in my studies and encouraged me.

Above all I am indebted to the Yanagita Bunko, the collection of Yanagita's library, which was later housed at Seiji University. The National Diet Library not only had rare books and journals, but catalogs of some university and prefectural libraries which opened the way for more search. Of the governmental and prefectural libraries, I consulted Kokuritsu Kokugo Kenkyū Sho and Fukui, Miyagi, Ōita, Okayama, Saitama, and Yamaguchi, and I searched in the city libraries of Fujisawa, Iida, Ina, Isawa, Morioka, and Ueda. The private libraries of K.B.S., Narita San, and Maison Franco-Japanaise were also helpful. The university libraries that permitted me to consult their catalogs and books were those of Ikeda of Osaka Gakugei, Tokyo Gakugei, Keio, Kokugakuin, and Tokyo Universities. In addition to libraries, there were scholars and collectors who were especially helpful. They were Ariga Kizaeomon, Hakoyama Kitarō, Iwaya Taishi, Maruyama Hisako, Moriguchi Tari, and Takeda Akira. They gave me permission to examine texts and were helpful in many ways. I should also mention the countless second hand book dealers who allowed me to browse among their shelves and who, in many instances, directed me to sources.

Without the generous permission of Yanagita, himself, I could not have undertaken this translation. In 1959 he gave me written permission to translate his *Nihon mukashibanashi meii* in any way I considered best. I leaned upon his encouragement over the years, right up to his death. Finally, I must express thanks to Ishiwara Yasuyo, who read my entire manuscript and helped me over difficult spots in the translation. I regret that I was never able to compensate her fully for her services and that she has not lived to see the work published.

Fanny Hagin Mayer

About Folk Tales
by Yanagita Kunio

To those who will make use of this volume I should present briefly some comments about the meaning of the study of folk tales and at the same time offer some words of caution to those who may undertake such study in the future.

The collection of folk tales in Japan has a history of only a little more than thirty years.[1] We could say this is a whole century behind the work of the Grimm brothers. Nevertheless, we cannot regard this delay as altogether unfortunate for several reasons—first, we are glad that Japan is a country that has been able to hand down such old style things until so very recently and then, all the study of the last century will be of use to us as we consider things anew, and will also make it possible through our efforts to present items that might have gone without notice in any other country.

There are any number of examples of Japanese folk tales that have been preserved in writing by chance since the beginning of the medieval period. To begin with, there is the greater part of the *otogi-zōshi*,[2] handed down since the middle of the Ashikaga era, and then, going further back into the past, we find what is called the parent of tales, *Taketori monogatari*.[3] I believe that this *Taketori monogatari* is an embellishment of a folk tale which was being transmitted at that time, and that it was set down by chance and not deliberately hunted out and recorded. Certainly, when I published *Tōno monogatari*[4] in 1910, a few folk tales of the Tōno region were included at the end of it. This was simply because the narrator happened to remember them since his childhood, while to me, who wrote them down, it had never yet occurred to wonder what a thing called a folk tale was. Within the next ten years or so, however, many folk tales in very complete form appeared from here and there in the region, and at present Iwate Prefecture has become unique in the whole land for the number of folk tales which has been recorded there. This was the beginning of a new life for Sasaki Kizen, who had been the first to introduce them.

Even someone like Seki Keigo, who is leading in the study of folk tales today, was at first deeply interested in legends and put all his efforts into publishing them, but I learned upon inquiry that his mother was a narrator of numerous tales. Besides, there had been an old man in his village who recalled many folk tales of unusual form and liked to tell them to people, which made me understand that Seki had been unconsciously influenced by folk tales. On the whole, legends and folk tales have different meanings and follow different courses, but

strangely enough, wherever the one is preserved there is a deep interest in the other. I think that we must consider anew the question of
the relationship between these two forms.

Many interesting facts have come to light as time goes on. It was
found that there were already a few people at scattered places in outlying regions who had a more than ordinary liking for folk tales. Even
though they were not inclined to set them down in writing, such
people in the course of their long lives instructed one or two of what
we might call disciples, and through them the stream of tales continued, and in some instances even grew. One of the pleasant discoveries
was that on Ikinoshima in the west there had been Yoshino Hidemasa,
a scholar who had made very detailed records of geographical
features of the island, and while his name was known to me and
others, we found among his notations there was a surprising number of
folk tales, a great exception in those days. This furnished the circumstance through which Yamaguchi Asatarō came to study folk tales.

I was inclined to think there would be still other such instances.
There was the unusual example of a person who went on a trip to
Mikawa and brought back a little picture book which he happened to
find in a secondhand book store, a book copied by hand, in which ten
tales were presented without a single word of explanation, only
pictures, but it showed that at the time they were drawn people could
recall and enjoy tales by only looking at pictures of them. These facts
made us feel we would not leave matters to chance, and we gradually
set up plans to collect tales all over Japan.

Our first step in undertaking this work was the journal *Tabi to
densetsu*.[5] It published two numbers devoted to folk tales, and from
these we could understand for the first time that throughout the land,
no matter which way we turned, there were little centers where
people were interested in folk tales, and we could not fail to see the
similarity in the tales which they recalled. There were no tales especially of Shikoku, for example, or of Hokuriku. By means of these two
issues of folk tales, our interest was aroused in a country-wide collection of tales. At the same time we realized we should take up the
study of tales according to their standard forms.

To be sure, among the books that gave us hints were some from
abroad that came to hand a few at a time. The detailed classification
of Aarne and Thompson came out later, but there was the work of
Miss Charlotte Sophia Burne,[6] published by the Folk-lore Society of
England, in which she presented seventy-two varieties of forms. Some
of them were not so popular in Japan as in her country, but on the
whole there was a similarity to ours. We were encouraged in our plan
by the fact that if we searched here for tales parallel to ones in distant lands, we could find them. Even now my estimate does not seem
wrong, for excluding some very short humorous tales, there are a few
more here than in England, making it possible to say that there are
around one hundred types of tales in Japan. Beyond that there are
traces of others, but we cannot vouch absolutely for them.

Encouraged by these unexpected circumstances, we set up two
more plans. The first was the publication of *Mukashibanashi saishū
techō*,[7] a guide for collecting tales. It was a comparatively small
piece of work, but one with which I took particular pains. I limited the

number to 100 well-known selections from folk tales and set down a
name for each. Since I thought that if I wrote the example in too
much detail it would be long and get in the way, I kept each down to
the main points. Opposite each I left a blank page for a place to
record newly collected variations. This work became the foundation
for the present *Nihon mukashibanashi meii*.[8] Perhaps it was a bit
pretentious, but in the first part of the *Techō* I explained something
of what a folk tale is and the significance of gathering tales for those
whose interest was still slight. We were assisted financially in this
work by a certain organization, so we distributed all the copies among
friends at no cost, and at present only two or three copies are left on
hand. Unfortunately, the samples in the little book, although given as
briefly as possible, proved to be such interesting reading that, contrary to the original plan, they were kept as personal possessions, and
not a single copy was returned with newly recorded tales. Even if the
books were not returned, nobody is going to deny that those who had
the *Techō* came to like folk tales more.

On nights when I would put up at some remote farmhouse on a
trip, sitting in the peaceful, silent light of the open hearth, I would
take out the *Techō* and begin to read aloud, or to pass it around, and
then I would notice a certain stir among those seated there. Looks
would be exchanged with a laugh, or a story would be begun by somebody who knew one, and suddenly feelings would relax and the atmos-
phere would soften, providing a pleasure we can say is reserved for
students of folklore, not only of folk tales but of other areas as well,
but I cannot say so without sympathizing at the same time with those
who knew tales. We came to learn indirectly that in the lonely farm
and fishing villages, other than festivals and anniversaries there was
only the folk tale for diversion among ordinary people.

Through this study we understood the history belonging to the
mass of common folk, and so as not to confine it to our pleasure
alone, we decided upon a further step, that of publishing the journal
Mukashibanashi kenkyū,[9] making it an activity in which the whole
country could join. This was published in the first year by Hagiwara
Masanori, the editor of *Tabi to densetsu*, with whom we were associated. In the following year it was taken over by a cerain other pub-
lisher, and because it became mixed up with other work of that firm,
it did not continue beyond the second year. There was no material to
print without manuscripts coming from readers, but while it was being
issued, specimens arrived that seemed written only for diversion, fake
tales or invented ones, making selection difficult. While it was being
published, at any rate, we were able to preserve part of the folk tales
that were cherished in the land. But strictly speaking, there are places
a magazine reaches and others it does not, and there were some
people who wanted to utilize ours for other purposes, so a systematic
plan could not be established for collecting the tales. We considered
other ways to collect, had circumstances permitted, but these were all
beset with difficulties. The number of persons who actually knew tales
was limited, and trying to run into a sincere narrator was as difficult
as the blind leading the blind.

For example, the Women's Normal School of Shizuoka was publishing something they called *Shizuoka-ken densetsu mukashibanashi shū*.[10]

If one looked carefully, he could see that the telling of a single tale differed from person to person, and among the women students there were two sisters from Izu and another from Enshū, I think it must have been, who made reports that left deep and vivid impressions. I am sure people like these had mothers or grandmothers living with them who were good story tellers, and it would have been better to have set out promptly to contact them, but we were hindered by various matters, and as times changed and we missed people. I should admit we had not reached the degree of enthusiasm attained by those Grimm brothers. But I felt more and more strongly that things could not go on as they had been, and we began taking some first positive steps.

We sent letters to people who were interested in our work, and through donations from the Keimei-kai, members of our group set out from time to time to do collecting. As a result, several volumes came out from places with which we had had no previous contact, and we gained noteworthy results by going to Sado Island and to Koshikijima. The reason folk tales of Kawagoe were published was that there were active people there. When these tales had been gathered and compared, a single tale showed extraordinary variations according to regions. At the same time, the same tale would exist in places separated by a distance of from five to seven hundred miles, between which there was no reason to think there had been much contact, all of which made our interest even deeper. In order to make this interest in the study of the folk tale more widespread, we took our fourth step, that of publishing *Zenkoku mukashibanashi kiroku*,[11] a series of collections from all over the country. It was just at war time when reading materials were scarce because of the austerities of the period, so we sold more copies than we had expected. By the close of the war we had published thirteen volumes, and it would be well worth it to continue putting them out. Since I still have a considerable amount of material at hand, I feel that this should be carried out speedily.

While engaged in collecting and publishing tales, I became keenly aware that in general they were known to old people, particularly to old women, and I was apprehensive lest when the narrators were gone, the links to the tales would disappear. But the inclination to enjoy folk tales takes root during youth, and I found that young people and those busy with daily duties, the housewives, appreciated the value of tales and were attached to them, although they did not express their feelings in words. However, in present day society there are many things that attract attention, their volume increasing since the war, so that even among those who are naturally gifted, their prewar power to concentrate is disturbed by outside influences—we might also say they lack occasion to recall what is in their memories—and there is a tendency, even a real danger, toward extinction of the tales. But under the severe circumstances of these times it is possible to think there are many whose souls seek peace, and we hope, therefore, that the publication of this volume will serve as a means of rehabilitating our people.

From the general inclination toward the historical approach, an approach which is not necessarily limited to the study of folk tales, emphasis at first was put upon the study of origins. Although folk tales are fiction, they probably were not enjoyed as such in the beginning. The fact that similar tales exist even among very primitive peoples, who have not yet reached the stage where they can create such art, shows that a foundation even older than the human desire to create art is present, and scholars in various countries and from various times have seen this germ in myths. The word "myth" is a term employed by scholars of philosophy and religion, hence we carefully avoid its use. But there are tales which could not have been believed without faith, and since myths were formerly both narrated and listened to by people who believed them, there are students of mythology who look to myths for the origin of folk tales. This may be correct, but it would be difficult to assert with finality that it is true. It would be difficult to prove because religious beliefs have already changed. It is pleasant to search for the old faith of our ancestors in folk tales, but this is a day in which some sort of proof must be the basis for scholarship, and there is a danger in tinkering with study simply as a hobby. It is a problem worth evaluation, but to study the folk tale with only this in mind would be unreliable, and we cannot advise it.

There are, however, still plenty of scholarly pleasures that can be enjoyed. One is the discovery that while making a comparative study of races that outwardly have had no relationship, tales of undeniable unity appear, for among those gathered by the Grimm brothers there are some in exactly the same form as in Japan and some with similar parts. It is estimated by a few that there are as many as fifty such stories. There are those who say that tales such as "The bean, the charcoal and the straw," "The cat and the rat," "The girl without arms," and "The handmill that ground out salt" have been imported, which might be so if it could be proved that the tales arrived after trade began with the "Southern barbarians," but some of them have older histories than that. Furthermore, the tales are found in regions where influence from the new trade was not felt, and their tales cannot be called importations offhand. The stepchild tale we call "Nukabuku, Komebuku" was certainly here before trade with the West.

Also, there are some tales which are said, in spite of the lack of proof, to be of Indian origin, crossing into China and arriving here from there. This is an interesting speculation, but we are still far from being able to conclude it is true. It is unthinkable that anyone who had read the Buddhist writings from beginning to end would have carried their contents to farmers and fishermen here, and even if they employed some tales in their sermons, those which would have been of use to such men were limited in number. Even considering China as an intermediary, it could have happened only around the time Japanese records had begun, and it would be impossible to determine which tales existed previously to that time, and which arrived subsequently.

It is difficult to imagine at this time that a single tale could have existed among peoples who had no natural relationship, but must this necessarily be so? Perhaps in a period not recorded in annals there might have been an exchange across borderlands between peoples, but when we consider the great barrier of language, that theory, too, has many difficult elements. However, the more we compare folk tales the more inclined we are toward the view that there may have been a

point at which exchange existed, and if that were true, we would have
to take a different view of world culture.

Transporting folk tales within a single land itself, was a miracle,
for it would be difficult to convey them actually from the limits of
Ōshū in the east to the islands of Okinawa in the south. Admitting
that people from separated places within the land came into touch
with each other on occasions other than at battles, such communica-
tion did not go beyond hurrying home as soon as the business at hand
was accomplished, and it must be recognized as a striking point in the
culture of the past that brought about such circulation of folk tales
throughout the country. For us who base our opinions upon what is
close by, research into the problem is directed to the consideration of
how tales were transported. It is beyond doubt that zatō,[12] miko,[13]
and itinerant entertainers carried them.

There are two forms in which folk tales have been transmitted,
one of which was carried by foot travelers, and we might say the odor
of these tales can be detected immediately. The other way was in the
form transmitted within the family, a grandfather or grandmother passing them on to a grandchild, and over a long period of years their
character adjusted to the family circle. When we compare the latter
to the former, it is like comparing hand-loomed fabric to that which is
mechanically woven, so great the difference between them has become. In other words, selection has been at work among those who
made use of the tales.

In order to deal with this problem, I am setting up a new scale for
judging tales. For example, a narrator is sensitive to the demands of
the listener, so that when hearers of a folk tale were children, it
became pure and simple, but in the mountains or aboard a craft where
only adult men associated, the tale became correspondingly vulgar, the
wishes of the hearers becoming apparent naturally. Pointing this out I
refer to the aesthetic level of readers, and in the case of folk tales, I
can see how the tales have changed as they have been told. What is
obvious to me as I consider the problem is that we can not say at
random that because the country is the same, it follows that the tale
is uniform.

Within a broader range which includes tales of various countries
and in a narrow range, tales within a single country, tales are modified, and this process, aside from the origin and transmission of the
tale, is an important theme for research. Even in literary circles of
this day authors may seem to pick up plots at random, but the current
that carries them along is the pleasure of their reading public. In like
manner, the development of the folk tale throughout an undetermined
length of time, but we might say for at least a thousand years, must
be recognized as evidence of a cultural level, beside their contents,
that was changing. That is why we intend to record the year and
month when we hear a tale as well as the place and region and the
age of the narrator as we pass it on.

There may be some matters involved which will escape the notice
of readers. If you are inclined to notice points similar to foreign
examples, you might receive a more vivid impression if we called one
of the stories "Cinderella" rather than "Nukabaku, Komebuku," but by
leaving the name used by someone somewhere who recalls it, we hope

to discover how the story turns out. When it came to giving names to tales, there were some stories that resembled ones in Europe, such as "Le Morte Reconnaisance" or "Singing Bones," and the like, so while there was not always a song in the tale, I decided upon "Utai gaikotsu (singing bones)" as a title. "Rat sutra" is a group found in various parts of Japan. However, it is known by that name in only one part of Kyūshū, but it was a good title and I picked it up.

We have said that there are about one hundred tales in Japan, but there may be others yet to be collected. The expectation that holds the greatest attraction for us is that in some corner of the land we can discover a tale which is about to become extinguished and bring it out into the light of the world. We want people who make use of this book to feel like trying to discover a story whose name and form are not included here and to give the editors a little surprise.

We have not reached all the corners of the land. As a by-product of this work, then, we would expect to find a tale somewhere like "Kokōjirō," for example, which is better and more beautifully arranged. Instead of the harsh, gloomy ending of "Urikohime," a version told as "Nishiki Chōja," as lovely as a picture, came from one remote corner of Senhoku in Ugo. If this book were to furnish such an opportunity, the discovery should be the means for folk tales to become more than a subject for scholarly research. They would become once more national treasures.

Yanagita Kunio
October, 1947

FOOTNOTES

The following footnotes have been added by the editor-translator.

1. This estimate was made in 1947.
2. *Otogizōshi* were tales which circulated from the time of Muromachi (1382-1573).
3. *Taketori monogatari* was written in the early 10th century.
4. *Tōno monogatari.* Enlarged edition, Tokyo: Kyōdo Kenkyūsha, 1935.
5. *Tabi to densetsu.* Begun in 1928 and continued through 1943. A total of sixteen volumes was published.
6. Charlotte Sophia Burne, *The Handbook of Folklore, Revised and Enlarged.* London, 1913.
7. *Mukashibanashi saishū techō.* Tokyo: Minkan Denshō-no-Kai, 1936.
8. *Nihon mukashibanashi meii.* Tokyo, 1948.
9. *Mukashibanashi kenkyū*, 1935-1937, two volumes.
10. *Shizuoka-ken densetsu mukashibanashi shū*, Shizuoka Joshi Shihan Gakkō Kyōdo Kenkyūkai, ed. Shizuoka: 1934.

11. *Zenkoku mukashibanashi shū.* Tokyo: Sanseidō, 13 volumes published between 1942 and 1944.
12. *Zatō.* A blind itinerant musician traveling a fixed route and often belonging to a group housed in a temple. *Zatō* told stories and entertained hosts where they were put up.
13. *Miko.* A woman with a special role in folk faith.

PART ONE

Folk Tales
in
Complete Form

1. Propitious Births

1. Momotarō

Once upon a time an old man and an old woman went to view cherry blossoms. While they sat on the ground to rest and eat their lunch, a peach came rolling to the old woman's seat. She picked it up and tucked it into her bosom. She wrapped it in cotton at home and put it into her bed. The peach broke open and a little boy came out. They named him Momonokotarō [Peach Boy] because he was born from a peach. He looked after the house and studied when his parents were working in their garden. While he was studying one day, a crow called from a persimmon tree by the back door that he had brought a letter from Hell. The letter demanded that the best millet dango in Japan be made and brought there. Momonokotarō asked his mother and father to make the dango and he took them to Hell. When he knocked at the gate of Hell, the demons came out and asked to sample the best millet dango in Japan. After they ate the dango they fell asleep drunk. Momonokotarō put the Princess of Hell onto a cart hurriedly and pulled it off. The demons awoke and set out after them on their fire cart, but by then Momonokotarō and the princess were far out at sea where the demons could not follow them.

Momonokotarō and the princess reached home at last. Word about his feat reached the Emperor, who gave him a great reward. Momonokotarō became a chōja and his household prospered.

Iwate, Shiwa-gun

Aomori: Tsugaru k 12. No title. Except that the peach came floating downstream in a box, it is the standard story.

Hachinohe: MK II 2 30, "Rikitarō." The child's name was Kuriko-tanpō [Chestnut Boy]. A chestnut was picked up in the mountains and turned into a baby on the seventh day. The last half of the story has disappeared.

Iwate: Shiwa 28, "Momonokotarō." Example.

Akita, Senhoku-gun: Ugo 39. No title. The boy was called Momonaiko-tarō in this region. He took a pheasant, a monkey, and a dog to attack Onigashima.

Fukushima: Iwaki 1, "Momotarō."

Tokyo, Kitatama-gun: MK II 1 48, "Momotarō." The ending is like "The battle between the monkey and the crab."

Ishikawa: Kaga 105, "A variant of the Momotarō story." (Momotarō no itan). Added to it are "The son-in-law tasks" and "Rikitarō."

Fukui, Sakai-gun: MK I 1 29, "Momotarō." The peach was set upon a mortar. A voice from inside said, "Split me open." Is this a fragment?

Yamanashi, Nishiyatsushiro-gun: Zoku Kai 244, 230, "The revenge of the crabs." (Kani no adauchi) and "Momotarō." The peach came floating downstream in a little case. The first tale says that a persimmon was in the case and its seed was planted. The second turns into "The battle between the monkey and the crab."

Nagano: Chiisagata 147, "Momotarō."

Gifu, Yoshiki-gun: MK II 10 25, "Momotarō."

Shimane, Oki: MK I 7 38, "The girl and the amanjaku" (Ane san to amanjaku). A peach came floating downstream. The last half becomes "Urikohime."

It is interesting because it is midway between "Urikohime" and "Momotarō."

Hiroshima, Asa-gun: Aki 56, "Momotarō." An unusual example. Is this a fragment? It is close to "Monogusatarō," an *otogizōshi*.

Kōchi: TD V 12 66, "Momokuritarō."

Ehime, Kitauwa-gun: MK II 3 35, "Momotarō." The followers who helped destroy the demons were a stone mill, a needle, horse dung, etc.

Fukuoka, Kiku-gun: Fukuoka 177, "Momotarō." This is the same version as is heard in Tokyo. It is probably based on a book version.

Nagasaki: Amakusa min 83. No title. What the old woman took from the river was a beautiful Benta doll. When she put it into the cupboard and left it, it cried in the night. She took it to bed with her. It was a kappa. Gotō 243, "The filial piety of Kurihime" (Kurihime no kōkō). A little girl came out of a chestnut. She wanted a nightingale's egg because her father was ill and she went to get one.

The story is broken for the most part.

Kagoshima, Satsuma-gun: MK I 12 37, "The snake's gratitude" (Hebi no hōon).

2. Rikitarō

A shiftless old man and old woman made a doll from their bodily sweat and grime. They called him Konbitarō. He was a big eater and grew fast. He asked for a 100 kan metal rod to be made and set out with it to learn feats of strength. Along the way he met Midōkoseoi carrying a portable shrine on his back and Ishikotarō, who was splitting stones. He matched strength with them and won. They became his followers. They arrived at a castle town. Although it was daytime, all the doors were closed and there was no sign of anyone. A beautiful girl was weeping alone in the house of what appeared to be the foremost chōja in town. When they asked why she was crying, she said that on the first day of each month a monster came to carry off a young girl. She was crying because it was her turn this time. Konbitarō said he would destroy the monster for her. He hid her in a chest and waited on guard with his two companions.

The monster came at night and swallowed Midōkoseoi and Ishikotarō in a twinkling. When Konbitarō set upon him with his 100 kan rod, he twisted it in the middle. The monster received a mortal wound as they grappled. It blew Midōkoseoi and Ishikotarō from its nostrils and expired. The people of the family were overjoyed. They invited the three young men to remain and marry their daughters. Konbitarō sent for his parents and they all lived a life of ease.

Iwate, Waga-gun

Aomori, Hachinohe: MK II 2 30, "Rikitarō." See entry for "Momotarō."
Iwate, Hienuki-gun: MK I 5 24, "Konbitarō."
    Waga-gun: MK II 3 41, "Konbitarō." Example.
    Esashi-gun: Kikimimi 80, "The three strong men" (Sannin no dairiki).
Ishikawa: Kaga 105, "A variant of the Momotarō story." (Momotarō no itan). See entry for "Momotarō."

Further reference:
Chōsen mintan shū 258.

3. Urikohimeko

Once upon a time there was an old man and an old woman. He went to the mountains to cut wood and she went to the stream to do her washing. One day while the old woman was washing at the stream, a melon came floating down. She picked it up and took it home. When she and her old man opened it a beautiful little girl came out. They called her Urikohime [Melon Maid] and took loving care of her. After she grew bigger, she wove at the loom every day. One year the old couple thought they would take Urikohime to the village shrine festival. They went to town together to buy a sedan chair. Urikohime wove at the loom while they were gone. An amanojaku came along and asked her to open the tightly closed door just a little. Urikohime thoughtlessly opened it just a little. The amanojaku thrust a terrible hand in and opened the door wide with a clatter. Then she came in. She led Uriko out behind the house, took off her clothes, and tied her to a persimmon tree. Then she put on Urikohime's clothes and sat at the loom as though nothing had happened. The old couple returned with the sedan chair they had bought in town. They put who they thought was Urikohime into the chair and set out for the shrine, but the real Urikohime cried out from behind the persimmon tree, "Don't put Urikohime in the chair! Only give the amanojaku a ride." Greatly surprised, the old man cut off the head of the amanojaku and threw it into the millet patch. The stalk of millet is red because of this.

Shimane

Aomori: Tsugaru m 99, "Urikohime and the amanojaku" (Urikohime to amanojaku).

Iwate: Kunohe 482, "Orikohimeko." The beginning is omitted. It starts with the weaving. It is her real mother. The tale is close to "Little Red Riding Hood."

Waga-gun: MK II 3 39, "Urikohimeko." The first part is the usual form. The amanojaku asked Uriko to climb the persimmon tree to pick fruit. She fell into the lake and drowned. The bird calls in this region have a special quality. Kikimimi 368, "Urikohime," No. 2.

Shiwa-gun: Shiwa shū 1, "Urikohimeko." The part where the girl is killed and fed to the old man and old woman is like "Kachi-kachi Yama."

Iwate-gun, Shizukuishi: Kikimimi 370, "Urikohimeko," No. 3.

Shimohei-gun, Iwaizumi: Kikimimi 376, "Urikohimeko," No. 6.

Kamihei-gun: Tōno No. 102. No title. A story about Orikohimeko and a yamahaha.

Yamagata, Kitamurayama-gun: MK II 5 24, "Ohimego." No part about coming out of a melon. While the old couple were gone to dig mountain yams, the amanojaku came and coaxed Ohimego to gather plums. The girl fell from the tree and died. There is a part where birds make it known. It closes with the reason the roots of thatching reed are red. Has the first part been omitted?

Akita, Hiraga-gun: MK II 10 21, "Urihimeko and the amanojaku" (Urihimeko to amanojaku). Two boxes came floating downstream. A melon was in one out of which a little girl came. It is between the stories in Rikuchū and Chūgoku.

Kazuno-gun: Dai-ichi 43, "Urikohimeko." Information about how she was born in missing. The story is rather abbreviated.

Senhoku-gun: Ugo 80, 105. The first is a poem. The second has no title.

Miyagi, Momoo-gun: Kyōdo den 2 123, "Urikohime."

Fukushima, Iwaki-gun: Iwaki 172, "The amanojaku and Urikohime"
(Amanojaku to Urikohime).

Niigata, Minamikanbara-gun: Kamuhara 202, "Amangyaku."

Ishikawa: Kaga 31 ff, "Urihime Kojorō." Two stories with the same
title.

Yamanashi, Nishiyatsushiro-gun: Zoku Kai 231, "Urihime." Urihime wove
for her family with the help of the weaving sparrow and the
weaving worm. The ending is happy and close to the story "Nishiki
Chōja" and it also resembles "The stork wife."

Nagano, Chiisagata-gun: Chiisagata 150, "Urihime"; MK I 1 34 and MK
I 7 30, "Urihime." The Chiisagata versions always end with a
wedding.
Kamiina-gun: Mukashibanashi 100, "Urikohimeko." The amanojaku
ate the girl and got blood on her face. When she washed, her skin
came off.
    No revenge and no return to life.

Gifu, Yoshiki-gun: MK II 10 27, "Urihime." There are four stories, but
none is complete. The last one says that it was a boy called Uri-
tarō.

Hyōgo, Himeji: Dai-ni 50, "Urikohimeko."

Okayama, Mitsu-gun: MK I 9 29, "Urikohimeko." Only the first half of
the story.

Hiroshima, Toyota-gun: Aki 38, "Orihime" No. 1. Also stories from
Kamo-gun, Takata-gun, Yamagata-gun, and Hiroshima City, total-
ling five versions.

Yamaguchi, Abu-gun: Bōchō I 2 18, "Urihime." When the melon was
taken from the stream and cut open, a maid came out of one side
and an amanojaku came from the other.

Shimane, Ōchi-gun: Ōchi 850, "Urihime" (Urihime no hanashi); MK II 9
31, "Urihime."
Oki: MN II 9 31, "Urihime." A girl born from a melon went to
attack Onigashima when she grew up and came back a chōja like
the story of Momotarō. Okinoshima 30, "The amanojaku and Himegimi" (Amanojaku to Himegimi san). See entry for "Momotarō."
Matsue: Nihon den 268, "Millet" (Kibi). Example. Nihon shū, jō 120,
"Urihime."

Tokushima, Miyoshi-gun: MK II 9 30, "Amanojaku." The first part is
entirely omitted. MK II 10 37, "Yurikohime." The maid came from
a mountain lily bulb. The enemy was a baboon.
Mima-gun: Awa Iyayama 72, "Urikohime."

Ehime, Kitauwa-gun: MK II 3 35, "The maid born from a melon" (Uri
kara umareta ohime sama). It is only about a girl who came from a
melon and wove.
    There may have been such a story with no danger to the girl
and a happy ending.

Fukuoka, Munakata-gun: Fukuoka 213, "The maid who wove at a loom"
(Hataori hime). The story develops around the sound of the loom as
the central interest. There is no amanojaku.

Ōita, Hayami-gun: MK I 12 42, "The melon that came floating (Uri ga
nagarete kita hanashi). The beginning is the same as "Urikohime."
Silver came out of melon instead of a girl. A bullfrog and snakes
came out for the old couple next door.

Kitaamabe-gun: MK I 3 40, "Urihime." She was fooled by a gamari-jako.

Nagasaki, Iki: Hōgen V 4 48. Noted. A phrase in the story about a melon which came floating downstream.

Tsushima: TD XII 9 13, "Urihime." Urihime is tied to a tall tree by a spirit.

Kagoshima: Koshiki 96, "Urihime." There are three stories.

Further reference:

Kiyū shōran 9 ge, 69 omote. This may be the earliest written reference.

4. Nishiki Chōja

Akita, Senhoku-gun, Obonai: MK II 2 8. In "Recalling folk tales" (*Mukashibanashi no omoide*) by Fujiwara Ainosuke. This is the story of Urihime with a happy ending. There is no part about her birth. A yamauba came where she was weaving. At the conclusion it tells of the beauty of her weaving as it floated in the stream.

From this we can see that there was formerly a version of the story with a happy ending.

5. Takenoko Dōji

Once upon a time when a cooper's apprentice went to cut bamboo, somebody inside the bamboo asked to be let out. When the apprentice cut the bamboo, a five-inch man called Takenoko Dōji came out. He was 1234 years old. He said he would grant seven wishes to Sankichi in thanks. He made Sankichi a samurai.

Kumamoto, Kuma-gun: MK I 8 37, "Takenoko Dōji." Example.

Kagoshima, Shimokoshiki-gun: MK II 9 20, "Takehime"; Koshiki 101 "Takehime." The same item. A beautiful girl came out of a bamboo which a poor man cut. When she was ten years old, she returned to heaven (no connection with suitors), leaving a red container for rice and a ladle.

This has some connection with "The old bamboo-cutter" story group, and it also reminds us of "The tongue-cut sparrow," in which a little bird is of central interest.

Kagawa: (no source). When a poor man dug up three bamboo sprouts, they thanked him and guided him to a town.

The feudal lord there was looking for bamboo sprouts for his sick daughter.

This is closer to "Singing bones" than to a story about a child.

Further references:

"Taketori-no-okina" *Gwaun nikken roku*, 2 (Second Month, Bunka 4) [1444]. The writer asked a well-versed zatō what the origin was of the phrase "smoke of Fuji," which was used often by poets, and he gave the following reply:

Long ago in the reign of Emperor Tenchi, an old man used to sell bamboo at the foot of Mt. Fuji. People were suspicious and followed him. They learned that he was from Uguisu-mura, a village half way up Mt. Fuji. A beautiful girl was at his house. She had been hatched from an egg in a cormorant's nest and had turned into a little girl. The old man was bringing her up lovingly. People called him Take-tori-no-okina because he was making a living by selling bamboo.

She was promised later to be a consort of the Emperor. She was called Kaguyahime. There are episodes about her going up to heaven and the potion of immortality being burned, and the rest of the story is like "Taketori monogatari."

"Uguisuhime" [Nightingale Princess]. As yet this is not found among legends of oral tradition.

The name Uguisuhime is mentioned in *Koeki zokusetsubon, sei* 3, 40. It is clear that Kaguyahime was Uguisuhime in *Shinetsu jiken shū* (in *Zoku Gunsho ruijū* 17, 154).

Gwaun nikken roku 1. The child came from a nightingale's egg and was called Kaguyahime.

Kaidōki. The Kaguyahime of "Taketori-no-okina" was from a nightingale's egg, and gold came out of green bamboo.

Kokumei fudoki (In *Nihon fuzoku shi, chū*).

Sangoku denki, maki 12 (In *Tōyō kōhi daizen* 151).

Konjaku monogatari, maki 31, No. 33. There is a part about finding gold inside the bamboo, just as in *Kaidōki*.

Shinrin saiyōshō. The story about a hawk and a dog of an old man called Hayashi Mitsukuri.

Ruijū meibutsuko, maki 17.

6. The Ghost that Cared for her Child

A woman came every night around midnight to buy ame at a little candy store in the village. She always put her hand through the door and she bought with the same coin. The owner of the shop thought it strange and followed her. After she went as far as the garden, she turned into a flame which went out beside a grave. The shopkeeper was sure she was a ghost. The next day when he went to look around where the fire had vanished, he found a hole opened in a new grave. He dug and found a baby boy with wide-open eyes sitting by a woman's corpse. The child had been born after the woman had died, and she was taking care of him with the ame she bought each night for him to eat. It is said that the child became a famous priest later.

Shimabara

This could be called a derived tale, one about births underground.

Fukushima, Date-gun, Hobara-machi: Shintatsu 61, "The ghost who had a child" (Komochi yūrei). It is about a woman buried at Tōkōji in Katsurada-mura. It is in the form of a legend.
    Iwaki-gun: Iwaki 2, 100, "How the ghost cared for her child" (Yūrei no kosodate).
Hyōgo, Himeji: Nihon zenkoku 245, "The ame at Shinkōji" (Shinkōji no ame).
    Hikami-gun: TD X 4 70, "The ghost that cared for her child" (Kosodate yūrei).
    Kinosaki-gun: MK II 8 32, "The ghost that cared for her child" (Kosodate yūrei). It is a story about a temple named Yūreizan Tsūgenji. (See Hyōgo-ken minzoku shiryō, No. 17.)
Nagasaki: Shimabara 76, "The ghost that cared for her child" (Kosodate yūrei). Example. (Old) Iki 88, "The woman who came to buy toasted mochi" (Yakimochi kai ni detekuru onna).
Kagoshima, Kikaijima: Shima I 5 72, "A dead woman who gave birth to a child" (Shinin ga ko o sanshita hanashi).
    Koshikijima: Koshiki 109, "The ghost that cared for her child" (Kosodate yūrei).

Further reference:
    Inu chōmon shū (in Tōyō kōhi daizen 629). The birth in the ground is not handled as a folk tale but as a legend. Many take the form of stories of destiny.
    Zoku Minakata zuihitsu 291.

7. The Eagle's Foundling

An eagle carried off a baby that was left in a basket while his mother was gathering mulberry leaves in the mountains. The child was saved and became the head priest of a large temple, and his aged mother met him after a long search.

Aomori, Hachinohe

Aomori, Hachinohe: MK II 2 31, "The child snatched away by an eagle" (Washi ni sarawareta ko). Example. Perhaps it was formerly a katarimomo.
Iwate, Kamihei-gun: Kikimimi 438, "Nagasuda Manko." This has an earlier part.
Niigata, Minamikanbara-gun: Kamuhara 126, Note No. 38. No title. The spider zatō is called Ryōben.
Nagasaki: Shimabara 169, 170, "The eagle's foundling" (Washi no soda-

tego). Both stories with the same title. One is confused. The other has the account of the meeting between mother and son.

Further reference:
At Shinohara, Shinoki-mura, Higashikasugai-gun, Aichi, a legend is told about Lake Kotori and Nishio Michinaga, Lord of Ōgusa Castle.

8. Issun Bōshi

After a childless couple prayed to Kannon, the wife's thumb began to swell. A little boy as small as a bean was born from it. They called him Mamesuke [Bean Boy]. Although they took good care of him, he did not grow. When he was 17 years old, he received permission from his parents to leave for a while. He set out carrying a little parched flour. He got work at a wine merchant's building fires for the vats. Three daughters were at that family, but Mamesuke wanted the middle one, the most beautiful one. When she was asleep one night, he smeared parched flour around her mouth and threw the rest into the river. The next morning he pretended to cry as though his heart were broken because his parched flour was gone. The family began to investigate and finally discovered the flour around the middle girl's mouth. She screamed that she did not remember eating the flour, but she was turned over to Mamesuke, who led her home. The angry girl looked for a chance to kill him on the way, but could not find one. Mamesuke's parents were delighted that he had returned safely with his master's daughter as his bride. They heated the bath, and Mamesuke was the first to get in. He called his bride to help him wash. She thought this was her chance and thrashed the bath water with a broom to stir it. Mamesuke's body burst open with a bang and out stepped a handsome young man. Both the bride and the parents were astonished and delighted. The young couple lived happy after that with the family.

Niigata, Sado

Aomori, Hachinohe: MK II 2 31, "Akutotarō." A child was born from his mother's heel. After he grew up, he took revenge on the yamauba who had eaten his mother. He was probably once called Chiisako [Tiny One].
   Kamikita-gun: Nobechi 48, "Shineko Tanpo." Said to have been a legendary monster.
Iwate, Hienuki-gun: MK II 5 29, "Suneko Tanpoko."
   Shiwa-gun: Shiwa shū 75, "Suneko Tanpako."
Fukushima, Aizu: Hōgen IV 8 105, "Mamechokotarō"; Techō 6, "Mamechokotarō." The story above.
   Iwaki-gun: Iwaki 4, 5, "Donguritarō" [Acorn Boy] and "Issun Bōshi."
Niigata, Sado: MK II 5 37, "Mamesuke"; Sado shū 211, "Mamesuke" (Mamesuke no hanashi). Example. MK II 4 30, "Issun Bōshi."

Minamikanbara-gun: Kamuhara 188, "The mudsnail son" (Tsubu musuko).

Ishikawa: Kaga 138, "Chibitarō."

Gifu, Yoshiki-gun: MK II 10 26, "Yubitarō" [Finger Boy]. He was born in answer to the prayers of a farmer and his wife. He got into the ear of a horse and led it. He was swept from a cowshed and eaten by a cow. People thought it was a bad sign to hear a voice from the cow, and so it was killed, and Yubitarō was found in its stomach. Next, he was eaten by a wild dog. He led the dog to a chicken pen. The master killed the dog because its belly was big.

Caution should be exercised because this seems to be a foreign tale.

Hiroshima, Hiroshima City: Aki 90, "Daizu and the demon" (Daizu to oni). Daizu [Bean Boy] went on an expedition, fought a demon and won treasures. The carpenter next door tried to imitate him but failed.

Aside from the name, this is like "Issun Bōshi."

Saeki-gun, Ōgaki-mura: Geibi 48, "The magic mallet" (Uchide no kozuchi). About Mameichi.

Toyota-gun: Aki 87, "Issun Bōshi."

Tokushima: Awa Iyayama 14, "Issun Bōshi."

Fukuoka, Kurate-gun: Fukuoka 71, "The ill-natured mother" (Shōne waruki haha). A fragment. The ill-natured mother had a baby like a bean. He got a sack of rice and went into the mountains. His parents followed him and saw him walk into the lake with his clogs on and sit on the sack of rice to rest. This may have some connection with the Hiroshima story, "Daizu and the demon."

Saga, Saga-gun: MK II 7 36, "Chinkoman-no-kohiyoro." A baby boy born from a log that floated downstream was named "Chinkoman-no-kohiyoro." He set out to destroy a demon with a needle, a measuring stick and a bowl. He tied the demon to the ceiling and treasures came dropping down. The old neighbor's failure to imitate him is included.

The tale is originally about a puppy and the part about destroying the demon has been inserted into it.

Nagasaki, Kitatakaku-gun: MK II 10 47, "Mametarō"; Hōgen shi 22 53 "Mametarō."

Shimabara: Shimabara 152, "The son-in-law called Issunbō" (Issunbō no muko). A man about the size of a one-shō bottle of sake became the son-in-law of a chōja, conquered Onigashima, brought home a magic mallet, turned into a handsome man, and prospered. The episodes about rice storehouses and burning one's own house go with it.

Ikinoshima: (Old) Iki 179, "Mamegō" (Mamegō no hanashi).

Kagoshima: Koshiki 70, "Issun Bōshi."

Kikaijima: Shima II 461, "Issun Kotarō."

Okierabu: Okinoerabu 227, "Issunbō."

Further reference:

Mukashibanashi kenkyū II 3 21, "Otogizōshi kaisetsu" by Okami Masao. He discusses the tales "Kootoko no sōshi" and "Himeyuri."

Shans at home 3. A Tom Thumb story which resembles "The mudsnail son-in-law" of Iwate.

Yearsley 218. A story about being swallowed by a fish.
Huet 140.
Imamura in *Okayama rekishi chiri*.

9. A Child Bestowed by a God

A child was born to a childless couple who obeyed an oracle and used a small ax as a pillow. One of the child's hands was like an ax. Because he used it to hurt other children in the neighborhood, he was abandoned in the mountains. The ending has been forgotten.

Kagoshima, Kikaijima

Kagoshima, Kikaijima: Shima I 5 72, "The child bestowed by a god" (Mōshigo banashi). Example. This story is related to the story of Ryūkichi. (See "The snake son".)

Further reference:
Riyō shū 563. The poem about the chōja dance of Awanonaka-gun.

2. The Lives of
Unusual Children

10. The Snake Son

A childless couple picked up a snake in the hills and brought it home. They named it Shidoko and took good care of it. The snake grew to be six feet long and as big around as a thick bamboo pole. The villagers asked the old couple to abandon Shidoko because they were afraid he would harm their children. The couple called him and explained. He shed tears of blood as he went far back into the hills. The old couple followed him. They saw him dig into the ground in a rice paddy. When they went again the next day, there was a big pond there. Such beautiful flowers bloomed around it in the spring that the villagers took their lunches and went to enjoy the view.

Later, the chōja's daughter missed her footing and fell into the pond. Villagers who were there for sightseeing milled around in excitement, but could not rescue her. They were astonished to see Shidoko appear on the surface of the water with the girl in his mouth. She began to breathe again immediately. The chōja offered gifts of thanks to Shidoko and took the old couple into his home to live. Shidoko went off somewhere happy.

Kumamoto, Kamoto-gun

Iwate: Shiwa 142, "The snake son" (Hebi no musuko). The snake was in the sedge hat when they returned to their garden. It is more of a story about marrying the chōja's daughter than one of unusual growth. There is a dialogue between the old man and each of his three daughters.

Fukushima, Iwaki-gun: Iwaki 3, "The snake son" (Hebi musuko). When the old couple went to cut grass, they picked up an egg from which a snake hatched. They named it Haru and cared for it lovingly. The snake had to be abandoned in the hills because the villagers disliked it. The rest of the story is broken up.

Yamanashi, Nishiyatsushiro-gun: Kai 1 13, "The snake son" (Hebi musuko). The story of Ryūkichi without his wanting a bride.

Shizuoka, Kamo-gun, Chikuma-mura: Shizuoka 438, "The snake egg" (Hebi no tamago). A snake hatched from an egg that an old woman picked up at the foot of a mountain. It hurt people after she turned it loose in the mountains. The villagers gathered for a snake hunt. The snake appeared small for the old woman so she could kill it. Then its corpse grew larger and larger to let her get the reward.

Perhaps this is one of the stories about unusual children growing up.

Tagata-gun, Nakazato-mura: Shizuoka 439, "The snake son" (Hebi musuko).

Yamaguchi, Suō Ōshima: TD VI 6 64, "Ichi." A snake hatched from an egg that was picked up on the grounds of Myōjin's shrine. It had a mark like the character for ichi [one] on its head. It was disliked by the villagers after it grew and it had to be abandoned in the hills. Ichi set out to destroy a monster in response to a big sign posted by the feudal lord. The creature itself turned into a snake. They were both mortally wounded as in the tale "Jūsan Tōge."

Kumamoto, Kamoto-gun: MK II 8 41, "Shidoko." Example. The rescue of the chōja's daughter suggests a trace of a son-in-law episode.

Kagoshima, Satsuma-gun: MK I 12 37, "The snake's gratitude" (Hebi hōon) by Saigō Shinji.

Koshikijima: Koshiki 154, "Sudō coins" (Sudō zen). Two stories.

11. Mudsnail Chōja

While an old couple were pulling weeds in their rice paddy, they heard a voice asking them to make him their son. It came from a mudsnail. The next day he had them saddle their horse. He mounted it and rode to a great house. He annoyed everyone by climbing onto the wooden ledge around the hearth and splashing boiling water and scattering ashes. He finally got the daughter of the family as his bride and took her home on the horse with him. The old couple was delighted, but the girl hated the mudsnail so much she couldn't stand it. He told her that if she hated him that much, she should take him to the stone courtyard where straw was crushed and crush him. When she did as he said, he turned into a handsome youth. They lived together very happy after that.

Aomori, Gonohe-machi

Aomori, Sannohe-gun: Tekkiri 112, "Mudsnail Chōja" (Tanishi Chōja). Example.

Iwate: Kikimimi 10, "Mudsnail Chōja" (Tanishi Chōja).
Waga-gun: Dōbutsu.* The beginning and the end are like the Kikimimi version. These must be called two ways of telling the same tale.

Akita, Hiraga-gun: MK II 8 30, "The mudsnail and the girl" (Tsubu to musume). There is no part about a child bestowed by a god. It begins with the call upon the chōja. He got the third daughter. He went into the sea and brought up a mallet of long life. He told the girl to shake it to turn him into a fine youth.
Senhoku-gun: Ugo 135. No title.

Miyagi, Momoo-gun: Kyōdo den 2 122, "The mudsnail son-in-law" (Tanishi muko dono).

Niigata, Minamikanbara-gun: MK I 3 30, "The mudsnail daughter" (Tanishi musume). The plot is the same, but the story is about a girl. Kamuhara 188, "The mudsnail son" (Tsubu musuko).

Hiroshima, Takata-gun: Geibi 1, "The mudsnail son" (Tsubu musuko).

Okayama: Okayama rekishi II 2 13, "The mudsnail son-in-law" (Tanishi muko dono).

Nagasaki: Shimabara 143, "The mudsnail son-in-law" (Tamina muko dono). The way of getting the bride is the same as in the Tōhoku story. There are episodes of an attack on Onigashima, the power of the needle, a boat made of reeds, and a magic mallet. He burned a village and shook out another with his mallet. With this there is the story of the neighbor and the rice storehouse.
Kitataku-gun: MK II 10 45, "The mudsnail" (Tanishi).

Further reference:
Mukashibanashi kenkyū I 9 17, "Nisshi mintan no hikaku." About Chinese tales.

12. The Frog Son-in-Law

The story parallels that of the mudsnail except that the main character is a frog.

Ōita, Hayami-gun: MK I 12 39, "The frog who took a bride" (Kaeru no yome morai). This is probably a fragment.

Nagasaki: Shimabara 148, "The frog son-in-law," (Kaeru no muko).

Kagoshima, Amami Ōshima: TD I 7 73, "The frog child" (Kaeru no ko).
Koshikijima: Koshiki 74, "The frog son" (Kaeru musuko).

---

* Items marked with an asterisk (*) have not been available for checking by the translator.

13. The Snail Son-in-Law

Shimane, Mino-gun, Hikimi-mura: Minzoku bun II 7, "The mudsnail son"
(Tanishi musuko). A snail was petted by an old couple. He received
a grain of rice and went to get the daughter of a chōja for his
bride. It resembles "Mudsnail Chōja" in this.

The girl gave him a needle. He annoyed demons who were
wrestling and stuck the needle into the nose of one of them. He
pricked the demon and got a magic mallet from him. The snail
asked the girl to use the mallet to change him into a youth six
feet tall. They shook out a house with the mallet and lived happy
together.

3. Unpromising Marriages that Became Happy

14. Netarō, the Lazy Man Next Door

Jinshirō lived on nothing but turnips. He got the daughter of Asahi Chōja as his bride with the help of the young men of the village. When the girl came to see, she found that he had only a little hut and no rice. Three times she gave him a bolt of silk to take to town to sell, but he was robbed twice. When he started home with the money the third time, he bought a lame hawk from children who were teasing it. He set it free and it dove into the river and caught a kappa. The kappa gave Jinshirō a magic mallet and magic bag because he set him free. Jinshirō thought the bag would be handy for turnips and took it home, but he left the magic mallet behind. His bride went for the mallet and started by shaking out a house. When Jinshirō tried to shake out a storehouse for rice (kome-kura) and rice, he failed and shook out a lot of blind children (ko-mekura) instead. His bride helped him to do it right. They invited her father to their home. After the feast, they threw the dishes they had used into the stream and burned their house to light his way home. When the chōja returned their invitation, he tried to imitate his son-in-law, but he could not set up another house after he burned it. Jinshirō shook out a new one for him.

Aomori, Hachinohe

Aomori, Hachinohe: MK II 2 31, "Kabuyaki Jinshirō." Example. There are four stories, but this is from a slightly different line than the

Sannohe "Kabuyaki Sasajirō." Although it is slightly complicated, it can be considered the pure form. Its connection to "Charcoal-maker Chōja" can be seen.

"Kaba-o-chōja." A man named Kaba married the younger of the chōja's two daughters. He became rich suddenly because money came from the roots of the turnips in his garden. The word kaba may be related to kabu (turnip), but it is not explained.

"Takoya Kyūbei." This is told as the origin of Chōjayama in Hachinohe. A man called Takoya Kyūbei lived in a vacant temple and ate nothing but octopus. Word of this spread around and, just as he hoped, the chōja's daughter came to be his bride. The store-house of the temple, which was said to be haunted, turned out to be full of money. He promptly became a chōja, too.

"Isaba-no Takozaemon." Isaba-no-Takozaemon from Osaka mar-ried the daughter of a rich Edo family. They received a haunted house to live in. Through his wife's cleverness, he learned that the ghosts in the twelve storehouses were big gold coins. He dug them out and became a chōja.

Sannohe-gun, Korekawa-mura: TD II 10 17, "Kabuyaki Chōja."

Iwate, Kamihei-gun: Kikimimi 3, "The pigeon lantern" (Hato chōchin). The plot is shortened.

Esashi-gun: Esashi 50, "How a lazy man became the son-in-law of a chōja by the help of his friends" (Namakemono ga hōbai no okage de chōja no muko dono to natta hanashi).

Akita, Senhoku-gun: Kyōdo den 2 133, "Lazy Tarō" (Nebō Tarō). This is not a story about becoming a son-in-law. A man who liked to draw cats stopped at a vacant temple. He drew many pictures of cats and destroyed ghosts there. He became head of the temple.

Toyama, Toyama City: MK II 6 29, "The lazy man" (Namakura ansa).

Tochigi, Haga-gun: Shimotsuke 22, "The lazy man" (Namakemono).

Yamanashi, Nishiyatsushiro-gun: Zoku Kai 182, "Just eating and sleep-ing" (Kutcha ne).

Gifu, Yoshiki-gun: Hidabito IV 4 40, "The lame son-in-law" (Chinba no muko). It resembles Ujishūi monogatari, No. 113. Hidabito V 3 24, "The cat's gratitude" (Neko no hōon). This resembles the tale on Suō Ōshima. Hidabito V 6 5, "The lazy son-in-law" (Netarō muko-iri). A bald-headed woman lied to get married. She climbed to the roof to say she was bald because the wedding was held on the night of Kōshin.

Hyōgo, Hikami-gun:: TD X 4 71, "The lazy man next door" (Tonari no Netarō).

Hiroshima, Jinseki-gun: Geibi 3, "The lazy man next door" (Tonari no Netarō).
This is about Sannen-Sangatsu-no-Tarō.

Hiba-gun: Geibi 4, "The lazy man next door." No. 2, (Tonari no Netarō).

Takata-gun: Aki 58, "Netarō Sansuke"; MK I 6 46, "The Kōnoike tale" No. 2 (Kōnoike no hanashi no ni). This has been changed into a humorous story of a beggar's dream.

Yamaguchi: Suō Ōshima 92, "Netarō." This story of the bald bride is close to the Ujishūi monogatari story.

Ehime, Nuwajima: (no source). A poor fisher named Takoya Sōbei met a girl from the Kōnoike family while on his way to visit the Grand Shrine of Ise. He was able to marry her by telling a lie.

Tokushima, Miyoshi-gun: Hokuto 31, App. 8 "Netarō."
Mima-gun: Awa Iyayama 128, "The lazy man who married" (Netarō mukoiri).

Nagasaki: Shimabara 195, "The pigeon god" (Hato no kami sama). This is not a story about marriage, but about a priest and his novice. The boy objected to his diet of cypress leaf soup.

Kagoshima, Kikaijima: MK I 6 23, "Netarō who was lazy for three years" (Sannen Netarō). Three stories have the same title. The first resembles "Sanpachi, the bath heater." A youth called Nananabe-no-shiki heated seven pans of water. He set aside a little from each, bathed in it, and became a handsome youth. He offered a wine cup to the daughter of the house and was accepted as son-in-law. In the second story, the man became yard sweeper for a chōja. When he was sent to pick flowers, he always brought such strange ones that he was followed. He was seen climbing a tall tree and talking to a god. The chōja decided he was not an ordinary man and took him as his son-in-law. The third story resembles "Yuriwaka." His son recognized him.

15. The Cow Bride

A young girl who offered prayers for a good husband was fooled, but a feudal lord took her out of her sedan chair on the way to her wedding. He substituted a calf. It came out in the parlor and rushed around where the young man was waiting.

Kikaijima

Aomori, Hachinohe: MK II 2 33, "A cow in the bride's chair" (Yome no koshi ni ushi).

Yamanashi, Nishiyatsushiro-gun: Kai 51, "A cow from out of the dark" (Kuragi kara ushi de gozaru). The last part turns into a humorous tale.

Kagoshima, Kikaijima: Kikai 52, "The calf in the bride's sedan chair" (Yome no kago ni koushi). Example. It is hard to account for the agreement in the tales. The steps are obscure.

Further reference:
Mukashibanashi kenkyū I 8 16, "The connection with the whispering bamboo" by Okami Masao.
Zōdan shū V 4 *omote*. Of the Kaei era [1849]. It is related to the story "Sasayaki take."

16. Shirataki of Yamada

A certain rich man had twelve beautiful daughters. A young man who worked for him set his heart upon Shiratakihime. The master heard about it. He called the young man to him one day and said he would give him Shirataki if he composed a suitable poem. The young man said:

Rice shoots wither in the drought;
Refresh them with water that falls from Shirataki.

He won her.

Niigata, Minamikanbara-gun

Aomori, Hachinohe: MK II 2 33, "Shirataki of Yamada" (Yamada Shira-taki). Three young men came to ask for her.
Iwate, Shiwa-gun: Shiwa shū 51, "Itonaga Shōji of Harima-no-kuni" (Harima-no-kuni no Itonaga Shōji).
Hienuki-gun, Hanamaki: Dai-ni 80, "The successful suitor" (Shusse muko). It is about three employees of a sake merchant. After a dialogue with them with poems, one was finally chosen as son-in-law. The common name Mokuzō was probably not known yet in the place.
Hienuki-gun, Yazawa-mura: MK II 5 32, "Gomogu, the son-in-law who was a poet" (Gomogu uta muko). The youth's name was Gomogu. It is influenced by a folk song.
Waga-gun: MK II 5 31, "The son-in-law who composed a poem" (Utayomi muko). The girl's name was Sakura. The young man with learning was Gomogu. Three servants are not there. The girl married him after the exchange of poems.
Miyagi, Momoo-gun: Kyōdo den 1 179, "The three letter carriers" (Sannin no kaifu mochi). The girl's poem shows that this story is the work of a zatō.
Niigata, Sado: MK II 4 31, "Shirataki of Yamada and Gorō, the char-coal-maker" (Yamada Shirataki, sumiyaki Gorō). A charcoal-maker called Sumiya-no-Gorō was taught a poem by a rokubu. He recited it and won the girl. What follows is like "Charcoal-maker Chōja."
Minamikanbara-gun: Kamuhara 152, 160, "Shiratakihime." Example. "Beneath Mokuzu" (Mokuzu no shita). A fragment. MK I 3 32, "Sarujirō." The first part of the story is about an abused stepchild. He was rescued and got work sweeping the yard of a chōja. He composed a poem and became the son-in-law there.
  These two episodes did not combine naturally, but should be considered the work of a goze.
Nagano, Shimoina-gun: Mukashibanashi 114, "Kinoha and Sakuhana" (Kinoha to Sakuhana no hanashi).
Hyōgo, Kasai-gun, Shimozato-mura: TD III 7 70, "Gensaemon of Yamada" (Yamada no Gensaemon).
Hiroshima: Geibi 163, "Shirataki of Yamada" No. 1 (Yamada Shirataki).
Tokushima: Awa Iyayama 31, "The son-in-law who composed poems"

(Utayomi muko); MK I 5 361, "Sakuhana and Gomoku" (Sakuhana to Gomoku). Usually there is an exchange of poems, but here they are in the form of a renga.

Nagasaki, Shimabara hantō: Shimabara 187, "The tasks of the son-in-law" (Nandai muko). There are six tales.

Ikinoshima: (Old) Iki 66, "Getting a bride by exchanging poems" (Utamondō de yome o morau hanashi).

Kagoshima: Koshiki 102, "Shirataki of Yamada" (Yamada Shirataki).

17. The Tasks of the Son-in-Law

Long ago the daughter of a chōja and a young man met at Arima hot springs in Settsu and immediately became very fond of each other. Finally, the girl had to go home, but both of them refused to tell their names or where they lived. The girl wrote a poem as she parted from the young man:

If you long for me, ask the insect that sings in the summer for botamochi [rice-cake].
At the bridge that never decays in the Land of Seventeen.

While the young man walked around town thinking about the lines, he met a blind masseur and asked him their meaning. The masseur said the "Land of Seventeen" meant young land or Wakasa, the bridge that never decays would be a stone bridge, and by it there was a family called Semiya [cicada] whose daughter was named Ohagi [ricecake]. The young man took off immediately to see and found that Semiya was a great chōja. He got work there as bath heater, but the girl was already promised to another man. The young man had to help carry the bride's sedan chair on her wedding day. She caught sight of him along the way and suddenly became ill. She had to be taken home and put to bed. A fortune teller was called. He said that all the men at the house should write something to show her. The young man wrote the love riddle. When the girl saw it, she lifted her head and smiled. Everybody understood then, and the young couple was given a splendid wedding.

Yamanashi

Aomori: Tsugaru m 4, "One bundle of straw turned into twenty" (Ippa no wara o nijuppa shita hanashi). The young man was chosen because he could solve the riddle. It turns into a story of cleverness.

Iwate, Shiwa-gun: Shiwa shū 32, 51, "A drum that sounded without being struck" (Utan taiko ni naru taiko), and "Itonaga Shōji of Harima-no-kuni" (Harima-no-kuni Itonaga Shōji).

Kamihei-gun: Rōō 146, "The bride who ate men" (Hitokui hanayome).

Hienuki-gun, Yazawa-mura: MK II 5 32, "The girl who ate a baby" (Bokkokui aneko). There were three young men. One was no better than the others at work. The third was not frightened when he saw the girl pull a doll made of mochi from a coffin made of white wood and eat it. He was chosen as son-in-law. The story is well told and may be in its old form.

Isawa-gun, Mizusawa-mura: Kikimimi 64, "The help of a bee" (Hachi no okage). A tall sign was set up announcing a husband was to be chosen for one of three daughters. The person selected would have to destroy a demon, earn 1000 ryō from a single straw, and count the bamboo in a Chinese bamboo grove. In the end, a bee showed the man which of the three girls was to be his bride.

Akita, Senhoku-gun: Kikimimi 62, "The son-in-law helped by a bee" (Hachi muko). The story of a bee's gratitude.

Yamagata, Kitamurayama-gun: MK II 6 40, "The tasks of the son-in-law" (Nandai muko). About the only daughter of a chōja and three suitors. They had to guess what was in a rice bag and to stop a log that was rolling downhill. Instructions for both trials were given through a nursery song.

Niigata, Minamikanbara-gun: Kamuhara 49, 186, 161, "One bundle of straw" (Ichiwa no wara); "The mountain where old women were abandoned" (Ubasute yama). An old woman solved the feudal lord's riddle and saved the beautiful bride for her son. Note No. 53.

Ishikawa, Enuma-gun: Kaga 137, 105, 100, 92, "The bride and Dōmo" (Yome to Dōmo); "A variant of the Momotarō story" (Momotarō no itan). This story is in the usual form. Momotarō was given many riddles by the chief of the land: the drum that sounds by itself, the sandals of ash, the demon's fang, etc. Along with these, he went to Onigashima. It turns into a story of cleverness. "Dōmo Kōmo" is a story about a priest and his novice. "Eight to, five shō" is a clumsy version, but the plot can be recognized. A child shows how to do tasks.

Nagano, Chiisagata-gun: Chiisagata 190, "Come when you're through" (Mattara koyō). This turns into "The three charms." He received help from a bee.

Yamanashi, Nishiyatsushiro-gun: Kai 78, "Hide your face and blow an ohiyaraka" (Ohiyaraka o fuite kao kakushi). It belongs to "The tasks of the son-in-law," but it is a derived tale. It is about a mean old woman and a man. Zoku Kai 197, 342, "The riddle poem" (Nazo no uta). Example. "The bee's drum" No. 2 (Hachi taiko). A story about a novice.

Kanagawa, Tsukui-gun: Dai-ichi 44, "The tasks of the son-in-law" (Nandai muko). Three stories. The first two have tasks and the third is like "Itonaga Shōji."

Aichi, Minamishidara-gun: Dai-ichi 61, "Itonaga of Harima" (Harima no Itonaga) and "If you want to see me" (Koishiku ba).

Gifu, Yoshiki-gun: Hidabito V 6 9, "The tasks of the son-in-law" No. 4 (Nandai muko). Seven stories; Hidabito IV 3 38, "The bee's gratitude" (Hachi no ongaeshi).

Hyōgo, Hikami-gun: TD X 4 72 "The trials of the son-in-law" (Nandai muko). About Egawa Magozaemon. It is like "Shirataki of Yamada." Three servants wanted to marry the girl.

Shimane, Ōchi-gun: MK II 8 46, "The tasks of the son-in-law" (Nandai muko). He won by his ability to write ten characters. A new style.

Okayama, Yakake: Dai-ni 81, "One mountain in nine" (Kokonotsu yama no hitotsu yama). From the poem "If you want to see me" to an explanation by a zatō and then to the story about the bath heater and then the story about selecting a son-in-law.

Yamaguchi, Suō Ōshima: Dai-ni 81, "Looking for a son-in-law" (Muko sagashi).

Tokushima: Awa Iyayama 92, "The tasks of the son-in-law" (Nandai muko). There is the poem "If you want to see me," but it is more of the bath heater story.

Miyoshi-gun: MK II 10 39, "The turtle's and bee's gratitude" (Kame to hachi no hōon dan). A complicated story about animal gratitude. The principal character is a drifter, but he saved the lives of a turtle and a bee. The turtle told him what medicine to take to the sick wife at a rich family, and the bee told him which of the maids was to be his wife. The latter part of the tale is the old form.

Ōita, Kitaamabe-gun: MK I 4 39, "The drum that sounds without being struck" (Utan taiko no naru taiko). It is changed into a humorous story about a priest and his novice.

Hayami-gun: MK II 1 44, "The priest and his novice" (Oshō to kozō). This is in the form of a humorous tale like the one above. MK I 12 43, "The tasks of the feudal lord" (Tonosama no nandai). This is like the latter part of "The wife from the Sky World" and can be considered a fragment.

Hayami-gun, Kizuki-machi: MK I 12 40, "A bee, a monkey, and a turtle" (Hachi to saru to kame). He became the son-in-law with the help of the three animals.

Kumamoto, Amakusa: Kyōdo ken V 4 46, "Three loads of stories" (Sanka no hanashi). The father said he would choose as son-in-law the man who could tell three wagon-loads of stories. It belongs to the category of endless stories.

Nagasaki: (Old) Iki 90, "Three tasks" (Mittsu no nandai). The tasks were set by a feudal lord for a mother and her child.

Kagoshima, Koshikijima: MK II 9 25, "The tasks of the son-in-law" (Nandai muko); Koshiki 26, "Comparing strong points" (Meijin kurabe). A sign was set up announcing that a man with talent would be chosen as son-in-law. A farmer was chosen. Besides this tale, there are three about hunting for a girl painted on a fan, two like Itonaga of Harima, and one where a man became a chōja by the help of a mosquito, a turtle, and a monkey that he had saved in their difficulties.

Kikaijima: Shima II 447, "Itonaga of Harima" (Harima no Itonaga); Dai-ni 46, "The child bestowed by a god" (Kami sama no mōshigo). The hero here is a child bestowed by a god. He heard the important story from a beggar while he was on a journey in search of a wife. He became the son-in-law of a feudal lord after various tasks.

Amami Ōshima: MK II 4 24, "The elder sister a demon" (Oni no ane). A mosquito which he had saved told him the number of grains in the storehouse.

Further reference:

Hasedera reigenki, ge 30, Minamoto Masmoto, an officer of Ōmi-no-kuni, met trials from the governor. He wrestled at Hasedera in Shinshū. This should be an oral tale.

Konjaku monogatari, maki 16, No. 15. In "Taketori-no-okina" a drum sounds without being struck.

Chōsen mintan shū 28. The beginning is like "The ungrateful man." The rescuers were a mosquito and a moth.

18. The Wife from the Sky World

Long ago a man who sold clay parching pans was walking in the mountains on the sixth day of the seventh month. He saw three maidens bathing and stole the robe of one of them. On his way home he found one of them crying. He took her home and married her. A child was born. While she was nursing her three-year-old child one day, she happened to notice a package wrapped in black paper and tucked into the rafters. She looked inside the package and found her lost robe. She realized for the first time that it had been stolen. She put it on hurriedly and held her child under one arm as she got ready to ride away on a cloud from behind the house. Her husband returned just then. She said she was Tanabata. If he wanted to see her, he should make 1000 pairs of straw sandals and climb up them to her. She went to the sky after she gave him these instructions. The husband set out with his whole heart to make the straw sandals, but when he finished the 999th pair, he could wait no longer. He went out his front door and saw a white cloud that had come to meet him. He went so high he could almost touch the Sky with his hands, but he could go no farther. His wife was weaving upstairs and noticed him. She felt sorry for him and reached out with the rod which she used for sending the shuttle back and forth and pulled him up. She presented him to her parents, but they hated him and made him do all sorts of hard tasks. His wife's cleverness helped him do them all. It was forbidden to eat melons in heaven, but his in-laws urged him so much that he did at last. When he bit into the melon, so much water flowed from it that he was about to be swept away. His wife called to him that she would meet him every month, but he was hard of hearing and thought she said once a year as he floated away. That is why the Tanabata [Vega and Alstair] meet only once a year.

Kagawa, Mitoyo-gun, Shishijima

Aomori: Tsugaru m 9, "The bean vine that reached the sky" (Ten sa nobita mame no hanashi).
   Hachinohe: MK II 2 34, "The most skillful flutist in three kingdoms" (Sangoku ichi no fue jōzu). The bride was the daughter of the Moon. The latter half is an adventure tale.
Iwate: Shima 186, 106, "The girl from the Sky and the youth" (Ten no ohime sama to wakamono) and "The feudal lord who sold peaches"

(Momouri tonosama)., The garment was hidden, but the story changes into "The wife's picture."

Kamihei-gun: Rōō 327, "Tohei, the flute player" (Fuefuki Tōhei). The wife wove a mandala. The tasks of the feudal lord were 1000 bundles of ash rope, getting a drum, and the Thunder God. Kikimimi 39, "The wife from the Sky World" (Tennin go). The form is close to a legend. It was originally a folk tale which has been made into a story about the foundation of Kōmyōji. It has been handed down in the family of the head of Hayachinezan Shrine.

Akita, Hiraga-gun: MK II 10 23, "The story about a man" (Ani no hanashi). It is close to the humorous tale about the cucumber in the Sky.

Fukushima: Iwaki 6, 102, "How the woman from the Sky was made the wife of an honest man" (Tennin ga shōjiki otoko no nyōbo to natte ita hanashi).

Niigata, Minamikanbara-gun: MK II 1 34, "The flute player" (Fuefuki otoko). A bride came from the Sky World to a skillful flute player. The feudal lord gave him tasks. The wife was carried away by the feudal lord and brought back, etc.

Sado: Sado shū 52, 65, "The beginning of Tanabata" (Tanabata no hajime) and "Waiting up for the 22nd Night" (Nijūniya machi no hanashi). The first story has many embellishments. It is the work of a professional story teller. The second story is an abbreviation, but the man was taken as son-in-law in the Sky World. He received a hen which laid golden eggs as a gift from his father-in-law. The deity waited for on the 22nd Night is called Ama Otome.

Nagano, Chiisagata-gun: Chiisagata 210, "Dōmo, Kōmo."

Kamiina-gun: Ono 210, "Tanabata" (Tanabata ni tsuite no mukashi-banashi). The version with the robe, the prohibited melon, and the origin of the stars.

Gifu, Yoshiki-gun: Hidabito V 2 33, "The wife from the Sky World" (Tennin nyōbō). The version with the robe. An old man showed her the robe and she returned to the sky, carrying her child.

Aichi, Hoi-gun: Aichi 224, "The pine tree of the feather robe" (Hago-romo matsu).

Tottori, Tōhaku-gun: Inpaku mukashi 47, "Uchifuki-yama." Her robe was not stolen, but when she took it off, she forgot about the Sky World and became a farmer's wife. When she happened to put it on later, she recalled the Sky World. She returned to the sky with the help of a calabash flower and a child.

Shimane, Ōchi-gun: Minkan. II 6 7, "The myth about Sanbai" (Sanbai no shinwa).

Hiroshima, Futami-gun: Geibi 5, "The wife from the Sky World" No. 1 (Tennin nyōbō). The Sky was reached by climbing the Tree of Happiness. Tasks were set by the girl's mother.

Hiba-gun: Geibi 11, "The wife from the Sky World" No. 2 (Tennin nyōbō). The sky was reached by climbing a pine tree. A dog went along. In this tale, as in the former two, the Milky Way came from the melon and was the beginning of Tanabata.

Saeki-gun: Aki 53, "The golden bucket" (Kin no tago). He saved a deer and it helped him go to the sky.

Yamaguchi, Suō Ōshima: Suō Ōshima 25, 26, "The wife from the Sky

World" (Tennin nyōbō). Both tales have the same title. The first begins with the rescue of a badger. After the wife returned to the sky, the badger went to the husband and gave him a horse bean. The vine grew to the sky. The story of animal gratitude is added. The wife left the bean in the second story. The man recognized his wife in the Sky World through the help of a bee, a fox, and a bird.

Tokushima: Awa Iyayama 43, 100, "The man carried off in the Milky Way" (Ama-no-gawa e nagasareta otoko no hanashi), and "The Tanabata wife" (Tanabata nyōbō).

Kagawa, Mitoyo-gun, Shishijima: MK II 12 18, "Tanabata." Example.

Kumamoto, Hōtoku-gun: MK II 6 23, "Inukai [the man with a dog] and Tanabata" (Inukai to Tanabata san).

Amakusa: MK I 10 41, "The wife from the Sky World" (Tennin nyōbō). The origin of the Inukai and the Tanabata stars. The story about 100 pairs of sandals with one missing, the snake gourd, etc.

Nagasaki, Minamitakaku-gun: Shimabara 127, "The wife from the Sky World" (Tennin nyōbō). The robe was stolen. The mother got the robe back after her child was born. The man had to bury 1000 yellow cows and sow squash over them. He climbed the vine to the sky, but there was one cow less than required. While he was helping make rain, he fell into Lake Biwa and became a fish.

Kagoshima: Kikai 18, 21, 22, "The wife from the Sky World" (Tennin nyōbō). All three tales have the same title. In the third, a cowherd hid the robe and married the girl. They went to visit her parents in the sky several years later. He cut the melon the wrong way. It is the story of the origin of the Milky Way. She learned where her robe was hidden by a nursery song her older boy sang in the second tale, close to the Okinawa version. The first is slightly different, one about a brother and sister who came down from the sky.

Koshikijima: Koshiki 108, "The Milky Way" (Ama-no-gawa), Only the latter half of the tale.

Amami Ōshima: Mukashibanashi bun 17. No title. In Yakiuchimura-yama-mura of Yamada. The old man and his black dog. The wife from the Sky World wanted to get tobacco.

Further reference:
Mukashibanashi Kenkyū II 5 22, The wife from the Sky World lived at Nishigōmura, Kitamurayama-gun, Yamagata.
Nihon mukashibanashi shū, ge 165. An Okinawa example.
Chōsen mintan shū 74,
Yukei no densetsu.
Otogizōshi: Bontenkoku.
Nihon dōwa hyōgoku shū, ge 218.
Yearsley 170, 172, 180.

19. The Wife's Picture

Long ago there was a farmer who was a little simple. Nobody wanted to marry him, so he lived alone in a little hut. One evening a beautiful woman came and asked him to take her as his wife and they married. She was so beautiful that Gonbei was completely charmed and lost interest in work. She had him draw a picture of her and take it with him to his garden patch. He hung it on the branch of a tree while he worked. One day a big wind blew the picture high, then dropped it into the yard of a feudal lord. When the feudal lord saw the picture, he wanted the woman as his bride. He sent his men out to look for her. They learned that she was Gonbei's wife, and they forced her to go with them to the castle. As his wife left, she told Gonbei to come to the castle gate to sell pine boughs on New Year's Eve. He took the pine boughs and stood before the gate, shouting, "Pine boughs, pine boughs!" The wife, who had not smiled since she had been taken away, broke into a laugh. The feudal lord was so pleased that he had the pine bough pedlar brought in. He traded clothes with him and imitated him to make the woman laugh. He then went out to the street to imitate him. In the meantime, the woman had the gates closed, and the feudal lord could not come back in. He was left on the outside while Gonbei and his wife occupied the castle and lived there together.

Niigata, Nakakanbara-gun, Gosen-mura

Iwate, Kamihei-gun, Tōno: Kikimimi 20, "Kabuyaki Sesajirō."
Niigata, Nakakanbara-gun: MK II 2 46, "The wife's picture" (Esugata nyōbō). Example.
  Minamikanbara-gun: Kamuhara 4, "A dream that came true" (Masayume). The first dream of the New Year came true. The man became a noble. How he got his wife is the same.
Hiroshima, Takata-gun: Aki 112, 117, "The wife's picture" (Esugata nyōbō). Both tales have the same title. Geibi 109, "The wife's plan" (Nyōbō shian).
  Yamagata-gun: Aki 118, "The wife's picture" No. 3 (Esugata nyōbō). These three stories are perhaps variants of "The tasks of the son-in-law."
Nagasaki, Minamitakaku-gun: MK I 11 22, "The wife's picture" No. 1 (Esugata nyōbō); Shimabara 121, "The wife's picture" (Esugata nyōbō). The beginning is like "The wife from the Dragon Palace" in Tōhoku. Trials are set by the feudal lord.
Kagoshima, Amami Ōshima: MK II 3 46, "The wife's picture" (Esugata nyōbō). It is about Bokka. The wife came from a different region. Her picture was blown away. Tasks set by the feudal lord, wagering on wrestling matches by two old men, and the hand of the image resemble the Hasedera tale in Shinshū.

Further reference:
  Mukashibanashi kenkyū II 6 7. Foreign examples can be found in

the article by Asada Isamu, but these do not have the part about the wife's picture being blown away.

20. The Stork Wife

Once upon a time an honest man who was cutting grass in the hills rescued a stork that had an arrow in its throat. In the autumn a young woman he did not know came to his house and asked to stay and they married. They had nothing with which to celebrate New Year as it approaches. The wife said she would do her best to weave something for her husband to take to the feudal lord to sell. He received a lot of money for this and was asked to bring another length of cloth. When he told his wife, she said she was not sure she could weave that much, but she would try. She told her husband not to look into the room until she was finished. He thought that strange and spied anyway. He saw a naked stork plucking the remaining few feathers from her body with her beak and weaving them into the cloth. She reminded him that she had told him not to watch her weave and asked why he had done it. She said that since she had been seen, she could no longer stay with him. She was the stork he had saved and had come to repay her debt of gratitude, but now she had to leave. She flew away completely naked as she spoke. The weaving she had done was known as shokukō brocade.

Nagano, Kitaazumi-gun

Aomori, Hachinohe: MK II 2 35, "The bird wife" (Tori nyōbō). This is a legend of the Kōnoike family. It has the story of the weaving and the forbidden room. Tekkiri 74 "The stork wife" (Tsuru nyōbō). There are three stories about the feather robe. It is in the form of Itonaga of Harima with the tasks set by the feudal lord and other episodes.
Iwate, Kamihei-gun: Rōō 288, "The wife from the wild goose nest" (Kō no su nyōbō).
Fukushima, Shinobu-gun: Shintatsu 119, "The stork's payment for kindness" (Tsuru on ni mukuyu). It is a legend about Tsurunuma in Niwatsuka-mura.
     Iwaki-gun: Iwaki 10, "The stork's gratitude" (Tsuru no ongaeshi); Dai-ni 53, "The stork wife" (Tsuru nyōbō).
Niigata, Minamikanbara-gun: Kamuhara 181, "The naked stork" (Tsuru tsuru hadaka."
     Sado: Sado shū 67, 171, "The stork wife" (Tsuru nyōbō). Both stories with the same title. No part about gratitude. An agreement to stop hunting.
Nagano: Kitaazumi 2 155, "The stork's gratitude" (Tsuru no hōon). Example.
     Chiisagata-gun: Chiisagata 262, 263, "The white rat" (Shiro

nezumi), and "The stork" (Tsuru). In one story, the rat pulled hair from its body.

Minamiazumi-gun: Nihon den 153, "Hachimen Daiō." A copper pheasant was rescued and lived as the daughter of an old couple.

Kamiina-gun: Mukashibanashi 125, "A length of weaving for 1000 ryō" (Hata ittan sen ryō). The wife was a pheasant. It is a combined tale.

Ishikawa: Nomi 1150, "The origin of the hair ornament" (Kōgai no yurai).

Yamanashi, Nishiyatsushiro-gun: Kai 7, "The rescued stork" (Tasuketa tsuru).

Hiroshima: Geibi 12, "The stork wife" No. 1 (Tsuru nyōbō).

Okayama, Mitsu-gun: MK I 7 33, "The gratitude of the stork" (Tsuru no ongaeshi). She came to live with an old couple as their daughter. No part about forbidding them to look into her room.   Going to inquire at Saraike in Harima.

Tottori, Iwami-gun: MK I 2 28, "The stork's weaving" (Tsuru no hata-ori). It is simply a story of gratitude told in great detail. A daughter instead of a wife.

Tokushima: Awa Iyayama 53, "The stork wife" (Tsuru nyōbō).

Kagawa, Takamatsu: Dai-ni 54, "Shōan and the stork" (Shōan san to tsuru). The first part is about gratitude. The bird flew around the grave of its benefactor for three years.   When he came back to life, the stork lost all its feathers and died.

Fukuoka, Kiku-gun: Fukuoka 167, "Kōnoike."

Kurate-gun: Fukuoka 94, "Helping a stork" (Tsuru o tasuku).

Nagasaki: (Old) Iki 164, "The stork" (Tsuru no hanashi). Simply a story of gratitude which could be called "Tsuru Jōdo" [Stork Jōdo].   It is close to the Dragon Palace story in *Konjaku monogatari, maki 16,* No. 15.

Kagoshima: Koshiki 63, "The stork wife" No. 1 (Tsuru nyōbō).

Further reference:
   Beifu koshi ruisan 60. A legend of a temple called Kakushizan Chinzōji at Yonezawa Higashi-tera-machi, Tsuruichiyama.

21. The Wild Duck Wife

The principal character is a rag buyer named Zen'emon. It is a story about the origin of the Kōnoike family.   The wild duck that was rescued became his wife.   There is the episode about weaving and the admonition not to look at her while she was weaving.   She made a riddle by putting her tail feathers in the measuring box and she left.

Fukui, Sakai-gun: MK I 1 31, "The wild duck wife" (Kamo nyōbō). Example.

22. The Copper Pheasant Wife

A man named Yasuke of Yamura was going to the year's end market at Hodaka on the 28th day of the twelfth month. He rescued a copper pheasant that was caught in a snare by the road, and left the 500 mon he was carrying in payment. The last part resembles a katari-mono.

Nagano: Minamiazumi-gun shi 927, "Yasuke of Yamura" (Yamura no Yasuke).
Ishikawa: Nomi 1150, "The origin of the hair ornament" (Kōgai no yurai). The latter part of the legend about Nakayama the Second of Nishijo-mura, Ogaya. A beautiful girl came and stayed. The man accompanied her as far as Hotoke Pass, and she turned into a white pheasant and disappeared. It is said that she was the incarnation of Hakusan Gongen. She left a comb and a hair ornament as tokens of gratitude and the ornament is still preserved. Pheasants are now never eaten by this family.

23. The Bird Wife

The story is told like the stork tale, but it is a wild goose. She came to the poor man who saved her. She wove cloth and bore him a child. The latter part is in the form of the Itonaga of Harima tale.

Akita, Senhoku-gun: Ugo 44, "The wild goose" (Kōnotori). Example.
Fukushima: Iwaki 11, "The gratitude of the wild goose" (Kōnotori no ongaeshi).
Tokushima: Awa Iyayama 24, "The bird wife" (Tori nyōbō). This includes an episode like the Itonaga of Harima story.

24. The Fox Wife

Once upon a time a man was having difficulties because his wife was ill and had gone home to her parents. He rescued a white fox from the stream where he was fishing one day and took it home with him. She said she would repay his kindness and left. Then a woman appeared and asked to work as his maid. He let her stay and presently she bore him a child. One day the child told his father that his mother was sweeping the yard with her tail. That puzzled the man. He climbed into the rafters for a look. He was surprised to see she really had a tail. He ran her off the place. Before she left, she wrote a poem telling him that if he wanted to see her, to hunt at the springs in the Shinoda forest for Urami Kazunoha.

Osaka, Izunami-gun

Aomori, Hachinohe: MK II 2 36, "The fox wife" (Kitsune nyōbō). The man's name was Abi-no-Yasuna and the child was Abi-no-Seme-tono. The place was Shiroda forest. It is clearly a katarimono.
Kamikita-gun: Kamikita 63.* He plagued the fox and it hid his horse on the day he was busy transplanting rice shoots.
Fukushima, Iwaki-gun: Iwaki 7, 103, "The fox who was a man's wife" (Kitsune ga hito no nyōbō ni natte ita hanashi).
Ishikawa: Ishikawa 978. No title.
Tochigi, Haga-gun: Shimotsuke 35, "The fox mother" (Hana wa kitsune). Only a trace exists, and it is not in the original form.
Nagano: Kitaazumi 2 26, "Kyūbeibun."
Minamiazumi-gun: Minamiazumi shi 937, "The fox at Shigenagi" (Shigenagi no kitsune). This is the tale at Shigenagi-mura. The fox came to help at rice transplanting and nursed her child. She left when her husband saw her tail.
Aichi, Hoi-gun: Aichi 263, "The fox disguised as a human" (Hito ni baketa kitsune).
Hyōgo: Nihon den Harima 117, "Kajigadō." The story of Shikama Fox. It is close to the story about Shinoda forest.

Further reference:
Honchō zokugen shi. The child of the fox was called Monogusa-tarō. It is told about Shinoda Shrine.
Hina no hitofushi. A story about Nabeko of Shida.
Zoku Azukagawa (In *Shin enseki jisshū* I 18). A fox mask is put on when a song is sung to celebrate the preparation of the rice field.
Kenchū mikkan. The Goddess of Miwa becomes the wife of a man.
Dōchō to tosetsu III 37.
Hyakka kikōdan. A story about Kuriyama Kakuzaemon from Hita-chi-no-kuni. The tale is also in *Tonegawa zushi.*
Toyama (Enzan) chōmon shū kōhen.
Nihon ryōiki. An ancestor of Kitsune Atae of Mino-no-kuni.
Shinano kidan (In *Dōbutsu yōkai dan* 312). Also in *Keimei manroku.*
Angya zuihitsu, chū kan 48.

25. The Clam Wife

Once upon a time a woman came to a man who was living alone and became his wife. His bean soup had not been very good until then, but after she came, it was very good. The man thought it strange. He pretended to set out for work, but he returned and hid behind the house to spy on his wife. She got out the mixing bowl and started to stir the bean paste, and then she climbed onto the edge of the bowl and did something dirty in it. When the man saw that, he was very angry and drove her away. Although she begged to be forgiven, he refused. She turned into a huge clam and dragged herself away slowly. The clam juice had made the soup delicious.

Nagano, Kamiina-gun

Nagano, Kamiina-gun: Minzokugaku I 2 50, "The clam's family" (Hamaguri no uchi). Example.
Nagasaki: Shimabara 130, "The clam wife" (Hamaguri nyōbō).

Further reference:
   Otogizōshi: "The clam wife (Hamaguri nyōbō).
   Nihon dōwa hyōgoku shū 260. "The clam princess" (Hamagurihime).

26. The Fish Wife

This is the same story as "The clam wife," but the wife is a fish.

Iwate, Iwate-gun: Kikimimi 361, "The fish wife" (Uo nyōbō). Example.
Akita, Senhoku-gun: MK I 6 39, 40, "The carp's gratitude" (Funa no ongaeshi) and "The carp woman" (Koijo).
Yamagata, Higashitagawa-gun: MK II 2 45, "The salmon wife" (Shake nyōbō).
Fukushima: Iwaki 12, "The mermaid's gratitude" (Ningyo no ongaeshi).
Niigata, Minamiuonuma-gun: MK I 7 24, "The carp's gratitude" (Koi no ongaeshi).
   The carp's gratitude and tasks set by the feudal lord.
   Nagaoka: Minzokugaku II 2 50 "The clam's family" (Hamaguri no uchi).
Toyama: Nihon zenkoku 188, "The festival of the cow's head" (Ushi-ga-kubi no matsuri).
   The origin of wrestling at the festival of Ushi-ga-kubi.
Ishikawa: Kaga 121, "The girl and the salmon trout" (Musume to kawamasu).
Gifu, Hida: Minzokugaku II 4 160, "Chinma-ga-ike." A legend about a lake.
Kagoshima: Koshiki 68, "The clam wife" (Hamaguri nyōbō).

Further reference:
   Chōsen mintan shū 235, "Winning a wife from the Dragon Palace by setting a carp free" (Koi o hanashite ryūjo o uru). It is close to "Urashimatarō." When the box was opened, a thin column of smoke came out.
   Chōsen mintan shū 122, "The carp and the poor man" (Koi to mazushii otoko.

27. The Wife from the Dragon Palace

A mother who had lost seven sons had only one left. He sold flowers, but one day he could not sell any. He said he would offer them to the Dragon Palace and threw them all into the sea. A turtle appeared and offered to take him to the Dragon Palace as thanks. He told the son to ask for a girl if he was offered a gift. What he thought had been three days had been three years in the human world. On the day he started home, the deity there gave him a girl. When he arrived home, he found that his mother had starved to death, but his bride stroked her head with a Life Whip and brought her back to life. She shook out a house and rice storehouse, and in a short time they became rich. The feudal lord heard about the beauty of the bride and demanded the man give him 1000 koku of rice or his wife. When the man told his wife, she obtained the rice from the sea, and he was able to deliver it without difficulty. Next, there was a demand for 1000 fathoms of rope, but she got it from the sea, too. Then the feudal lord announced that he would come on New Year's Day with 699 followers to see the bride, so 77 jars of foaming wine should be prepared for them. The wife had the wine set out and waited. The feudal lord demanded that she prepare lively entertainment. She brought out hundreds of identical little men from a box and they sang and danced. Then he demanded that she put on a quieter entertainment. She protested that it would be dangerous, but he insisted. She drew out hundreds of men with swords from another box, and they cut off the heads of the feudal lord and all his followers.

Kagoshima, Kikaijima

Iwate: Kunohe 474, "Tarō and the Dragon Palace" (Tarō to Ryūgū).
Niigata: TD II 7 37, "Rankei kikō." A legend of the Sakai family and the Dragon Princess of Useinoike.
Gifu, Yoshiki-gun: Hida fūbutsu 87, "Yomegafuchi" (Yomegafuchi no hanashi). It is also in *Nihon densetsu shū.*
Shimane, Ōchi-gun: MK II 9 33, "Potato-digger Chōja" (Imohori Chōja), No. 1. A simple form. The Dragon Princess came as a bride to a bamboo hut in the mountains and wove at a loom.
Nagasaki: Shimabara 121, "The wife's picture" (Esugata nyōbō). The first half of the tale.
Kagoshima, Kikaijima: MK I 5 40, "Ryūjin and the flower peddler" (Ryūjin to hanauri). Example; Dai-ni 23, "The Ryūjin's girl" (Ryūjin no onna).
Koshikijima:: Koshiki 61, "The wife from the Dragon Palace" (Ryūgū nyōbō).

Further reference:
The well-known Toyotamahime tale. It is told clearly in *Hachiman gudōkun.*

28. The Snake Wife

The word snake is used, but it is a great Water Spirit, nearer to a Dragon Woman than a big snake.

A beautiful woman appeared at the home of a man who was griev-ing over the death of his wife. They married and presently a child was born. When it came time, the wife asked her husband not to look under any circumstance. After making doubly sure, she went into the room to deliver her baby. The man could not endure his worry and looked in secretly. There he saw a great snake coiled around a baby. He was dumbfounded, but he withdrew and said nothing about it. The woman came out on the seventh day carrying a lovely little boy, but she was weeping bitterly. She said she could stay no longer because her true form had been seen. She scooped out her left eye and gave it to her husband. She told him to let the baby suck it if it cried. He cared for the baby by letting it suck the eye, but the eye began to grow smaller after a while until it was completely gone. The father put his child onto his back and went to the pond in the hills to look for his wife. The great snake appeared and took out her remaining eye and gave it to him. She asked that a bell be hung near the lake and rung at the sixth hour of the morning and evening. She hid in the lake again. The father furnished the temple by the pond with a bell and arranged to have time marked. When the child grew up, he learned about his birth and went to the pond to meet his mother. She appeared in human form as a blind woman. He put her on his back and carried her home and lived with her as a dutiful son.

Iwate, Esashi-gun

Aomori: Tekkiri 78, "The snake wife" (Hebi nyōbō).
Iwate, Esashi-gun: Kikimimi 182, "The mother's eyeballs" (Haha no medama). Example.
    Hienuki-gun: MK I 10 23, "The precious snake scales" (Kogera dama). The snake's gratitude. It turns into the story about a dog, a cat, and a rat.
Akita, Kazuno-gun: MK I 3 26 "Caring for a child" (Kodomo sodate). A fragment of the snake wife story.
Miyagi, Natori-gun: Kyōdō den 3 172, "Ryūwaka."
Fukushima: Iwaki 8, 103, "The snake that was a man's wife" (Hebi ga hito no nyōbō ni natte ita hanashi).
Niigata, Sado: MK II 6 39, "The snake wife" (Hebi zuma). The tale resembles "The snake bridegroom." She climbed the tree to get the eagle's eggs. It is different from the love of a child.
Fukui, Mikata-gun: MK I 8 11, "The blind Water Spirit" (Mekura no mizu no kami). A woodcutter was charmed by a beautiful Water Spirit and went into the pond. He left his eyes for his wife and child.
Ishikawa: Kaga 51, 64, "The thanks of the frog" (Kaeru no orei) and "Saving the old woman" (Tasuke baba).

Nagano: Chiisagata 200, "The snake's child" (Hebi no ko). It is a fragment.

Gifu, Yoshiki-gun: Hidabito V 2 33, "The snake wife" (Hebi nyōbō). One gives the origin of the bell at Miidera and the other is close to the Shimabara story. These tales may have been carried by zatō. Hidabito IV 10 40 "The snake wife" (Hebi nyōbō). It is a Niugawa tale. It is like the story about a wife without a mouth. There is no part about giving an eye for the child to suck.

Shizuoka, Hamana-gun: Shizuoka 432, "The origin of the divided skirt" (Hakama no yurai). No part about the gift of gratitude. The skirt was put on to cover the part she had not finished licking clean.

Tōtōmi (Shizuoka, Iwata-gun), Gansuiji: Nihon den 165, "Koyasu Son of Gansuiji" (Gansuiji no Koyasu Son). Is it about the origin of the temple? An old story about Tamura Shōgun.

Shiga: Nihon den 169, "The bell at Miidera" (Miidera no kane). This is a folk tale. Or it was formerly a katarimoto.

Kyoto, Minamikuwate-gun: MK I 9 46, A notation. Only a fragment.

Wakayama, Higashimuro-gun: MK I 9 45, "The blind Water Spirit" (Mekura no mizu no kami). She gave an eyeball each of the first two times and her navel the third time to nurse her child.

Hiroshima, Mitsuki-gun: Geibi 17, "The snake wife" No. 1 (Hebi nyōbō). The opening episode is not there. It starts with seeing his wife give birth to the baby.

Takata-gun: Aki 35, "The mother's eyeballs" (Haha no medama).

Tokushima: Awa Iyayama 60, "The snake wife" (Hebi nyōbō). Firewood was thrown into the river in the first part and the woman came from the Dragon Palace. The combination should be noted. The child was reared by letting it suck the eyeballs. When he was five years old, he became the main image worshipped at Sanjūsangendō in Kyoto.

Fukuoka, Kiku-gun: Fukuoka 161, "The snake mother" (Hebi no haha). It follows the usual version, but it does not say the jewel that was sucked was the mother's eye.

Nagasaki: Shimabara 131, "The blind Water Spirit" (Mekura no mizu no kami). Uzen's eruptions are explained; a snake's gratitude without marriage; rescuing a sea snake; and one in the form of a legend. Shimabara 34, "Taking a snake bride" No. 1 (Hebi yomeiri). Using a thread and needle appears.

Kagoshima: Kikai 28, "The snake wife" (Hebi nyōbō).

29. The Frog Wife

The principal character is a candle seller. A woman came on a rainy night and asked to stay. He married her, but day after day she ate no rice. One day she said it was the 100th Day anniversary of a death in her family, so he gave her candles and let her go. He followed her and saw her jump into a pond. Then he heard voices of many frogs and he realized his wife was a frog. He tossed a rock into the pond and went home. His wife returned toward evening and said that during the sutras there had been a big earthquake and many were killed or injured. The man took a close look at his wife and saw she was a frog.

Yamagata, Higashitagawa-gun

Aomori, Hachinohe: MK II 2 36, "The frog wife" (Kaeru nyōbō). A frog came disguised as a man's dead wife. She went to see sacred dances often. It is a fragment.
Yamagata, Higashitagawa-gun: MK II 7 29, "The frog wife" (Kaeru nyōbō) Example. It has a hint of the story "The wife who didn't eat."
Fukushima, Iwaki-gun: Iwaki 13, "The frog's gratitude" (Kaeru no ongaeshi).
Niigata, Sado: MK II 11 31, "The frog wife" (Kaeru nyōbō). It resembles "The snake wife." The wife came home lame because of the rock thrown into the pond. There is the sadness of her leaving her eyeball for him and going away.
Tokushima: Awa Iyayama 28, "The singing frog wife" (Kajiki nyōbō).

30. The Snake Son-In-Law

A certain farmer tried to save a frog from a snake that was trying to swallow it by promising one of his daughters to the snake. The three daughters saw that their father was worried and urged him to tell why. His two older girls refused to marry the snake. The youngest, her eyes full of tears agreed to marry it. She asked for 1000 gourds and 1000 needles for her preparation. The farmer went to town and bought them. The snake came that evening, appearing like a handsome young man, with many followers. He led the girl across meadows and hills, far back into the mountains. A thousand fellow snakes were swarming around, waiting to devour her. She asked that the thousand needles be floated and the thousand gourds be sunk in the lake. When the snakes leaped into the water and tried, they became worn out. The girl took that opportunity to run away and go home. She lost her way and asked an old woman who was spinning alone in a hut to stay over night. The old woman was happy to let her stay and prepared a good meal for her. It happened that the feudal lord had proclaimed at that time that he was looking for a bride. The old woman took the girl to the castle town where many girls had gathered. She was chosen from among them and became his bride. She sent for her parents and they lived with her in comfort. That kind old woman was really the frog that the farmer had saved.

Tochigi, Haga-gun

Aomori, Shimokita-gun: TD IX 2 71, "A trip to seaside villages" by Nakaichi Kenzō. The wine cup of a kappa. Tsugaru m 57, "The

filial little daughter" (Kōkō na unbako); Tekkiri 68, 71, "The snake
son-in-law" (Hebi mukoiri).
Iwate, Kamihei-gun: Tōno 137 No. 26. No title; Kikimimi 177, 179,
"The snake son-in-law" Nos. 3 and 4 (Hebi no muko). Two tales
with the same title; Kikimimi 168, "The bride of the snake" (Hebi
no yomego); Rōō 20, 38, "The snake son-in-law" (Hebi muko) and
"The gratitude of the crab" (Kani no hōon). The snake came as the
bridegroom after the frog was rescued. The frog came as an old
woman and asked him to get the eggs of a wild goose.
    Shimohei-gun, Iwaizumi: Kikimimi 175, "The snake son-in-law" No.1
    (Hebi muko).
    Shiwa-gun: Shiwashū 83, "The snake who came visiting a maid"
    (Musume sa kayōta hebi).
    Nishiiwai-gun: TD XII 11 36, "The snake son-in-law" (Hebi mukoiri).
Akita, Senhoku-gun Kakunodate: Kikimimi 173, "The snake's bride" No.
    2 (Hebi no yomego).
Miyagi, Sendai: Kyōdo ken I 8 26. No title.
    Natori-gun, Tamura: Kyōdo den 3 171 "Ryūwaka."
Fukushima: Iwaki 15, 105, "The snake son-in-law" (Hebi no muko).
Niigata, Minamiuonuma-gun: MK I 10 37, "The gratitude of the frog"
    (Kaeru no ongaeshi).
    Minamikanbara-gun: Kamuhara 209, "The egg in the fragrant tree"
    (Kōno ki no tamago).
    Sado: Dai-ni 48, "The big sack of the frog" (Kaeru no danbukuro).
Fukui, Sakai-gun: MK I 1 31, "The snake son-in-law" (Hebi mukoiri).
Ishikawa: Fugeshi 925. No title.
Nagano: Chiisagata 166, "The old woman's skin" (Ubagara).
    Kitaazumi-gun: Otari 145, "An old tale" (Mukashi mukashi).
    Kitasaku-gun: MK I 12 35, "The chōja's daughter and the Lake
    Spirit" (Chōja no musume to ike no nushi).
    Kamiina-gun: Dai-ichi 54, "The snake son-in-law" (Hebi mukoiri);
    Mukashibanashi 7, 136, "The snake son-in-law" (Hebi muko domo)
    and "The iris and mugwort" (Shōbu to yomogi).
Tochigi, Haga-gun: Dai-ni 17, "A thousand gourds and a thousand
    needles" (Hyōtan sen to hari sen bon no hanashi). Example. Shimo-
    tsuke 31, 63, "The thousand gourds and thousand needles" (Hyōtan
    sen to hari sen bon) and "The gratitude of the crab" (Kani no
    ongaeshi). In the first there is the old woman's skin and no choos-
    ing a bride. The other is about a crab repaying a kindness.
Yamanashi, Nishiyatsushiro-gun: Kai 103, 107, "The snake man" (Hebi
    otoko) and "The snake son-in-law" (Hebi muko); Zoku kai 92, 95,
    96, "The snake son-in-law" (Hebi muko) and "The snake man" Nos. 2
    and 3 (Hebi otoko).
Gifu, Yoshiki-gun: Hida den 116, "Ubagaike"; Hidabito V 2 37 "The
    snake son-in-law" Nos. 3 and 4 (Hebi mukoiri).
Shizuoka, Shida-gun, Yaitsu: Shizuoka 429, "The snake's wedding" (Hebi
    no konin no hanashi).
    Tagata-gun: Shizuoka 421, "The snake's wedding" (Hebi no konin
    banashi); MK I 12 19, "The snake son-in-law" (Hebi mukoiri) The
    same tale.
    Ibara-gun, Ryōgawachi-mura: Shizuoka 424, "The snake's wedding"
    (Hebi konin banashi).

Suchi-gun: Shizuoka 431, "The snake's wedding" (Hebi no konin banashi).

Kamo-gun: Shizuoka 419, "The snake's wedding" (Hebi konin banashi).

Hamamatsu: Shizuoka 433, "The origin of the divided skirt" (Hakama no yurai).

Hyōgo, Hikami-gun: TD X 6 40, "The eagle's egg" (Washi no tamago). The snake bride went to get the eggs. This example is also found on Izu.

Kinosaki-gun, Sanshō-mura: MK II 8 33, "The snake and the frog" (Hebi to kaeru).

Wakayama, Ito-gun: Kōshō 10 19, "The snake son-in-law" (Hebi no mukoiri).

Okayama, Mitsu-gun: MK I 9 35, "The girl wearing a frog's hood" (Kaeru no zukin musume).

Hiroshima, Yamagata-gun: Aki 27, 29, "The snake son-in-law" Nos. 1 and 2 (Hebi muko banashi).

Shimane, Oki: Okinoshima 27, "The snake girl" (Daija no musume); Kyōdo bun I 3 27. "How the crabs in the mountain destroyed the great snake" (Yamakani no daija taiji). This is a legend.

Yamaguchi, Suō Ōshima: Suō Ōshima 46, "The snake son-in-law" (Hebi mukoiri banashi); Kōshō 11 19 "A snake story" (Hebiko dan).

Bungo (Ōita): Minzokugaku V 10 86 "Asahi Chōja" (Asahi Chōja no hanashi).

Kitaamabe-gun: MK I 4 37, "Gakkai Chōja."

Nagasaki, Shimabara: TD II 11 25, "The snake's bride" (Hebi no yomeiri); TD III 5 14, "The snake's bride" (Hebi no oyome); Shimabara 36, "The snake bride No. 2 (Hebi yomeiri). This can be considered in the old form. The episode about the old woman's skin turns into a legend about a great snake. Shimabara 28, 30, 31, "The snake son-in-law" Nos. 1 and 2 (Hebi mukoiri) and "The snake and the eagle" (Hebi to washi). The advice of a yamabushi.

Ikinoshima: (New) Iki 15, 16, "The snake son-in-law" (Hebi muko). This is the old form of the spool of thread. Both tales with the same title.

Kagoshima: Koshiki 75, 77, "The snake son-in-law" (Hebi mukoiri). The first is about eavesdropping and the second is like "The ash girl"; Kikai 25, 27, "The snake son-in-law" (Hebi mukoiri). Both with the same title. One is in the form of eavesdropping and the other, "The ash girl."

Okierabu: MK II 7 26, "The three sisters" (Sannin shimai). There is an episode about the jealousy of the two sisters who would not agree to marry and lost out.

Okinawa: Yambaru 149. No title. Close to a legend; Nantō 6, "Akamata" (Akamata no densetsu).

Further reference:

Chōsen mintan shū 40. Destroying a great snake. The rescue of the girl was done entirely by the bullfrog that had been saved. No story of a bridegroom.

Nihon dōwa shū 585. An otogizōshi, "Amewakahiko monogatari."

Nihon dōwa hyōgoku shū, ge 254.

31. The Demon Son-In-Law

A demon became the bridegroom. It is made up of three tales. There is no promise about the demon and watering the rice paddy. He married the youngest of eight sisters. She went off with wild violet seeds and said she would return when they bloomed. The girl danced for the demon and he drank water and died.

Aomori, Hachinohe: MK II 3 25, "The wild violet seed" (Keshi no tane). Example.

32. The Kappa Son-In-Law

This belongs to the stories of the monkey bridegroom and the snake bridegroom groups. The principal character is a kappa.

Iwate, Iwate-gun, Shizukuishi: Kikimimi 357, "The eel man" (Unagi otoko). An old eel from the bottom of the pond went visiting a girl.
Isawa-gun: Kogane 94, "The girl who became a mudsnail's bride" (Musume ga tsubu no yome ni natta hanashi).
Nagasaki: Shimabara 41, "The gourd and the kappa" (Hyōtan to kappa). Iki: TD IX 4 171, "Notes on folk tales" (Mukashibanashi zakko) by Yamaguchi Asatarō. About monkey, snake, and kappa sons-in-law.

33. The Monkey Son-In-Law

Long ago there was a farmer. He was so worried over the drought that dried up his paddies that he said to himself that he would be willing to give one of his daughters as a bride to anyone who would help water his fields. A monkey suddenly appeared from out of the thicket and then went back into the hills and sent water flowing down to the fields. The old man was too worried over his promise to do anything and went to bed without eating his supper. His oldest girl urged him to eat, but she ran away angry when she heard his story. The second girl got angry, too, but when the youngest heard, she said she would go as a bride and asked her father to get right up and eat his supper. He got up quite happy and ate it. On the next day the monkey came wearing a red sleeveless jacket to claim his bride. They set out for his home back in the hills. They lived together in a friendly way. When spring came next year, they decided they would take mochi flavored with burdock leaves to her family. If they put the mochi in a lacquer box, it would smell of lacquer; if they put it in a kettle, it would smell of the kettle; so they left it in the mortar and the monkey carried it on his back. Along the way, there were lovely cherry blossoms beside the river, and they decided to take some as a gift. If the mochi were left on the ground, it would smell of dirt, so the monkey climbed the tree with the mortar on his back. As he climbed up and up, a branch broke, and he fell into the river with the mortar on his back and he was washed away. He called the following song:

My life washed away in Sarusawa without a regret!
Later the girl will surely weep.

When the girl reached home at last, her father shed tears of joy. The two older sisters were punished for being unfilial by being turned into rats.

Yamagata, Mogami-gun

Aomori: Tsugaru m 28, "The girl who became a monkey's bride" (Saru san yomeko ni natta hanashi).
Hachinohe: MK II 4 44, "The monkey son-in-law" (Saru mukoiri).
Sannohe-gun, Gonohe-machi: MK I 7 21, "Putting water on the rice paddy" (Ta no mizukake), "Pulling weeds in the millet patch" (Awa no kusatori), and "The big furoshiki and the wisteria" (Ōfuroshiki to fuji no hana).
Iwate, Kamihei-gun, Tōno: Kikimimi 246, "The monkey son-in-law" (Saru no muko); Kikimimi 472, "The priest and the mortar" (Bōsama to suriusu). The man would give one of his daughters as wife to a priest if he could chant a joruri until morning. He succeeded, but he was deceived and was carried off in the current of a river and drowned. There is also a dying song. This is found in *Masumi yūran*. Perhaps there is influence from that on "The monkey bridegroom."
Shiwa-gun: Shiwa shū 111, "The bride of the monkey" (Saru no yomego).
Isawa-gun: Kogane 91, "The girl who became a monkey's bride" (Musume ga saru no oyome ni natta hanashi).
Akita, Senhoku-gun, Kakunodate: Kikimimi 254, "The monkey son-in-law" (Saru no muko). A note.
Hiraga-gun, Asamai-machi: MK II 5 26, "One grain, 1000 grains" (Hitotsubu sentsubu).
Yamagata, Mogami-gun: MK II 4 40, "The monkey son-in-law" (Saru no mukoiri). Example.
Kitamurayama-gun, Nishigō-mura: MK II 5 23, "Watering the field" (Mizuhiki no hanashi).
Miyagi, Momoo-gun: Kyōdo den 2 119, "The monkey's bride" (Saru no yome).
Fukushima: Iwaki 17 109, "The monkey son-in-law" (Saru no muko).
Niigata, Nakakanbara-gun, Shirone: Nihon zenkoku 195, "The bride of the monkey" (Saru dono no yome).
Sado: MK I 4 41, "The monkey son-in-law" (Saru mukoiri).

Minamikanbara-gun: Echigo Sanjo 115, "The old man and the monkey" (Jiji to saru); Kamuhara 15 "The monkey son-in-law" (Saru mukoiri); MK I 5 21, "The monkey son-in-law" (Saru mukoiri).

Nakauonuma-gun: Dai-ichi 47, "The monkey son-in-law" (Saru mukoiri).

Kitakanbara-gun: Koshiji VI 10. No. 90, 4. The story in a grinding song. There are two or three such songs in *Shōnai riyōshū*.

Ishikawa: Kaga 1, "The three sisters" (Sannin shimai); Kaga 124, "The girl wrapped in tanned paper" (Shibugami ni tsutsumareta musume). It is the first part of "Ash girl," but it does not say whether it is a monkey or a snake.

Nagano: Chiisagata 172, "Longing for the maid" (Ohime koishii).

Kitaazumi-gun, Minamiotari: Kitaazumi 2 161. No title.

Kamiina-gun: Mukashibanashi 39, 77, "The monkey son-in-law" (Saru no muko dono) and "The girl and the monkey" (Musume to saru). A humorous tale.

Shimominochi-gun: Shimominochi 198, "The monkey's bride" (Saru no yome).

Tochigi, Haga-gun: Dai-ni 16, "The monkey son-in-law" No. 1 (Saru mukoiri); Shimotsuke 30, "The monkey son-in-law" (Saru no mukoiri).

Gifu, Yoshiki-gun: Hidabito III 6 28, "The monkey and his bride" (Saru to hanayome).

Hidabito V 2 36, "The monkey son-in-law" (Saru mukoiri). Not complete. Only that the tale exists.

Shizuoka, Kamo-gun: Shizuoka 434, "The monkey son-in-law" (Saru no mukoiri).

Shiga, Takashima-gun: MK I 10 47 "The monkey son-in-law" (Saru mukoiri).

Hyōgo, Kanzaki-gun: Dai-ichi 66, "The monkey son-in-law" (Saru no mukoiri).

Kinosaki-gun: MK II 8 32, "The monkey son-in-law" (Saru no mukoiri).

Hikami-gun: TD X 6 39, "The monkey son-in-law" (Saru mukoiri).

Osaka, Sennan-gun, Higashikatsuragi-mura: Kōshō 10 29, "The monkey son-in-law" (Saru no mukoiri).

Wakayama, Ito-gun: Kōshō 9 15, "The monkey son-in-law" (Saru mukoiri). This is a fragment.

Bichū (Okayama): Minzoku I 6 180. No title.

Hiroshima, Yamagata-gun: Aki 19, 25, "The monkey son-in-law" No. 1 (Saru muko banashi) and "The deer son-in-law" (Shika muko banashi).

Takata-gun: Aki 20, "The monkey son-in-law," No. 2 (Saru muko banashi).

Asa-gun: Aki 22, "The monkey son-in-law," No. 3. (Saru muko banashi).

Saeki-gun: Geibi 19, "The monkey son-in-law" No. 1 (Saru mukoiri). The beginning is like "Kachi-kachi Yama."

Hiba-gun: Geibi 27, "The wild boar son-in-law" No. 2 (Muko wa inoshishi). He was burned to death as the badger in "Kachi-kachi Yama."

Sera-gun: Geibi 25, "The wild boar son-in-law" No. 3 (Inoshishi muko). He drank water and became a handsome man.

Okayama, Oku-gun: Okayama bun III 5 33, "The monkey" (Osaru goke).

Yamaguchi: Bōchō I 2 18, "The monkey son-in-law" (Saru mukoiri).

Tokushima, Miyoshi-gun: MK II 10 37, "The monkey son-in-law" (Saru mukoiri); Ōawa 432, "The origin of Genpeida" (Genpeida no yurai). It is a legend.

Kagawa, Takamatsu: Dai-ni 17, "The monkey son-in-law" No. 2 (Saru mukoiri).

Mitoyo-gun, Shishijima: MK II 2 42, "The wild boar son-in-law" (Inoshishi mukoiri).

Fukuoka, Chikujō-gun: Fukuoka 215, "The monkey's great wish" (Saru no taibō).

Kumamoto, Aso-gun: MK I 2 42, "The monkey son-in-law" (Saru mukoiri). Two stories, one about digging burdock and the other about watering the rice paddy. MK I 6 30, notes on various versions in villages of Aso-gun.

Amakusa-gun: MK II 1 42, "The monkey son-in-law" (Saru mukoiri).

Nagasaki, Kitatakaku-gun: MK II 10 44, "The monkey son-in-law" (Saru no mukoiri).

Kagoshima: MK I 6 28, "The monkey son-in-law" (Saru no mukoiri); Kikai 31, "The monkey son-in-law" (Saru mukoiri); Koshiki 72, 81, "The mudsnail son-in-law" (Tamina mukoiri). After the mudsnail put water into the rice paddy, he became a handsome youth. The other story is the usual tale.

Further reference:

Nihon dōwa shū 691. This may be taken from "The maid from the wisteria bag" (*Fujibukuro otohime*), an *otogizōshi*.

Minzokugaku V 11 25. In China there is a monkey bridegroom story.

Nihon dōwa hyōgoku shū, ge 493.

4. Stepchildren Stories

34. Nukabuku, Komebuku
[Awabuku, Komebuku]

Once upon a time there were two sisters in a certain place. The older, Komebukuro, was the stepchild and the younger, Awabukuro, was the real daughter. The mother hated the older girl and constantly abused her. One day they were going to gather chestnuts with the village girls. The mother gave the older girl a bag with a rotten bottom and gave the younger daughter a new bag. Komebukuro did not fill her sack even by nightfall, so the rest left her and went home. She went down to a stream to drink because she was hungry. Then her real mother appeared as a white bird and gave her a silk dress to wear when she needed it, a hollyhock flute, and a new sack. The girl filled the sack with chestnuts and went home.

When the festival day came, the mother dressed her child in a beautiful dress to go, but she told the older girl she would have to spin three skeins of linen before she could go. Friends helped the older girl finish her task. She put on the dress the white bird had given her and played the flute as she went to the shrine. The mother and her child were watching the doll dance there. Komebukuro tossed the manjū wrappings and bamboo bark at her sister and hit her cheek. The girl recognized her, but the mother would not believe the older sister had come because she had so much work to do.

The older girl went home first, hurriedly changed into her old clothes and waited for her mother and sister to return. The next day somebody from the neighboring village came to ask for the older girl as his bride, but the mother tried to persuade him to take her child.

The girls got fixed up to be compared, but, of course, the older was lovelier and was chosen. The younger girl said she wanted to ride a splendid sedan chair and go off as a bride, too. Her mother dressed her up and set her on a hand cart and pulled it along, calling, "Anyone want a bride?" Her girl fell off the cart into a rice paddy and turned into a mudsnail, and the mother fell into the sluice and turned into a sluice clam.

Aomori, Tsugaru, Nanatsuishi

Aomori: Tsugaru m 72, "The girl who became a mudsnail" (Tsubu ni natta aneko no hanashi). Example; Tsugaru k 21, 23. No titles; Nihon shū, jō 122, "Komebukuro, Awabukuro."
Hachinohe: MK II 4 44, "Nukabukuro, Awabukuro." Four stories.
Iwate: Kunohe 492, "Komeko, Nukako."
Waga-gun: MK I 4 33, "Nukafuku, Akezara." Tasks include gathering acorns, gathering invisible shellfish, breaking a branch with a sparrow on it, etc. Akezara turns into a mudsnail at the end.
Shiwa-gun: Shiwa-shu 23 "Nukabuku, Komebuku"; Shiwa 140, "Nukabukuro, Akezara."
Isawa-gun: Kogane 70, "How the yamababa saved the girl" (Yamababa ga musume o sukūta hanashi).
Hienuki-gun: MK I 6 33, "Nukabukuro, Benizara."
Kamihei-gun: Tōno 103 No. 118. No title.
Iwate-gun: Dai-ichi 31, "Komebuku, Awabuku."
Akita, Kazuno-gun: Dai-ichi 40, "Komebuki, Awabuki."
Fukushima, Futaba-gun: MK II 4 38, "Nukabukuro, Benizara."
Iwaki-gun: Iwaki 27, 188, "The child by a former marriage and the stepchild" (Tsurego to mamako).
Niigata, Minamikanbara-gun: Kamuhara 66, 144, Notes 23 and 44. There are not two sisters in the latter. Its boundaries are clear.
Nagano: Shimominochi 196, "Nukaboko, Komeboko."
Minamiazumi-gun: Dai-ichi 51, "Nuka, Kome."
Yamanashi, Nishiyatsushiro-gun: Zoku Kai 149, "Snow Maid and Crow Maid" (Yukimusume, Karasumusume).
Kazusa (Chiba): Minzokugaku IV 3 30, "The Kazusa Cinderella" (Kazusa no Shinderera no monogatari). The names are Kushime and Tokume.
Ibaraki, Inashiki-gun: Kōshō 8 8, "Awabukuro, Komebukuro."
Shizuoka, Ogasa-gun: Shizuoka 406, "The stepmother and her stepchild" (Mamahaha to mamako no hanashi).
Ibara-gun: Shizuoka 398, "The stepmother and her stepchild" (Mamahaha to mamako no hanashi).
Shiga, Takashima-gun: MK I 10 47, "The stepchild and the real child" (Mamako to honko no hanashi). Two stories.
Nara, Soekami-gun: Yamato 298, "The selfheal flower" (Utsubogusa no hana). It tells the reason for the flower's shape.
Hyōgo, Mikata-gun: MK II 7 38, "When the stepchild gathered chestnuts" (Mamako no kuri hiroi).
Tottori, Yazu-gun: MK I 10 35, "Nukabuku, Akezara."
Okayama: Okayama bun II 2 60, "About the stepchild" (Mamako no hanashi).

Yamaguchi: Suō Ōshima 18, "Komebuku, Awabuku."
Nagasaki, Kitatakaku-gun: MK II 10 42, "Ōfu and Hagesen" (Ōfu to Hagesen).
Ikinoshima: Dai-ichi 82, "Chiyogoko."
Kagoshima: MK I 6 29, "Abusing the stepchild" No. 2 (Mamako ijime).

Further reference:
Nihon mukashibanashi shū, ge 60, "Bajji and Konguji." Helped by a Korean bird.
Huet 141.
Tabi to densetsu IV 6 8. An application of Freud.

35. Benizara, Kakezara

See previous entry, "Komebuku, Nukabuku."

Iwate, Hienuki-gun: MK I 6 33, "Nukabukuro, Benizara." These are the names of the two sisters.
Tokyo, Kitatama-gun: MK II 1 47, "Benizara, Kakezara."
Shizuoka, Hamamatsu: Shizuoka 411, "Benizara, Kakezara."
Ogasa-gun: Shizuoka 404, "The stepmother and her stepchild" (Mamahaha to mamako no hanashi).
Wakayama: Kii 8 [missing page in the book].

Further reference:
Nihon mukashibanashi shū, ge 60.
Minakata zuihitsu 60-80.
Yūyō zasso zoku shū.
Nihon dōwa shū 134. The girl wearing a bowl.
Yearsley 213. A Magarashii tale.

36. Sara-Sara Yama

Once upon a time there were two sisters, the older a child by a former wife. The mother sent them to fetch water while their father was away. She gave the younger girl a good dipper so she could dip water quickly, but the older girl's dipper was broken and she could not get any water. A feudal lord's procession passed by and the feudal lord took a fancy to the older girl. He wanted to take her with him to his castle. The girl requested that he ask her mother, so one of his men went to the mother's house. The mother said the younger one was nicer and begged them to take her instead. The man returned to the feudal lord with this message. The feudal lord decided to compare their intelligence to choose. He told the woman to prepare a tray with some salt, a dish, and a sprig of pine. She was to put the dish on the tray, the salt on the dish, and the pine on the salt. Then the two girls were to compose a poem about it. He would chose the one who did the best. The younger girl said:

On the tray is a dish; on the dish is salt; on the salt is some pine.

The older girl thought for some time and then said:

Oh, tray and dish, some snow has covered your mountain to nourish the roots of the pine!

With that, the older girl was placed into a sedan chair and carried back to the castle. The angry mother put her child into the lower part of a mortar and rolled it around until her eyes popped out and she turned into a mudsnail.

Nagano, Kitasaku-gun

Aomori: Tsugaru m 105, "The girl who composed poems" (Uta yomi ane sa no hanashi).
Nagano: Chiisagata 227, "Oh, bowl" (Banzara ya).
    Kitasaku-gun: MK I 12 34, "The girl and the mudsnail" (Musume to tanishi). Example.
Niigata, Minamikanbara-gun: MK I 1 26, 2 27, "Sara-sara Yama." Two stories with the same title.
    Sado: Dai-ichi 50, "Sara-sara Yama"; Sadogashima 14, 15, "Sara-sara Yama." Two stories with the same title. There is considerable design in the plot of the second. The girls were called Ohira and Otsubu. The tale is like the work of a professional.
Gifu, Yoshiki-gun: Hidabito V 5 21, "Sara-sara Yama."
Hyōgo, Mikata-gun: MK II 7 37, "The stepchild" (Mamako no hanashi).
Tokushima: Awa Iyayama 4, "Sara-sara Yama."
Fukuoka, Onga-gun: Fukuoka 48, "The stepmother" (Mamahaha no hanashi).
Ōita, Hayami-gun, Kitsuki-machi: MK I 12 39, "Sara-sara Yama."
Kumamoto, Aso-gun: MK I 6 31, "Sara-sara Yama."
    Tamana-gun: MK I 5 32, "Oh, tray and dish; oh, tray and dish" (Bonsara ya, bonsara ya).
    Hōtaku-gun: MK II 6 22, "Tray and dish" (Bonsara).
Nagasaki: (Old) Iki 113, "The mountain on the dish" (Sara sa no yama); Dai-ichi 83 "Sara-sara Yama."
Kagoshima: Koshiki 91, "Sara-sara Yama." No. 1.

Further reference:
    Nihon dōwa shū 155.
    Mukashibanashi kenkyū I 2 17. Poems in "Sara-sara Yama" in various regions.

37. The Old Woman Skin

The young wife of a certain wealthy man died and left an only daughter. The man married again and had many children by his next wife, but that woman hated the girl of the former wife. She told the nurse to get rid of her. The nurse gave the girl something called an old woman skin and told her to put it on when she was in danger. The girl put the old woman skin on and left home looking like an old woman. She wandered around here and there and finally became the water-carrier at the home of a gentleman. She always wore the skin except when she took a bath. The young master happened to see her once when the skin was off, and he suddenly became ill. The worried father asked a fortune teller to make a divination. The fortune teller said that there was somebody in the household that the young master liked. If he could meet her, he would recover. The master had each of the women, one after the other, take medicine to the young man, but he did not like any of them. At last it was the turn of the old woman who carried water. She said there was no point in going and tried to get out of it, but she was persuaded to go. When she arrived at the young man's room, he immediately saw through her disguise. She took off the old woman skin and turned into a beautiful girl. She was taken as his bride, and they lived happy together.

Niigata, Minamikanbara-gun

Aomori, Hachinohe: MK II 3 24, "The girl who went as a bride to the snake's house" (Hebi no toko sa yome ni itta mukashi).
Iwate, Kamihei-gun: Kikimimi 168, "The snake's bride" No.1 (Hebi no yomego).
   Shiwa-gun: Shiwa shū 60, "The old woman skin" (Uba kawa). It is a part of a story about the snake son-in-law.
Akita, Senhoku-gun: Ugo 209. Only a trace is present.
Fukushima: Iwaki 20, 111 "The old woman skin" (Baba kawa).
Niigata, Minamikanbara-gun: Kamuhara 117, "The old woman skin" (Babakkawa). Example; Kamuhara 178, "The frog skin" (Fuku no kawa). This is follows the snake son-in-law story.
   Sado: Sado shū 220, "The frog's gratitude" (Kaeru no ongaeshi); Dai-ni 48, "The frog's bag" (Kaeru no danbukuro).
Ishikawa: Kaga 1, "The three sisters" (Sannin shimai). It is at the end of the monkey bridegroom story.
Nagano: Chiisagata 116, "The old woman skin" (Ubagara).
Kai (Yamanashi): Nihon zenkoku 66, "The house of the yamauba" (Yamauba no ie).
   Nishiyatsushiro-gun: Zoku Kai 204, "The frog mask" (Gāru men). She receives a frog mask on her way to become the snake's bride.
Shizuoka, Ibara-gun: Shizuoka 424, "The snake's marriage" (Hebi no konin banashi). A frog saved from being swallowed by a snake repays his debt of gratitude. He appeared in the disguise of an old woman and gave the girl a dirty towel.

Okayama: Mitsu 87, "The girl with the frog's hood" (Kaeru no zukin
    musume).
Ōita, Kitaamabe-gun: MK I 4 37, "Gakkai Chōja."
    Bungo (Ōita): Minzokugaku V 10 86, "Ashi Chōja" (Asahi Chōja no
    hanashi). Here it is a cat skin.
Kagoshima, Kikaijima: MK I 6 24, "The gratitude of the fox" (Kitsune
    no ongaeshi). The story of how a fox skin, a kind of invisible
    cloak, is given as thanks by a fox.

Further reference:
    Nihon dōwa hyōgoku shū, ge 188.
    Yearsley 101.
    Kakisute 325.
    Aira chihō no kenkyū II 352. From the Suwa Shrine in Kamii-mura,
Kagoshima.

38. The Girl Who Tended Fires

This belongs to "The old woman skin" group.

Iwate, Kamihei-gun: Rōō 152, "A outline of the Deer Maid" (Shika
    musume no kōgai).
Ishikawa: Kaga 124, "The girl wrapped in tanned paper" (Shibugami ni
    tsutsumareta musume). This is added to a monkey bridegroom tale.
Shizuoka, Hamamatsu: Shizuoka 415, "Osan, Otomi, and Oichi" (Osan,
    Otomi, Oichi no hanashi). There were three girls. Otomi was the
    stepchild, and Osan and Oichi were the mother's real children.
    While Otomi was digging in a large rice field, she got tired and
    thought of her dead mother. Kannon appeared, looking like her
    mother, and told her to dig around the roots of the pine tree. She
    found good things to eat when she dug. She enjoyed them while
    her sisters slept. Oichi had one eye, so she could not see, but
    Osan had three eyes and slept with one of them open, so she saw
    what happened. She told her mother. The angry woman struck
    Otomi with a hoe and the handle broke in half. Otomi had a reve-
    lation from a god telling her that if she planted the pieces in the
    garden, a gold tree would grow. The feudal lord heard of this and
    came to take Otomi as his bride.
        This is a very different version or perhaps an old form.

39. Haibōtarō

This is about a boy, but it resembles "The girl who tended fires."
See entry for that story.
        Once upon a time there was a man named Sanpachi who was the

bath heater at the home of a warrior. Sanpachi was really a samurai, but circumstances made him become a bath heater.

One day the whole family set out to see the noh drama, leaving instructions for Sanpachi to have the bath heated by the time they returned in the evening. After they left, he heated the bath and got into it himself, dressed as a splendid samurai and went to the noh himself. There he joined in the festivities and performed a dance. He did so well that his master and everybody admired his dance. Sanpachi hurried home before the rest and dressed once more as the bath heater. He had the bath ready for the rest by the time they returned. When they got back, everybody was talking about how fine the unknown samurai's dance was. The daughter of the family became ill the next day and refused to eat. Although a doctor was called, he could not cure her. A fortune teller was asked the cause of her illness. He said if a certain person there would bring her food she would eat, and if that person cared for her, she would recover. Everyone tried in turn until only Sanpachi, the bath heater was left. When he took food to her, she ate well, and she recovered as he cared for her.

Nagasaki, Ikinoshima

Iwate: Esashi 46, "The girls who became rats" (Nezumi ni natta musume no hanashi).
    Kamihei-gun: Rōō 223, "Kannojō, the flute player" (Fuefuki Kannojō). The composition can be considered a katarimono. Kikimimi 164, "The poem written on a fan" (Ōgi no uta).
    Shiwa-gun: Shiwa shū 60, "The old woman skin" (Uba kawa). This version is about a girl. Refer to "The old woman skin."
Niigata, Minamikanbara-gun: MK I 3 32, "Sarujirō."
    Sado: Sadogashima 56, "Itonaga of Harima" (Harima no Itonaga). Quite a bit of embellishment has been added to this tale. It is evidently the work of a zatō.
Ishikawa: Kaga 34, "Haibo, the flute player" (Fuefuki Haibo). The beginning of the story is unusual.
Nagano, Kamiina-gun: Mukashibanashi 149, "Nonoya's daughter" (Nonoya no musume).
Okayama, Okayama City suburbs: Dai-ni 81, "One mountain in nine" (Kokonotsu yama no hitotsu yama); Mitsu 68, "One mountain in nine" (Kokonotsu yama no hitotsu yama). The above item. Refer to the section about the tasks of the son-in-law.
Hiroshima, Hiba-gun: Geibi 34, "The girl without hands" No. 3 (Tenashi musume). The principal character is Gonsuke and the story is changed considerably.
Tokushima, Miyoshi-gun: MK II 11 47, "Haibōtarō."
Fukuoka, Miyako-gun: Fukuoka 42, "The stepchild" (Mamako monogatari). It is not clear whether the principal character is a boy or a girl, but it seems like a girl.
Nagasaki: Shimabara 79, "The snake's bride" No. 2 (Hebi yomeiri) and "The demon who carried off a child" (Kosari oni); (Old) Iki 94, "Sanpachi, the bath heater" (Furotaki Sanpachi). Example.

Kagoshima: Kikai 45, 47, 48. The first two are "Haibōtarō" and the
last is "The son-in-law's tasks" No. 1.
Okierabujima: Okinoerabu 15, "The cat's face" (Neko no tsura).
Refer to "Haibōtarō" and "The older sister a demon" on pages 155
and 219 of the same book.

Further reference:
Tōō ibun 67.
Refer to "The old woman _skin," "Gakkai Chōja," and "The snake
son-in-law" of Kitaamabe-gun, Ōita.
Eiji who built fires for Koshiba Chōja.
Nihon densetsu shū 189. Haibōtarō was the name of the dog used
in destroying the monkey gods. The story is about the origin of Giken-
zuka at Kōzenji in Akaho-mura, Kamiina-gun, Shinshū (Nagano).

40. When the Child Gathered Acorns

A stepmother gave her stepchild a sack with a torn bottom and
her own child a good sack and sent them to gather chestnuts. Her
child filled hers quickly and went home, but the stepchild could not
fill hers. She began to cry as night came on, but she saw a light in the
distance. She found an old woman spinning alone in a house. That was
a demon's house, but the girl got the old woman to let her stay. The
old woman was afraid the demon would eat the girl, so she gave her a
magic cloak and hat to make her invisible and hid her in a corner of
the yard. When the demon came home, he said it smelled of a human,
but he could not find the girl. The girl ran away while the old woman
put the demon to bed. The feudal lord praised the girl because she had
a magic cloak and hat, and he gave her a reward.

Nagano, Kamiina-gun

Akita, Senhoku-gun: MK I 11 27, "Miyoko and Yaeko" (Miyoko to
Yaeko).
Fukushima: Iwaki 21, 111, "When the stepchild gathered chestnuts"
(Mamako no kuri hiroi).
Fukui, Sakai-gun: MK I 1 28, "The stepchild" (Mamako banashi).
Nagano, Kamiina-gun: Minzokugaku I 4 276, "The real child and the
stepchild" (Honko to mamako); Mukashibanashi 51, "The stepchild
and the true child" (Mamako to honko). Example. Does not have
the episode in which the girl becomes the wife of a chōja.
Yamanashi, Nishiyatsushiro-gun: Kai 14, "Awabuki, Komebuki." It is the
last part of the story "Awabuki, Komebuki."
Gifu, Yoshiki-gun: Hidabito V 5 21, "The three charms" (San mai no
ofuda). Two stories seem to have been carelessly combined.
Gunjō-gun: MK II 6 25, "When the stepchild gathered chestnuts"
(Mamako no kurihiroi).
Shizuoka, Kamo-gun: Shizuoka 392, 394, "The stepmother and her step-
child" (Mamahaha to mamako no hanashi). The first story is like
"Jizo Jodo." It resembles the Kai version.

Abe-gun, Osada-mura: Shizuoka 400, "The stepmother and her step-child" (Mamahaha to mamako no hanashi). Proceeds to the point when the real daughter follows the stepdaughter, picking up the chestnuts that fall out of the bottomless bag.

Suchi-gun, Shironishi-mura: Shizuoka 409, "The stepmother and her stepchild" (Mamahaha to mamako no hanashi). One was given a parched flour lunch and the other a pear lunch.

Osaka, Nakakawachi-gun: MK I 10 47, "The stepchild and the real child" (Mamako to honko no hanashi). Two stories.

Wakayama, Nishimuro-gun, Tanabe: Kyōdo ken III 3 47, "Joriki jōmon." Words in a child's game.

Arita-gun: Kii.

Ito-gun: MK I 12 21, "When the stepchild gathered acorns" (Mamako no shii hiroi); Kōshō 10 21, "Masako and Kiyoko" (Masako to Kiyoko).

Hyōgo, Mikata-gun: MK II 7 38, "When the stepchild gathered chest-nuts" (Mamako no kuri hiroi). Two sisters went to gather chest-nuts, but when night came, the stepchild stayed at a Jizō shrine. She received some beans and went home. When the younger sister tried to imitate her, she was eaten by demons. The younger girl shows some sympathy in the first part but not in the last.

Hiroshima City: Aki 49, "Otsuru, Okame".

Tokushima, Myōsai-gun: MK I 3 35, 36, "Gathering acorns" (Shii hiroi) and "The demon" (Oni). The first is somewhat modified as a child's story, but it is likely that this type of variant once existed. The second resembles "The ox-leader and the yamauba."

Mima-gun: Awa Iyayama 116, 131, "When the stepchild gathered acorns" (Mamako no kashi no mi hiroi) and "When the stepchild gathered chestnuts" (Mamako no kuri hiroi).

Fukuoka, Itoshima-gun: Fukuoka 52, "When the stepchild gathered acorns" (Mamako no shii hiroi). It goes like "Jizō Jōdo." This could be an early form.

Ōita, Kitaamabe-gun: MK I 4 35, "When the stepchild gathered acorns" (Mamako no shii hiroi).

Hayami-gun: MK I 12 43, "When the stepchild gathered acorns" (Mamako no shii hiroi).

Kumamoto, Tamana-gun: MK I 5 33, "The bottomless bag" (Sokonashi bukuro).

Saga, Kanzaki-gun: Tabi kyō 1.*

Saga-gun: MK II 7 35, "The torn bag" (Hage bukuro). The story is about an old man and an old woman gathering acorns. Either this story was originally like "Monkey Jizō," with the point about laughing or not laughing, or the stepchild theme has been forgotten.

Nagasaki: (Old) Iki 61, "When the stepchild gathered acorns" (Mamako no shii hiroi).

Kagoshima, Kikaijima: MK I 5 39, "The deity and the riceball" (Kami sama to o-musubi). This about gathering firewood. The older girl went to the hills to gather wood and received a demon's treasure. The younger tried to imitate her but failed.

Further reference:
Shizuoka-ken densetsu mukashibanashi shū 399, "Dipping water with a basket" (Mekago de mizu kumu hahashi). This episode is found in "The girl who built fires" and "The stepchild and the flute." The relationship between these two stories can be seen here.

41. The Bottomless Bag

This belongs to the group about the stepchild gathering acorns. See entry for that story.

Saga, Saga-gun: MK II 7 35, "The torn bag" (Hoge bukuro).
Kumamoto, Tamana-gun: MK I 5 33, "The bottomless bag" (Sokonashi bukuro).
Kagoshima: MK I 6 29, "Abusing the stepchild" (Mamako ijime).

Further reference:
Mukashibanashi kenkyū I 10 12, Seki Keigo discusses this group in "Mamako no shii hiroi."

42. Otsuki, Ohoshi
[or Ogin, Kogin]

This title has probably been used either because the story is like the Korean story in which the two climb to the Sky, or because it shows the connection with the escape to the Sky in "O Sun, the chain."

It should be considered different from the Nukabuku story because of how the younger girl protects her stepsister. Besides, it is a well told story.

Once upon a time there were two girls called Orinko and Korinko in a certain family. Orinko was a child by an earlier marriage. The stepmother hated Orinko so much that when her father was away in Kyoto, she had a box made and ordered Orinko to be buried alive in the forest. The younger girl heard about that and secretly had holes made in the bottom of the box. She gave Orinko poppy seeds.

Orinko dropped the seeds a few at a time while she was being carried away in the box and buried. After there had been enough time for the poppies to sprout, Korinko followed their course into the forest, calling to her sister. She dug her sister out with the help of an old man who came along, and the two children were allowed to stay with him.

When the father finally came home, he was so grieved over the fact that both girls were gone that he lost his sight. He looked like a blind pilgrim as he wandered around, singing and searching for his daughters.

He came across them unexpectedly at a certain village. His eyes opened when Orinko called him with a voice full of yearning. The three went home together and lived a happy life.

Akita, Hiraga-gun

Aomori, Hachinohe: MK II 4 46, "Ogin, Kogin." Here they are called Kariko and Uriko. Tsugaru m 47, 50, "Yurikohimeko" and "Chahinko and Chachirinko"; Tsugaru k 17. No title.
Iwate, Morioka: Susō I 130, "Chasenko, Chawanko."
  Waga-gun: MK I 3 24, "Otsuki, Ohoshi."
  Hienuki-gun: MK I 4 30, "Otsuki, Ohoshi"; MK I 8 44, "Otsuki, Ohoshi"; Kōshō 10 12, "Aranko, Ranko."
  Kamihei-gun: Kikimimi 395, "Otsuki, Ohoshi"; Rōō 139, "The later story of Ashiko and Kayako" (Ashiko to Kayako no kodan); Rōō 149, "A stepchild called Chawanko" (Mamamusume Chawanko). No younger sister. She must build a fire below the kitchen hearth and dip water with a bamboo basket. An old woman came and showed her how, which makes this close to "The girl who build fires."
  Shiwa-gun: Shiwa 150, 201, "Otsuki, Ohoshi" and "The pitiful sisters" (Aware no shimai); Shiwa-shū 68, "Okichi, Otama."
  Isawa-gun, Mizuswa-machi: Kikimimi 400. A note; Isawa*; Kogane 75, "Otsuki, Ohoshi."
Akita, Kazuno-gun: MK I 2 46, "Aranko, Koranko."
  Hiraga-gun: MK II 8 30, "Orinko, Korinko". Example.
Miyagi, Shita-gun: MK I 12 21, "Otsuki, Ohoshi."
  Momoo-gun: Kyōdo den 2 124, "Otsuki, Ohoshi."
Fukushima: Iwaki 23, 26, 113, "Otsuki, Ohoshi" and "Ogin, Kogin."
Niigata, Minamikanbara-gun: Kamuhara 79, 191, 183, "Osugi, Otama" Nos. 1 and 2. The second is close to "Nukabuku" which shows their relationship. The third is a note.
Fukui, Onyū-gun: Kōshō 8 8, "Ogin, Kogin."
  Echizen (Fukui): Nihon zenkoku 174, "Ogin, Kogin."
Ishikawa: Kaga 29, "Orin, Korin."
Nagano: Shimominochi 197, "Ryūwakamaru and Sayohime" (Ryūwaka-maru to Sayohime). It is composed like a romance. The younger sister's wisdom saves her brother.
  Chiisagata-gun: Chiisagata 247 "Faith in Kannon" (Kannon shinkō). About a brother and a sister. The brother was suspended from a tree but saved by forming a dog ladder.
Yamanashi, Nishiyatsushiro-gun: Kai 59, 214, "Fukuhara Chōja" and "The stepchild boiled in a kettle" (Mamako no kama yude). The first is like a katarimono.
Shizuoka, Abe-gun: Shizuoka 397, 400, 402, "Stepmother and stepchild stories" (Mamahaha to mamako no hanashi).
Gifu, Yoshiki-gun: Hidabito V 8 18, 19, "Ogin, Kogin" Nos. 1 and 2. They are two brief stories with only the part about being abandoned in the mountains.
Hiroshima, Hiba-gun: Geibi 30, "The girl without hands" No. 1 (Tenashi musume). The girl's name is Ogin, but the plot of story is that of "The girl without hands."

Takata-gun: Aki 47 "Otsuruji, Otaraji."
Hiroshima City: Aki 49 "Otsuru, Okame."
Fukuoka, Kurate-gun: Fukuoka 81, "The stepmother" (Mamahaha). The
older girl was called Haru and the younger, Aki.

43. The River That Rose Each Day

This is a story about stepchild abuse that belongs in the group
with "Nukabuku, Komebuku," "Otsuki, Ohoshi," and others. Refer to
them.
Could such a title belong to stories about abusing stepchildren?

Nagano: Chiisagata 225, "The river that rose each day" (Himasari
gawa). Example. When the stepdaughter was abandoned in the
river, the younger sister came every day with food for her and
asked how far the river had reached. At last, the older girl was
weakened in the water and died.

Further reference:
There is an old tale in Bulgaria called "How far has the river
come."

44. When the Stepchild Dug a Well

One of the stories about abusing a stepchild.

Kagoshima, Kikaijima: Shima I 5 75, "The hole at the side" (Yokoana).
A stepchild who was put into a well was instructed by an old man
in the neighborhood to put a piece of money into each bucket of
dirt that was pulled up. The child dug a hole in the side in the
meantime and escaped danger.

45. A Thousand Bundles of Thatch

Iwate, Kesen-gun: Tōō 145, "A thousand bundles of thatch" (Senba
kaya no hanashi).

46. The Stepchild Flower

Nara: Yamato 298, "The selfheal flower" (Utsubogusa no hana).
Nagasaki: (Old) Iki 99, "The stepchild flower" (Mamakobana). A legend
about selfheal.

47. The Stepmother Ghost

The "Otsuki, Ohoshi" story as changed into an anecdote.

Shizuoka, Suchi-gun: Shizuoka 408. No title. An inquiry was made about a child who always dozed at school. It was found that the stepmother disguised herself as a ghost to abuse him.

48. The Stepchild and the Flute

After Osono's mother died, a stepmother came bringing a child of her own. While Osono's father was away in Kyoto, her stepmother made Osono fill a kettle of water with a bamboo basket and build a fire under it to heat it. When the water was boiling, the stepmother put a pole over the kettle and told Osono to cross it if she wanted to see her father. The stepmother shook the stick when Osono was midway across and dropped her into the boiling water. The father asked about the girl when he reached home, but his wife said she did not know about her. When he went out into the yard, a nightingale flew out of where the child was buried and sang, "I dipped the water a thousand times with the basket and at last I was boiled in the water and turned into this form." The mother was frightened and tried to chase the bird away with a broom, but it continued to sing. The father found Osono's bones in the yard. The stepmother was taken by the authoriies.

Fukushima, Iwaki-gun

Aomori: Tsugaru m 16, 22, 48, "How the flea, the mosquito, and the louse were made" (Nomi to ka to shirami ga dekita hanashi). The same title on 19; "Senko, Manko" and "Sodome and the flint" (Sodome to kadoishi). The Sodome story is valuable because it falls between "Ogin, Kogin" and "The stepchild and the flute." The younger sister rescued her stepsister who had been abandoned in the mountain, and they stayed at a she-demon's house. She ordered them to dip water with a basket. A bird call told them how to do it. The she-demon tried to boil them alive, but she was the one who died. Their parents came looking for them.

This story is mixed up a bit, but the latter part is older than the stepmother story. Tsugaru k 19. No title.

Hachinohe: MK II 4 46, "The stepchild and the bird" (Mamako to tori).

Iwate, Hienuki-gun: Kōshō 10 12, "Aranko, Ranko" (Aranko to Ranko).

Akita, Hiraga-gun: MK II 8 30, "Orinko, Korinko"; MK II 10 22 "The three daughters" (Sannin musume).

Fukushima, Iwaki-gun: TD IX 5 75, "Osono who turned into a nightin-
    gale" (Uguisu ni natta Osono). Example; Iwaki 25, 116, "The step-
    child and the bird" (Mamako to tori).
Niigata, Kitauonuma-gun: Fushi 3 97, "Abusing the stepchild" (Mamako
    ijime). It is told as a true story.
Nagano, Shimominochi-gun: Shimominochi 196, "The three stepchildren"
    (Sannin mamako no hanashi).
    Chiisagata-gun: Chiisagata 224, "The weak toy bow and arrow"
    (Hama yumi yowaki). A fragment.
    Kamiina-gun: Mukashibanashi 64, 121, "I long for my father,
    hōyarehō" (Toto sama koishi ya hōyarehō) and "The three step-
    children" (Sannin mamako no hanashi).
Yamanashi, Nishiyatsushiro-gun: Kai 63, "The three flutes" (Sanbon no
    fue). The story is about the killing of three stepchildren. Three
    stalks of bamboo sprouted from their graves. They were cut and
    made into flutes. It is close to "Singing bones." Zoku Kai 147, "The
    stepdaughter" (Mamamusume). A girl who was abandoned in the
    mountains wrote a note and asked a sparrow to take it to her
    uncle. He saved her. We can see by this its relationship to "Ogin,
    Kogin" and "Ash girl."
Tochigi, Haga-gun: Dai-ni 51, "The chrysanthemum doll" (Kiku ningyō
    no hanashi). A girl was put into a box and abandoned. She wrote a
    note and asked a pigeon to take it to her father.
        This type of story seems unique to Japan. In stories in which
    the stepchild is put into a kettle, as well, they often die and turn
    into a bamboo flute or sing with the voice of a nightingale. Shimo-
    tsuke 40, "The strange flute" (Fushigi na shakuhachi).
Gifu: Utsushibana 70, "The three stepchildren" (Sannin no mamako). A
    bamboo grew from the grave of children who had been killed. It
    cried "piihoroo" when the father was about to cut it.
Shizuoka: Shizuoka 395, 399, 403, 407, "Stories about stepmothers and
    stepchildren" (Mamahaha to mamako no hanashi).
Hiroshima, Asa-gun: Aki 51, "Abusing the stepchild" (Mamako ijime).
Tokushima: Awa Iyayama 55, "The stepchild and the flute" (Mamako to
    fue).
Kagawa, Takamatsu: Dai-ni 52, "The bamboo flute" (Takebue).
Fukuoka, Ukiha-gun: Fukuoka 47, 48, "Stepmother hates me, chinchiro-
    rin" (Mamahaha urameshi chinchirorin), and "The stepmother"
    (Mamahaha no hanashi).
    Itojima: Fukuoka 49, "Killing the stepchild" (Mamako koroshi no
    hanashi).
Ōita: Buzen.*
Kumamoto, Amakusa-gun: MK I 11 43, 12 22, "The stepchild and the
    flute" (Mamako to fue). Two stories with the same title. Kyōdo
    ken V 3 4, "Folk faith in Banshū" (Banshū nōshin tan) by Sasaki
    Kizen.
Nagasaki, Kitatakaku-gun: MK II 10 40, "Going to Kyoto" (Kyō nobori).
    The flute sounded, "I want my father, chin-chirori." It is evident
    that the phrase was emphasized when the tale was told.
Kagoshima: MK I 6 28, "Abusing the stepchild" No. 1 (Mamako ijime);
    Kikai 59, "The seven white birds" (Shichiwa no shiradori). This
    resembles a foreign story to a strange degree.

Part of "Ash girl" started from here.

Is the bamboo flute of a later date than the bird's song?

Hearing a bird rather than the flute shows the influence of the Nukabuku story, and the motif of child being made to cross the kettle on two chopsticks seems derived from the she-demon tale.

Further reference:

Yearsley 47, 48.

Grimm's stories about stepchildren.

49. The Father's Gift

This belongs to stepchildren stories. The part about asking for a gift seems to be a recent innovation in stories about killing stepchildren.

Tochigi, Haga-gun: Shimotsuke 41, "The gold scissors and the little gold box" (Kin no hasami ni kin no tebako). A stepmother made the stepchild perform many difficult tasks, but an old woman next door kindly showed her how to do them. The fact that this assistance does not result in saving the child's life is evidence for this being an old version. However, neither a bird nor a flute appears in the tale.

50. The Girl Without Hands

Once upon a time there was a girl named Oharu whose stepmother hated her bitterly. The woman considered all kinds of ways to deal with the child, and finally she told her husband that she could no longer live with such a clever girl as Oharu and she wanted to leave him. The man believed his wife and decided to kill Oharu. He told her he would take her to a festival and led her far back into the mountains. He cut off her hands and went home with her crying with pain. Oharu managed to live by eating fruit and grasses. One day a handsome youth found her and asked why she had been treated that way. He felt sorry for her and took her home on his horse. His mother took care of her as if she were her own child. After a while the young man married Oharu, but he had to go to Edo before her baby was born. When the baby, a fine boy, was born, his mother sent a courier to Edo to let her son know. The man stopped on his way for a drink of water at a certain house. It happened to be Oharu's former home. When the stepmother heard about his errand and all about Oharu, she suddenly showed great hospitality. She made the man drunk and then exchanged the letter in his case for one that read, "A child like a demon or snake, something beyond describing, has been born." At Edo the young husband wrote, "Even if it is a demon or a snake, take good care of it till I return." The courier stopped at Oharu's former home to rest on his way back. The stepmother exchanged his letter for one that read, "Drive her and the child out." The mother was surprised over the letter and waited without showing it to Oharu. Days passed without the young master's return, so finally the mother wept and showed the letter to Oharu. Oharu asked to have her baby tied onto her back, and she set out from the house with nowhere to go. As she walked around aimlessly, she became thirsty. She leaned over a stream to drink, but her baby started to slide off her back. She tried to check his fall although she had no hands. Strange to say, her hands grew out suddenly. In the meantime, the young father returned from Edo and found both Oharu and his baby gone. When he looked into matters, he suspected the courier. He examined the letter and saw that it had been substituted. His mother urged him to lose no time in setting out to look for Oharu. When he reached a shrine at the edge of a stream, he saw a beggar that looked like Oharu. He spoke to her and found it was she. He was delighted over how her hands had been restored. They went home together happy. The father and stepmother were punished for abusing Oharu. The local official had them put to the sword.

Iwate, Hienuki-gun

Aomori, Hachinohe: MK II 4 46, "The girl without hands" (Tenashi musume). It is told as the origin of the nishiki tree.

Iwate, Hienuki-gun: MK I 5 25, "The favor bestowed by the thousand armed Kannon" (Senju Kannon no riyaku); MK I 8 40, "Oharu without hands" (Teboko Oharuko). Example. The original was clearly a katarimono.

Shiwa-gun: Shiwa shū 96, "Chohenko, Chahenko."

Waga-gun: MK I 3 21, "The girl without hands" (Tenashi musume).

Niigata, Minamikanbara-gun: Kamuhara 191, "Osugi, Otama."

Sado: Sadogashima 81, "The girl without hands" (Tenashi musume).

Yamanashi, Nishiyatsushiro-gun: Kai 304, "Hinoya of Kyoto and Hinoya of Osaka" (Kyō no Hinoya to Osaka no Hinoya).

Gifu, Yoshiki-gun: Zoku Hida 161, "The girl without hands" (Tenashi musume). No marriage and no child. Perhaps only a fragment is remembered. Hidabito V 5 20, "The girl without hands" (Tenashi musume).

Shizuoka, Kamo-gun, Inatori-machi: Shizuoka 390, "A stepmother and her stepchild" (Mamahaha to mamako no hanashi).

Hyōgo, Hikami-gun: TD X 6 40, "The girl without hands" (Tenashi musume).

Shimane, Ōchi-gun: Dai-ichi 74, "Abusing a stepchild" (Mamako ijime); MK II 9 30, "The girl without hands" (Tenashi musume).

Fukuoka: Fukuoka 43, "A stepchild story about Omatsu" (Mamako no monogatari Omatsu no hanashi).

Nagasaki: Shimabara 43, "The stepdaughter without hands" (Tenashi mamamusume).

Kagoshima: Kikai 56, "The girl without hands" (Tenashi musume).

Further reference:
Yearsley 199. It is interesting that everything even to the substitution of the letter is found in foreign lands.

5. Brothers Not Alike

51. The Brothers

Long ago at Yoshiachi in Shimokawara, Kakunodate there was a deep pool called Akafuchi which was filled with cinnabar. In those days two brothers at Shimokawara went every day to gather cinnabar. They made a living by selling it in town. The younger brother was quite different from his older brother and was wicked. The evil thought came to him that there was no telling how much he could earn if he gathered the cinnabar alone. One night he made a frightful looking dragon's head with red trays he fastened together. He took it to Akafuchi and set it afloat and then went off.

Not knowing that, the older brother came as usual to gather cinnabar, but when he saw the huge dragon with its mouth wide open as if to swallow him, he turned pale and ran away.

It all happened as the younger brother had planned, and he made lots of money by himself. One day when he went as usual to the pool and started into the water, he noticed that the dragon he had made looked alive. Since he had made it himself and set it afloat, he thought there was no reason for that. He made ready to dive in. The dragon had really come alive and swallowed him in one gulp.

Akita, Senhoku-gun

Iwate: Shiwa 58, "Gourd Chōja" (Yūgao Chōja).
Akita, Senhoku-gun: Dai-ni 27, "The cinnabar at Akafuchi" (Akafuchi no shu). Example.

Hiroshima, Takata-gun: Aki 181, "The Myōjin who blew out money"
(Kanefuki Myōjin).

Tokushima: Awa Iyayama 74, "The brothers who drew bows" (Yumihiki
kyōdai).

Nagasaki: Shimabara 109, "The horse that dropped gold" (Kin o hiru
uma). This is a humorous tale like the one about the two Muku-
suke. (Old) Iki 9 Note No. 4. The older brother brought back a
mikanko cat from the Dragon Palace.

Kagoshima, Amami Ōshima: MK II 5 44, "The greedy elder brother"
(Yoku no fukai ani).

Koshikijima: Koshiki 46, "The two brothers" (Futari Kyōdai). It
turns into a tale of "Singing bones" in the legend of "Koga Saburō."

Okinawa: Nantō 53, "The origin of the mandarin orange" (Kuganii no
yurai); Nihon shū, ge 147, "Until the golden tree grew fruit"
(Kogane no ki no naru made). About mandarin oranges.

Further reference:
Karin ryōzai shū, ge (In *Zoku gunsho ruijū* XVII 229).
Shisetsu tsukimi shū, ge (In *Zoku gunsho ruijū* XVII 138).
Konjaku monogatari, maki 31, No. 27. About asters and licorice
plants.
Kesen fūdogusa, ge 196. The origin of Hyappiki-zuka. The older
brother was poor and had only one cow. The younger was rich and had
99. He was jealous of him and burned the cow. Told here as a legend.
Perhaps this is older in form than the envious neighbor.

52. The Younger Brother's Success

This is part of "The Brothers" group. See entry on "The Brothers."

Miyagi, Momoo-gun: Kyōdo den 2 125, "The three brothers" (Sannin
Kyōdai). Each of three brothers was given five ryō and sent forth
to find his way in the world for three years. Ichirō threw his coins
at wild geese in the marsh, and while he slept in a shrine, he was
called by an old bowl. He put it into his bosom and practiced
thieving.

However, he was the oldest, not the youngest brother. It is a
zato's tale well told.

Yamanashi, Nishiyasushiro-gun: Kai 265, 273, "Morning tea" (Asacha).
A story ending with a play on words. "Disliking the character for
shi [death]" (Shi no ji kirai).

Tokushima: Awa Iyayama 78, "The three brothers" (Sannin Kyōdai).

A tale about seeing something in a dream is found in western
countries, too. See Yearsley 169. Three go on an expedition. It does
not say they were brothers.

53. The Sister and Her Younger Brother

First story:

A poor sister and brother lived together. There was a fan contest to be held at school one day. The boy went home and told his sister. She found an old frame and pasted paper on it and painted a plum tree and a nightingale.

The boy was ashamed because all his friends had magnificent gold and silver fans, and waited until the last to show his fan. When he opened it, the nightingale flew out and perched on the edge of the fan.

His fan was judged the best. His friends said that they would compare boats this time. He asked his sister to make him a boat. She made a little boat and put three clay dolls into it. The boat looked crude, but when the boy put it into the race, the three dolls set up the oars and rowed the boat. The little brother took first place again.

Second story:

Once there was a girl named Hana-no-senmatsu and her younger brother. He was the best student among his friends at school. They said they would give him a banquet one day. When he told his sister, she warned him to take the lid off each bowl and to look for steam on it. He was not to eat what was in the bowl if there was no steam.

The boy took the lids off the bowls at the banquet, but there was no steam on any of them. He remembered what his sister had said and did not eat anything except for a grain of rice that had stuck to his hand. He died when he went home.

His friends came to see, but his sister disguised herself to look like her brother and acted as though nothing had happened. They went back and ate the banquet, and all of them died. Then the sister gathered one thousand kinds of flowers and spread their juices over her brother and brought him back to life.

Kagoshima, Koshikijima

On Amami Ōshima and Okierabujima the two stories are preserved and handed down orally in perfect form.

Sanuki (Kagawa), Nakatado-gun, Honshima: Setonaikai 193. No title.
Nagasaki: (New) Iki 26, "The tree that grew gold coins" (Zeni naru ki).
Kagoshima: Koshiki 56, "The sister and her brother" No. 1 (Ane to otōto). Example. Two stories.
   Amami Ōshima: MK II 2 36, 38, "The big sister and her little brother" (Nēsan to otōto). Two stories.
   Okierabujima: Okinoerabu App. 1, "Lord Shimota" (Shimota dono no hanashi).

Further reference:

Mukashibanashi kenkyū II 12 20, "The sister and her younger brother" (Ane to otōto) by Iwakura Ichirō.

54. The Three Brothers

Each of three sons was given 100 ryō and sent out for three years to see who could lay up the most in his storehouse. The one who had things of the most value would inherit his father's wealth. The youngest set out for Kyoto and bought all kinds of silk. The middle son started to trade in rice and stored lots of it. The oldest set out for wherever his feet took him. He came to the Kannon temple at Kurokawa. The building was so dilapidated that he wanted to repair it and he put new thatch on it. The same for Gongen by the gate. But people who came to worship were put to great trouble because there was no bridge there, so he hired carpenters and put up a bridge, and spent all the money he had received. After the bridge was built, the man was pleased to see worshippers come flocking. He spent the night at the temple and had a dream. He dreamed he had gotten a fishing pole, and when he woke up, there was one by his pillow. He kept it and spent the next night at Gongen. He received a fan there that would restore youth and a tin flask of sacred wine. He decided to try his fishing pole from the new bridge he had had made. He caught a little bag, and when he shook it against the railing, money came jingling out. At home his wife was worrying because his storehouse would be examined on the next day, but he came along and told her not to worry. He took out his tin flask and poured her some wine. No matter how much he poured, it did not give out. He went to his storehouse and began to shake the little bag until he filled the place with money. The next day he served his relatives wine from the flask that would not run dry. Because his storehouse was filled with money, of course the oldest son inherited his father's wealth. He took out the fan that restored youth and used it on his mother and his wife. His mother wanted to become still younger and got out the fan when her son was away. She made herself too young and turned into a baby crawling around the place.

Iwate, Shiwa-gun

Aomori: Tsugaru m 32, "Blear-eyes, Scabby, and Louse-bitten" (Mekusare Ganbe, Shiramitagare no hanashi).
　　Hachinohe: MK II 4 47 (Sannin kyōdai) Two stories.
Iwate, Kamihei-gun: Rōō 12, "A thousand ryō to see a girl" (Ichimoku sen ryō no hanashi). Two stories seem to have been combined.
　　Shiwa-gun: Shiwa shū 16, "The fan that restored youth" (Wakagi no hōgi). Example.
　　Kamihei-gun: Kamihei 64, "Destroying the snake woman" (Hebi onna taiji).
Miyagi, Momoo-gun: Kyōdo den 2 125, "The three brothers" (Sannin kyōdai); Kyōdo den 3 122, "The three brothers" (Sannin Kyōdai). Both are humorous tales.
Gifu: Hidabito III 10 11, "Choosing the oldest son" (Ani erabi).
Nagasaki, Kitatakaku-gun: MK II 10 46, "The three brothers" (Sannin kyōdai). It is like a moral tale.

Kumamoto, Amakusa-gun: MK II 4 27, "The three sons" (Sannin musu-
　　ko). It resembles the Kikaijima version. It is well constructed and
　　like one used by a priest in a sermon.
Kagoshima, Koshikijima: Koshiki 38, "The three brothers" No. 1 (Sannin
　　kyōdai).
　　Kikaijima: Kikai 62, 150, "The inheritance of the third son" (San-
　　nan ga atotori) and "The three brothers" No. 1 (Sannin Kyōdai). In
　　the first story the three brothers set out to hunt for brides. The
　　corpse of the demon's mother that one of them was asked to carry
　　home on his back turned to gold. It is like "The hearth fire on New
　　Year's Eve." The second is like the Amakusa tale.
　　Okierabujima: Okinoerabu 217, "The three brothers" (Sannin
　　kyōdai). This story resembles a large number of legends, especially
　　that of Koga Saburō.

6. Finding Treasures

55. Gorō's Broken Bowl

A certain man gave each of his sons, Tarō, Jirō, and Saburō, money and told them to become successful at something and to come home in three years. Saburō became a dealer in cotton and Jirō became a dealer in rice, but lazy Tarō just stuck his money into his bosom and went far back into the mountains. There he met a yamauba, to whom he told everything. He worked for her for three years. When the time was up, she said he had worked well and gave him a dirty bowl. He accepted it and went home where Jirō and Saburō had already returned as independent merchants. The father looked at Tarō arriving in his dirty clothes and asked him what he had learned. The bowl in his bosom told him to say he had learned thieving. At that, the father told Tarō he would have to steal his horse that night to show him. The father hired young men to guard the horse and tied a scallop shell to his dog's mouth to prevent the theft. Tarō put his bowl into his bosom and went to the stable. The bowl fell out and dug a hole so he could go inside. He shouted, "I'm going to steal the horse now!" While everyone was rushing around in excitement, he led the horse out and took it to his father.

Aomori, Sannohe-gun, Gonohe-macl

Aomori, Sannohe-gun, Gonohe-machi: Dai-ichi 36, "The thieving bowl" (Nusubito wanko) Example. There is also a version in which he received a little chick instead of a bowl.

Iwate, Kamihei-gun: Kamihei 162, "The robber god" (Dorobō gami). A man heard music below a bridge and looked down. He saw a little doll. He picked it up and took it home. Whenever he looked at it, he felt like stealing. Nobody knew that he stole when he carried it in his pocket. He reformed later and threw the doll away. Rōō 22, "A chōja from a wooden Buddha" (Kibotoke Chōja).

Isawa-gun: Kogane 47, "The son who studied to become a thief" (Nusuto no shugyō shite kita musuko no hanashi).

Esashi-gun: Esashi 56, "How Gorō succeeded with the help of his broken bowl" (Gorō ga kakewan no okage de shusse shita to iu hanashi).

Tochigi, Haga-gun: Shimotsuke 58, "The origin of nostrils" (Hana no ana no yurai). A man picked up a broken bowl. He could make his nose get higher or lower when he hit the bowl.

Hiroshima: Geibi 40, "The three brothers" (Sannin kyōdai).

Kumamoto, Tamana-gun: Dai-ni 28, "Hinasan, the thief" (Nusubito Hinasan). The way he stole was like the way in the story of Goemon.

Nagasaki: Shimabra 104, "The tumbler toy" (Okiagari kobōshi).

Kagoshima: Koshiki 32, "The three brothers" (Sannin kyōdai).

Further reference:
Sangoku denki (In *Tōyō kōhi daizen* 151).

56. The Power of Treasures

Iwate, Waga-gun, Kurosawajiri: Kikimimi 231, "The bean story" No.3 (Mameko banashi). An old man followed a bean that rolled into a hole and received an ugly looking child from the Little Folk. He was about to throw it away when it said, "Don't throw me away, Grandpa!" The old man's family gradually prospered until he became the foremost chōja in his village.

Nagasaki: Shimabara 104, "The tumbler toy" (Okiagari kobōshi). A man bought a tumbler toy and performed all kinds of feats by its instructions. See "Gorō's broken bowl."

57. Hachikoku Yama

There once was a rich older brother who was stingy and a poor younger brother who was very good. One year the younger brother wanted to borrow rice seed from his brother, but the older brother put the seed into hot water before he gave it. The younger brother planted it, but none sprouted. Instead, a single calabash appeared. It spread out over his whole field and many gourds formed on it. He decided to eat gourds instead of rice. He picked the first one that ripened and tried to cut it open with a knife, but he couldn't. He split it open with an ax. A huge mound of rice poured out as high as a mountain. He became a famous chōja.

Iwate, Shiwa-gun

Aomori, Hachinohe: MK II 6 43, "Hachikoku Yama"; Tsugaru k 27. No title; Tsugaru m 9, "The bean vine that reached the Sky" (Ten sa nobita mame no hanashi). The wife in the story was from the Sky World. She gave a single bean to the child's nurse. After the nurse planted it, it grew to the Sky. She and the child climbed it to the Sky.

Iwate: Shiwa shū 58, "Calabash Chōja" (Yūgao Chōja). Example; Esashi 96, 33, "The teakettle lid that jumped" (Chagama no futa ga tonda to iu hanashi) and "The son who climbed to the Sky to become the son-in-law of Raijin" (Tenjō ni nobotte Raijin no muko to narō to shita musuko no hanashi).

Niigata, Kariwa-gun, Hōjō-mura: Echigo yashi I 6 147, "Hachikoku Yama"; Densetsu Echigo II 159, "Hachikoku Yama."

Kashiwazaki: Nihon den 206, "Yone Yama and Hachikoku Yama" (Yone yama to Hachikoku Yama).

Sado: Sadogashima 51, "Hachikoku Yama."

Ishikawa: Note 60, 101. No titles. One is a legend of a great drum at Matsuokadera and the other a legend of Sengoku Yama in Kashima-gun. Examples of folk tales becoming legends.

Shizuoka, Kamo-gun: Shizuoka 395, "A stepmother and her stepchild" (Mamahaha to mamako no hanashi).

Shimane, Ōchi-gun: Shimane I 4. [The reference is not clear.]

Hiroshima, Kamo-gun: Aki 82, "The tiger's eyes" (Tora no medama).

Saga, Saga-gun: MK II 7 34, "Roasted millet seed" (Itta awa dane).

Nagasaki: (Old) Iki 157, "Roasted millet seed" (Itta awadane).

Further reference:
Mukashibanashi kenkyū I 9 17. The Chinese versions.
Yearsley 206.
Huet 180.
There are many stories on Okinawa and in *Seiban densetsu shū* in which one grain of rice fills a kettle. The story has been turned into one of exagerations such as "Hachikoku Yama" and others.
Esashi-gun mukashibanashi 33. It is added to the story of Gengorō.
Shiwa-gun mukashibanashi 58. Rice from the gourd in "Calabash Chōja."
Kogane no uma 81. The bean story. Finding a single bean. Put into a kettle, it fills it to the brim. A single bean pounded fills the mortar.

58. Hold Fast or Stick Fast

Once upon a time a good old man and a bad old man lived in a certain village. When the good old man went into the mountains to work by himself one day, he heard a voice from somewhere call, "Shall

I hold fast or stick fast?" It called so many times that he answered, "If you're going to hold fast, hold fast. If you're going to stick fast, stick fast!" Strangely enough, gold and silver came flying from both sides in the forest and stuck to his shoulders and back. He took it home. While he and his wife were looking at it, his bad neighbor came and wanted some, too.

He lost no time imitating his neighbor. He went into the mountains the next day. Just as he expected, voices came from his right and left, calling, "Shall I stick fast or hold fast?" He answered, "If you're going to stick fast, stick fast. If you're going to hold fast, hold fast!" He turned his back and waited while pine pitch fell from the pines until his back was loaded. He called to his old woman to hurry with the pine torch so he could show her. She brought the torch too close. The pine pitch caught fire and burned the old man badly.

Wakayama, Arita-gun

Aomori, Hachinohe: MKII 6 43, "Carry me on your back" (Obareyō). An old man who was having a hard time at the end of the year set out to the home of a relative to borrow something. As he passed through a meadow at dawn, something called, "You can't borrow any money. Go home, instead, and boil red beans in your oil kettle." He went home and did as he was told. While he was doing it, a voice above the hook said, "Are you ready?" Then something jumped into it. Because of this, he became a chōja. Tsugaru m 67, "A ghost that said, 'Carry me on your back!" (Obasaru obosaru to iu bakemono.

Fukushima: Iwaki 30, "Shall I hold fast or stick fast" (Tottsuku ka hittskua ka).

Wakayama: Kii 11, "The honest old man" (Shōjiki na ojii san). Example.

Hyōgo, Kanazaki-gun: Dai-ichi 67, "Shall I hold fast or stick fast" (Tottsukō ka kuttsukō ka).

Tottori, Yazu-gun, Saigō-mura: Inpaku min III 2 22. No title. When a good old man went into the mountains to cut grass, a bird called and drew gold to him. Dust landed on the bad old man who imitated him. another story says he was told to put it on his old woman's seat. Also, there is one in which pine pitch sticks to the man.

Shimane, Ōchi-gun: Dai-ichi 73, "If you're going out, go out" (Deba dei). A voice asked, "Shall I go out?" He answered, "If you're going out, go out!" Then his teeth stuck out.
This has been made into a humorous tale.
Matsue: Kyōdo ken II 6 59, "Long ago in Izumo" (Izumo no mukashi, mukashi) by Shimizu Hyōzō.

Hiroshima, Hiba-gun: Hokuto 31 [The reference is not clear.]
Takata-gun, Yamagata-gun, Toyota-gun: Aki 175, "Shall I stick fast or hold fast" (Hittsukō ka mottsukō ka). Three stories with the same title.

Ehime, Kitauwa-gun: MK II 3 35, "Shall I stick fast, shall I stick fast" (Hittsukō ka hittsukō ka).

Ōita, Kitaamabe-gun: MK I 3 40, "I'll stick fast" (Suitsukō).

Hayami-gun: MK I 12 42, "I'll stick fast, I'll stick fast" (Hittsukō hittsukō). This is related to "Yarōka flood." In Akinokuni mukashi-banashi shū 270 it is told in the form of a hayamonogatari.

59. Carry Me on Your Back

This group belongs to "Hold fast, stick fast."

Aomori: Tsugaru m 67, "A ghost that said 'Carry me on your back'" (Obosaru obosaru to iu bakemono). It said, "I'll climb onto your back! I'll climb onto your back!" The man said, "Climb onto my back!" Something came crashing down. He saw the next morning that it was gold coins.
Hachinohe: MK II 6 43, "Carry me on your back" (Owareyō). Three brothers went out to the radish patch. It follows the pattern of "Picking Nara pears."
Iwate, Kamihei-gun: Tōno 234 No. 136. No title. A voice from a tuft of grass said, "Carry me on your back." The old man looked at it when he went home and found it was an image of Buddha. Rōō 196, "The shining gourd" (Hyōtan no hikarimono). A beautiful girl on a mountain peak said, "I want to be carried on the back of a man who is like wild boar."
Miyagi: Kyōdo den 1 168, "Daimi." An old man, the ancestor of a certain family, heard a voice from an old tree in the meadow say, "Carry me on your back! Carry me on your back!" This is handed down as a legend.
Niigata, Minamikanbara-gun: Kamuhara 127, "Barō Fox" (Barō gitsune). Kitakanbara-gun: MK I 12 19 "Baron, the ghost" (Baron bakemono). There are two stories. An old man came home bringing a ghost called Baron on his back in one and it turned to gold. There are traces of the old woman's participation in the other. It is in the form of an anecdote.
Koshi-gun, Jōjō-mura: (no source) Something kept saying, "Baron, baron," at the foot of a great nettle tree. It was a badger.
Aichi, Kitashidara-gun: Inoshishi 175 "The newly cut off head on the grave marker" (Tōba ni namakubi). The badger at Nokkoshi Pass. This also was only a ghost.
Hiroshima, Hiroshima City: Aki 163, "Osan Fox at Enami" (Enami no Osan Gitsune). This is a story of disguises.
Nagasaki: (Old) Iki 98, "The child who carried gold on his back" (Kin o ōta kodomo).

Further reference:
There was a stone outside the city of Awa in Tokushima that called "Oppasho." It gradually grew heavier when Hoshiai Mozaemon carried it on his back. He threw it with a great shout and it split into two. It no longer said "Oppasho" after that. Originally the strong man's tombstone, it has become a story of the test of a hero.

There is some connection with the story of the woman with a newborn babe. It may be an old ghost story.

60. Heaven's Blessings and Earth's Blessings

Once a good old woman and a bad old woman lived as neighbors. The good old woman was going to celebrate and go to worship Buddha on the 8th day of the Fourth Month, but when she went to invite her neighbor to go with her, the bad old woman said there was no use praying to Buddha. The good old woman set out alone. Along the way she picked up a purse filled with gold that had been dropped and left it tied to the railing of a bridge. When the bad old woman heard about it, she set out for the temple because she was greedy. When she reached the bridge, there was no purse, but a dead snake was wrapped around the railing. Angry, she split a piece of bamboo to pick up the snake and flung it into the good old woman's house. The good old woman heard a noise outside her window and saw something thrown in with a clatter. She looked to see what it was and found the little money bag she had left tied to the rail of the bridge. Money came spilling all over the house. She told her old man about what happened when he came home. He said that if something she had left tied to the bridge came flying into the house, it was bestowed by a god, and they both were very happy.

Yamanashi, Nishiyatsushiro-gun

Iwate, Kamihei-gun: Rōō 311, 310, "The frog's jar" (Kaeru tsubo) and "The fortune from birth" (Umaretsuki un).

Yamagata, Higashitagwa-gun: MK I 12 47, "Heaven's blessings and earth's blessings" (Tenfuku chifuku).

Niigata, Kitakanbara-gun: MK I 12 30, "Heaven's blessings and earth's blessings" (Tenfuku chifuku). There are three stories. The third is about fishing money up in a box. No snake but probably a variant of the same story.

Nagano, Kitaazumi-gun: Otari 59, "Morning sun, evening sun" (Asahi yūhi). A certain Mr. Okamoto in Nōsei, Nishikubiki-gun, Echigo [Niigata] had the same first dream at New Year for three years. He dreamed that there was gold at Yamazaki on the shore of Lake Aoki. When one of his employees ran ahead to dig it out, it just flew away. When he returned to his master's house, he found that it was filled with gold.

This is told in the form of a legend.

Kitasaku-gun: Kitasaku 207, "The transformation of the great snake" (Keshin no daija). It is said that the gold flew to Jōshū. A different version is in Kitaazumi-gun kōhi shū. A story about a dead snake. The motif of fate assigned at birth must account for this change. A variant is in Shiwa-gun mukashibanashi shū 106 and others.

Yamanashi, Nishiyatsushiro-gun: Zoku Kai 354, "The money bag and the snake" (Kane bukuro to hebi). Example.

Further reference:
Minakata zuihitsu 268.

61. The Snake and the Treasure of Gold

This belongs to the "Heaven's blessings, earth's blessings" group. See entry above.

Iwate, Kamihei-gun, Tōno: Kamihei 33, "The jar of gold" (Kogane no tsubo). The form is well preserved.
Yamanashi, Nishiyatsushiro-gun: Kai 25, "The snake and the treasure of gold" (Hebi to kin no tama). Stories like this and "Shall I hold fast or stick fast" or "The golden jar that came flying" are treated humorously in "If anyone sees you, turn into a frog."
    This is about an old priest who could not be satisfied. A golden jar went flying away. It is found in Kitasaku-gun kōhi shū and others.

62. Finding a Treasure

This belongs to the "Heaven's blessings, earth's blessings" group. See entry for that story.

Iwate, Kamihei-gun: Rōō 307, 311, "The old man and the jar of gold" (Jiji to kogane no tsubo). A jar of gold said, "Danger, danger" to warn that a cliff was crumbling. "The fortune from birth" (Umare-tsuki no un). Gold appeared as a snake to a neighbor, but when he threw it out the window it turned to gold.
Shiwa-gun: Shiwa shū 106, "Born with gold" (Umitsuki kane). There is nothing about a snake, but gold went flying off to a neighbor.

63. The Jar of Gold Coins

Aomori: Tekkiri 255, "Money that turned into snakes" (Kane ga hebi no naru hanashi). A mother and her child dug up gold coins. When the old woman next door saw them, she thought they were blue snakes. When she threw them through the roof they became gold.

Iwate: Kamihei 33 "The jar of gold" (Kogane no tsubo); Rōō 310, "The frog jar" (Kaeru tsubo).
Fukushima: Iwaki 154. No title. A voice called, "I'm afraid," in the night. When they went to see they found a jar of gold about to fall into the stream.
This can be a variant of the ghost of treasure at the roadside.

64. The Snake in the Jar

In Kyūshū it is not called "Heaven's blessings, earth's blessings."

Kumamoto, Amakusajima: MK II 4 28, "The old man next door" (Tonari no jiji). When the neighbor saw it, it was a bee.
Tottori, Iwami-gun: Inpaku min I 2 74, "A record about a treasure" (Takara no okibun) by Tanoguchi Tetsumi. A true story about an old villager named Matsukawa. It is an exact example of a folk tale that has become an anecdote. An old jar was found in that area in the hills back of Shoshiji. When it was opened, a beautiful little snake was there. After the neighbor received it, he became a chōja in a short time.

65. "If Anyone Sees You, Turn into a Frog"

There was a somewhat foolish novice at a certain temple. Once when he received a coin with a hole in it for going on an errand, he strung it onto a piece of straw and buried it in a corner of the yard. While he buried it, he said over and over, "If I dig you up, be a coin. If somebody else digs you up, turn into a frog." Whenever he received a coin after that for an errand, he always buried it with the same admonition. The old priest noticed this. He dug up all the coins one day and put a frog into the hole instead. When the boy came as usual to bury a coin, he discovered the coins were gone and a frog came jumping out. He cried, "Wait wait, I'm not somebody else! I'm me, I'm me! If you jump like that, the string will break." He ran after the frog as the old priest held his sides laughing.

Kōshū [Yamanashi], Nishiyatsushiro-gun

Iwate, Kamihei-gun: Rōō 310, "The frog jar" (Kaeru tsubo).
Ishikawa: Ishikawa 940, "The legend about a chōja" (Chōja densetsu). Shichiemon of Ōnogi in Kitaōnomi-mura had a dream about a coin bag. Following the instructions in the dream, he put a frog into

the bag and left it in a long chest. He looked after a number of days, and, sure enough, the chest was filled with coins.
    A fragment?

Yamanashi, Nishiyatsushiro-gun: Kai 173, "The coins and the frog" (Zeni to kaeru). Example.

Tochigi, Haga-gun: Shimotsuke 82, "The mochi that turned into a snake" (Hebi ni natta mochi). When the villagers saw it, it was good wine, but when the priest saw it, it was a snake. These stories are close to those in *Nihon ryōiki* and *Konjaku monogatari*.

Okayama: Mitsu 165, "The ohagi and the frog" (Ohagi to kaeru).

Fukuoka, Asakura-gun: Fukuoka 112, "Heaven helps a true heart" (Magokoro wa ten tasuku). A mother-in-law hid mochi and told it to turn into a frog if the bride found it. Then she found it.
    There is no part about substituting a frog.

Kurate-gun: Fukuoka 79, "The greedy old woman" (Gajitsubo baba ga). In this the bride substituted a frog for the mochi. The old woman cried, "Don't jump! The bean powder will fall off."

Kumamoto, Amakusa-gun: Kyōdo ken V 4 47, "The ohagi and the frog" (Ohagi to kaeru). About a mother-in-law and bride.

Nagasaki: Shimabara 240, "The frog botamochi" (Kaeru no botamochi).

Further reference:
    Tabi to densetsu I 4 72. A Kishigo story. In this it is a snake. He said, "It's me! Have you forgotten what I look like!"
    Honchō koji innen shū (In *Kōhi daizen* 634). At Iwami Ichiki a man had a dream in which he saw coins at the foot of a tree. When he dug them up they were iron, but when his neighbor dug them up they were gold.
    Seisuishō II 68. The line "Here, snake, have you forgotten how I look" is repeated a number of times to be entertaining.

66. Misokai Bridge

Once upon a time there was an honest charcoal-maker named Chōkichi at Sawaage in Niugawa, Hida. He dreamed that if he went to Misokai Bridge at Takayama, something good would happen, so he set out immediately. A tōfu maker came up to him and asked what he was doing. He laughed when he heard Chōkichi's answer. He said that anyone who took dreams seriously was foolish. He said he had been dreaming for some time that there was gold buried beneath a crypto-meria tree by the house of Chōkichi at Sawaage at the foot of Nori-kura, but it was only a dream and he took no notice of it. When Chōkichi heard that, he went home and dug around the tree. He promptly became very wealthy.

Gifu, Hida

Fukushima, Iwaki-gun: Iwaki 37, "Luck's treasure" (Un no tama).

Gifu, Hida [Yoshiki-gun]: Zoku Hida 134, "One dream and another" (Yume to yume). Example. This is exactly like a story about London Bridge.

Kagawa, Nakatado-gun: Nishisanuki 35, "The Gojō bridge of Kyoto" (Kyō-no-Gojō no hashi). There are two stories.

Further reference:
Mukashibanashi oboegaki 213, "Misokaibashi."

67. The Boy Who Had a Dream

A tutor asked his twelve students to tell the dreams they had on the 2nd Day of New Year, but one of them refused. This made the tutor angry and he had the boy put into a dugout boat and set adrift. The boat arrived at Onigashima on the 16th Day of New Year. The child deceived the leader of the demons cleverly and took his Thousand ri Stick, his Life Stick and his Listening Stick. He jumped to Osaka with the Thousand ri Stick. He saw two crows perched and with the help of his Listening Stick, he heard one say, "It looks as though the only daughter of West Chōja will die." The lad hurried to West Chōja's house and brought the girl back to life with his Life Stick. Since he had saved her life, and thus become the master of her soul, he was taken as her husband. The daughter of East Chōja died suddenly. Somebody came to ask the son-in-law of West Chōja to come. He took his Life Stick and restored her life, too. Then East Chōja insisted that he become his son-in-law but he refused. Finally, the feudal lord was asked to settle the matter. The feudal lord's decision was that the lad should be son-in-law of East Chōja for the first 15 days of the month and the son-in-law of West Chōja for the last 15 days of the month. In this way he received two households. Every 15 days one girl would accompany him to a bridge and the other would come to meet him. In that way his New Year dream of holding hands with two girls as he crossed a bridge came true.

Koshikijima

Aomori, Sannohe-gun, Hachinohe: MK II 6 43, "The chōja who had a dream" (Yumemi chōja). A chōja's son who would not sell his good dream was disinherited, but he became happy later.

Iwate, Kamihei-gun: Kikimimi 85, "The boy who had a dream" (Yumemi musuko). At the conclusion it is said that it was a dream, but it seems like something different. It may be turned around with the last part first.

Akita: Akita 119, "The whale" (Kujira). The village head, Daikoku, and an old she-demon wanted to hear the dream, but he would not tell it. He got treasures by tricks and had good fortune.

Fukushima, Iwaki-gun: Iwaki 35, "Gaining by refusing to tell a First Dream" (Hatsuyume o oshienai de toku shita hanashi).

Nagasaki, Tsushima Nita-mura Kuhara: TD XII 8 12, "The boy who had a dream" (Yumemi kozō).
Kagoshima: Koshiki 12, "The chōja who had a dream" (Yumemi chōja). Example.

68. The Bee and the Dream

Two merchants living in a certain place set out together to sell things. While they rested along the way, the older fell asleep. The younger man looked absently at the other's face and saw a horsefly come out of his nose and fly off toward Sado. The man woke up and said he had had a wonderful dream. It was about a wealthy man on Sado who had a yard full of white blooming camellias. A horsefly flew up from the root of a camellia and told him to dig there and he found a jar full of gold. The younger man asked him to sell him his dream. The older man thought it strange, but he sold it for 300 coins.

After their journey was over and they had returned to their village, the younger man secretly crossed over to Sado. He hunted out the wealthy man and lived as yard sweeper for him until spring. When the flowers bloomed, they were all red, not a single white one. He waited another year, and this time there was one tree covered with white flowers. He was delighted. He probed with fire tongs at its roots secretly in the night and heard a click. A jar of coins came out when he dug. He hid it where nobody could find it, and after half a year had passed, he asked to go home. He took the jar back to Echigo and he became a chōja. He lived the rest of his life in ease.

Niigata, Minamikanbra-gun

Niigata: Minamikanbara 94, "The white camellia on Sado" (Sado no shiroi tsubaki). Example. Densetsu Echigo II 58, "The golden bottle" (Kin no bin). About Jinsuke of Maze-mura in Nishikanbara-gun. The treasure was on Sado.
Nagano, Kitaazumi-gun: Kitaazumi 2 100, "The jar of gold" (Kin no tsubo). There is nothing about selling a dream in this.
  One of two men had a dream when he took a nap while resting. When the one who heard about the dream dug, a blue light came flying out and went into the house of the one who had the dream, where it became a snake in front of the alcove. It crumbled into gold when stabbed.
Ishikawa: Ishikawa 975. No title. A man went to the seashore according to the instruction of a dream. A golden magpie came flying and left two brocaded bags.
Yamanashi, Nishiyatsushiro-gun: Zoku Kai 160, "The jar merchant from the east and the jar merchant from the west" (Higashi no tsuboya, nishi no tsuboya); TD IV 2 39, "The merchant from the east and the merchant from the west" (Higashi no tsuboya nishi no tsuboya). The two men rested at the foot of a great lotus tree. One saw a

bee go in and out of the nose of the other. He dug out two jars, just like the dream, but this was a set of seven jars. When the other man hunted, he found the other five.

Could this be a katarimono?

Aichi, Kitashidara-gun: (no source), "The horse leader's dream" (Mago no yume).

Tokushima: Awa Iyayama 123, "The dream and the bee" (Yume to hachi).

Ōita: Bungo den 12, "Sanya Chōja." A peddler named Sanya Sansuke of Hagiwara bought a dream with ginger and a sifter.

Kagoshima, Kikaijima: Shima II 457, "The boat's captain who bought a dream" (Yume o katta sendō). The captain of a ship from Yamato bought a dream about a treasure at the foot of a gajimaru tree. He dug and found the body of his father for which he had been searching for years. Kikai 155, "The child who had a dream" (Yumemi dōshi). A child who had a good dream would not tell it and it came true.

Koshikijima: Koshiki 119, "Sanya, the rich man" (Sanya daijin) and 117, "The dream at Hachiman Shrine" (Hachimandō no yume). Both men became wealthy in the story on p. 117.

Further reference:
Stories about buying dreams.
Ujishūi monogatari No. 165, "Kibi to makibi."
Tōgoku yochi shūran 12.
Shasekishū VIII 23.
Sanya daijin (In *Eitaigura, maki* 3).
Shokoku monogatari 69.
Tabi to densetsu III 5 21. About Sanya Chōja by Ichiba Naojirō.
Shosai hikki 2. In the form of an anecdote.

69. Chōja from a Straw

Long ago a certain man prayed to Kannon that he would prosper. He received a revelation instructing him to accept the first thing that touched his hand if he fell as he left the temple. As he went through the gate, he stumbled on a stone and fell. A single piece of straw touched his hand. He carried it along and caught a horsefly. He tied it to the straw. As he continued his way, he met a nobleman's procession. A child in that procession, being held in someone's arms, began to cry suddenly and so the nobleman said he wanted the man's horsefly tied to the straw. The man gave it to him and received three oranges in return. He went on with his three oranges and met a cloth merchant who was suffering from thirst. He gave the man the oranges and received three bolts of cloth as thanks. He went on carrying the cloth and came across a group of men standing by a dead horse at the roadside, trying to think what to do with it. The man offered his cloth for it. When he gave the horse a drink, it was restored to life and proved to be a splendid mount. He continued on his journey with it. He asked to stay at a wealthy man's home one evening. The master there sent for him and asked to borrow his horse. He said the man could look after his place while he was away in payment. If something happened to prevent his return, he would give the man his estate. The master set out and did not return, so the poor man became the owner of the estate and lived for the rest of his life in comfort.

Hiroshima, Kure

Iwate: Shiwa 169, "Dragonfly Chōja" (Tonbo Chōja). It is a fragment of "Chōja from a straw." Most of it is close to the story in *Ujishūi monogatari*.

Kamihei-gun: Rōō 235, 299, "Laughing bones" (Warai gaikotsu). In the first part of "Singing bones" a man received a piece of straw as a symbol of disinheritance. He exchanged it for a plain leaf and then for bean paste, which he ate. This is followed by the story of the laughing bones. "Ichimonjiya Tōshichi." A child received a single coin and ended up a tobacco merchant.

Hienuki-gun, Yazawa: Dōbutsu 21.*

Iwate-gun, Mizusawa-machi: Kikimimi 64, "The help of a bee" (Hachi no okage). It goes into "The son-in-law's tasks."

Fukushima, Iwaki-gun: Iwaki 31, 121, "Chōja from a straw" (Warashibe chōja).

Gifu, Hida: MK II 11 35, "Chōja from a straw" (Warashibe chōja).

Hiroshima, Kure: Aki 110, "Chōja from a straw" (Warashibe chōja). It is exactly like *Ujishūi monogatari*. It is apparent that significance is given to the horsefly.

Shimane, Ōchi-gun: MK II 10 33, "Chōja from a straw" (Warashibe chōja).

Yamaguchi, Suō Ōshima: Suō Ōshima 30, "Chōja from a straw" (Warashibe chōja). The last half is forgotten.

Tokushima: Awa Iyayama 16 76, "A single strand of rope" (Hitosuji no nawa) and "Chōja from a straw" (Warashibe chōja).

Nagasaki: Gotō 244, "One thousand three hundred yen from three straws" (Wara san bon ga sen sanbyaku en).

Ikinoshima: (New) Iki 34, "Chōja from a straw" (Warashibe chōja).

Kagoshima, Koshikijima: MK II 12 23, "Chōja from a straw" (Warashibe chōja); Koshiki 8, "Chōja from a straw" (Warashibe chōja); Kikai 72, "The two brothers" (Futari kyōdai). The start is not like the usual story. The brothers were Sun and Sō. It is close to the Ikinoshima story.

Okinawa: Nantō 93, "Repaid for a kindness by a golden corpse" (Kabane kogane o motte on ni mukuita hanashi).

Further reference:
Ujishūi monogatari No 96. A man spending the night at Hasedera.
Konjaku monogatari, maki 16. No. 28.

70. Success through a Bee

There are many varieties of tales about being helped to success by
a bee.
One tells of becoming the son-in-law of a chōja by selecting the
girl that the bee signaled by a buzz.
Another is the son-in-law task type. From this type has developed
the story about the drum that sounds by itself and the story called
"Covering the drum with a sleeve."

Akita, Senhoku-gun: Ugo 142. No title. This becomes a humorous tale
ending in a word play. A lazy fellow wrapped a beehive in gold
paper to make it look like a gold ball and left it at a pawn shop.
The owner was suspicious and opened it. He was stung and scolded
his clerk, saying, "Even if we take pledges (shichi), we don't take
bees (hachi)." [Shichi also means "seven" and hachi means "eight,"
a double word play.]
Tokushima, Mima-gun: Awa Iyayama 10, "The drifter" (Gokudō mono no
hanashi). After a man saved a monkey and a bee, they helped him
cure the chōja's daughter, and he became the chōja's son-in-law.
Kagoshima: Koshiki 27, "Help from animals" (Dōbutsu no enjo). A beggar rescued a mosquito, a tortoise, and a monkey. He performed
tasks set by a chōja with their help, then married the chōja's
daughter.

71. Dragonfly Chōja

Aomori: Tsugaru k 30. No title. A girl went out to cut grass and found
spring of wine. When her parents went, they found only water. It
is a fragment.
Iwate, Iwate-gun, Nagahara-mura: TD III 11 33, "Dragonfly Chōja"
(Tonbo Chōja). It is handed down as a legend.
Something that was shining at a ferry proved to be gold. There
is no part about learning something from a dragonfly.
Another story is about Mano Chōja. It is the same as the
legend in Nagahama at the main family of Iwai Hana. Refer to
Mukashibanashi kenkyū II 5 8, "About a soul turning into an
animal" (Reikon ga dōbutsu to naru hanashi) by Asada Isamu.
Akita, Kazuno-gun: Nihon shū, jō 93, "Dragonfly Chōja (Danburi
Chōja).
Ishikawa: Ishikawa 979. No title. A legend of Moromi Hill in Notobe-
mura.
Okinawa: Iro 78, No. 99. No title. A fisherman washed his feet in
Sakugawa at Nakagusuku Anri. He received a bottle of wine from a
beautiful woman. His wife saw only regular water. Even now at
the Ina Festival water from this river is offered by a priestess.

72. Charcoal-Maker Chōja

In a certain place there were two fathers who were friendly neighbors. They went into the hills to cut wood together and stayed overnight at a little shrine for the Mountain Deity and they had similar dreams. They dreamed that many deities were waiting for the Mountain Deity to return from the village. When she came back, she said that two children had been born to neighbors. The girl had been born with the fortune of one shō of salt and a bottle of wine, but the boy's luck was only one shō of rice. The deities wanted to know about their marriages. She said since they were neighbors she had thought of having them marry, but would wait and give it more thought. The two men awoke and compared dreams. They thought it very strange. When they went home, they found that a girl had been born at one's house and a boy at the other's.

When the children grew up, they married. They prospered with the good fortune the wife had received, but the husband was unhappy over the way his wife used one shō of salt a day and never let the wine bottle out of her hand. He finally drove her away.

The woman walked along with nowhere to go. She felt hungry and pulled a radish growing by the road. Wine came springing up from where she pulled it. She drank some and was refreshed. She walked toward a light shining in the hills beyond and found a blacksmith's house, and asked him to let her stay. He refused because he was too poor. All the seats and paving stones at his place, however, were made of gold. The woman persuaded him to take them to town to sell. There was gold all around the smithy's house, and wherever they dug, wine would spring up. In less that no time the old man became a chōja, and a town built up around his home. The woman's former husband became poorer and poorer. At last he and his son came to sell firewood at that town.

Iwate, Waga-gun

Characteristics of this story are the blessings through the wife.

The two patterns here are the good wife and finding treasures.

These are related to the idea of destiny foretold.

In the second part of the story we have the element of the wife who makes good wine.

These episodes are followed by storehouses of rice.

The story takes a humorous turn sometimes, such as throwing gold at birds or rice at a shadow.

The versions are distributed widely as legends, perhaps because they were katarimono.

Aomori, Hachinohe: MK II 6 44, "Charcoal-maker Chōja" (Sumiyaki chōja). There are four stories. Also, see Okunan Shinpō, August 7, 1930.

Iwate, Kamihei-gun: Rōō 9, "Charcoal-maker Chōja" (Sumiyaki Chōja). The former husband was a blacksmith and he later came to work at her house. All around the smithy's house was gold. He did not throw coins at birds, but he threw rice at his shadow. On page 322 of this book there is a story called "The chōja with a charcoal storehouse." (Sumi-no-kura chōja).

Shiwa-gun: Shiwa shū 28, "Uemon Tarō and Saemon Tarō" (Uemon Tarō to Saemon Tarō). A well-preserved story. It must be related to "Kowashimizu."

Waga-gun, Kurosawajiri: Kikimimi 27, "Charcoal-maker Chōja" (Sumiyaki Chōja) Example.

Akita, Senhoku-gun: Ugo 35, Mentioned; MK I 6 40, "How a poor man got a bride" (Binbōnin no yometori).

Fukushima, Futaba-gun: MK II 4 37, "Charcoal-maker Chōja" (Sumiyaki Chōja). This may have been carried around by itinerant singers.

Miyagi, Karita-gun, Tōkarita: Minzoku sō 90.*

Niigata: Densetsu Echigo II 33, "Gongasawa." It is in the form of a legend.

Sado: MK II 4 31, "Charcoal-maker Gorō of Yamada Shiratake" (Yamada Shirataki Sumiyaki Gorō); Aikawa 173. No title.

Minamikanbara-gun: Kamuhara 158, 196, "Chrysanthemum wine" (Kiku no sake) and "Charcoal-maker Chōja" (Sumiyaki Chōja). Wine is found in both stories.

Ishikawa, Nomi-gun: Dai-ichi 51, no title.

Nagano, Ina-gun: Ina 5, 213, "The willow tree at Lake Sugatami" (Sugatami ike no yanagi) and "Kitōji, the charcoal maker" (Sumiyaki Kitōji).

Chiisagata-gun: Chiisagata 136, "Charcoal-maker Chōja" (Sumiyaki Chōja).

Nishichikuma-gun, Kisō: Kyōdo ken V 4 42, "The legend of Charcoal-maker Chōja at Mino" (Mino no Sumiyaki Chōja no densetsu). About the chōja's estate at Mikasa Pass.

Yamanashi, Nishiyatsushiro-gun: Kai 3, 176, 182, "The long-lived chōja" (Enmei chōja), "Hōkiemon of Hōki-no-kuni" (Hōki-no-kuni no Hōkiemon sama), and "Fortune from birth" (Umaretsuki no un); Zoku Kai 184, "Tōjirō, the charcoal maker" (Sumiyaki Tōjirō).

Shizuoka, Fuji-gun: Nihon den 77, "Chōja-ga-ike." A story about waving back the sun. This may be a katarimono.

Gifu, Yoshiki-gun: MK II 11 37, "Charcoal-maker Chōja" (Sumiyaki Chōja).

Gujō-gun: MK II 6 26, "God of Gold and God of Fortune" (Kane-no-kami to Fuku-no-kami).

Hyōgo, Kinosaki-gun: MK II 8 34, "The origin of the gold mine on Sado" (Sado no kinzan no okori).

Hikami-gun: TD X 6 40, "Charcoal-maker Chōja" (Sumiyaki Chōja). This is the first part of "Wearing a bowl" (Hachi katsugi). In Bungo this story is the first part. Emphasis is put on the latter part when it is recited.

Hiroshima, Mitsuki-gun: Geibi 172, "Charcoal-maker Chōja" (Sumiyaki Chōja).

Shimane, Ōchi-gun: MK II 8 48, "Charcoal-maker Chōja" (Sumiyaki Chōja). The chōja's daughter was married 49 times, but was not settled happily until the 50th time.

Tokushima, Mima-gun: Awa Iyayama 51, "The beginning of Sumitomo" (Sumitomo no okori).
Miyoshi-gun: MK II 9 39, "Charcoal-maker Chōja" (Suimiyaki Chōja).

Kagawa, Mitoyo-gun, Shishijima: Sanuki I 2, "Gorōbei, the charcoal-maker" (Sumiyaki Gorōbei).

Kōchi, Hata-gun, Abiike: Report by Mr. Sakurada. "Gorō, the charcoal-maker" (Sumiyaki Gorō). Later he became Sumi-no-kura of Kyoto.

Fukuoka: Chikuzen 25.* A legend about Katsuyama Chōja. There is a part about throwing rice at a shadow. An example of an idiot who prospers.

Kumamoto, Kikuchi-gun, Shirokita-mura: Higo VI 190-o, "The chōja's estate" (Chōja yashiki). It is about Kosaburō, the mat weaver, but like charcoal-maker Kogorō.

Nagasaki: Shimabara 173, "The cat's benefactor" (Neko no onjin). This is a fragment of "Charcoal-maker Chōja." It is strange because there is a fight between the cat and an octopus.
Ikinoshima: (Old) Iki 34, "The millet that was kicked" (Ashige ni sareta awameshi). Stories of how a former husband was ruined and became a basket seller are found in many places. There is a definite connection between this and the tale of the reed cutter in *Konjaku monogatari, maki* 30, No. 5.

Kagoshima, Kikaijima: MK I 4 23, "Charcoal-maker Chōja" (Sumiyaki Chōja); Kikai 38, "Bankoi from the west" (Nishi no Bankoi). There is a part about throwing coins at a swan, an attack on Onigashima, a magic mallet that shakes out things, and the chōja who set fire to his house. See "Gorō, the charcoal-maker" (Sumiyaki Gorō) on p. 33 and "The gratitude of the kappa" (Kappa no ongaeshi) in the same book.
Koshikijima: Koshiki 1, "Charcoal-maker Chōja" (Sumiyaki Chōja).

Okinawa: Nanto 98, "Becoming the wife of the Charcoal-maker Chōja by the help of a sparrow go-between" (Suzume no nakōdo de Sumiyaki Chōja no tsuma ni natta hanashi). The wife who had been driven away by a sparrow catcher married a charcoal-maker. She met her former husband again after he became a basket seller. She shamed him and he died.

Further reference:
Kanei shoka keifuden. (In *Shi ryō* XI 3 78).

73. Potato-Digger Chōja

A man-servant at a certain house was told to dig potatoes. He went to the hills to dig and found gold nuggets here and there in the dirt, thus becoming a chōja.

Iwate: Kamihei 23, "The golden cow" (Kogane no ushi). A man who dug potatoes found a vein of gold and became a chōja. The story is concluded by the story of a liar. This may be one kind of derived tale.

Gifu, Ōno-gun, Niugawa-mura: Utsushibana 119, "Potato-digger Tōhei" (Imohori Tōhei).

Wakayama, Arita-gun: Nanki 4, "Potato-digger Chōja" (Imohori Chōja). The story of Chōja-ga-mine at Tsugi-mura. A homely girl from a neighboring village came to be the bride of Chōgorō, the potato-digger. He threw gold coins at ducks at the mouth of the river and said, "We have as many of these at home as the potatoes we dig." The name came from this.

Shimane, Ōchi-gun: MK II 9 33, "Potato-digger Chōja" (Imohori Chōja). There are two tales. The first is a fragment of "The wife from the Dragon Palace." The other is about how the daughter of Gakkai Chōja of Shimonoseki took her maid with her and went as a bride. When her maid Chiyo washed rice, the water turned to wine. That is said to be the beginning of the Kōnoike family. The name Chiyo appears in rice-planting songs sung when carrying lunches to planters. In Rikuchū the tale of Charcoal-maker Chōja says that a maid was taken along by the bride.

Tsuchi iro XIII 1 (No. 76) 11, "Kamoe Kannon." The origin of Kamoe Kannon. A woman from Chūgoku was always unfortunate. Her father gave her a jewel and told her to select a place where the soil was the color of the jewel to die. She met an old man selling yams at Shichiken-machi in Hamamatsu and asked him. He said he knew of a place and took her into the mountains where coins came out when they dug. They married and built a shrine according to a revelation from Kannon. When they finished building it, they still had ten ryō left.

74. The Hearth Fire on New Year's Eve

Once upon a time there was a maid called Ofuji. Her master told her on New Year's Eve she should be careful not to let the fire go out, but somehow it went out before she realized what had happened. She went to borrow coals from another house. Everywhere she went the people were already asleep. As she went farther and farther, she saw a fire burning in the mountains. When she asked for live coals, she was told she could have them, but she was asked to look after a coffin for a while as a favor. That troubled her, but there was no help for it. She got the coals and went home with the coffin on her back. She hid it in the corner of her room where nobody could see it. The 4th and 5th Day of New Year came, but nobody arrived to claim the coffin. Ofuji was worried and opened the coffin to look. It was filled with gold. When she told her master, he said he would give her the money. She decided to build a temple with it. After it was finished, she and her master were invited to come to it together. On the way, Ofuji stepped onto a purple cloud and went into the temple. There she turned into the image of Kannon. She was called Toshikoshijin [Deity of the New Year].

Hyōgo, Mikata-gun

Aomori, Hachinohe: MK II 6 45, "The hearth fire on New Year's Eve" (Ōtoshi no hi).
Fukushima, Iwaki-gun: Iwaki 34, "Receiving a treasure on New Year's Eve" (Ōmisoka ni takara o sazukerareta hanashi).
Gifu, Ōno-gun, Niugawa: Utsushibana 64, "The New Year pine and the maid" (Kadomatsu to gejo).
Hyōgo, Mikata-gun: MK II 9 37, "The origin of Shōgatsu San" (Shōgatsu San no okori). Example.
Hiroshima, Takata-gun: MK I 6 45, "Kōnoike" No. 1 (Kōnoike no hanashi).
Okayama: Mitsu 109, "New Year's Eve" (Ōmisoka no yoru).

75. The Guest on New Year's Eve

Once upon a time a horse leader had no customers on the day before New Year. He thought as he started home that he would have nothing with which to celebrate. Trees stood in a row along his way. He noticed a leper lying under them alone and groaning. He had felt sorry for himself, but he saw that here was somebody worse off. He lifted him kindly onto his horse and took him home. The man's body smelled so vile that he laid him on straw matting in a corner of the room with a dirt floor to spend New year's Eve. His guest did not get up in the morning of New Year's Day. Although he shook him, he did not answer, so he thought the man must have died. When he looked closely, he saw that the man had changed into a huge lump of gold.

Aichi, Minamishidara-gun

Aomori, Hachinohe: MK II 6 47, "Turning into money" (Zeni ni natta hanashi).
Iwate: Esashi 30, 63 "How a zatō was connected with improved fortune" (Zatō ga shinjō ni kakawatta to iu hanashi) and "Five pilgrims all turned into money boxes" (Rokubu gonin ga mina kanebako ni natta to iu hanashi).
Niigata, Minamikanbara-gun: Kamuhara 22 31, "The guest on New Year's Eve" (Ōmisoka no kyaku), Nos. 1 and 2.
Fukui, Sakai-gun: MK I 1 31, "The New Year's Eve Man" (Toshitori otoko). How the New Year firewood came to be called "toshitori otoko" [New Year's Man].
Aichi, Minamishidara-gun: Dai-ichi 60, "The guest on New Year's Eve" (Ōmisoka no kyaku). Example.

Hiroshima: Geibi 43, "The guest on New Year's Eve" (Toshi no kyaku). Four stories. The beggar was given a place to stay in one and in the other three there is a fire that goes out. In the Takata-gun story the beggar came and said he would give them live coals if they let him stay. This combines the live coals with putting up the beggar, showing that originally the two parts belonged to one story.

Tokushima: Awa Iyayama 9 126, "The three chōja" (Sangen chōja) and "The guest on New Year's Eve" (Ōtoshi no kyaku). The son of a poor man who lived between two chōja climbed onto their roofs and began to recite ill omens. The astonished chōja divided rice and money with the poor man, so he became the third chōja. In the other story the seven guests which the maid allowed to spend the night at a chōja's house proved to be Shichifukujin [the Seven Gods of Happiness]. The dead man they carried on their backs was a sack of gold coins, but there is no part about getting fire.

Kagoshima: Koshiki 156, "The guest on New Year's Eve" (Ōmisoka no kyaku).

Okierabu: Okinoerabu 109, "The guest on New Year's Eve." No. 3 (Ōtoshi no kyaku).

Okinawa: Yambaru 182, "The man who turned into a monkey" (Saru ni natta hito); Nantō 16, "Fire at New Year" (Hi shōgatsu no hanashi).

76. Sedge Hats for Jizō

Once upon a time there was a poor old man and old woman. Soon it would be New Year, but they had no money for mochi. The two of them made sedge hats to sell, and the old man set out on a snowy day for town to sell them. He saw twelve Jizō standing with snow on their heads and looking cold by the road along the way. He felt sorry for them and put one of his hats on each, but he lacked one hat. That was too bad for the remaining Jizō, so the old man took off the hat he was wearing and put it onto Jizō's head. Then he went home. His old woman came to meet him and asked about the mochi, but when he told her about the Jizō, she praised what he had done and rejoiced with him. She said they could build up a good fire and go to bed after they had warmed themselves at it. The next morning they were awakened by voices calling. They drew open their door and found lots of fresh pounded mochi. The surprised couple saw the backs of the twelve Jizō wearing sedge hats as they went away, led by the Jizō wearing the old man's hat.

Fukushima, Iwaki-gun

Aomori, Hachinohe: MK II 6 45, "Sedge hats for Jizō" (Kasa Jizō).
Iwate: Shiwa 67, "The gratitude of the six Jizō" (Roku Jizō ga on o kaesu); Shiwa shū 119, "Seven Jizō" (Shichinin Jizō Sama).

Esashi-gun: Esashi 4, "Being kind to the stone Jizō" (Ishi Jizō ni on o okurareta to iu hanashi).
Isawa-gun: Isawa.*
Akita, Senhoku-gun, Kakunodate: Kikimimi 233, "Sedge hats for the stone Jizō." No. 1 (Ishi Jizō no kasa).
Yamagata, Mogami-gun: Toyosato 258, "The six Jizō" (Roku Jizō); MK II 4 40, "The gratitude of the Jizō" (Jizō no henrei).
Fukushima: Iwaki 32, "Sedge hat Chōja" (Kasa Chōja). Example.
Niigata, Nakauonuma-gun: Dai-ichi 45, "Sedge hats for Jizō" (Kasa Jizō).
Minamikanbara-gun: Kamuhara 143, "Sedge hats for Jizō" (Kasa Jizō).
Minamiuonuma-gun: MK I 7 27, "The gratitude of the six Jizō" (Roku Jizō no henrei).
Sado: MK II 4 32, "Sedge hats for Jizō" (Kasa Jizō).
Nagano, Chiisgata-gun: Dai-ni 55, "Sedge hats for Jizō" (Kasa Jizō). A rat dragged the gifts from the Jizō to the old couple. This is not in any other version. It is the result of turning it into a child's tale.
Yamanashi, Nishiyatsushiro-gun: Kai 9, "The gratitude of Jizō" (Jizō no hōon).
Chiba, Ichihara-gun, Goi-machi: Ichihara 480, "Jizō" (Jizō Sama).
Shimane, Ōchi-gun: MK II 9 33, "Sedge hats for Jizō" (Kasa Jizō). The tale is not clear. MK II 12 34, "Sedge hats for Jizō" (Kasa Jizō).
Tokushima, Mima-gun: Awa Iyayama 62, "Shōgatsu Sama" (Shōgatsu Kami Sama).
Saga, Kishima-gun: Kōshō 10 16, "Sedge hats for Jizō" (Kasa Jizō); Techō 35. The above reference. The appealing sight of the retiring Jizō, the old woman praising what her old man had done, their peaceful joy—it is in the same group as the "Owari sedge hats" in *Tōkaidō meisho zue*, and it also belongs to the same group as "The hearth fire on New Year's Eve."

77. Kōbō's Loom

An itinerant priest came with his bowl to a certain house where the woman was weaving busily at her loom. She got down and gave him alms. Although he returned a second and third time, she stopped each time and gave him something generously. He was impressed by her good nature and said he would give her a treasure in thanks. He left her a shuttle and went on his way. She had only to wind the warp and use the thread in her shuttle to weave, and it would last her for the rest of her life. Sure enough, even after three years had passed, the thread in the shuttle did not give out. She had been warned not to put her finger into the opening where the thread came out, but it seemed so strange that it had not diminished in the three years she had used it that she put her finger in to see. The shuttle disappeared instantly with a clatter. It is said that the itinerant priest was Kōbō.

Aomori, Hachinohe

Aomori, Hachinohe: MK II 6 47, "Kōbō's loom." Example. There are
   four stories. The woman was good in the first, the example. This is
   close to the original form. The other three are fragments. Or
   perhaps they are faulty transmissions.
Tōtōmi [Shizuoka], Igawa: TD XIII 11 10. In "Jibata" by Iwai Saburō.
Nagasaki: (Old) Iki 118, "The little shuttle that never gave out" (Izumi
   no kokuda).

78. The Magic Towel

   Once upon a time a shabby beggar stopped at a house. The housewife was busy weaving and she drove him away because she did not
like to hear him. Her maid secretly gave him some riceballs, and in
thanks he gave her a towel. When she wiped her face with it, everybody was surprised at how beautiful she looked. They asked her why,
and she told them what had happened the day before. Her mistress was
bitterly disappointed. The beggar came again some days later. This
time the housewife welcomed him politely and gave him all sorts of
things. He gave her a red sash and left. When she put the sash on, it
turned into a snake.

Ikinoshima

Aomori, Hachinohe: MK II 7 41, four stories. In the first, "The origin
   of the monkey" (Saru no hajimari), a good woman received something like a thin piece of silk from an itinerant priest. When she
   wiped her face with it, she looked younger, but when her pitiless
   master and mistress used it, they turned into monkeys. The second
   is "Kōbō Daishi" (Kōbō Daishi Sama no hanashi). Kōbō Daishi tore
   off one of his sleeves and gave it to a good-natured but homely
   maid who cooked rice for him. The third is "An old priest" (Oshō
   sama no hanashi). This is about a bride and her mother-in-law. The
   mother-in-law's face turned into a horse face. The old priest told
   the bride that if she would use the other side of the towel, she
   would recover. The fourth is "Kōbō Daishi and the maid" (Kōbō
   Daishi to jochū). The servant became beautiful, but her mistress
   turned into a horse. It is a humorous story here.
Niigata, Sado: Sado no shū 190, "The woman whose face was cured of
   pockmarks by Kōbō's power" (Kōbō Daishi Sama no ontoku abata ni
   oyobu).
Shizuoka, Shita-gun: Shizuoka 129, "The ghost's revengeful spirit"
   (Tatari to onryō yōkai).
Tokushima: Awa Iyayama 104, "The magic towel" (Takara tenugui).
Nagasaki: (Old) Iki 116, "The magic towel" (Takara tenugui). Example.
   (New) Iki 46, "The magic towel" (Takara tenugui).

79. Water That Restores Youth

Once upon a time there was an old man and an old woman. The old woman became thirsty when she went into the hills to gather wood. She went farther back into the hills and found a spring where she took a drink. When she did that, she turned into a girl seventeen or eighteen years old. Her old man was surprised when she went home, and asked what had happened. When he heard, he decided to be young, himself. He set out to look for the spring, but no matter how long his wife waited, he did not return. She went to look for him and found him by the spring. He had drunk too much and turned into a baby.

Tochigi, Haga-gun

Tochigi, Haga-gun: Dai-ni 32, "The old man who turned into a baby" (Kodomo ni natta ojii san no hanashi). Example.

Nagano: Chiisagata 161, "The water of youth" (Wakamizu).

Hiroshima, Jinseki-gun, Toyomatsu-mura: Geibi 79, "The water of youth" (Wakamizu). The origin of mugwort. A dutiful son went to Ise Shrine to dip up the First Water of New Year for a sick parent. When he returned, he found that his father had been dead for 30 days, but he restored him to life with the water. His wife thought the water was a bother and threw it out. A strange tree and plants grew from the medicine. They were called **yonogi** ["mugwort" or "one night tree"] because they grew in a single night.

Shimane, Ōchi-gun: MK II 10 32, "The water of Higan" (Higan no mizu no hanashi). This is turned into a humorous tale with a play on words and extreme exaggeration. Perhaps that is because of how it was heard originally, probably from an unknown traveller.

80. The Golden Hatchet

When an honest woodcutter was working by the edge of a pond, he accidentally dropped his hatchet into it. As he stood troubled, a beautiful girl came up out of the water with a golden hatchet in her hand. She asked him if he had dropped his. He said that his was a rusty one, not that. She went back into the water and brought up the rusty one. She praised the old man for his honesty and gave both hatchets to him. With that, he became a chōja.

When the old woman next door heard about the golden hatchet, she sent her lazy old man out to cut wood. His hatchet did not fall into the water, no matter how long he waited, so he threw it in. The beautiful girl appeared with a golden hatchet. The old man said that it

was his and started to take it from her. She called him dishonest and
cut his head with it. He went home covered with blood, and he became
poorer and poorer.

Iwate, Shimohei-gun, Iwaizumi

Iwate, Shimohei-gun: Kikimimi 70, "The golden hatchet" (Kogane no
    chōna). Example.
    Esashi-gun: Esashi 82, "The man who received a strange jewel from
    the Pond Spirit" (Fuchi no nushi kara fushigi na tama o moratta
    otoko no hanashi). Instead of a hatchet, it was a strange stone
    that caused rain when it was touched.
Fukushima, Iwaki-gun: Iwaki 39 172, "A palace that was under the
    water" (Mizu no naka ni goten no atta hanashi) and "Dig here,
    bow-wow" (Koko hore wan wan).
Aichi: Mikawa 526, "The ax from the Dragon Palace" (Ryūgū no ono).
    An ax from the Dragon Palace is treasured at the home of Mr.
    Suzuki in Oka, Miai-mura. It is said to have been traded for an ax
    made in the human world by someone who found that one marvel-
    lous.
Ōita: Naori 27, "The silver ax and the golden ax" (Kin no ono to gin
    no ono).

81. The Little Boy from the Dragon Palace

Once upon a time there was an old man in Higo who made a living
by going into the mountains to cut wood and selling it in town. One
day he could not sell any wood, no matter how much he tried. He came
to the bridge in the center of town all worn out. He tossed his bundles
of wood, one after the other, into the deep pool in the stream. After
praying to Ryūjin [the Dragon Deity], he started home. Just then a
beautiful girl holding a child in her arms came up out of the pool and
told the old man the child was a gift from Ryūjin in repayment for the
wood. She handed him the little boy and said his name was Little
Runny-nose Boy. She said he would give the old man anything he asked
for, but the old man was to prepare a dish of fresh shrimp for the
little boy three times a day as an offering. After she had explained,
she went back into the water.

The old man carried the child home and set him at the side of his
alter shelf. He took good care of him. The boy would bring out anything the old man asked for with a single blowing sound from his nose.
In a short time the old man became such a rich man that people hardly
knew him.

The old man went to town every day to buy the shrimp and prepared the dish for the little boy, but finally that became a bother. He
said to Little Runny-nose Boy that there was nothing more that he
wanted and asked him to go back to the Dragon Palace and give his
regards to Ryūjin. Little Runny-nose Boy went outside without a word,

but for some time he could be heard snuffling. In the meantime, the storehouse and the house gradually disappeared and only the former shabby house remained. The terrified old man rushed out to stop the boy, but he could see no sign of him by then.

Kumamoto, Tamana-gun

Aomori, Hachinohe: MK II 7 42, 43, "The New Year pine of the Dragon Palace" (Ryūgū no kadomatsu) and "Giri flew off" (Giri ga tonda hanashi).

Iwate: Esashi 13, 23, "The beginning of Hyottoko" (Hyottoko no hajimari) and "The Lucky God Untoku who came from the pool" (Fuchi kara agatta Fukushindō Untoko).

Shiwa-gun: Shiwa shū 8, "The Lucky God, Yonegai" (Fuku no kami Yonegai).

Niigata: Minamikanbara 89, "The little boy from the Dragon Palace" (Ryūgū Dōji).

Kumamoto, Tamana-gun: TD II 7 20, "Little Runny-nose Boy" (Hanatare kozō sama). Example; MK I 5 35, "Little Runny-nose Boy" (Hanatare kozō sama).

Kagoshima, Kikaijima: Dai-ni 25, "Ryūjin and the flower pedlar" (Ryūjin to hana uri); Kikai 3, "Ryūjin and the flower pedlar" (Ryūjin to hanauri).

Further reference:
Momotarō no tanjō 59.
Mukashibanashi kenkyū I 4 7 and I 5 12.

82. The Golden Puppy

Aichi, Nukata-gun: Aichi 252, "Mafuku Chōja and the green snake" (Mafuku Chōja to aohebi). The origin of Mafuku Chōja at Iwatsumachi. He rescued a little snake and dreamed he would get a little dog. It would be a sea treasure, etc. He cooked three shō of rice every day for the dog, and it disgorged three shō of gold dust. That made the old man a chōja. This may be a recorded tale.

Nagasaki, Ikinoshima: Dai-ichi 81, "The turtle that disgorged gold" (Kin o hiru kame).

Kagoshima, Kikaijima: Shima II 440, "The dog that disgorged gold" (Kane o hiru inu).

83. The Boy Magician

Nagano, Shimoina-gun, Yamamoto-mura: Fukihara No. 3 49, In "Folk tales of Yamamoto-mura, Shimoina" by Inoue Masafumi. A little boy called Abe-no-dōji was the child of a fox. He was led to the

Dragon Palace for saving a tortoise. He brought back treasures called tora-no-maki and ryūsengen. When he wore the tora-no-maki next to his skin, he could not feel heat or cold. When he put on the ryūsengen, he could understand what the birds said. He went to Kyoto to make his fortune because of what he heard. He went through the streets calling, "I pity those who do not know there will suddenly be a great calamity." Soon he was called the boy magician. He cured the emperor's illness.

84. The Visit to the Dragon Palace

Aomori, Hachinohe: MK II 7 42, "The visit to the Dragon Palace" (Ryūgū iri). A man called Zensuke at Sotogahama rescued a flatfish. A tortoise came to meet him and took him to visit the city in the sea. He received a box which he was not to open, but opened it and turned into an old man just as Urashimatarō did.

Iwate, Kamihei-gun: Kikimimi 463, "The instructions of Ryūjin" (Ryūjin no denju). He cured illnesses with the jar of sacred water Ryūjin gave him. When the jar was broken by mistake, plants grew where the water spilled. They were called mugwort. It reminds one of "The water of youth" and other such humorous stories.

85. The Magic Mallet

This belongs to the same group as "The little boy from the Dragon Palace."

After an old man threw his pine boughs for New year into the river a messenger from the Dragon Palace appeared and took him to the Dragon Palace. He enjoyed all kinds of feasts there. He was given a magic mallet when he started home. He was told that anything he wanted would come out of it. He tried striking it and ordering rice ["kome"]. Lots of it came out. He asked for a storehouse ["kura"] next and got storehouses to put rice into. His neighbor was envious and inquired how it happened. He borrowed the mallet. He wanted to get a lot of storehouses at one time and said "komekura, komekura" as he shook it. Out came many little blind men ["ko-mekura"]. They chased him and killed him.

Kumamoto, Yatsushiro-gun

Aomori, Hachinohe: MK II 7 45, "The little blind men" (Komekura hōshi).
Hiroshima: Geibi 70, "Jizō Jōdo." When he shook the mallet and said, "Komekura come out," blind children came out and said, "We want rice, old man. We want cakes, old woman." This is a child's idea of the blind, and it is turned into a children's story.

Okayama: Okayama bun II 6 32, "Komekura."
Kumamoto, Amakusa: Kyōdo ken V 6 37, "The mudsnail man" (Tamina otoko).
Yatsushiro-gun: Dai-ichi 77, "Rice storehouses, little blind men" (Kome-kura, ko-mekura). Example. If one considers that the narrator was a blind hōshi, the play on words is more amusing.

86. The Handmill that Ground out Salt

Once there were two brothers at a certain place. The older was a sympathetic, good man, but the younger was a greedy gambler.

One year when a famine came, the older man gradually spent all his savings to help villagers around him until he became poor. While he was troubled one day because he had nothing to eat, a white-haired old man came and said that since he had been doing what he could for the villagers, he had brought something good for him. He gave him a handmill that would grind out anything he wanted and then he left. The older brother said for rice to come out or money to come out, it would come out when he turned the mill. He divided it all with the poor people around him. His brother heard about the strange handmill and wanted to get possession of it. He invited his brother to bring it along and took him with it into a boat. Then he rowed out to sea. There he killed his brother. The younger man was short of salt and asked for it as he turned the mill, but he did not know how to stop the mill. Finally, he sank with it to the bottom of the sea.

The reason the sea is salty is that the little handmill is still grinding.

Tokushima, Mima-gun

Iwate, Kamihei-gun: Rōō 293, "The handmill that ground out salt" (Shiofuki usu). It tells of meeting Little People and trading a wheat manjū for a handmill. There is an element of "Issun Bōshi."
Fukushima, Iwaki-gun: Iwaki 169, "Why the sea is salty" (Umi no mizu no shoppai wake).
Okayama: Mitsu 171, "The handmill that ground out salt" (Shiofuki usu).
Tokushima, Mima-gun: Awa Iyayama 87, "The stone handmill in the sea" (Kaichū no ishiusu). Example.

Further reference:
Mukashibanashi kenkyū I 9 21, Chinese stories. Good and bad brothers are taught by a mountain god. They receive a handmill from a little spirit. It is stolen by a thief, etc.
Chōsen mintan shū 30, "Why the sea is salty" (Kaisui no shiokarai riyū). Stealing a treasure mill. It does not say how it was obtained. The first part is dropped.

7. Overcoming Evils

87. Demon Stories

Fukushima: Hōgen IV 5 12, "Mamechokotarō." In "Dialect and Aizu tales" (Aizu mintan hōgen) by Takei Takashi. It is a variety of stories about fighting demons. There are others called "Fox stories" (Kitsune mukashi).

88. Picking Nara Pears

Long ago there were three brothers. Their father had been ill for a long time and somehow never could recover. Somebody said that if he ate Nara pears that grew back in the hills, he could get well. The oldest son set out to pick some. Along the way he met an old woman gathering firewood and asked her the road to take. She told him there was a monster in those mountains and nobody who had gone into them had ever returned. He did not heed her warning and started on. She told him that he would see a black bird and a white bird flying around a little farther on. If the black bird called, he should not go ahead, but if the white bird called, he could go on. A black bird and a white bird were really there. The black bird called for him not to go, but the boy was so intent upon helping his father get well that he went on until he came to a pond. A single Nara pear tree with sweet-looking ripe fruit stood there. He was happy and climbed the tree. While he was picking the fruit, a monster rose up out of the pond and swallowed him. The second son decided to go next, but he, too, was swallowed by the monster. The third son would not heed his father's plea for him not to go. He made a straw image and set out with it. He met the old woman along the way and asked her what had become of his brothers. She said that they must have been swallowed by the monster. She warned him not to go, but he went for his father and to take revenge for his brothers. This time the white bird told him to go ahead. He tied the image he had brought to the Nara pear tree by the pond. He hid himself as the monster came out. It thought the image was a man and tried to swallow it, but it was tied fast. The boy came out and leaped upon the monster while it was trying to get the image. He gripped its throat. It begged to be forgiven, but the boy would only if he restored his two brothers. The monster disgorged them. The three sons picked lots of Nara pears and took them to their father. Then his illness was cured.

Iwate, Hienuki-gun, Hanamaki

Aomori, Sannohe-gun, Hachinohe: MK II 9 43, "Picking Nara pears" (Nara nashi tori). There are four stories. The first three are like "The gourd that made sounds," the following tale group. The words in the stories are interesting, but the first and last parts are not well connected. They are fragments.

Iwate: Shiwa 66, "The ghost of mountain pears" (Yamanashi no bake-mono).

Kamihei-gun: Rōō 197, "Nara pears" (Nara nashi). The father and two sons went to get pears for the pregnant mother. They were helped by all sorts of warnings along the way. The form is that of a genuine folk tale.

Hienuki-gun: Dai-ni 30, "When the three brothers picked Nara pears" (Sannin kyōdai no Nara nashi mogi). Example.

Yamagata, Higashitagawa-gun: MK I 12 46, "Narita plums" (Narita no sumomo no hanashi). This is rather broken up.

Akita, Senhoku-gun: Ugo 281. No title. About three brothers and a priest. The priest destroyed an old badger that was disguised. It is like "Hōin and the fox."

Niigata: Sado shū 148, "Picking Nara pears" (Nara nashi tori no hana-shi).

Tochigi, Nasu, Toriyama-machi: Nihon zenkoku 122, "The ghost pear tree" (Bakemonon nashi no ki).

Kagoshima, Amami Ōshima: MK II 8 40, "The sympathetic third son" (Nasake bukai sannan).

Further reference:
Yearsley 76.

89. The Gourd that Made Sounds

This belongs in the group with "Picking Nara pears."
Two brothers were frightened by a calabash that sang and they ran home. The third took it and it proved to be a treasure.

Aomori, Hachinohe: MK II 9 44, "The gourd that made sounds"
    (Sayazuri fukube).
Iwate, Kamihei-gun: Rōō 196, "The gourd that shone" (Hyōtan no
    hikari mono); Kamihei 26, "Gourd Chōja" (Fukube Chōja). There is
    some relation to "Singing bones."

90. The Flower that Reflected a Human Form

    This is found in stories called "Crossing to Onigashima," "Rescuing
a beautiful girl," "The wife from the Sky World," and others. In Saeki-
gun, Hiroshima, they say it was a male flower and a female flower.

Aomori, Hachinohe: MK II 9 44, "Crossing to Onigashima" (Onigashima
    watari).
Hiroshima: Geibi 119, 196, "The origin of the song" (Uta no yurai) and
    "Destroying the baboon" (Hihizaru taiji).

91. Kotsuna, the Demon's Child

    An old man and an old woman had a daughter, but she was carried
off by a demon. The old man searched for her for a long time, and at
last he met a child far back in the hills. He realized suddenly that he
was his daughter's child. While the father, his daughter, and child
were rejoicing together, the demon came home. They hid the father in
the closet. The demon declared the place smelled of a human and he
looked all around for him. Finally, he knew the man was there. The
woman and her child brought the old man out and begged the demon
not to eat him. The demon wanted to eat him so badly that he decided
to boil him in the bath. He had his child heat the water. The boy
showed the old man a secret way to escape and went on firing the
bath as though he knew nothing. After he thought the old man had
enough time to escape, he put the lid on the bath and set a big stone
onto it. The daughter and her child escaped by the secret way and
took a dipper with them. When the demon came to see, his child was
not there and nobody was in the tub. He concluded they had run away
and started after them angrily. The old man, his daughter, and her
child were at the seashore in a boat and starting to row away when
the demon caught up. He began to drink the sea water, complaining all
the while. Little by little the water in the sea went down and drew
the boat to the shore, almost within reach of his hands. Then the
demon's child took the dipper and saucily imitated the way the demon
was drinking. The demon burst out laughing and spat up the sea water.
The boat got away safely out to sea, and they reached home.

Nagano, Minamiazumi-gun

Iwate, Kamihei-gun: Rōō 135, "Kotsuna, the demon's child" (Oni no ko Kotsuna). There is a latter part to this. The demon's child was burned to death and his ashes became horseflies and mosquitoes.
Iwate-gun: Kikimimi 113, "A good dream" (Yoi yume). A little novice who said he had a good dream was put into a boat and drifted to Onigashima. He got away by making demons laugh and spit up water. He took treasures called Floating Shoes and a Life Needle home. The tale is rather abbreviated and combines episodes.
Niigata: Minamikanbara 143, "A mother, a child, and a demon" (Boshi to oni). The first part of the tale on 147, "The demon's child," is about a son-in-law.
Nagano, Minamiazumi-gun: Dai-ichi 52, "Making the demon laugh" (Oni o warawaseru). Example.
Yamanashi, Nishiyatsushiro-gun: Kai 91, "The seven kettles" (Nanatsu no kama). There is no part about making a demon laugh. Where this is connected to a success story is like many examples in Grimm.

92. Rescuing a Beautiful Girl

This is in the same group as "Kotsuna, the demon's child." It is in the style of an escape story.

Aomori, Sannohe-gun, Hachinohe: MK II 9 44, "Crossing to Onigashima" (Onigashima watari). There are two stories. In the first, the boy was swallowed by a demon. He made it laugh while in its stomach. The part about a white dog helping him is like "Momotarō." The beginning of the second story is like "The monkey bridegroom," but the girl is given to a demon. The one who went to rescue her was a bosama [blind minstrel].
Iwate: Shiwa 138, 186, "The girl who was carried off by a demon" (Oni ni sarawareta onna). Since the husband was a famous flute player, it can be recognized as a fragment of "The wife from the Sky World." "The girl from the Sky World and the man" (Ten no hime to wakamono).
Iwate-gun: Kikimimi 94, 98, "The sister's plans" (Ane no hakarai) and "The demon's beans" (Oni no mame).
Akita, Senhoku-gun: Ugo 87. A notation.
Miyagi, Momoo-gun: Kyōdo den 3 108, "The demon and the girl" (Oni to musume).
Ishikawa: Kaga 126, "The god and the wine drinker" (Kami sama to sakenomi).
Nagano, Chiisagata-gun: Nagakubo 4-0, "The legend of the demon's eye" (Oni no me no densetsu). The opening of the snake bridegroom story. It is a legend about the demon's eye on the last day of January.
Shizuoka, Shita-gun, Yaitsu-machi: Shizuoka 463, "Holly drives out demons and brings luck into the house" (Hiiragi oni wa soto fuku wa uchi no hanashi).

Gifu, Yoshiki-gun: Hidabito V 5 20, "Kotsuna, the demon's child" (Oni
  no ko Kotsuna). A traveling medicine peddler put a drug into wine
  to kill a demon and saved a wife. This is like Raiko Ōeyama, but
  there is no name Kotsuna in the story.
Hyōgo, Hikami-gun: TD X 4 74, "The wife's plan" (Nyōbō no hakarai).
  The man was Iseshirō. He rescued a woman who had been sold to
  bandits far back in the hills and held for ransom. There is an episode with a drop of dew on a lotus leaf.
Kagoshima, Kikaijima: Shima I 4 72, "Hana-no-maguzumi." It is the
  wife's name. She went to the after world to save her husband's
  soul and returned with him. Kikai 105, 113, "The asunarō flower"
  (Asunarō no hana) and "The demon's child" (Oni no ko); Shima I 6
  83, "The asunarō flower" (Asunarō no hana); Shima II 436, "The
  demon's child" (Oni no ko). The younger brother went in search.
  His sister hid him in a toragame. She and her child and her brother
  escaped when they saw their chance. There is an amusing part
  about standing 1000 needles in turds for an answer. There is no
  part about drinking sea water to dry things up nor striking the
  buttocks to make the demon laugh. There is a sad part where the
  demon's child is flung into the sea before he reached the island.
  The changes in mood give it a musical quality. Kikai 110, "The
  wife from Shiinokiyama" (Shiinokiyama no tsuma). The couple set
  out to call upon the bride's parents. While the husband was
  gathering acorns along the way, the wife was carried off by a
  great bandit. The man set out as a sardine peddler and saved his
  wife.

Further reference:
Yearsley 93.

93. The Flight from Onigashima

These are stories about wandering into a demon's house by mistake, killing him, and escaping.

Tokushima, Myōsai-gun: MK I 3 36, "The white bird" (Shiroi tori).
  Sisters lost their way and stayed at an old woman's house. (This is
  like the story of gathering acorns.) After the old man came home,
  they heard him talk with the old woman about eating them. They
  heated water in a kettle and pushed the old woman into it and ran
  away. The old man turned into a demon and chased them. A white
  bird came to their rescue and took them onto its back. The bird
  was their Ujigami [tutelary deity]. Up to where the old woman is
  pushed into the kettle is like "Hansel and Gretel."
Kagoshima: Kikai 70, "The two brothers" (Futari kyōdai). The two boys
  were hated by their mother and driven from home. They parted
  from each other after agreeing that if one's bow string broke, the
  other would know he was dead. The younger one became an

apprentice and received something that could be used as a Death Whip. He wandered into a demon's house by mistake. He killed the demon with the sword a beautiful girl showed him. He traded it for a Life Whip and left. The string on his bow broke, so he knew his brother was dead. He was in time for the funeral and brought his brother back to life with his Life Whip.

94. The Seven Cauldrons

This is a variation of "Onigashima."

Yamanashi, Nishiyatsushiro-gun: Kai 91. A father went to his son-in-law's house and was asked to see his seven cauldrons. He had been told that everyone who looked at them had been killed. He looked at them one at a time, praising them and retiring one step after each. The demon admired his father-in-law's cleverness and sent him home safely. The last part is broken.

Kagoshima: Kikai 105, "The asunarō flower" (Asunarō no hana). He was asked to see wine jars.

95. The Thousand-ri Boots

Yamanashi, Nishiyatsushiro-gun: Zoku Kai 155, "The abandoned children and the demon" (Sutego to oni). Once upon a time a poor mother abandoned her three children in the mountains because she could not care for them. The two older brothers began to cry when night came on, but the youngest comforted them. They went toward a light and found a demon's house. The old woman there hid the children, but when the demon came home, he said he smelled humans. She fooled him. He put on his 1000-ri boots and set out to look for them. After he left, the children escaped by another path. Along their way they came across the demon asleep and snoring loudly by the road. They wrenched his boots off his feet through the cleverness of the youngest and returned safely to their mother.

Are the thousand-ri boots something from a foreign country? There is the exactly the same story in *Pentamerone*, where a poor mother abandons her children in the mountains.

96. The Water Spirit's Letter Carrier

One evening a man was hurrying along a path on the bank of a river when a man fishing there called him to stop. He said there should be somebody fishing at the pool below. He handed the man a letter and asked him to deliver it to the fisher. The man took it unsuspectingly and delivered it to the man at the pool. The fisher looked at it and then said he had dropped something into the water. He asked the man to wait while he went into the water to get it. He came back presently. He said he really was the kappa who lived there in the pool. He said the letter was from the kappa above, and he had written that the man had a purple buttocks and told him to eat him. He couldn't because the man was too honest. The kappa gave him a golden package as a reward for his good heart. He said not to tell anyone and jumped back into the pool. The man became rich from the time.

Iwate, Iwate-gun

Aomori, Sannohe-gun, Hachinohe: MK I 7 43, "The errand for the Water Spirit" (Mizu no kami no otsukai).
Iwate, Kamihei-gun: Rōō 16, "Koganemaru Inu"; Kamihei 19, "The string of cash that never gave out" (Tsukinu zenisashi).
Isawa-gun: (Old) Kogane 3, "The golden horse" (Kogane no uma).
Iwate-gun: Kikimimi 44, "The two kappa" (Jōge no kappa). Example.
Shimohei-gun: Kikimimi 42, "Brother pools" (Kyōdai buchi). A legend of two pools. There is a part where a pilgrim reads the letter and changes it.
Shiwa-gun: Shiwa-shū 105, "The Spirit of the great marsh" (Ōnuma no nushi).
Miyagi: Tome II 811, "Anetori Marsh" (Anetori numa).
Ibaraki Namekata-gun: Minzoku sōwa 62, "The lone princess at Nabutsu Pond" (Nabutsu-ga-ike no hitori hime).
Ishikawa, Nomi-gun: MK II 8 36, "The chōja at Yokoyama" (Yokoyama Chōja). The principal character is an eight year old child. An ascetic changed the message.
Kyoto, Kuwata-gun: Kuchitanba 37, "The River Spirit" (Kawa no nushi).
Wakayama: Chihō.*
Ōita, Hita-gun: Shumi 229, "The female dragon at Shimokotsu Pond" (Shimokotsu ike no meryū).

97. Destroying the Monkey Gods

Long ago there was a temple called Shōhōji at Kuroishi. No matter how many priests served there, they were all eaten by ghosts, and everybody was troubled about it. A priest came begging once and asked to spend the night at the empty temple. He recalled that his instructor had told him that when staying at an empty house, he should sleep where there was only one opening. He crawled under the iron pot in the kitchen to sleep. In the night he heard some things come out of the main hall with a clatter and say they would celebrate before the evening's feast. As they danced, they sang, "Don't let Denjōbō in Tanba-no-kuni hear about it, chiu-u-u." Then they said they smelled a human around and looked all over. They found nothing and went off. The villagers came in the morning, thinking there would be nothing but bones left of the priest, but they found him alive. They admired him as a great priest and asked him to take over the temple. He said that in such a case he would ask them to wait until his return. He set out for Tanba-no-kuni to look for Denjōbō. It proved to be a cat. He borrowed it and started back. When he arrived, the villagers were gossiping and saying he would never return, but they were glad to have him start living there. The cat was beside the priest wherever he walked and never left him. When he asked why, it explained that the ghosts were old rats. If it left the priest, they would eat him immediately. It said it needed the help of its brother cat to destroy the ghosts. The priest pasted up a picture of the cat to take its place, and it left for ten days. It returned with its brother. That night the two of them fought the rats for some time, but finally the cats and the rats killed each other. The priest made a stand for sacred scrolls from the rat legs. It is still treasured at the temple. He buried the cats carefully and stayed on and worked at the temple.

Iwate, Hienuki-gun

Iwate, Hienuki-gun: MK I 11 29, "The old rats at Shōhōji" (Shōhōji no furunezumi). Example. Maybe the reason there are so many folk tales at this temple is that it sheltered hōshi [minstrels].
   Kamihei-gun: Kikimimi 74, "The woodcutter feudal lord" (Kikori no tonosama).
Akita, Hiraga-gun: MK II 8 28, "Soheitarō of Tanba" (Tanba-no-kuni no Soheitarō).
Yamagata: TD VII 6 21, "The dog shrine" (Inu no miya). About a three colored and a four colored dog.
   Nishitagawa-gun, Ōyama: TD I 8 62, "The dog festival at Ōyama" (Ōyama no inu matsuri) by Itō Hijirō. The festival is held on the 15th Day of the Fifth Month.
Miyagi, Momoo-gun: Kyōdo den 3 113, "Shikuheitarō." That was the dog's name.
Fukushima, Iwaki-gun: Iwaki 59, 151, "A ghost story" (Bakemono no hanashi).
Ishikawa: Ishikawa 951, "Destroying the monkey god" (Sarugami taiji). The human sacrifice at Nanao Sannosha. Fugeshi 1056, "Iwayado."
Niigata, Minamikanbara-gun: Kamuhara 34, 200, "About Oyama Taishō" (Oyama no Taishō) and Note 78. There is a cat story on 206 and a note on 207.
Yamanashi, Nishiyatsushiro-gun: Kai 48, "Osakujo of Tanba" (Tanba no Osakujo). It is connected to the priest's story at Kenchōji.
Nagano, Kamiina-gun: Kyōdo ken I 3 42. No title. There is a monument of Hayatarō at Kōzenji in Akaho-mura, Kamiina. Some call it Heibōtarō. It was a dog. According to a legend in Fushimizato in Mino, it bit a ghost.
   Shimoina-gun: Den Shimoina 122, "The maid who was sacrificed at a shrine" (Hime miya no hitomi goku sonae).

Kitasaku-gun: Kitasaku 227, "The ghost at Onshōji" (Onshōji no bakemono). The ghost was an old cat. They knew ghosts came out and sang when there was a priest occupying the temple called Onshōji in Mochizuki. A dog called Tanpororin of Takasaki was taken there and it destroyed the ghost.

Hyōgo, Kinosaki-gun: MK II 9 34, "The human sacrifice" (Hitomi goku). The dog has no name. The story is a fragment.

Shimane, Ōchi-gun: Dai-ichi 72, "Destroying the monkey" (Saru taiji).

Tokushima: Awa Iyayama 5, "Suppeitarō of Tanba" (Tanba-no-kuni no Suppeitarō). On the 7th Day of New Year it came out and lived in a conch shell that could be heard for 1000 ri in four directions. There is a song about "Don't tell Suppeitarō," but there is no story about destroying something.

Fukuoka, Kurate-gun: Fukuoka 106, "Hyūgajirō of Hyūga" (Hyūga no Hyūgajirō).

Itojima-gun: Fukuoka 107, "Destroying the ghost" (Bakemono taiji).

Nagasaki, Minamitakaku-gun: Shimabara 93, 95, "Jizō and the traveler" (Jizō to tabibito) and "The village deity" (Mura no kami sama). Both are short anecdotes.

Kumamoto, Ashikata-gun: MK I 7 46, "The monkey disguised as an old woman" (Baba ni baketa saru). The old woman at a house where a man stopped was really a monkey, and she ate his dog. Another dog was brought. She said, "Come to the beach and let me fight a dog that has lived 40 years." They were matched and killed each other. The story is broken up, but it is undoubtedly connected with destroying monkey gods. In "Mokukendō" of Sankoku denki there is a famous dog of Kamakura.

Kagoshima: Koshiki 148, "The dog called Santarō" (Santarō inu).

98. Travelers Turned into Horses

In the form of Hankyō sanjōshi.

A priest was going along a mountain road with six young men when they got lost. They stopped at a lonely house. The old man there said he would prepare supper. After he set the kettle of rice gruel on the fire, he went into the next room. The priest looked through a crack and watched him put dirt into a tub, scatter some kind of grass seed on it, and then cover it with straw matting. The grass sprouted after a short time. The priest pretended that he knew nothing about it as the old man brought out the grass and put it into the kettle to boil. He served them all some, but the priest did not eat any. He poured it into his bosom instead. Then the man offered them a bath. When the young men got into it, they turned into horses. In the meantime, the priest ran away. When the old man noticed that, he turned into his true form of a demon and chased him. The priest called, "Namu Amida Butsu," as he ran. Dawn came at last and the demon had to give up and turn back. The priest escaped danger and made his way to where people lived.

Yamanashi, Nishiyatsushiro-gun

According to another version, the priest helped the youths turn back into men with the assistance of friends.

Iwate, Kamihei-gun: Rōō 274, "The men turned into horses" (Uma ni natta otoko). It is said that they turned back into men when they ate striped shear grass. Since the ending is happy, maybe this should be considered the original story.

Akita, Senhoku-gun: MK I 10 30, "The pilgrim who grew horse hair" (Umage no haeta rokubu). A pilgrim stopped at a haunted temple. What he thought was the priest was really a horse. It threw a horse shoe at the pilgrim and hit his heel. Horse hair grew there.

Fukushima, Iwaki-gun: Iwaki 51, 139, "Putting a traveler up and turning him into a cow" (Tabibito o tomete ushi ni shita hanashi).

Yamanashi, Nishiyatsushiro-gun: Zoku Kai 130, "The men turned into horses" (Hito ga uma ni naru). Example.

Kagoshima: Kikai 97, "Travelers turned into horses" (Tabibito uma). There are many points that seem to have been adapted from abroad, but it does not seem to be a direct translation.

Koshikijima: Koshiki 124, "Travelers turned into horses" (Tabibito uma). There is magic in it.

Okierabu: Okinoerabu 170, "Travelers turned into horses" (Tabibito uma). The story builds up like a thriller.

Further reference:
Minakata zuihitsu 228.
Kii sōdan shū.
Clouston I 97.
Rōō yatan 274. And others with accompanying revenge. These are not as close to *Konjaku monogatari* as to *Gen'ishi.*
Konjaku monogatari, maki 31, No. 14. There is no revenge here. He runs away and hides in a demon's house and is saved. Where the demon comes back in the middle of the night is like an old folk tale.
Gen'ishi. There is the story of *Hankyō sanjōshi.*
Hōmotsu shū. An Indian tale says the mother who turned into a horse saved her child.

99. Kōketsu Palace or Extracting Oil

This belongs in the same group as "Travelers turned into horses." Men are carried off and fattened and their fat or blood is pressed out. Refer to tales of exaggeration.

Iwate: Shiwa shū 141, "The lazy man" (Namake mono). It is a story about pressing fat out of men like the Kōketsu story, and the conclusion is that it is a dream. Considering the ending, the story is likely of recent date. Perhaps it is a bosama's tale. There is a Blue Beard episode, but no forbidden room. The woman alone in the house resembles the Hankyō sanjōshi story. When the man is

saved by the old woman, she said she was working for the house,
etc. This is like *Konjaku monogatari*.

Tokushima: Awa Iyayama 95, "The house where blood was wrung out"
(Chi o shiboru ie).

Kagoshima, Kikaijima: MK I 7 43, "Izumikawa, the wrestler" (Rikishi
Izumikawa). When Izumikawa went to the bandit's house, he found
men were being fattened and heard that they were being sold to
demons. He rescued them and sent them home. Kikai 108, "Extracting oil" (Abura tori).

100. The Three Charms

When the novice at a certain temple asked the priest to send him
into the mountains to gather flowers, the priest told him that demons
might come out and that it was dangerous. The novice insisted upon
going. The priest gave him three charms for his protection and told
him to throw one if he were in danger. While the boy was breaking off
branches, an old woman came out. She said she would give him something good and took him to her house. He decided to spend the night
there. It began to rain in the night. As he lay there listening, it
seemed to say, "*Tan-tan* splashes the water from the rafters. Rise and
look at granny's face." He looked cautiously toward the old woman and
saw she had turned into a demon. That was terrible. How could he run
away! He decided to say he had to go to the privy. She agreed to let
him go, but first she tied a rope around his waist and fastened it to
the grindstone. When she would call, "Are you through, boy?" he would
answer, "Not yet!" In the meantime, he untied the rope and tied it to
the upright post. He fastened one of his charms to it and asked it to
answer for him. Then he ran away. Since the boy kept on saying he
was not through, the old woman tried pulling the rope and discovered
he was not there. She started after him in a rage. When she nearly
caught up with him, he threw one of his charms and shouted, "Big
river, come out!" A big river came between them. She nearly caught
up with him again, but he threw the other charm and called a big
mountain out. The novice reached the temple while she was trying to
cross the mountain. The priest hid him in a cupboard. The old woman
came leaping into the temple and started to argue with the priest,
even threatening to eat him. The priest proposed that they compare
tricks. He told her to turn into a bean. She promptly turned into one.
The priest stuck it into a piece of mochi and ate it.

Akita, Senhoku-gun, Kakunodate

Refer to "The privy at the demon's house," "The priest and the
ghost," "Dan'ichi whose ears were cut off," and others. A priest takes
a role in these.

Aomori, Minamitsugaru-gun, Kuroishi: Tsugaru k 29. No title. This says
he hid in a patch of iris and it is tied to the festival on the 5th
Day of the Fifth Month. Tsugaru m 96, "Are you through, boy"
(Konbo baba iiga).

Iwate: Esashi 41, "The bad demon who turned into a poppy seed and
was stuck onto mochi and eaten by a priest" (Akki ga keshi tsubu
to natte oshō ni mochi ni tsukerarete kuwareta hanashi); Isawa*;
Shiwa 78, "The yamaonna" (Yamaonna). In this there was one
charm, and the priest was eaten by the yamaonna. The novice who
was hiding in a Chinese chest came out as a little white dog.

Akita, Senhoku-gun, Kakunodate: Kikimimi 91, "The she-demon and the
novice" (Onibaba to kozō). Example.

Kazuno-gun, Miyakawa-mura: MK I 2 44, "The novice and the
yamauba" (Kozō to yamauba).

Hiraga-gun, Asamai-machi: MK II 3 28, "The novice and the she-
demon" (Kozō to onibaba). The demon turned into a bean and the
priest ate it. A lot of flies came from his turds. That flies all over
Japan came from a she-demon originally resembles the story about
the beginning of fleas and mosquitoes.

Miyagi, Momoo-gun: Kyōdo den 3 112, "The novice and the she-demon"
(Kozō to onibaba).

Kurihara-gun, Uguisugawa-mura: Kyōdo den 1 174, "The priest and
his novice" (Oshō sama to kozō no hanashi).

Fukushima, Iwaki-gun: Iwaki 52, 141, "The three charms" (Sanmai no
ongofu).

Niigata: Minamikanbara 136, "The yamauba and the novice" (Yamauba
to kozō).

Minamiuonuma-gun: MK I 10 36, "The yamauba and the novice"
(Yamauba to kozō).

Nagano: Chiisagata 250, 190, "The Privy Deity" (Benjo no kami) and
"Come when you're through" (Mattara koyō).

Yamanashi, Nishiyatsushiro-gun: Kai 100, "The novice and the yamababa (Kozō to yamababa).

Tochigi, Haga-gun: Shimotsuke 36, "The three letters" (Sanbon no
tegami). The beginning is like "The snake son-in-law." A man
promised to give his daughter to a demon for fixing a broken place
in his yard. The frog gave her three letters in the privy. She hid
among iris and mugwort by their instructions to escape difficulties.
It tells the beginning of the festival of the 5th Day of the Fifth
Month.

Gifu, Yoshiki-gun, Kamitakara-mura: Hidabito V 5 21, "The three
charms" (Sanmai no ofuda). There are two stories. The first is
about brothers. The second goes like the latter part about the
stepchild gathering chestnuts. Nihon zenkoku 108, "The two
charms" (Nimai no gofu).

Kumamoto: Amakusajima den "Yamauba stories" Part I (Yamauba no
hanashi). See Shokoku m; Techō 63, "The three charms" (Sanmai no
ofuda).

Nagasaki, Minamitakaku-gun: Shimabara 77, "The griffin that carried
off a child" (Kosari kirin). He escaped with the help of a horse,
three jewels, and a magic mallet. Is the griffin a demon god?

Kagoshima, Kikaijima: MK I 7 39, "The demon mother" (Oni no haha).

The mother was a she-demon. The child escaped by the help of a charm he received from a priest. MK I 7 41, "The priest and his novice" (Oshō to kozō). A great snake 33 fathoms long came to have its head cut off. The priest destroyed the snake with three charms. It was a musk snake, a treasure bestowed by the Sun.

Further reference:
There is an example in northern Africa of spittle answering in place of a man.
Yearsley 122.

101. The Privy at the Demon's House

This is the story about the three charms with the charms omitted. It is close to "O Sun, the chain."

Gifu, Yoshiki-gun, Kamitakara-mura: Hidabito V 5 21, "The three charms" (Sanmai no ofuda). Two tales. In the first, the brothers stopped at the hut of an old woman and escape through the window of the privy. They tied the rope to the post and prayed fervently as they left. It answered for them. There seems to be interest in this point, but there are many regions which have stories of the Privy Deity's acting as substitute. The second tale is like the last part of the stepchild gathering chestnuts. The stepchild tied the rope to a broom and went home. The child herself answered, "Not yet."

102. Eating a Demon in One Bite

This is the latter part of "The three charms." A demon who is deceived by a priest is always destroyed by agreeing to compare tricks.

Iwate, Isawa-gun: Kogane 55, "The she-demon who turned into a bean and was eaten" (Mame ni natte kuwareta onibaba no hanashi).
Kamihei-gun: Tōno 276 No. 165. No title. A man called Nue at Hataya went into the mountains. He matched wits as the priest did with a blue ghost. He made it small and put it into a tinder box. When he got home and opened the box, a blue spider came out.
Tochigi, Haga-gun: Dai-ni 38, "The yamajii who turned into a flea" (Nomi ni natta yamajii no hanashi). Shimotsuke 51, "The yamajii who turned into a flea" (Nomi ni natta yamajii no hanashi). The demon turned into a flea and the priest crushed him.
Niigata, Minamikanbara-gun: (no source). A lazy man who deceived a demon by persuading it to turn into a small piece of mochi ate it.

Tokushima: Awa Iyayama 26, "The fox and the boy" (Kitsune to musu-
_ ko). The fox was told to turn into a manjū and was eaten.
Ōita: Naori 84, "The fox story" (Kitsune no hanashi).

Further reference:
  Seisuishō 15.

103. Dan'ichi whose Ears were Cut off

The first part of this is like "The three charms." At the end, the
priest wrote sutras all over the novice except his ears, so the demon
took his ears off.

Fukushima, Iwaki-gun: Iwaki 54, 147, "How ears were bitten off by a
  she-demon" (Onibaba ni mimi kara kuwareta hanashi).
Niigata, Minamikanbara-gun: MK I 10 37, "The yamauba and the
  novice" (Yamauba to kozō).

104. The Staring Match with a Demon

Ōita: Bungo den 10, "The grave of Prince Yuriwaka at Moto-machi,
  Ōita" (Ōita-shi Moto-machi no Yuriwaka Daijin no tsuka). He put
  gongs in his eyes and defeated the demon. This is also found on
  Iki. Perhaps it is from a katarimono version.

Further reference:
  Azuma kagami has a phrase about winning with the eye. Also in
Kanbun gyoki.

105. "O Sun The Chain"

Once upon a time there were three brothers. Their mother called
them to her before she set out and told them to be good till she
returned. A man-eater might come, so they should be very careful. In
the evening somebody came and knocked at the door. The oldest boy
went to the door to see and his mother was there, but when he looked
closely, he saw hair all over her hands. At that, he shut the door
tight. Then the man-eater scraped the hair off her hands with a potato
grater and knocked again. This time the boy thought she was his
mother and let her in. The boy woke up in the night and heard his
mother eating something. When he asked what she was eating, she
answered that she was eating something because she was hungry, and

she tossed him a finger she was gnawing. The boy woke his next younger brother immediately and the two of them ran out and climbed a peach tree. After the man-eater had finished eating the youngest boy, she went to look for the other two. She saw them in the peach tree and started to climb up after them. The frightened boys cried, "O Sun, O Sun, save us!" A chain came down from the sky. They climbed it. The man-eater imitated them and cried, "O Sun, O Sun, save me!" A chain came down and the man-eater started up, but the chain broke and she fell. She hit her head on a stone and died. The man-eater's blood went onto the roots of corn that was growing there and they turned red. The roots of corn became red from the next year.

Hiroshima, Asa-gun

This story in Japan is like "Little Red Riding Hood" or "The seven lambs."

Fukushima, Futaba-gun, Kawata-mura: MK II 4 36, "Hanako and Jirō" (Hanako to Jirō). This is about a girl and her little brother, but the brother ran away. No part about a chain.

Iwaki-gun: Iwaki 55, 147, "O Sun, the chain" (Tentō San kane no tsuna).

Tochigi, Haga-gun: Shimotsuke 48, "The yamauba and the three children" (Yamauba to sannin no kodomo).

Saitama, Kawagoe: Kawagoe 93, "O Sun, the chain" (Tentō Sama kane no kusari). This is about brother stars.

Nara, Kitakatsuragi-gun: Fushi 2 74, "The old she-demon" (Onibaba no hanashi); Techō 64, "O Sun, the chain" (Tentō San kane no tsuna).

Hiroshima: Geibi 182, "O Sun, the chain" (Tentō San kane no tsuna). Three stories.

Asa-gun: Aki 97, "Why the roots of corn are red" (Tōmorokoshi no ne wa naze akai). Example.

Kure: Aki 99, "O Moon, thirteen and seven" (Otsuki San Jūsan nanatsu).

Kagawa, Takamatsu: Dai-ni 38, "The yamauba" (Yamauba no hanashi).

Tokushima: Awa Iyayama 70, "O Sun, the chain" (Tentō San kane no kusari).

Fukuoka, Chikujō-gun: Fukuoka 223, "The yamauba" (Yamauba no hanashi).

Munakata-gun: Fukuoka 225, "The brother stars" (Kyōdai boshi). One story each from Kiku-gun and Kurate-gun are also recorded. The latter is about the wolf and the sheep. This could be considered a translation. There is also a tale in the appendix about a yamauba and three sisters. The girls climbed to the sky and became stars. Buzen,[*] "The yamauba and the brothers" (Yamauba to kyōdai).

Ōita, Nishikunisaki-gun: Dai-ni 37, "The children and the wolf" (Kodomo to ōkami).

Kumamoto, Amakusa-gun: MK I 10 42, "O Sun, the chain" (Tentō San kane no tsuna). Two stories; Nihon den 267, "Buckwheat" (Soba). Very much like the Buzen version.

Nagasaki, Kitatakaku-gun: MK II 11 41, "The yamauba" (Yamauba); Shimabara 65, "O Sun, the chain" (Tentō San kane kusari). Four stories. The third is "Becoming a star" (Hoshi ni natta). The fourth is "One-eyed Gorō will come and eat you" (Me hitotsu Gorō ga kite kuu).
Kitatakaku-gun, Isahaya: Kōshō 8 4, "The fox and the children" (Kitsune to kodomo). The beginning is like "The ox-leader and the yamauba." Nothing about a chain.
    Minamitsuura-gun: Gotō 258, "The yamauba"; (Old) Iki 51, "The yamauba" (Yamauba no hanashi).
Kagoshima: Kikai 115, "The sisters and the demon" (Shimai to oni). The beginning is like "The ox-leader and the yamauba." Where they cut open the yamauba and bring out their mother is like "The seven lambs."
Amami Ōshima: MK II 8 38, "The brothers and the demon" (Kyōdai to oni).
Okierabujima: Okinoerabu 164, "O Sun, a strong chain" (Tentō San tsuyoi tsuna).

Further reference:
Nihon mukashibanashi shū, ge 71. An example from Korea.
Chōsen mintan shū 5, "The sun, the moon, the stars" (Hi to tsuki to hoshi). In the Supplement 1.

106. The Ox-Leader and the Yamauba

    Long ago an ox-leader packed a load of salt mackerel and started into the mountains to sell them at settlements. He met a yamauba at the pass on his way. She kept begging for mackerel until he had thrown all of them to her, but she still followed him and demanded his ox to eat. When she had finished off the ox, she declared she would eat the ox-leader. He ran away frantically and climbed a big tree to hide. Unfortunately, there were no leaves below him, and his form was reflected in the marsh below. The yamauba thought the man was in the marsh and she went in to look for him. He took that chance to run off and rush into a lonely house at the foot of the mountain. That proved to be the yamauba's house. He climbed into the rafters overhead and hid. Presently the yamauba came home. She built up the fire and started to toast mochi. When she fell into a doze, the ox-leader took a piece of thatch from under the roof and picked up a piece of mochi to eat. The yamauba woke up and roared, "Who took my mochi!" The man answered softly, "Fire God, Fire God!" The yamauba declared that if it was the Fire God, there was no help for it and she ate a piece of mochi that was burned on its side. She then got out a kettle and set it over the fire to heat some sweet wine, but she fell asleep again. The ox-leader took another piece of thatch and sucked it all up. The yamauba woke up and yelled again, asking who drank the wine. The ox-leader answered again that it was the Fire God. She declared that on such a night it was better to sleep. She said to herself, "Will it be the stone chest or the wooden chest? The stone chest is cold, so it will be the wooden chest." She climbed into it and closed the lid. She went to sleep and snored. When the ox-leader saw that, he came down carefully and built up the fire. He boiled lots of water. Then he took a drill and bored holes in the lid of the wooden chest. The yamauba inside heard it and said, "Tomorrow will be good weather. I hear the drill bugs sing." In the meantime, the ox-leader brought the scalding water over and poured it through the holes to revenge himself at last on the yamauba.

Echigo, Minamikanbara-gun

There is this ending where he takes revenge himself and one in which he climbs a tree as in "O Sun, the chain."

Aomori, Sannohe-gun: Minzokugaku V 12 55, "The ox-leader and the yamauba" (Ushikata to yamauba).
   Hachinohe: MK II 9 45, "The she-demon and Tarasuke Sābu" (Onibaba to Tarasuke Sābu). The part about eating the cow is omitted. "The yamauba" (Yamauba). This seems to be a more complete form than the first. "The ox-leader and the mountain spider" (Ushikata to yamagumo). The unusual part in this is that a child was crying in the little mountain shrine by the side of the road. When the ox-leader put the child onto his ox, it turned into a big she-demon (or mountain spider).
Iwate, Kamihei-gun: Tōno 99, No. 16. No title. It begins like "Uriko-hime." A girl who was chased by a yamauba was sheltered by a girl in a lonely house. The two of them killed the yamauba and ran away. Rōō 215, "Kohei Chōja." In the form of a legend.
   Shiwa-gun: Shiwa 87, "The ox-leader and the yamauba" (Ushikata to yamauba). An ox-leader who was sleeping at night in an open field was chased by a yamauba. He fled to a farmhouse where the housewife hid him. That she in turn killed him is an unusual form. She poured hot water onto him, but this is the way the yamauba is usually killed. It is either a mistake or the story has been changed.
   Kunohe-gun: Kunohe 481, "The yamauba and the ox-leader" (Yamauba to ushikata). This is a slightly different form. An ox-leader who gambled with a yamauba and lost was chased, and he ran to a lonely house where a girl was living. The girl fooled the yamauba and killed her. The grains of rice turned into as many coins as there were hairs on the seven cows she had eaten. The girl and the man became a wealthy couple.
   Iwate-gun, Takizawa-mura: Kikimimi 100, "The yamajii and the ox-leader" (Yamajii to ushikata). Three oxen were eaten. The man was saved by a towing boat. The yamajii climbed a tree. He fell and was killed. This resembles "O Sun, the chain."
   Iwate-gun, Nagaoka-mura: Iwate 2, "The ox-leader and the yamajii" (Ushikata to yamajiji). This is practically the same as the *Kikimimi sōshi* story.

Akita, Senhoku-gun: Ugo 246. A notation. The ox-leader hid in the
   yamauba's house.
Yamagata, Higashitagawa-gun: MK II 7 30, "The mackerel peddler"
   (Sabauri no hanashi). A man went to sell mackerel at a yamauba's
   house, but he was not an ox-leader.
Fukushima, Iwaki-gun: Iwaki 56, 148, "The horse-leader and the she-
   demon" (Umakata to onibaba).
Niigata Minamikanbara-gun: Echigo Sanjo 119, "The she-demon and the
   fish peddler" (Onibaba to sakanauri). Example. Minamikanbara 139,
   "The mackerel peddler and the she-demon" (Sabauri to onibaba).
Toyama, Kaminiigawa-gun: MK II 6 30, "The fish peddler and the she-
   demon" (Sakanauri to onibaba). There is no ox. The man sold
   salted yellow tail.
Ishikawa: Kaga 44, "The fox and the horse-leader" (Kitsune to umakata). It is a fox instead of a yamauba, and it demands the horse's
   legs. The man ran home. The ending is missing.
Tochigi, Haga-gun: Shimotsuke 46, 50, "The fish peddler and the yamauba" (Sakanaya to yamauba) and "Tome who destroyed the yamaub-
   a" (Yamauba o taiji shita Tome san). The first of these is close to
   "O Sun, the chain."
Yamanashi, Nishiyatsushiro-gun: Kai 147, "The horse-leader and the
   demon" (Umakata to oni). The man went to the demon's house for
   revenge. When he took the lid off the kettle in which he burned
   the demon to death, it was filled with pine pitch. He sold it and
   became a chōja. The ending could be a recent story.
Nagano, Kitaazumi-gun: Otari 19, "Sanjūrō" (Sanjūrō no hanashi).
   Sanjūrō was the ox-leader. He had a load of dried cod when the
   yamauba met him at the pass. After he scalded her to death, he
   found a great mountain spider.
Gifu, Yoshiki-gun: Hidabito V 3 21, "The ox-leader and the yamauba"
   (Ushikata to yamauba).
Okayama, Oku-gun: Okayama bun III 4, "The horse-leader and the she-
   demon" (Mago to onibaba). She asked for salt and ate all of it. No
   part about eating the horse. The horse-leader followed her to her
   home and killed her in the bath.
Hiroshima, Toyota-gun: Aki 95, "Chōta and the demon" (Chōta to oni).
   Asa-gun: Aki 92, "Chōkichi and the she-demon" (Chōkichi to onibaba). A man went to buy salt and met with danger on the way
   home. After he destroyed the she-demon, he buried her in the corn
   patch. The roots of the corn turned red.
   Yamagata-gun: MK I 9 33, "The horse-leader and the she-demon"
   (Mago to onibaba). After he burned the she-demon to death, he
   discovered she was a badger. What follows is like "Kachi-kachi
   bird." Geibi 82, "The ox-leader and the yamauba" (Ushikata to
   yamauba). About Keisaijirō. He invited the yamauba to his house,
   put her into a kettle, and killed her. He reached from the rafters
   to take mochi. There is another kind of story on the same page.
Tottori: Inpaku min I 5 258, "The yamauba and the horse-leader"
   (Yamauba to mago).
   Yazu-gun: Inpaku mukashi 75, "The yamauba" (Yamauba).
Yamaguchi, Suō Ōshima: Kōshō 11 18, "Why the stem of buckwheat is
   red" (Soba no kuki no akai wake).

Kagawa: Shōdojima.*
Tokushima: Awa Iyayama 45, "Yajirō and the old woman" (Yajirō to obaba).
Chikuzen (Fukuoka): Nihon zenkoku 318, "The yamauba and Umakichi" (Yamauba to Umakichi). This is the same story as in Nihon dōwa shū.
Ōita: Bungo min* 24, "The horse-leader and the yamajii" (Mago to yamajii). Dried mackerel were taken from the horse-leader, but he ran away and got home. He planned with his wife and they made millet dango for him to take. He was helped in his revenge by a chestnut, a crab, a needle, a bee, and a handmill.
Kumamoto, Kuma-gun: Enzoku 106, No. 29. No title. A monkey licked up his salt. A crab, a handmill, etc. went along to take revenge.
  Tamana-gun: Dai-ni 34, "Itchome" The yamauba had only one eye.
Saga, Kishima-gun: Kōshō 11 12, "The horse-leader and the yamauba" (Umakata to yamauba). The middle and the ending are omitted. The horse-leader went home dragging the head of his horse—all that was left of it.
Nagasaki: Shimabara 62, "The horse-leader and the yamauba" (Umakata yamauba). The story is pretty much broken up. (Old) Iki 36, "The demon" (Oni no hanashi); (New) Iki 77, "Boiling the yamauba to death" (Yamauba o nikorosu).
Kagoshima: Koshiki 140, "The horse-leader and the yamauba" (Umakata to yamauba).
  Kikaijima: TD III 6 67, "The demon" (Oni no hanashi). A demon came to a man's house. He ate his pig, he ate his horse, and said he would eat the man. The man climbed a tree by the edge of a lake and climbed to the Sky on a chain that came down. The demon fell and was killed.
Okinawa, Tokunoshima: TD I 8 51, "The demon" (Oni no hanashi).

Further reference:
  Kiyū shoran 9, "Kohada no Koheiji." A legend about Myōjinzaka at Namase-mura, Kuji-gun, Hitachi (Ibaraki). Since the term she-demon is used, it is close to a folk tale. Sansuke had a load of dried bonito on his horse when he met the yamauba. He ran away to her house, ate mochi, and left stones in its place. He killed the yamauba as she slept in her chest.

107. The Wife Who Didn't Eat

Once upon a time an unmarried man went into the hills to cut wood. He said to his companion that he wished he had a wife who didn't eat. Four or five days later a woman came to his house and asked him to marry her because she did not eat. Once they were married, she certainly did not eat, but after she came, the rice and bean paste was disappearing. He thought it strange. One day he pretended to set out for town, but he took the time his wife went to the privy to climb into the rafters of the stable to hide. His wife got out a kettle that held one shō of rice and cooked it. Next, she took out bean paste and made soup. She covered a straw mat with rows of riceballs and put the soup into a bucket to cool. She took her hair down, and there on the top of her head was a mouth. She tossed the riceballs into it and then poured in the bean soup. When she had finished, she combed her hair once more to look as usual. While she was putting things back in order, the man climbed down carefully and pretended to have returned and went into the house. The next morning he said he would send her home. She asked him for something as a gift. He told her to take a tub that was there. She said there were bugs in it and asked him to take them out. She fooled him and pushed him into the tub. She swung it up to her shoulders and ran with it back to the mountains. She called, "I've brought something good to eat, so everybody come!" Voices replied from trees here and there, and the man felt more dead than alive. Branches of trees beside the path brushed the tub as she went along. The man caught onto one and pulled himself out. He started to run back down the mountain as fast as he could. The woman went on till she came to where everybody was waiting and set the tub down. Then she saw it was empty and concluded he had run away. She started after him. When she was about to catch up with him, the man hid where mugwort and iris were growing. The yamauba followed, but when she saw him there, she declared her hands would rot if she put them among the plants. There was nothing she could do about it, so she went back up the mountain. The man had been saved from danger. He put iris and mugwort onto his head and stuck some into his belt and went home. He put some of the plants onto his roof and at the entrance, too, so the yamauba would never come again.

Iwate, Shiwa-gun

Aomori, Kitatsugaru-gun, Kira-mura: Tsugaru m 67, "Becoming the head of 1000 men" (Sennin no kashira ni taterareta hanashi). The wife was a snake in disguise. They had one child. The mother left one of her scales for the child and went away. This belongs to "The snake wife."

Iwate, Iwate-gun, Shizukuishi: Dai-ichi 33, "The wife who didn't eat" (Kuwazu nyōbō). The couple made mochi and went to the wife's home for a festival. The wife was a demon. The man ran away and hid from danger among iris and mugwort.

Kunohe-gun: Kunohe 464. No title.

Shiwa-gun: Shiwa shū 94, "The wife who didn't eat" (Mono kuwazu ogata) Example.

Isawa-gun: Isawa.* "The she-demon" (Onibaba).

Akita, Senhoku-gun: Ugo 193. Mentioned. It is about a cooper and a yamauba. MK I 11 27, "The wife who didn't eat" (Meshi kuwanu nyōbō). When he killed her with the fire tongs, he found she was a red demon. Kikimimi 383, "Turds that became brocade" (Fun ga ayanishiki). It starts like "Urikohime." There is a part where the yamauba made riceballs and threw them into a hole on her head.

Hiraga-gun: MK II 8 28, "The demon of the Fifth Month" (Gogatsu no oni). The story has the two plants, but no tub.

Yamagata, Higashitagawa-gun: MK II 7 30, "The wife who didn't eat" (Kuwazu nyōbō). The principal character is a rice dealer. He made a coffin and put his wife into it and abandoned her, but she came back. The part about the origin of the use of iris and mugwort follows. MK II 2 44, "The wife who didn't eat" (Kuwazu nyōbō). The wife was a demon. The reason for the use of iris and mugwort follows the story.

Miyagi: Tome II 803, "Kuchinashi Pond at Yoshida" (Yoshida Kuchinashi numa).

Fukushima, Iwaki-gun: Iwaki 57 149, "The wife who didn't eat" (Mono o kuwanu nyōbō).

Niigata: Minamikanbara 141, "The wife who didn't eat" (Meshi kuwanu nyōbō).

Ishikawa, Nomi-gun: MK II 8 36, "The bride who didn't eat" (Mono kuwanu yome). Aside from her putting five *go* of rice into the kettle, the story is like "The wife from the Sky World."

Enuma-gun: Kaga 86, "The bride who didn't eat" (Mono o kuwanu yome).

Fukui, Sakai-gun: MK I 1 30, "The wife who didn't eat" (Kuwazu nyōbō). There are two stories. One is about a spider and the other about a yamauba.

Nagano: Chiisagata 200, 201, "The snake's child" (Hebi no ko) and "Mugwort and iris" (Yomogi shōbu). Hiding upstairs in the second makes it like "The ox-leader and the yamauba"

Shimoina-gun: Mukashibanashi 90, 135, "The snake bride" (Hebi no yome sama no hanashi). There is no part about the rice and her not eating. It says the house filled with water and the snake swam around in it. "Iris and mugwort" (Shōbu to yomogi).

Minamiazumi-gun: Minamiazumi nen 153. No title. There are a number of stories about the origin of iris and mugwort. They are told as legends, not folk tales.

Yamanashi, Nishiyatsushiro-gun: Kai 66, "How light since I rested" (Yasundara karui naa). No part about the mouth in the head. Only about the origin of using the plants.

Tochigi, Haga-gun: Shimotsuke 47, "The bride who didn't use her mouth" (Kuchi o kikanai yome). Besides telling the beginning of using the two plants for the festival of the Fifth Month, it tells of the start of decorating with maple leaves and wisteria on the 8th Day of the Fourth Month.

Shizuoka, Suntō-gun: Shizuoka 456, "The spider bride" (Kumo yome).

Fuji-gun: Shizuoka 457, "The night spider" (Yoru no kumo).

Aichi, Kitashidara-gun: Dai-ichi 55, "The night spider" (Yoru no kumo).

Gifu, Yoshiki-gun, Kamitakara-mura: Hidabito V 5 23, "The wife who did not eat" (Kuwazu nyōbō). There are four stories. In the fourth, the wife was a frog. A rock thrown at it struck a priest's head.

Wakayama, Ito-gun: Kōshō 10 20, "The wife who didn't eat" (Kuwazu nyōbō). For the most part, it is the usual story, but the old man next door disclosed the secret.

Arita-gun: Kii 24 u, "Putting iris and mugwort on the roof on the 5th Day of the Fifth Month" (Gogatsu itsuka ni shōbu to yomogi o fuku koto).

Nara: Nara 18, 21. No title.

Hyōgo, Kinosaki-gun, Sanshōmura, Mihara: MK II 9 34, "The bride who didn't eat" (Kuwanu yome). Instead of telling about iris and mugwort, it says that he caught onto branches of a kaya tree and pulled himself out. He freed himself from the wrapping around him and hid in the tree. This tale is connected with ceremonies on the 6th Day of New Year. It may be that folk tales were tied to such ceremonies to explain them.

Kawabe-gun: Hokuto 31 [The reference is not clear]. Techō 66, "The wife who didn't eat" (Kuwazu nyōbō).

Shimane: Okinoshima 12, "The yamauba" No. 1 (Yamauba). Contrary to not having a mouth, she was a great eater and was told she would have to go home. She turned into a spider after she was abandoned and came back. When she was burned to death, she turned into a yamauba.

Okayama, Jōdō-gun: Okayama bun III 1 49, "A folk tale" (Mukashibanashi). It says nothing about a mouth on her head. Many spiders gathered and cooked oats to eat while the man was away.

Shizuki-gun: MK I 8 26, "Burning night spiders to death" (Yogumo wa yaki korosu hanashi).

Mitsu-gun: Mitsu 107, "The spider is scary" (Kumo wa kyōtee). Nothing about her eating rice alone. She led the man into the mountains and turned into a spider. She wrapped her web around him.

Hiroshima: Aki 125, "The wife who didn't eat" No. 1 (Kuwazu nyōbō). He learned her secret through the hint of a friend. She killed his friend and carried her husband off, but he ran away.

Asa-gun: Aki 128, "The wife who didn't eat" No. 2 (Kuwazu nyōbō). She was a snake that later turned into a spider.

Takata-gun: Aki 130, "The wife who didn't eat" No. 3 (Kuwazu nyōbō). She was a snake wife. The man went to a temple to ask for a divorce. It is a fragment.

Yamaguchi, Suō Ōshima: Kōshō 11 15, "The wife who didn't eat" (Kuwazu nyōbō). It gives the origin of the saying, "It's no use because it is a citron tree." It ends with the night spider, but there is nothing about iris.

Tokushima: Kyōdo ken II 6 58, "The yamachichi and yamaonna" (Yamachichi to yamaonna); Awa Iyayama 67, "The wife who didn't eat" (Meshi kuwanu nyōbō).

Kagawa: Shōdojima.* There was a hole on her head as big as a kettle. When he saw it he was so shocked that he died.

Mitoyo-gun, Shishijima: MK II 12 38, "The wife who didn't eat" (Meshi kuwanu nyōbō).

Fukuoka, Sōra-gun: Chikuzen* 33. It gives the reason for using citron leaves at New Year ceremonies.

Kumamoto, Kuma-gun: MK I 8 38, "The wife who didn't eat" (Kuwazu nyōbō).

Tamana-gun: Dai-ni 35, "The reason roots of corn are red" (Tōmorokoshi no ne no akai wake). It ends like "O Sun, the chain."

Amakusajima: Amakusa min 57, "Festivals of Yama-no-kami [Mountain Deity]" (Yama no kami matsuri). One folk tale is mentioned.

Nagasaki, Ikinoshima: Dai-ichi 82, "Thatching rush and mugwort at the

Fifth Month festival" (Gogatsu no sekku no kaya to yomogi). It states clearly that the wife was a snake.

Kitatakaku-gun, Isahaya: Kōshō 8 2, "The wife who didn't eat" (Kuwazu nyōbō); Shimabara 84, "The wife who didn't eat" (Kuwazu nyōbō). The last two stories are vague.

Kagoshima: Koshiki 142, "The spider wife" (Kumo nyōbō).

Kikaijima: Shima II 479, 424, "The cat wife" (Neko no tsuma). She would go out in the night and kill rats to eat. He poured the juice of tsuki grass and miha grass into her ears to kill her. "The demon and iris" (Oni to shōbu). A demon came to eat everyone in the house, but they ran away to where iris grew in the mountains. It happened on the 5th Day of the Fifth Month.

Amami Ōshima: MK II 7 26, "The three sisters" (Sannin shimai).

Okinawa: Nantō 88, "Chased by a demon and hiding in an iris patch" (Oni ni owarete shōbu e kakureta hanashi).

108. The Wife without a Mouth
or "The wife who didn't eat"

The principal character is a stingy priest. He wanted a wife who didn't eat. At last he found a woman without a mouth. It was strange however, that she cooked lots of rice every day. He spied on her from a tub in the yard where he hid. She took her side-locks down and ate with a big mouth that was in the part in her hair. When the priest cried out in astonishment, she grabbed him, tub and all. She started to run with the tub on her shoulders. When she set it down by the side of the road, it rolled over and dropped the priest into a place where lots of iris were growing. She could not follow him because of the plants. Iris was put under the eaves of houses and floated in bath water after that on the 5th Day of the Fifth Month.

Miyagi, Tome-gun

Aomori, Hachinohe: MK II 9 46, "The wife without a mouth" (Kuchi-nashi nyōbō). Two stories. The man was saved by iris in both. For some reason, the principal character in the second story is an egg peddler.

Miyagi, Tome-gun: Kyōdo den 3 116, "The bride without a mouth" (Kuchi no nai yomego). Example.

Igu-gun: Igu 26, "The origin of Shimokuzaka" (Shimokuzaka no yurai). It is turned into a legend. (In *Nishine-mura kyōdo shi* 26).

109. The Younger Sister a Demon

Once there was a family with a son and a daughter. The girl would leave the house every night after she made sure her brother was asleep. The brother thought it strange and followed her to see. She turned into a demon at the edge of the village and carried off a horse to eat. This went on every night, so he told his father and mother. They would not believe him and drove him away from home. He wandered around as a beggar until a chance came for him to be adopted into a family as a son-in-law. After five years passed, he wanted to go home to see how things were. He gave his wife a mirror and told her that if it became clouded, she would know that his life was in danger and for her to set the male and female falcons in the yard free. When he neared his home, he looked down from a hill at his village, but there was no sign of a house. His sister was sleeping face up and looked like a dreadful monster. When he cleared his throat, she changed back to her usual form and saw her brother. She said that in the many years he had been away their parents had died in an epidemic. She asked him to beat on a drum she gave him for their comfort while she went to boil rice. When he beat the drum, the ghosts of his parents came out like rats and beat the drum for him. His sister noticed the difference in the sound of the drum and came to see. She found the rats beating it. While she was chasing the rats off angrily, the brother managed to run away. She started after him. In the meantime, the wife at home noticed the mirror was clouded, so she set the two falcons free. The brother had climbed a tree and his sister was digging at its roots to topple it when the birds arrived. They pecked out her eyes, but both of them had been touched by the demon's breath and died. The young man destroyed the demon and made a grave for the birds. Then he went home safely to his wife and parents.

Kagoshima, Koshikijima

Gifu: Zoku Hida 141, "The great snake and the tiger" (Daija to tora).
Fukuoka: Fukuoka 165, "The bear that saved a bride" (Yome o tasuke-shi kuma no hanashi).
Nagasaki, Kitatakaku-gun: Hōgen shi 22 35, "The big snake" No. 1 (Daija); (Old) Iki 69, 72, "The younger sister who turned into a snake" (Hebi ni natta imōto) and "The snake bride" (Hebi yome no hanashi).
Kagoshima, Amami Ōshima: MK iI 4 24, "The elder sister a demon" (Oni no ane). The gratitude of a tiger is added.
   Kikaijima: MK I 7 39, "The demon mother" (Oni no haha).
   Koshikijima: Koshiki 126, "The younger sister a demon" (Oni no imōto). Example.
   Okinoerabujima: Okinoerabu 219, "The elder sister a demon" (Oni no ane).

Further reference:
   Chōsen mintan shū 110, "The fox younger sister and her three brothers" (Kitsune imōto to san kyōdai).

110. A Thousand Wolves

A certain merchant of Kōshū had gone on a trip to Suruga and was on his way back. The sun set when he reached the broad plain at the foot of the mountain at the border between Suruga and Kai. There was no house around. It was at the end of autumn, so there were stacks of straw here and there. He decided to climb into one to spend the night. A pack of mountain dogs scented the man in the night and gathered around, sniffing and growling. The man started to run away in excitement and climbed a tree nearby. The mountain dogs came running after him, but they could not climb the tree. While they were milling around they began to talk over what to do. They decided to call Old Lady Magotarō. Two or three went off somewhere while the rest guarded the man. He was wondering what Old Lady Magotarō could be when they returned with an old tiger cat. The dogs seemed impatient as they asked her what to do. Presently, she said she thought they could make a dog ladder. One dog crouched low while another mounted him and did the same. Then another and another climbed on until they were nearly high enough to reach the merchant's feet. The frightened man tried to climb higher, but it was no longer possible. The dogs reached higher and higher. The frantic man drew his sword at his side and for some reason thrust it with all his might into a nest that was above his head. It proved to be a bear's nest. The sleeping bear was startled and went tumbling down to the ground and rushed off. When the dogs saw that, they were sure it was the man. They pulled their ladder down and rushed after it. They were dumbfounded to find it was a bear. They said the man must still be in the tree and hurried back. In the meantime, dawn was coming on. Old Lady Magotarō and the dogs said they would have to give up because of the dawn and they went off. The merchant came down from the tree fearfully at last and ran home.

Yamanashi, Nishiyatsushiro-gun

Niigata, Minamikanbara-gun: Minamikanbara 135, "Old Lady Yasaburō" (Yasaburō baa san).
Fukui, Sakai-gun: MK I 1 29, "Old Lady Baben" (Baben baba). Two stories but no ladder.
Yamanashi, Nishiyatsushiro-gun: Kai 296, "Old Lady Magotarō" (Magotarō baba). Example. Zoku Kai 71, "Old Lady Tarō" (Tarō baba). They were badgers, not wolves. They made a ladder by climbing onto each other's shoulders.
Nagano, Shimoina-gun: Mukashibanashi 14, "The mountain cat disguised as an old woman" (Baa san ni baketa yamaneko no hanashi). The beginning is like "The ox-leader and the yamauba."
Hyōgo, Kinosaki-gun: MK II 9 35, "The wolf's gratitude" (Ōkami no ongaeshi).
Tottori, Hino-gun: Inpaku dōwa 95, "The yamabushi" (Yamabushi). They

said to go for Old Lady Gorōta. The conclusion is different. The villagers decided they should be on their guard.

Yazu-gun, Wakasa-machi: Inpaku min I 187, "Old Lady Gorōta" (Gorōta baba).

Kedata-gun: Inpaku min I 188, "Old lady Gaadai with a metal tail" (Kane no o no Gaadai baba). It was a wolf's name.

Shimane, Matsue: Nihon den 149, "Old Lady Koike" (Koike baba).

Oki: Okinoshima 20, "The mountain cat and the merchant" (Yamaneko to shōnin). What was called Old Lady at Shōya was a big white cat. They say it wore a sleeveless coat and tied a towel around its head. Perhaps there were no wolves on that island.

Yamaguchi, Suō Ōshima: Kōshō 11 25, "Eaten by a wolf" (Ōkami ni kuwareru hanashi). In this there is something about throwing a mirror and turning everything upside down.

Tokushima: Awa Iyayama 22, "A thousand wolves" (Senbiki ōkami).

Kagawa, Mitoyo-gun, Shishijima: MK II 12 44, "The old woman smithy at None" (None no kaji no baba).

Further reference:

There is a famous tree called Dog-Ladder (Inuhashigo) at Nishihara, Kaminohara-mura, Kitatsuru-gun, Yamanashi.

In Echigo it is called a dog chain (ōintsunagi). It is dreaded by villagers, but nobody has seen one.

Chōsen mintan shū 96, "Mikotora." The first part is this story.

111. The Cat and the Lid of the Teakettle

A hunter in a certain place counted out his bullets before going into the mountains one morning. His pet three-colored cat pretended to sleep, but it watched him. The hunter set out without any worries. He met a ghost there which was nothing like he had ever seen or heard of. It was a one-eyed ghost. No matter how many times the hunter shot it, the ghost seemed unconcerned. When he had shot all the bullets he had brought, the ghost turned into a huge cat and came leaping at him. The hunter brought it down with a secret bullet he had with him. When he examined the cat, he found a teakettle lid beside it. He realized that the cat had held it in its mouth to protect itself from the bullets. Somehow the cat looked very much like the one at his house. He took the teakettle lid home. He found that the teakettle lid was missing and the cat was not there.

Iwate, Kamihei-gun

Iwate, Kamihei-gun: Kikimimi 344, "The monster cat" (Kaibyō no hanashi). Example.

Fukushima, Iwaki-gun: Iwaki 173, "The cat that counted the bullets" (Neko ga teppō dama o kazoeta hanashi).

Ishikawa: Ishikawa 949. No title. At Dōnokawa there is a ghost story about "Chikkin Kaburi." It is not a detailed story.

Nomi-gun: MK II 6 34, "Nekomata of Tanitōge" (Tanitōge no Nekomata).

Fukui, Fukui City: MK II 3 44, "Destroying the ghost cat" (Bake neko taiji). A cat in the tree-tops ate people at night. A samurai destroyed it with more arrows than the cat could see. It does not say how the cat protected itself. This is a fragment.

Nagano, Shimoina-gun: Mukashibanashi 49, "The mountain cat and the hunter" (Yamaneko to ryōshi). The mountain cat was disguised as an old woman. It is close to the story on Kikaijima.

Yamanashi, Nishiyatsushiro-gun: Kai 299, "The cat and the hunter" (Neko to karyūdo).

Aichi, Minamishidara-gun: Inoshishi 42, "The hunter long ago" (Mukashi no karyūdo). In one story the cat curled up on the teakettle lid, counting the bullets. It carried the lid when it went into the mountains.

Fukuoka, Chikujō-gun: Buzen,* "The badger with a bell on his head" (Kane o kabutta tanuki).

Bungo (Ōita): Sangaku XIX 3 79, "A legend about Kurogatake" (Kurogatake no densetsu). It says an old monkey on Kokonoe Yama Kurogatake wore a temple bell on its head.

Kitaamabe-gun: MK I 4 35, "Old Lady Shōbe" (Shōbe baba). A hunter saw cats wrestling when he set out to hunt in the morning. He shot Old Lady Shōbe. He followed the trail of her blood to the village and called at her house because of her injuries. He shot her through the quilts and destroyed her.

Kagoshima, Kikaijima: Shima I 2 27, "The iron bullets" (Kurogane no tama). Some parts are close to the Ina story. It is about shooting wild boar and a pet cat. The hunter's wife came to meet him in the mountains. He thought it was strange and shot her, but she ran away. He traced the blood and found she was the pet cat. It was dead at the altar of Hi-no-kami [Fire God] in the kitchen. It does not say it counted the bullets.

112. Cat Mountain
or Nekomata

A certain man planned to cross the mountain on his way home from Osarisawa to Kemanai, but when he got as far as Shinden, he became confused and went back into the mountains. Farther on, he saw a big, brightly lighted house and went to ask to stay there for the night. The kitchen was crowded with women and children. When he asked to stay, they agreed willingly. Presently a sliding door was drawn back and an aged woman came in. She greeted him and said, "I am the three colored cat which your grandfather kept for many years. This place is called Nekomata where the unwanted cats of the village gather. They have gone for your bedding for tonight, but if you stay, they will kill you. Please hurry away. There is a small hole in the corner of the alcove. Go through it onto the porch. There is a river outside the gate. If you can manage to cross it, the cats can not follow you, and you will be safe. Please hurry!" The man recalled that there had been an old three-colored cat at his grandfather's that had got lost, and he thought this cat must be the one. He went out of the estate as he had been directed and was starting across the river when a big crowd of cats came howling after him. He managed frantically to cross to the other side. When dawn came, he looked around and found himself in a mountain he had never seen before. Finally, he found his way and reached home.

Akita, Kazuno-gun

Akita, Kazuno-gun: Dai-ni 21, "Cat Mountain" (Nekomata). Example.
Niigata, Minamikanbara-gun: Kamuhara 170, Note No. 58. About the gratitude of a cat.
Ishikawa, Nomi-gun, Shiromine-mura: MK II 6 33, "Sentarō." A man named Sentarō hid a gourd given him by a pet cat he had had a long time before, and he escaped danger at Nekomata.
Yamaguchi, Suō Ōshima: Dai-ni 19, "Cat Mountain" (Nekoyama no hanashi). The story is about the gratitude of a cat that had gone away to Cat Mountain. She showed gratitude to a former maid, but she ate the mistress who had tormented her. The story is close to "The tongue-cut sparrow," and there is a part about the old man next door. This might have been the original story.
Kumamoto: (no source). This Nekomata story is about adventure. There is no part about receiving treasure and going back the second time.

113. Cat Mountain or Cat Island

The maid at a certain house was kind to the cat, but its mistress abused it. The cat disappeared suddenly. This grieved the maid. A pilgrim who came along told her the cat was in the mountains of Inaba on Kyūshū, and she set out to look for it. Night overtook her in the mountains. She asked to stay over night at a splendid house. It proved to be the cat house. When it was night, the cat she loved came out to greet her looking like a woman except for her cat face. She handed the maid a paper parcel and warned her the place was where cats gathered. She asked her to hurry away. The next morning, the place was full of cats, just as she had been told. She waved the parcel she had received at them and was able to go home safely. There was a picture of a dog holding a real 10-ryō coin in its mouth in the package. Her mistress was envious and went to visit the cat. She was bitten to death because she had not loved it.

Yamaguchi, Suō Ōshima

Akita, Kazuno-gun, Miyakawa-mura: Dai-ni 21, "Nekomata."
Niigata, Minamikanbara-gun: Kamuhara 168, "The cat's gratitude" No. 1 (Neko no ongaeshi).
Ishikawa, Nomi-gun, Shiramine: MK II 6 33, "Sentarō."
Yamaguchi, Suō Ōshima: Dai-ni 19, "Cat Mountain" (Nekoyama no hanashi). Example.
Fukuoka: Nihon den 232, "Nekogatake." It is a legend of Nekogatake in Kurate-gun, Chikuzen.
Kagoshima: Kikai 82, "The cat's gratitude" (Neko no ongaeshi).

114. The Ghost of the Treasure

On a certain island there was a deserted house with pots and pans and everything prepared for travelers who might want to stay over night, but nobody who came would stay a second night. Then a traveler came to the island and stayed over night to see. In the middle of the night a beautiful woman came out and seemed to say something and then disappeared. The man thought it strange. The next night a big snake came out. The next night a man came out and said something and disappeared. On the fourth night the former woman came out. She asked the man who he was and where he had come from. After he answered, she said, "No matter what region a traveler comes from and stays here, he never stays the second night. I happen to be money that has been buried under this house for many years. I wish to go out into the world soon and to bring pleasure to people, but I cannot go on my own power, and I suffer. Please dig me up quickly." The next morning the man asked the villagers to help, and they dug out the money hastily. He gave half of it to the villagers and kept the other half and went home. They say that money buried for several hundred years can appear as a ghost and say something.

Kagoshima, Kikaijima

Aomori: Tsugaru m 6, "Dancing with ghosts" (Bakemono to odoru hanashi). It is like "The old man who got a tumor."
Iwate: Shiwa shū 45, "The Ise pilgrim" (Ise maeriko). A ghost came out and danced at a house where a pilgrim stayed on his way to Ise. It was gold coins. It shows the secret happiness of a hero who is not afraid.
Fukushima: Iwaki 154. A note.
Niigata: Sadogashima 130, 131, "The ghost of treasure" (Takara bakemono) and "The spirit of gold" (Kin no rei). A girl came to an ascetic named Ōkubo in a town in Izumo to ask him to marry her. The couple rented a haunted estate and met the ghost of gold. What follows is like "Charcoal-maker Chōja."
Yamanashi, Nishiyatsushiro-gun: Zoku kai 164, "The tea jar under the tea tree" (Cha no ki no shita no chatsubo).

Okayama: Mitsu 84, "The ghost of coins" (Zeni no bakemono no hana-shi).

Shimane, Ōchi-gun: MK II 9 31, 12 35, "The ghost of treasure" (Takara bakemono). Both stories with the same title. The first is about stopping over night at a diplapidated house and seeing a ghost. In the other, the ghost of the chōja's daughter came out and asked for a hōji [a Buddhist memorial service]. The whole way in which the story is told is somehow professional.

Tokushima, Miyoshi-gun: MK II 9 41, "The ghost of treasure" (Takara bakemono). The origin of the Mitsui family. The middle part is omitted.

Ōita, Kitaamabe-gun: MK I 4 39, "Two ghost stories" (Bakemono futa-tsu). The second.

Kagoshima: Kikai 136, "The ghost of treasure" (Takara bakemono) Example.

115. The Ghost of Mountain Pears

This is a variant of stories about showing the real form of a ghost.

Iwate: Shiwa 66, "The ghost of mountains pears" (Yamanashi no bake-mono). A filthy ghost called an ōnyūdō came out and told the novice at the temple to eat its feces. He followed it and found a great mountain pear tree. A huge mound of fruit that had dropped year after year was at its foot.

Akita, Senhoku-gun: MK I 10 32, "The ghost of apples" (Ringo no kai).

116. The Man-Eating Mushroom

A mushroom at a deserted house ate people. The house was falling into ruin. A man stayed there and saw the true form of the ghost and destroyed it.

Iwate, Kamihei-gun: Rōō 27, "The mushroom ghost" (Naba no bake-mono). A drifter stopped over night at a great empty house. The mushroom told him how he got ahead in the world. It disliked salt and heat.

Niigata, Minamikanbara-gun: Kamuhara 204, "The mushroom ghost" (Kinoko no bakemono). There is a bit of humor where it says it disguises itself as a man. There is a dialogue about what is dis-liked the most.

Nagasaki: (Old) Iki 55, "The man-eating mushroom" (Hitokui naba). The youngest of three brothers destroyed it. He put salty bean soup onto it.

117. The Haunted Mountain Temple

This is like a ghost of treasure, but finding gold does not come into it.

Long ago an itinerant priest came to a certain village and asked to stay over night. He was told that no priest traveling alone could be put up at the village, but since they felt sorry for him they would let him stay at a vacant temple. When he went there, five or six villagers were building a fire and making preparations for him. They left, saying there was rice and wine for him. He heard something in the night in the main hall, so he put a kettle that was there onto his head and waited silently. A three-eyed ōnyūdō with two sets of teeth came out from the living quarters and thumped the man's head, pachin, and remarked it was a strong, hard one. The priest said, "It's my turn now!" He took an ax and split the ghost's head, gachari, and tossed it outside and left it there. The same kind of ghost came out three times, and he destroyed each and tossed it outside. The next morning the villagers came, saying the priest had surely been eaten the night before. They found him sitting safely by the fire, warming himself. When they asked him if anything had happened the night before, he told them and that he had thrown the ghosts outside. If they were held up to the morning light, their real form could be seen. They looked and found the three dead ōnyūdō and held them up to the sunlight. They were old wooden geta. The people told the priest that many times a priest had come to take over the temple, but each time he had been eaten by a ghost. They asked him to take charge of the place. The itinerant priest agreed.

Bestowing a fortune along with a ghost story is very old. Ghosts in old tales are always something in disguise.

Iwate, Shiwa-gun

Iwate, Shiwa-gun: Shiwa shū 14, "The haunted temple" (Bakemono dera). Example.

Akita, Senhoku-gun: MK I 11 24, "The old straw cloak, a furoshiki, and an old drum" (Furumino ni furoshiki ni furudaiko). It resembles the Ōshū story about getting a tumor.

Niigata, Minamikanbara-gun: Kamuhara 201, "The mortar and the mallet" (Usu to kine). The ghosts of a mortar and a mallet showed a man who was not afraid where gold was at a temple.

Nagano: Chiisagata 266, 269, "Gold and silver and copper coins" (Kin gin bita sen) and "The carp, the chicken, and the fox" (Koi, niwatori, kitsune). In the second, the ghosts wore red, gray, or brown hoods. The man took everything the next morning and ate them all. **Kitasaku-gun:** Kitasaku 219, "How Baienbō destroyed the ghost" (Baienbō no bakemono taiji). The ghost was in the temple at Uenoyama, Fuse-mura. The priest was called Baienbō. **Shimoina-gun:** Mukashibanashi 28, "Sokuheitan." The ghosts were the head of the horse of Tōgen, Saishō cock of Saichikurin, the

big fish at Nanki, and the toad at Hokuchi. The Kitasaku item and
this belong to a period when Chinese characters were esteemed.
Yamanashi, Nishiyatsushiro-gun: Kai 97, "The buried bottle" (Iketa bin).
Gifu, Yoshiki-gun, Kamitakara-mura: Hidabito V 6 6, "The ghost of
treasure" (Takara bakemono). The ghosts were an old straw cloak,
a carved wooden fish, and a drum. The story is about ghosts, but
they were not treasures.

118. The Ghost in the Deserted House

A man spends the night at a lonely house and is asked to look
after a corpse and sees a ghost. In many such stories it is said to be
nothing. The following might be one form of the story.
A traveler was overtaken by night and managed to reach the house
of somebody he knew. His host said he had arrived at a good time.
There was somebody dead there and he needed somebody to keep
watch. He asked him to take over and then he left. The traveler was
annoyed, but there was no help for it. He sat by the hearth to have a
smoke. The corpse of the dead woman began to stir and rise. The man
was startled, but he kept his head and looked around. He saw something like a fox had stuck its head through the opening below the
drain and was watching the corpse intently. The man went outside and
around to the back stealthily to investigate. A fox was actually there,
standing on its hind legs with its head thrust through the opening. The
traveler picked up a stick that was handy and beat the fox to death.

Iwate, Shimohei-gun, Toyomane-mura

Iwate, Shimohei-gun, Toyomane-mura: Tōno 88 No. 101. No title.
Example. It is told as a true story. It is like other examples where
the true situation is discovered later.
Yamagata, Higashitagawa-gun: MK I 10 34, "The gold coins in the
coffin" (Hayaoge no naka no koban). The principal character was
Yaro, who gathered mushrooms. He was put in charge of a coffin
with a corpse in it. He was asked to carry it on his back later.
What follows is like "The hearth fire on New Year's Eve." He
opened the coffin at dawn and found it full of coins.
Yamanashi, Nishiyatsushiro-gun: Kai 286, "The deserted house" (Ikkenya).
Kagoshima: Kikai 137, "The corpse and the salt buyer" (Mōja to
shiokai). An old man and old woman agreed to signal each other
when one of them was put into a coffin. The old woman died first.
The old man did as he had agreed, but he got tired of it. He fooled a salt buyer who came along and asked him to look after things
and to answer for him. The dead woman asked, "Who are you?" She
came out and the salt buyer tried to run away. She chased him and
went off somewhere.

8. Help from Animals

119. The Listening Hood

Once upon a time when a good old man went to pray to Inari, his tutelary deity, he received a treasure that was a red hood. When he wore it, he could understand right off what birds or animals said. The delighted old man put the hood into his bosom and went along to where there was a big tree. He sat beneath it and went to sleep. A bird came flying from the direction of the seashore and another from an island. They lighted upon the tree. The old man decided this was the time to try his hood. He put it on his head and began listening to the birds. The bird from the seashore said it had been five or six years since the village chōja had built a storehouse. When the roof was being thatched, a snake had crawled up and was nailed down. Half dead and half alive, it was being cared for by the female with food she brought it. Its resentment, however, had built up and caused a long illness for the chōja's daughter. If the snake were rescued, the girl would surely get well, but it was a pity that men could not understand such things. Then the two birds parted and flew away. The old man thought he had heard something fine. He wanted to hurry and save the lives of the chōja's daughter and the snake. He disguised himself as a fortune teller and went to the chōja's house. He pretended to lay out his fortune sticks and repeated what he had heard the bird say. The snake was rescued. Then to the chōja's delight, his daughter gradually recovered. He gave the old man a great sum of money, making him a rich man. The old man rebuilt Inari's shrine and celebrated a splendid feast.

The old man set out again and rested under the former tree. Those same birds came again and began to talk. This time it was about the illness of the chōja in town. It was because when the guest room had been built, a camphor tree that grew under the eaves had been cut. The rain dripped off the roof onto it, keeping it alive by watering its roots, and it continued to suffer. Its resentment caused the master's illness and distress among its friends, the trees in the mountains who came to comfort it. The old man disguised himself once more as a fortune teller and went to the chōja's house. He heard various trees from the mountains come to offer sympathy when he spent the night in the guest house. In the morning, the old man pretended to lay out his sticks and told about the camphor tree. He asked for it to be dug up from its roots. When this was done, the master recovered day by day. The old man received a great sum of money again, but he stopped being a fortune teller and lived as a chōja.

Iwate, Kamihei-gun

Aomori, Hachinohe: MK II 7 44, "The Listening Hood" (Kikimimi).
Iwate, Kamihei-gun: Rōō 86, "The Listening Hood" (Kikimimi). Example.
    Nihon shū, jō 163, "The Listening Hood" (Kikimimi).
Gifu: Masuda 569, "Eight hundred [years] Bikuni" (Happyaku Bikuni). The story is about Jirōbei, the wine merchant, at Nakagiri, Masemura.
Kumamoto, Kamoto-gun: MK II 8 42, "The kunotsu" (Kunotsu). The bird called a kunotsu was given the man at the Dragon Palace. When he put it to his ear, he could understand what birds said.
Kagoshima, Amami Ōshima: MK II 3 45, "The Listening Hood" (Kikimimi). A man who saved a red snapper was invited to the Dragon Palace. He received a Listening Hood which let him understand what birds said. He became the chōja's son-in-law.

120. The Golden Fan and the Silver Fan

Long ago a poor man spent days petitioning the kami to get rich. On the final day of his prayers, a white-haired old man came out and bestowed two fans upon him. One was gold and the other, silver. He was told that if he fanned a nose with the gold fan, the nose would grow higher, and with the silver fan, it would grow lower. He was told to use them cleverly and to become rich. At the time the chōja's daughter went to see cherry blossoms, he used the fan to make her nose three feet high. Although a doctor was called, he could not cure it. The chōja and his wife worried. Finally, they declared they would take as son-in-law anyone who could cure her. The poor man disguised himself as a masseur. He was called into the house and he used his silver fan to cure the girl. Then he became the son-in-law. One day he fell asleep while fanning his nose. It grew all the way to the sky and pierced the fire-box at Raijin's house [Thunder God]. That made Raijin uneasy. He stuck his fire tongs through it. The man was startled when his nose was burned. He fanned himself with the silver fan, but his nose was held fast as it shrank and his body was drawn up. He is dangling somewhere in the sky even now. He will probably stay there until Raijin releases the tongs.

Yamanashi, Nishiyatsushiro-gun

Fukushima, Iwaki-gun: Iwaki 41, 130, "Making a nose high or low" (Hana o takaku shitari hikuku shitari hanashi).
Saitama: Kawagoe 113, "Gengorō's trip to the sky" (Gengorō no ten nobori).
Yamanashi, Nishiyatsushiro-gun: Kai 30, "Gonemon's nose" (Gonemon no hana). Example.
Tokushima: Awa Iyayama 115, "Nose, get high" (Binbana takō nare).
Kagoshima: Koshiki 181, "Making a nose high" (Hana o takaku shita hanashi).

121. The Magic Ladle

There was once a man in a certain place who was such a liar that he had no friends. He reformed and petitioned the kami. On the final day of his petitions, he came down the hill in front of the shrine and found a little red ladle that had been dropped below the torii. He picked it up and went along with it. One side was painted red. When he stroked his seat with it, out came a big noise. When he stroked himself with the other side, which was painted black, the noise stopped. He tried stroking the seat of the chōja's daughter, and big noises came out and did not stop. Her father called in doctors and hōsha, but she did not get better. He put up a big sign on which he wrote that he would give the one who cured her anything he wanted. The liar mingled with the crowd of doctors and hōsha at the chōja's house. He stroked the girl's seat with the ladle and cured her. Then he became the son-in-law there and was a great success. He declared that whatever he had done was by the help of the ladle. He worshipped it as a deity and called it Ohera Daimyōjin [The Great Manifestation in the Ladle].

Iwate, Kamihei-gun

Aomori, Hachinohe: MK II 7 45, "The magic ladle" (Shirinaki no hera). Two stories.
Iwate, Isawa-gun: Kogane 84, "The girl whose seat started to make noises" (Musume no shiri no nakidashita hanashi); Techō 43, "The magic ladle" (Shirinaki hera).
    Kamihei-gun: Kamihei 51, "The Daimyōjin Ladle" (Ohera Daimyōjin). Example.

Akita, Hiraga-gun, Asamai-machi: MK II 5 28, "The strange ladle"
  (Fushigi na hera).
Miyagi, Momoo-gun: Kyōdo den 1 181, "The golden ladle" (Kin no
  hera).   The man was a bamboo cutter.   It is connected to "The
  bamboo cutter" and "The old man who broke wind."

122. Bumbuku Teakettle

Once there was a junk man in a certain village who was so poor
that he went to a friendly badger to ask it to disguise itself as a teakettle.   He took it to the priest and sold it for three ryō.   The priest
told his novice to scour the kettle.   When the novice started to scour
it with sand, it cried, "It hurts, novice, it hurts.   Scour gently!"   When
the novice told the priest, he tried scouring it himself.   Sure enough, it
said the same thing.   When the novice filled it with water and set it
over the fire, it said, "It's hot, it's hot, novice.   Fire it up slowly!"
When the fire grew very hot, out came the badger's head and then its
tail.   It turned into a big badger and ran off to the mountains.   With
that, the priest lost all his three ryō.

Nagano, Shimoina-gun

Aomori, Hachinohe: MK II 7 46, "The fox harlot" (Kitsune yūjo).
Iwate: Esashi 95, "The bumbuku teakettle at Shōhōji" (Shōhōji no
  bumbuku chagama).
Akita, Hiraga-gun, Asamai-machi: TD XIII 2 40, "The fox and the
  badger" (Kitsune to mujina).   A badger was fooled by a fox.   He
  disguised himself as a temple bell and was sold to a temple.   When
  the novice rang it, it cried out.
Fukushima: Iwaki 169, "The bumbuku teakettle" (Bumbuku chagama).
Niigata, Minamikanbara-gun: Kamuhara 94. Note No. 28. The story is
  about a fox harlot.   On p. 168 in the same book is a story about a
  cat.
Nagano, Shimoina-gun: Mukashibanashi 1, "The badger and the teakettle" (Tanuki to chagama).   Example.
Aichi: Shidara No. 15 26, "Bonboko teakettle" (Bonboko chagama).
  There are many stories about old teakettles in this region.
Tokushima: Awa Iyayama 20 98, "The magician" (Majutsusha) and "The
  bumbuku teakettle" (Bumbuku chagama).   The first story follows the
  part about four magicians.

123. The Fox Harlot

This should be considered as the same kind of tale as "Bumbuku
teakettle."
The fox is sold as a horse and then as a harlot.   The horse is the
earliest, the teakettle is next, and the woman episode can be consi-

dered the newest. They all belong to the same type. There may be three motives. It may be a debt of gratitude or just friendliness or repenting when revenge is about to be carried out.

Aomori, Hachinohe: MK II 7 46, "The fox harlot" (Kitsune yūjo). The fox offered to be sold as a harlot to show its repentance. The written characters and the seal on the deed were footprints of a fox.

Iwate: Kamihei 98, "The gratitude of the fox" (Kitsune hōon). In gratitude it changed into three things—a kettle, a harlot, and a horse.

Niigata, Sado: MK I 4 42, "The gratitude of the fox" (Kitsune no ongaeshi).

124. Animal Gratitude

Many of these are brief anecdotes or in the form of a legend.

Nagano, Shimoina-gun: Mukashibanashi 138, "Helping a wolf" (Ōkami o tasuketa hanashi). The wolf gave the man a pheasant as thanks for taking a big chicken bone out of its throat.

Hyōgo, Kinosaki-gun, Kiyotaki-mura: MK II 9 35, "The gratitude of the wolf" (Ōkami no ongaeshi). The man pulled a bone out of a wolf's throat. It drew him into a cave to protect him from 1000 wolves.

Hiroshima, Takata-gun: Aki 137, "The gratitude of the black dog" (Kuroi inu no hōon). After the man saved one of the dog's pups, the father dog invited him to his house and made him son-in-law for one of his daughters. The story is pretty much broken.

Nagasaki: Gotō 240, "The gratitude of the monkey" (Saru no ongaeshi). A poor man rescued a monkey when he set out on New Year's Eve to gather snails. The monkey showed him a spring of wine in the mountains as thanks and he became rich. His neighbor who lived down the hill put a straw snake into the spring and planned to take the wine for himself. The snake came alive and swallowed him.

125. The Dog, The Cat, and the Ring

Long ago there were two families on opposite sides of a river, one on the east side and one on the west, and in each there was an old man and an old woman. The old man to the east was honest. He received a monkey farthing from the Dragon Spirit. Day by day his fortunes improved until the old man on the west became envious. He borrowed the monkey farthing and would not return it. Then the old man on the west prospered and the old man on the east became poorer and poorer. He told his pet cat to go and get the coin. The cat rode a dog's back across the river. He found a rat and told it if it wanted to be spared it would have to get the monkey farthing. The rat brought it promptly. The cat took the coin in its mouth and started back across the river, but accidentally dropped it. The cat came safely home with it by the help of a kite, a cormorant, and a trout.

Shimane, Ōchi-gun, Hinuki-mura

Aomori, Sannohe-gun, Hachinohe: MK II 9 44, "The dog, the cat, and the ring" (Inu to neko to yubiwa). It tells only the reason dogs and cats are unfriendly.

Iwate, Hienuki-gun: MK I 10 23, "The precious snake scales" (Kogera dama).

Yamagata, Higashitagawa-gun: MK I 10 33, "The white macaw" (Shiroi inko). Two old men were neighbors. It is combined with "komekura" and is overdone.

Akita, Senhoku-gun: MK I 6 38, "Returning the magic mallet" (Enmyō kozuchi o torimodoshi). There is no dog. It resembles the Ryūkichi story.

Niigata, Minamikanbara-gun: MK I 1 21, "The dog, the cat, and the rat" (Inu to neko to nezumi). There are two stories. The first tells of saving the life of a snake and the ring from the Dragon Palace. What was lost was returned by the help of three animals. The second is like "Sedge hats for Jizō." A purse was received from Jizō. There is the reason why dogs and cats are unfriendly.

Nagano, Shimoina-gun: Mukashibanashi 103, "Ishi-no-Shōbei." It starts from the snake son.

Osaka, Senhoku-gun: Dai-ni 10, "The dog and the cat" (Inu to neko). It only says that long ago dogs and cats were friendly. The rest of the story is broken up.

Shimane, Ōchi-gun: MK II 10 29, "The old man on the east bank and the old man on the west bank" (Tōgan no jiji to seigan no jiji). Example. Nihon zenkoku 215, "The monkey's thanks" (Saru no henrei). The dog is not present. This is an unusual example. It resembles the story in Inpaku dōwa 68.

Nagasaki, Minamitakaku-gun: Shimabara 156, "The dog, the cat, and the ring" (Inu to neko to yubiwa). The principal character is Netarō, a man who was lazy for three years. He went to the Dragon Palace and received a ring, but his stupid wife lost it. There is help from a dog, a cat, and a kappa.

Kagoshima: Koshiki 133, "The dog, the cat, and the ring" (Inu, neko, yubiwa).

Further reference:

Nihon mukashibanashi shū, ge 98. A Korean example. "The stone from which wine flowed" (Sake no wakideru ishi).

Chōsen mintan shū 240, "The dog, the cat, and the jewel" (Inu to neko to tama). An old man who lived by the seashore rescued a carp. He was invited to the Dragon Palace and received a jewel. A bad old woman substituted something for it, but it was brought back by the help of a dog, a cat, and a rat. In App. 42, a note with the same title. An example from the Buriat tribe in Siberia.

Ainu minzoku shiryō I 31, refers to B.H. Chamberlain, "The language, mythology, and geographical nomenclature of Japan viewed in the light of *Ainu Grammer* by John Batchelor and a catalogue of books relating to Yezo and the Ainu," Tokyo Imperial University, 1887.

Mukashibanashi kenkyū I 1 13. Seki Keigo, "A comparative study of material in tales called 'The dog, the cat, and the ring'" (Inu to neko to yubiwa hikaku shiryō).

126. The Tongue-Cut Sparrow

Once there was an old man and an old woman who kept a sparrow in a cage. One day when the old woman made dango and left them on the roof, the sparrow ate them all. The old woman was angry and cut the sparrow's tongue. She told her old man when he came home from the mountains. He set out calling, "Sparrow, sparrow, where have you gone?" He saw a man cutting bamboo and asked him which way the sparrow had gone. The man said he would tell if he would help him, so the old man helped. Next he saw a man dipping up fertilizer, and he helped him. In this way he found the sparrow's home. (What follows is the usual story and it will be omitted.)

Fukui, Sakai-gun

Fukushima: Iwaki 169, "The tongue-cut sparrow" (Shitakiri suzume).
Niigata, Sado: Sado shū 15, "The tongue-cut sparrow, the old man who swallowed a bird" (Shitakiri suzume, torinomi jiji). There is a part where the old man asks the way of a man tending a dog and one tending a cow and a horse. In the last part it says the sparrow was roasted and eaten, so it may be only here that it is confused with the story of the old man who swallowed a bird.
Fukui, Sakai-gun: MK I 1 27, "The tongue-cut sparrow" (Shitakiri suzume). Example.
Ōita: Naori 28, "The tongue-cut sparrow" (Shitakiri suzume). He asked a cow washer and a horse washer the way to the sparrow's house.
Kumamoto, Kamoto-gun: MK II 8 45, "The sparrow's gratitude" (Suzume hōon).
Ishikawa (Noto) Kashima-gun, Nanao: Dai-ni 60, "The tongue-cut sparrow" (Shitakiri suzume).

127. The Sparrow with a Broken Back

An honest old woman and a greedy old woman lived in the mountains. The honest old woman rescued a sparrow whose back had been broken by children. It gave her a single gourd seed as thanks. She planted it in her yard and soon it sprouted and spread all over, loaded with big gourds. When she tried eating one, it was so good that she divided the gourds with her neighbors. She hung the big ones below the eaves to dry. These suddenly became very heavy. When she tried shaking one, lots of rice came out. After that, she could eat rice every day and her life became happy, and it continued until she became rich. The greedy old woman looked on and was very envious. She hunted for a sparrow with a broken back, but since she could not find one, she caught a sparrow and deliberately broke its back. She set it free after she had cared for it. That sparrow, too, brought a gourd seed. The old woman planted it in a hurry. Seven or eight gourds formed. Instead of dividing with her neighbors, she hung them under her eaves to dry. She gloated over them as they grew heavy. One day she decided to take one down to see. It was much too heavy for her to handle alone. She thought it was full of rice, but when she opened it, only vipers, centipedes, and frogs came out. She was so shocked that she died.

Ōita, Usa-gun

Niigata, Minamikanbara-gun: Kamuhara 39, "The gratitude of the sparrow" (Suzume no ongaeshi).
Shimane, Ōchi-gun: MK II 12 34, "The sparrow with a broken back" (Koshiore suzume).
Ōita, Usa-gun: Dai-ni 58, "The gourd that produced rice" (Kome no naru hisago). Example.
Kumamoto, Kamoto-gun: MK II 8 45, "The sparrow's gratitude" (Suzume hōon). This is exactly the same version as Ujishūi monogatari No. 48. It is also found in Korea. It is distributed widely in Japan and cannot be considered the result of modern books.

128. Kokōjirō

Once there was an old man and an old woman. The old man went to the mountains every day to cut wood. He always gave what was left over from his lunch to crabs in the marsh. Then wine began to come out of the marsh. He always dipped up some to take home. His old woman thought it strange and went to the marsh to see. She ate all the crabs before the old man knew. The next time the old man went, there was not a single crab left in the marsh. He was worried. A bird in a tree top sang: "Shells in the wood patch, meat in Granny's belly, Gaa gaa!" The old man went home to the seed patch and found heaps of empty shells by the roots of the tree. (The rest is forgotten.)

Aomori, Hachinohe

Aomori, Kamikita-gun, Nobechi: TD XII 7 17. No title. The second of three tales. Example.

Hachinohe: MK II 8 22, "The crabs and the old man" (Kani to jii).
It resembles "The tongue-cut sparrow" somewhat.
Akita, Senhoku-gun, Kakunodate: TD XI 7 34, "The bird call" (Tori no
oto). This is about a crab wife. The old woman killed the crabs.
When the old man went looking for them, a crow called, "The
claws are on the roof, the shells in the garden, karon, karon";
Akita 7, "The old man and the crab" (Jichiya to kaniko).
Miyagi, Sendai: Kikimimi 257, "Kokōjirō." The name of the crab was
Kokōjirō.
Kagoshima: Koshiki 189, "The crab shell" (Kani no kōra).

129. The Temple Patron Who was a Cat

There once was a very old priest at a certain temple. He kept a
cat that was very old, too. They did nothing but sit by the hearth and
doze. One day the cat suddenly declared that as thanks for its long
care it would like to make the temple prosper once more. It said that
the chōja's only daughter would die shortly. It would raise her coffin
into the air during the funeral. When the old priest would go to offer
sutras, it would lower the coffin when he said, "Namu Tora-ya." The
chōja's daughter did die, and since she was an only daughter, the
priests from all around were called for her splendid funeral, but the
old priest in the mountains was overlooked. When the funeral procession was formed to proceed around her coffin, the coffin suddenly rose
into the air and hung there. The people milled around and the priests
exhausted all their arts by intoning sutras and rolling their strands of
beads, but nothing seemed to work. The chōja grieved and the people
began to complain about the priests. The chōja said he would remit
the rice tax for the rest of the life of anyone who could lower the
coffin, he would repair his temple, he would contribute anything to
him, but nobody could budge the coffin. Somebody recalled the old
priest and went for him. He came tapping along with his staff and sat
down quietly on the grass. He began his sutra. At the right time he
intoned, "Namu Tora-ya," and down glided the coffin and came to rest
on the grass. All cried out and marveled. The chōja prostrated himself
in thanks. He had his red lacquered sedan chair prepared and sent the
old priest home to the mountain in it. He made all kinds of donations
and had the temple repaired as he had promised. It prospered so much
that a market sprang up outside its gate.

Iwate, Kamihei-gun

Aomori, Hachinohe: MK II 8 22, "The temple patron who was a cat"
(Neko danka). Two tales. Both are changed into legends to tell the
origin of temples. This story is also told at Jōhōji.
Iwate: Kamihei 118, "The yellow cat and the priest" (Tora neko to
oshō). Example.
Fukushima: Iwaki 42 131, "The cat's gratitude" (Neko no ongaeshi).

Nagano, Kitasaku-gun: MK I 12 36, "The cat patron" (Neko danka no hanashi).
Yamanashi, Nishiyatsushiro-gun: Zoku Kai 83, "The cat temple" (Nekodera).
Tokushima, Mima-gun: MK II 1 29, "The cat at Takidera" (Takidera no neko); Awa Iyayama 57, "The temple patron who was a cat" (Neko danka).

130. The Cat Temple

There was a chōja with an only daughter in a certain place. She became ill suddenly. She would groan and suffer in the middle of the night, but the doctors and hōsha could do nothing for her. It was noticed that the pet cat never left her side and that seemed strange. Although it was chased away, it would come back. The cat appeared in a dream and said that the reason he could not leave the girl was that there was a big tenko above the ceiling that wanted to kill the girl. She would be in danger if the cat were not there. He said he could not destroy the tenko by himself. He wanted to get his brother cat at a certain house many miles away. The two of them could destroy it. The family was not sure the dream was true, but they dispatched a messenger, who came back after a number of days with a cat that looked like theirs. They gave the two good things to eat and let them be. When the cats were asked what to do, there was another dream. The cat asked that they be put in a certain one of their storehouses at a certain moment of a certain day and month. The dream ceased as the voice seemed to be heard. The two cats were put into the storehouse at the right time. The family waited. Nothing happened at first, but presently there was a big noise, "dotan batan," and the scuffle began. Things quieted for a while, but the noise started again. They thought it was all over and opened the door a little to see. The other cat came out followed by theirs carrying a silver haired tenko in its mouth. They had killed it, but the two cats died in a short time. The girl's illness disappeared. The chōja had two tombs erected for the cats.

Okayama, Tomata-gun

Iwate, Kamihei-gun: Rōō 125, "The cat temple" (Nekodera). The cat belonged to seven different priests since the founding of the temple. It is the start of Nekoza Daimyōjin.
Shiwa-gun: Shiwa shū 53, "The cat on a pilgrimage to Ise" (Isemaeri neko).
Niigata, Minamikanbara-gun: Kamuhara 206, "The cat's gratitude" (Neko no ongaeshi).
Yamanashi, Nishiyatsushiro-gun: Kai 37, "The cat and the girl" (Neko to musume). There is another story about a cat's grave and a rat's grave.

Okayama, Tomata-gun: Mitsu 77, "How cats destroyed the tenko" (Neko no tenko taiji). Example.
Mitsu-gun: Mitsu 79, "The cat's protection" (Neko no shugo).

131. The Forbidden Room

When a young farmer set out to look for work, he reached the mountain pass just at sunset. He saw a light ahead and barely managed to reach it. He found a splendid house. A beautiful girl came out and agreed to let him stay overnight. Then she decided to hire him to look after things when she was away. As she set out on a horse the next morning, she said there would be anything he wanted to eat in the cupboard if he opened it. She said for him to eat if he was hungry. She asked only that he not open the door to the interior room, and then left. The young man just stayed there as caretaker finding whatever he wanted to eat by opening the cupboard. Thus a full year passed. When he said that they would be worrying about him at home and asked to go, he was given a roll of white cotton cloth and money wrapped in paper. He opened the wrapping when he got home and found only a single strange coin. He thought it unusual and took it to the village head. He was told it was a great treasure called a nightingale farthing. The village head bought it for 1000 ryō. The young man became suddenly rich. The man next door heard about it and hunted for the house at the pass. He was hired as caretaker, but he looked into the forbidden room. It was empty. The girl came back and went into the room as usual, but came out disappointed. She said, "By just opening that door, you let out all the hokekyō I have been collecting for years in the mountains." She sighed and sent the man away without giving him anything.

Niigata, Minamikanbara-gun

Iwate, Hienuki-gun: MK II 1 38, "The forbidden room" (Miruna no zashiki).
Yamagata, Mogami-gun: MK II 4 41, "The nightingale's court" (Uguisu no dairi).
Fukushima: Iwaki 43, 132, "Looking into the forbidden storehouse" (Mite naranai kura no naka o mita hanashi).
Niigata, Minamikanbara-gun: Kamuhara 44, "Hokekyō." Example.
Gifu, Hida: Hidabito V 3 20, "The forbidden room" (Miruna no zashiki). A woman said not to look into the storehouse. While she was away, the man tore a hole in the plaster and looked through the wall. He saw many tubs with fish swimming in them. Merits that were worth 3000 years were lost in a single moment. They flew toward the mountains crying hohokekyō. They could no longer return to the human world.

Further reference:
Mukashibanashi kenkyū II 12 2. A study of "The forbidden room"
by Suzuki Tōzō.

132. The Monkey Farthing

This is in the same group as "The nightingale farthing." The coin
was received as a gift of gratitude from a monkey. When it was put on
a money box, money was made. When put on a rice chest, rice was
made. (Refer to the passage in "The dog, the cat, and the ring.")

Yamagata, Higashitagawa-gun: MK I 10 33, "The white macaw" (Shiroi
inko).
Niigata: Sado shū 81, "The old man who scattered ashes" No. 2 (Haimaki jiji). This belongs to the group, "The old man who made
flowers bloom."
Hiroshima, Takata-gun, Kita-mura: Geibi 54, "Chōja from a monkey"
(Saru Chōja). Here it is called monkey's money. The money was
taken by the old woman next door. A dog and a cat went to bring
it back. The cat brought it and that is why the cat and dog are
unfriendly.
Inaba (Tottori): Nihon zenkoku 215, "The monkey's thanks" (Saru no
henrei).
Shimane, Ōchi-gun: Minzoku bun II 7, "The monkey's thanks" (Saru no
orei). It is a little broken up, but there is a part about a monkey
being tormented by children at the beginning. MK II 10 29, "The
old man on the east bank and the old man on the west bank"
(Tōgan no jiji to seigan no jiji).

133. Rat Jōdo

Once upon a time an old man took a toasted buckwheat cake with
him to his garden patch when he went to dig. While he was digging a
rat came out cautiously. The old man broke off half of his cake and
gave it to the rat. It picked it up and crawled back into its hole. The
rat came out again, and the old man gave him some of his cake again.
He picked it up and went back into its hole. Then the father rat came
out and thanked the old man. He invited him to his house. The old man
closed his eyes as he was told and followed the rat. He found himself
in a splendid parlor. The children that he had seen before came out
and thanked him. He was given a fine feast. When he started to leave,
they gave him money. The old man next door tried to imitate him. He
took a toasted buckwheat cake to his garden patch to dig. He gave
some of his cake to the little rats and was invited to their home.
While he was eating, he saw rats put gold into a mortar. As they

pounded it, they sang, "We don't want to hear a cat's voice!" The old man wanted the gold, so he imitated a cat. All the rats ran away, and the place became pitch dark. The old man looked around and found himself in his own garden patch with his head stuck into a rat hole.

Iwate, Shiwa-gun

Aomori: Tsugaru m 61, "The old man who went into a rat hole" (Nezumi sa no ana haitta jisa no hanashi).
  Hachinohe: MK I 8 32, "Rat Island" (Nezumi no shima).
Iwate, Shiwa-gun: Shiwa shū 107, "When the old man dug in his garden" (Jiina no hatakeuchi). Example.
  Kamihei-gun: Kikimimi 220, "The bean" No. 1 (Mameko banashi).
Yamagata, Higashitagawa-gun: MK I 9 43, "When the rats pounded mochi" (Nezumi no mochi tsuki).
  Kitamurayama-gun: MK II 6 42, "Rat Jōdo" (Nezumi Jōdo).
Akita, Hiraga-gun: MK II 5 27, "When the rats pounded mochi" (Nezumi no mochi tsuki).
  Kazuno-gun: Dai-ichi 42, "Rat kingdom" (Nezumi no kuni).
Fukushima, Iwaki-gun: Iwaki 44, 113, "The rats and the dango" (Nezumi to dango).
Niigata: Minamikanbara 30, "Rat Jōdo" (Nezumi Jōdo).
Nagano, Chiisagata-gun: MK I 1 36, "Invited to the rat's house" (Nezumi ni yobareta hanashi).
  Shimominochi-gun: Shimominochi 197, "Rat Jōdo" (Nezumi Jōdo).
  Matsumoto: Kyōdo ken IV 8 54, "Children's stories from the Matsumoto region" (Matsumoto chihō no dōwa).
Hyōgo, Mikata-gun: MK II 7 38, "Rat Jōdo" (Nezumi Jōdo).
  Kinosaki-gun: MK II 8 35, "Rat Jōdo" (Nezumi Jōdo).
Hiroshima, Yamagata-gun: Aki 72, 73, "Rat kingdom" (Nezumi no kuni); Geibi 59, "Rat Jōdo" No. 1 (Nezumi no Jōdo).
Shimane, Oki: MK I 8 32, "Rat Island" (Nezumi no shima).
Ōita, Hayami-gun: MK I 12 40, "Rat Jōdo" (Nezumi no Jōdo).
Kumamoto, Hōtaku-gun: MK I 9 36, "Rat Jōdo" (Nezumi no Jōdo).
Kagoshima, Amami Ōshima: MK II 8 38, "Rat Jōdo" (Nezumi Jōdo).
  Koshikijima: Koshiki 169, "Rat Jōdo" (Nezumi no Jōdo).

134. Jizō Jōdo

An old man who went into the mountains to cut wood started to eat his lunch. He happened to drop his riceball and it rolled away and dropped into a hole. The old man crawled in after it and found Jizō eating it. The old man said, "That's the only riceball I have. Please give it back to me." Jizō apologized and told the old man a demon would come presently. He said, "Get under my seat and when I shake it, imitate a rooster's crow." Soon the demon arrived and declared he smelled a man. Jizō shook his hips three times. The old man imitated a rooster three times, and the demon thought it was dawn and ran away, leaving his iron rod behind. The old man took it home with him. It was a treasure that would bring out anything the old man wanted if he shook it. Suddenly he became very rich. His neighbor saw what happened and wanted to imitate him. He took a riceball to his garden patch. From there he went to Jizō's place. However, when the demon came and Jizō shook his hips, he was so amused that he laughed. The demon found him and said, "You're the one who fooled me yesterday, aren't you!" He stuck his iron rod through him and carried him off to Hell.

Hiroshima, Saeki-gun

Aomori, Sannohe-gun: MK II 12 26, "The crowing insect" (Kakerō mushi).
Fukushima, Iwaki-gun: Iwaki 46, 134, "Jizō and the dango" (Jizō sama to dango).
Niigata: Koshiji VI 7 14. No title.
Hiroshima, Saeki-gun: Aki 65, "The riceball that rolled away" (Korogeta nigirimeshi). Example.
    Yamagata-gun: Aki 69, "The mochi that rolled away" (Korogeta mochi); Geibi 66, "Jizō Jōdo." They call small holes demon holes or crab holes here, but in the tale it is a rat hole. The same is in the story about the monkey and the crab. There is also the exaggeration that a single grain of rice and a single bean were used to make ohagi.
Shimane, Oki, Chibu-gun: MK I 8 30, "The old man with toasted mochi" (Yakimochi jii san); MK I 9 25, "Dango Jōdo." Chasing toasted mochi to Onigashima, getting a golden ladle, and bringing it back.
Kagoshima: Koshiki 172, "The demon gamblers" (Oni bakuchi).

135. Dango Jōdo

This is a more humorous type of story than "Jizō Jōdo." For example, the dango was made from a single bean, and other points.

Iwate, Higashiiwai-gun: Fujisawa 267, "The rolling dango" (Koro-koro dango).
Niigata, Minamikanbara-gun: Dai-ichi 49, "Dango Jōdo"; Minamikanbara 24, "Dango Jōdo."
Etchū (Toyama), Mizuhashi: Hidabito VII 12 10, "Dango Jōdo." It is like the Hida example with "Jiji wa kororin."
Kumamoto, Amakusa-gun: MK II 1 40, "Dango Jōdo."
Ōita, Hayami-gun: MK II 1 43, "Dango Jōdo." Kyūshū versions are well arranged and in the old style.

136. The Old Man Who Made Flowers Bloom

"The little dog" (Inuko banashi), "The old man above and the old man below" (Kami no jii shimo no jii), "The old man who scattered ashes" (Hai maki jiji), "The old man who caught geese" (Gan tori jiji) and such stories are included in this group.

Long ago in Ōshū a good old man and a bad old man lived as neighbors. Each left a basket in the river to catch fish. The old man who lived upstream went early in the morning to see. He found a little dog in his basket, but there were a lot of little fish in the basket of the old man who lived downstream. He exchanged the contents of the two baskets and went home. When the old man from below went, he found the little dog caught in his basket. He picked it up and took it home. If he fed it from a bowl, it grew as big as a bowl. When he fed it from a pot, it grew as big as a pot. One day it went with the old man to hunt deer. He helped the old man catch lots of them. The neighbor borrowed the dog, but where the old man should have said shishi [deer], he said hachi [bees], and he was stung by many of them. He was angry and killed the dog and buried it under a rice-tree and went home. The lower old man wondered why his dog was not returned. He went to ask for it and heard that it had been killed and buried under the rice-tree. He went to the mountain and cut the rice-tree. He made a handmill from it and as he turned it, he sang for rice and money to come out. Rice and money really came out and his life became easy. His neighbor borrowed the handmill, but he and his wife forgot the song. Instead of rice and money, filthy things they sang about came flowing and filled their house. They declared it was the fault of the handmill and they burned it. When the lower old man heard that his handmill had been burned, he asked for the ashes, at least. He threw the ashes into the eyes of geese and they fell dead one after another. The old couple were eating goose soup when the old man from next door came and asked how it happened. When he learned how they had thrown ashes, he asked for some. He climbed onto his roof on a night when there was a strong wind, and looking up the sky, he sang by mistake, "Ashes go into Grandpa's eyes." The ashes flew into his eyes and blinded him. He went rolling off the roof to where his old woman was waiting. She thought he was a goose and hit him on the head with a big mallet.

Iwate, Esashi-gun

Aomori: Nihon zenkoku 153, "The little dog Shirotae" (Koinu no Shirotae); Tsugaru k 33. No title; Tsugaru m 43, "The old man who scattered ashes" (Haimaki jii sama).

Hachinohe: MK II 8 26, "The old man who caught geese" (Gan tori jiji no hanashi).

Iwate, Esashi-gun: Esashi 15, "The old man who scattered ashes" (Hai maki jiji no hanashi). Example.

Shiwa-gun: Shiwa 73, "The upper old man and the lower old man" (Kami no jii to shimo no jii).

Kamihei-gun: Kamihei 68, "The upper old man and the lower old man" (Kami no jii to shimo no jii); Rōō 130, "What happened to the old man who caught geese" (Gan tori jii no gojitsu dan).

Iwate-gun: Dai-ichi 27, "The old man from the lower field and the old man from the upper field" (Shimo ta no ōji to kami ta no ōji).

Yamagata, Kitamurayama-gun: MK II 11 34, "The old man who made flowers bloom" (Hana saka jiji).

Akita, Hiraga-gun: MK II 10 24, "The upper old man and lower old man" (Kami no jiji to shimo no jiji).

Miyagi, Kami-gun: Jinruigaku XII (No. 128) 58. In "Rikuzen-no-kuni Kami-gun" by Arima Shinji.

Fukushima, Iwaki-gun: Iwaki 172, "Dig here, bow-wow" (Koko hore wan-wan).

Niigata, Sado: MK II 4 32, "The old man who made flowers bloom" (Hana saka jiji).

Nakakanbara-gun: MK I 9 40, "The old man who showered blossoms" (Hana furi jiji).

Minamikanbara-gun: Minamikanbara 34, "The old man who scattered ashes" (Hai maki jiji); Kamuhara 60, "The old man who scattered flowers" (Hana maki jiji).

Fukui, Sakai-gun: MK I 8 34, "The old man who made flowers bloom" (Hana saka jiji).

Gifu, Ōno-gun, Niukawa: Utsushibana 47, "The man and the fox" (Otoko to kitsune no hanashi).

Okayama, Mitsu-gun: MK I 9 30, "The dog's kindness" (Inu no hōji). No part about scattering ashes.

Ehime, Kitauwa-gun: MK II 3 36, "The old man who made flowers bloom" (Hana saka jiji).

Saga, Ogi-gun: MK II 7 32, "The turtle that talked" (Mono iu gūzū). Often it is a turtle rather than a treasure dog.

Nagasaki, Kitatakaku-gun: MK II 9 27, "The upper old man and the lower old man" (Kamin jii to shimon jii); Hōgen shi 22 12, "The upper old man and the lower old man" (Kamin jii to shimon jii).

Kagoshima: Koshiki 167, "The upper old man and the lower old man" (Kami no jiji to shimo no jiji).

Okierabu: Okinoerabu 48, "The child who scattered ashes" (Hai maki dōji).

137. The Old Bamboo Cutter

Once upon a time a feudal lord heard the sound of someone cutting bamboo as he passed a thicket. He demanded, "Who is that fellow cutting my bamboo?" The man who was cutting it answered, "The greatest in all Japan at breaking wind." And he let go with a "chinpui, chinpui, goyo no sakazuki ochichin pu." The feudal lord admired him and gave him a big reward. A bad old man in his neighborhood heard about that and went to cut bamboo in the feudal lord's thicket to imitate him. He failed and was arrested.

Shiga, Takashima-gun

Aomori, Hachinohe: Dai-ichi 63, "The man who broke wind" (Hehiri jiji); MK II 9 42, "The old man who broke wind" (Hehiri jiji). The sound, "hiza agare kata agare" (Climb to my knees, climb to my shoulders) has been changed. It does not belong to the story "The old man who swallowed a bird."
Yamagata, Kitamurayama-gun: MK II 6 40, "The chōja who broke wind" (Heppiri chōja).
Akita, Hiraga-gun: MK II 12 31, "The old man who broke wind" (Heppiri jiji).
Niigata, Minamikanbara-gun: MK I 2 25, "The old man who broke wind" (He hanari jiji). Two stories about eating a bird.
Nagano, Kitaazumi-gun: Otari 147. No title. The principal character is in "The satori and the hoop."
Aichi, Kitashidara-gun: Dai-ichi 56, "The old man who broke wind" (Hehiri jiji). There are 17 other examples.
Shiga, Takashima-gun: Dai-ichi 62, "The old bamboo cutter" (Takekiri jiji). Example.
Hiroshima: Geibi 71, "The old bamboo cutter" (Takekiri jiji).
Shimane, Ōchi-gun: MK II 12 35, "The old man who broke wind" (Hehiri jiji).
Tokushima: Awa Iyayama 91, "The old woman who broke wind" (Hehiri baba).
Kagawa, Mitoyo-gun, Shishijima: Sanuki 8.*

Further reference:
Mukashibanashi kenkyū I 8 16. The relation of this story to *Fukutomi sōshi* is discussed.

138. The Old Man Who Swallowed a Bird

An old man swallowed a bird by mistake. Funny sounds came from his seat, and that brought him a fortune. The latter half is like "The old bamboo cutter." Refer to it.

Fukushima, Iwaki-gun: Iwaki 47, 136, "The old man who swallowed a bird" (Tori nomi jii san).
Niigata, Minamikanbara-gun: MK II 5 34, "The old man who sang" (Utautai jiji).
Ishikawa: Kaga 73, 77, 79, "The old man who broke wind" (Heppiri jiji). The three stories have the same title.

Fukui, Sakai-gun: MK I 1 30, "The old man who swallowed a bird" (Tori nomi jiji).
Gifu, Hida (Ōno-gun), Niukawa: Utsushibana 50, "The old man who sounded like a bird" (Torinaki jiji).
Kagoshima: Koshiki 170, "The old man who swallowed a bird" (Tori nomi jii).

139. Monkey Jizō

Once upon a time there was a good old man in a certain place. One day when he went to the mountains to cut wood, he saw monkeys had gathered at the sandbar in the river beyond. They were carrying a stone image of Jizō across to the opposite bank. That amused the old man. He went to the sandbar, rubbed rice flour all over himself, and turned a mortar over for a stand. He climbed onto it and posed as Jizō. The monkeys noticed him and thought he was another Jizō. They put him onto a hand cart and carried him over to the other side. They sang a jolly song as they went. Once across, they set him up and worshipped him. The old man disguised his voice and ordered them to get stone pillows and a mallet ready. The monkeys did as he said and all of them went to sleep. When they were sound asleep, the old man took the hammer and smashed their heads. He took them home and his wife made monkey soup to enjoy.

Akita, Kazuno-gun

Aomori, Hachinohe: MK II 9 42, "Monkey Jizō" (Saru Jizō). There are four stories. In all four the old man went to his garden patch to work. He whitened his face with flour. In the first three, the old neighbor failed to imitate because he laughed. There is no neighbor in the last.
Iwate, Isawa-gun: Kogane 28, "The old man worshipped as Jizō" (Jii ga Jizō son to ogamerareta hanashi); Isawa.*
    Esashi-gun: Esashi 28, "The monkeys and the two old men" (Saru dono to futari no jiji no hanashi).
    Shiwa-gun: Shiwa 94, "The old man and the monkeys" (Jiji to saru).
Yamagata, Kitamurayama-gun: MK II 5 22, "Watering the rice paddy" (Mizuhiki no hanashi).
Akita, Kazuno-gun: Dai-ni 67, "The old man and the monkeys" (Jii sama to saru). Example.
    Senhoku-gun: Kikimimi 241, "The monkeys and the old man Jizō" (Saru to jiji Jizō).
Fukushima, Iwaki-gun: Iwaki 49, 139, "Mistaken for Jizō by monkeys" (Saru ni Jizō sama to machigaerareta hanashi).
Nagano: Chiisagata 253, "Jizō's balls" (Jizō honguri).
Wakayama, Nishimuro-gun, Tanabe: Kyōdo ken II 4 50. No title.
Shimane, Ōchi-gun: Dai-ichi 73, "The wine from Buigadani" (Buigadani no sake).

Hiroshima: Geibi 179, "Monkey Jizō." There are three stories and in each, the one who laughed failed. In one story they were demons and not monkeys.
    Yamagata-gun, Shinshō-mura: Aki 80, "Monkey Jizō" (Saru Jizō).
Ōita, Hayami-gun: MK I 12 41, "Monkey Jizō" (Saru Jizō).
Nagasaki, Tsushima-gun, Saru-machi: TD XII 8 22, "Monkey Jizō" (Saru Jizō). An old man went to dig mountain yams. Instead of monkeys, there were badgers.

140. The Old Man Who Got a Tumor

Once there was an honest old man and a bad one, and each had a tumor on his cheek. The honest old man went to the mountains to cut wood one day, but when it was time to go home, it began to rain. He crawled into the hollow of a tree and fell asleep. When he awoke and looked around it was the middle of the night. All kinds of ghosts had gathered in front of the hollow tree and were having a drinking bout. Some were drunk and started to dance. Carried away by the fun of the dance, the old man came out without thinking and joined it. The ghosts were all surprised, but they accepted him into their company until dawn. Then as they left boisterously, they declared, "Because you are a jolly old man, we'll make sure you will come again by taking a pledge." With that, they took the tumor from his face. The old man went home and told his wife, and they rejoiced together. The bad old man wanted his tumor taken off, too. He went to the hollow tree and waited. The ghosts gathered again in the middle of the night. The old man trembled from fright. The ghosts looked for the old man of the night before and found the old man in the hollow tree. They pulled him out, but he wouldn't dance even a little. The ghosts were angry and put the tumor they got the night before on the other cheek of the old man. He went home with a tumor on each cheek.

Yamagata, Mogami-gun

Iwate: Esashi 25, "The old man who got a tumor" (Kobu tori jiji).
    Waga-gun: Kikimimi 210, "The old man who got a tumor" No. 1 (Kobu tori jiji).
    Nishiiwai-gun: Kikimimi 214, "The old man who got a tumor" No. 2 (Kobu tori jiji).
    Kamihei-gun: Rōō 319, "The old man who got a tumor" (Kobu tori jiji).
Yamagata, Mogami-gun: MK II 2 42, "Getting a tumor" (Kobu tori). Example.
Fukushima, Iwaki-gun: Iwaki 50, 139, "The old man who got a tumor" (Kobu tori jii san).
Niigata, Minamikanbara-gun: Kamuhara 14. Note No. 3.
Shizuoka, Hamana-gun: Shizuoka 462, "Getting a tumor" (Kobu tori no hanashi).

Wakayama, Ito-gun: Kōshō 9 16, "The old man who got a tumor" (Kobu tori jii san). There is nothing about the old man's good dancing. It can only be seen that the tale exists. The telling is ruined.

Hiroshima, Kamo-gun: Aki 84, "The old man who got a tumor" No. 1 (Kobu tori jiji).
Yamagata-gun: Aki 85, "The old man who got a tumor" No. 2 (Kobu tori jiji). It is close to a story of finding happiness, close to the old form of ghost stories.

Ōita, Kitaamabe-gun: MK I 3 39, "The old man who got a tumor" (Kobu tori jiji). It starts with an episode about a riceball in the garden. Tengu were in the hole.
Naori-gun: Naori 41, "Getting a tumor" (Kobu tori).

Saga, Saga City: MK II 7 34, "The rice ball that rolled away" (Korōda nigirimeshi). It is only about seeing demons dance and has nothing about tumors. If it is compared to "Dango Jōdo," we find no dango and no rice ball. By this we can see the two stories belong to the same group.

Further reference:
Nihon mukashibanashi shū, ge 88. A Korean example.
Seisuishō.
Mukashibanashi kenkyū I 9 20.

9. The Power of Words

141. A Dialogue with a Ghost

A doctor came to a certain village in the mountains and decided to stay, but there was no house for him. It was decided that he would stay in a vacant temple a little way off in the mountains. In the night something came to the outside doors by the porch and climbed up. In a voice that sounded like a broken bell, it shouted, "Suteten-koten on the doctor's head! Suteten-koten on the doctor's head." It pounded on the doors until they nearly broke. The frightened doctor crawled deep into his quilts. In the morning he found footprints of a big animal all over the porch. When he told the villagers, they said it was probably a prank of a bad old badger. That night a number of young men from the village decided to stay at the temple. They secured the doors with poles and sat around the hearth to wait. Something came again in the middle of the night and pounded on the doors. It shouted, "Suteten-koten on the doctor's head!" They matched it from the inside with, "Suteten-koten on the head of what says that!" The badger and the young men exchanged shouts and made a great uproar. After that continued for some time, the badger seemed to give up and remained silent. The next morning they found the old badger. He had been so humiliated at being outshouted that he had torn his belly open with his teeth and died. Then they all made badger soup and ate him.

Yamanashi, Nishiyatsushiro-gun

Iwate, Kamihei-gun: Rōō 80, "The three-eyed one-legged ghost" (Mitsume ipponashi no bakemono).

Yamanashi, Nishiyatsushiro-gun: Kai 40, "The doctor's head" (Isha don no atama). Example.

Gifu, Yoshiki-gun: Hidabito IV 6 35, "The zatō and the badger" (Zatō to tanuki). When the badger shouted, "Sutten-ten on your head," the zatō gave him in return, "Suppera-ponja on your head," adding notes from his shamisen to his shout.

Aichi, Kitashidara-gun, Furigusa-mura: Aichi 258, "The badger" (Tanuki).

Minamishidara-gun: Inoshishi 158, "The badger who called" (Yobaru tanuki).

Tōtōmi (Shizuoka): Nihon zenkoku 52, "The mountain yam" (Yama no imo). After the big ghost of mountain yams ate a priest and his novice, a zatō destroyed it with words as he accompanied himself on the biwa.

Fukuoka, Kurate-gun: Fukuoka 98, "The fox, the old woman, and Uso" (Kitsune baba to Uso). An old woman, her daughter, and Uso lived together. While Uso was away, a fox came and shouted, "Uso hit Granny, ten-ton-ton." When Uso heard about it, he said to answer, "Ten-ton-ton on whatever is saying that." In the morning they got up to look. They found a dead fox with its tongue chewed off. The question is whether Uso can be considered the same sort of person as Kichigo. There is a latter part to this story, but it is not altogether clear. However, the original form can be made out. Or it may just be as a zatō recited it.

Further reference:
At Kenkōin in Hirai, Munakata-gun, Chikuzen one priest after another lost out and died in contests with words with a voice in the ceiling. An itinerant priest came along and outdid it with, "Kenkōin is bokkurisho, a thousand, ten thousand bokkurisho." A badger as big as a colt was defeated.

142. A Dialogue with a Crab

A famous itinerant priest was overtaken by night in the mountains. He found a wretched looking woodcutter's hut where he asked to spend the night. He was refused. He was told to go farther to an old temple where ghosts appeared, so he went there to stay. In the middle of the night an ōnyūdō came out from somewhere with a clatter and declared that if the priest did not solve a riddle which he would propose, he would eat him. It shouted, "Little legs, eight legs, big legs, two legs, red in color, eyes facing the sky like the sun and moon." The priest replied that it was a crab and gave the ōnyūdō a whack, *pishari*, on its head with his staff. It went off with a clatter. Nothing more came out before morning. At dawn the priest went to look in the direction the ōnyūdō had gone. He found a huge dead crab under the porch. No more ghosts came out at that temple after that.

Saitama, Kawagoe

Ishikawa, Suzu-gun: Noto 53. No title. Getsuan at Kanidera (Echizen) in Iida knew that "Four legs, eight legs, both legs, eight legs, goes right, goes left, eyes above" meant a crab.

Yamanashi, Nishiyatsushiro-gun: Kai 290, "The crab priest" (Gani bōzu); Zoku kai 319, "The crab priest" (Gani bōzu). A story of Chōgenji, Kanioizaka, Manriki-mura, Higashiyamanashi-gun.

Saitama, Kawagoe City: Kawagoe 100, "A dialogue with a ghost" (Bakemono mondō). Example.

Kumamoto, Amakusa-gun: Kyōdo ken V 3 26, "The crab shell" (Kani no kō). A hermit priest encountered a strange light on the road at night. A voice demanded, "Four legs, eight legs . . ." to which he replied, "You are a crab." He whacked it with his bamboo flute. The crab has had cracks on its shell since that time. "Crab yamabushi" (Kani yamabushi) is also a kyōgen, so it is probably an old story.

143. The Poem about Ashes

"Raked ashes are the color of the seashore" was the first line of a poem. The ghost of a priest suffered and could not attain Buddhahood because he could not match it with a second line. His novice laid the ghost by the line "At the hearth I watch the open sea [live coals]."

Ōita, Naori-gun

Akita, Senhoku-gun: MK I 11 26, "Raked ashes are . . ." (Hai narashi hai wa).

Hiraga-gun: TD XIII 3 39, "The poem and the priest" (Haiku oshō). There is a story about a poem by a priest about ashes in *Ugo Asamai-machi kinbo kikigaki*.

Niigata: Sadogashima 160, "The closing line" (Shimo no ku). This is not about a priest. He is the host at an inn. A guest furnished the closing line of the poem.

Ōita: Naori 74, "The poem and the ghost" (Uta to yūrei). Example.

144. The Carpenter and Oniroku

At a certain place the current in the stream was so strong that no matter how many bridges were built across it, they were all washed away. It was decided to hire a most famous carpenter who lived in a neighboring district. While the carpenter was frantic with worry after he accepted the order, he stood on the bank of the river and stared at its current. A demon appeared in the foam that floated on its surface. He asked the carpenter what he was thinking about, and he laughed when he heard the reason. He said, "No matter how skillful you are, you are not likely to succeed in building a bridge here. If you are willing to give me your eyeballs, I will build it for you." The carpenter went home intending to hand over his eyeballs. The next day the bridge was half built and on the next it was finished. As the man stood there surprised, the demon demanded his eyes. The carpenter begged him to wait and he fled to the mountains. While he was wandering around he heard children singing. They sang, "If only Oniroku would hurry with the eyeballs, wouldn't that be fine!" The carpenter went home when he heard that. The next day he went to the river. The demon came out and demanded his eyes. If he did not want to give them, he should try to guess his name. The man declared it was Oniroku. The demon vanished instantly and never returned.

Iwate, Isawa-gun

Iwate, Isawa-gun: Kikimimi 106, "The carpenter and Oniroku" (Daiku to Oniroku). Example. This story and those like it are probably the old form with knowing the name Oniroku by hearing it in the children's song. The same story is recorded in *Mukashibanashi saishū techō* 70. It is from *Iwate nippō* material.

Iwami (Shimane): TD IV 7 50, "Teitei Kobushi." Carp from the south pond came and asked, "Is Teitei Kobushi stopping here?" Teitei Kobushi was the name of a camellia tree. What at present has become only "The one-eyed rooster at Shichikurin" and the like was made up after the introduction of Chinese characters with commentaries. Formerly they were just known as ghosts.

145. The Warning in the Lullaby

Someone can escape through learning of danger from words in a nursery song.

Fukuoka, Chikujō-gun: Fukuoka 232, "Helped by knowing writing" (Gakumon no okage). The tale is said to be from Gōshū. A man stopped at a teahouse in the mountains. A woman tending a child sang repeatedly, "If you try writing it in word." Perhaps this was a way to teach one kind of word. However, learning through a nursery song can be traced to plots in "The carpenter and Oniroku," "Hirabayashi," and other such tales. They are like the "Tom Tit Tom" group.

Nagasaki, Minamitakaku-gun: Shimabara 244, "The nursery song in the mountains" (Yama no naka no komori uta). The song is a poor attempt by somebody, but the tale can be considered old. There is a song about the stone pillow in the story of the lonely house in Owari. The central interest in the song from Asakusa, also, may be the song. Information is learned from a nursery song in the story about a bargain with a demon and the tale of the wife from the Sky World.

146. Zuitonbō

This is a story about a badger calling somebody by name.

Nagano: Chiisagata 269, "Zuitonbō" When the man looked through a knothole, he saw a badger hit the door with its tail. He pulled the tail till it broke off. He followed the badger far back into the mountain and caught it.

Shimoina-gun: Mukashibanashi 30, "The priest named Zuitonbō at the mountain temple" (Yamadera no bōsama Zuiton no hanashi). This is how the badger was outtalked and died. It does not say how it said the words, but the rhythm of the words lends flavor to the melody. It is a composition of a bosama.

10. Cleverness at Work

147. Destroying the Fox

This is in the same group as "The fox in the straw bag." It is about fooling a fox and destroying it.

Aomori, Hachinohe: MK II 9 47, "Destroying the fox" (Kitsune taiji). Two versions. It is also found in Rikuchū.

In the first story an old man and woman hide a dog for protection and dance. In the second, foxes who came to call were fooled and put into a sack and beaten to death. Each story contains an episode in which one fox escaped and went home. People overhear foxes planning revenge and so protect themselves. Both versions may be the work of a zatō.

Iwate: Shiwa 31, "The fox and the novice" (Kitsune to kozō). A fox disguised as a priest was destroyed.

Yamanashi: TD III 5 77, "Fooling a fox" (Kitsune o damashita hanashi).

Senshū (Osaka), Izunami-gun, Sugahara: Kōshō 10 25. A note.

Nagasaki, Minamitakaku-gun: Shimabara 45, 48, "Fooling a fox" Nos. 1 and 3 (Kitsune o azamuku hanashi). Both stories have the same title. There is nothing in the first about the wrong eye. In the second story it is a badger which was tied to a horse. The ending is embellished.

148. The Fox in the Straw Bag

This is a story about fooling a fox, putting it into a straw bag and then destroying it.

In rural areas the fox is tied to a horse instead of being put in the bag. See "The fake image of Buddha."

Aomori, Hachinohe: MK II 10 14, "The fox in the straw bag" (Kamasu gitsune). Four stories.

The first is "Fooling a fox" (Damasare gitsune). The story follows the plot of the story about the one-eyed old man through the point where the fox is put into a straw bag and beaten.

The second is "Fooling a fox" (Kitsune o damashita hanashi). The sons defeat the fox, and there is nothing about the one-eye.

Third is "Fooling a fox" (Damasare gitsune). When the old woman went out, the fox disguised itself as her grandchild.

Fourth is "The salty old man from Niida" (Niida no shoppa jiji). There is a straw bag, but the fox eats the salt in it. This is a story of admitting defeat.

Iwate, Kunohe-gun: Kunohe 477, "The fox who turned into a handsome man" (Bidan to natta kitsune). The fox disguised himself and arrived as the son-in-law. His disguise was discovered and he was put into a straw bag. The fact that they shouted "Look inside, look inside" as they beat it shows that the story is the work of a bosama accompanying himself on a shamisen as he recited it.

Kamihei-gun: Kaminei 103, "The bosama and the fox" (Bosama to kitsune). A blind minstrel came along where a fox hunt was going on. He got the fox into a straw bag through his cleverness and killed it.

Yamagata, Mogami-gun, Toyosato-mura: Toyosato 251, "Cooking the fox whole" (Kitsune no maruni). There are two images of Buddha as in the Zuiten story.

Nagano, Kitaazumi-gun: Kitaazumi I 85. No title. The story of how a young zatō killed a fox.

Yamanashi, Nishiyatsushiro-gun: Chihō.* It is the old badger at Konbukuro Pond.

149. The Wrong One-Eye

There once was an old man and an old woman. The old man was blind in his right eye. He met an old badger when he was making his rounds to give New Year greetings. The badger imitated him, but with his left eye blind, and went to the old man's home. The old woman realized the old man was fake. She heated the bath and put him into it. Then she put the lid down and set a heavy stone on it. The badger inside the tub said he was not the real old man, but she would not let him out. After the real old man came home, they took the badger out, but it was dead by then.

Kamihei-gun, Iwate

Iwate, Kamihei-gun: Rōō 188, "The left-eyed old man" (Hidari katame no jiji). The conversation with the fox progresses amusingly, and children enjoy the mistake about the eye.
Hienuki-gun: Kōshō 9 2, "Fooled by a fox" (Kitsune ni damasareta hanashi). The old man who was imitated by the fox was right-eyed. The old woman tested him by trying to get him to wash his feet in hot water. At the end, he is put into a straw bag.
Isawa-gun: Kogane 104, "The real Heiroku" (Moto no Heiroku no hanashi). This may be a fragment.
Nagano, Shimoina-gun: Mukashibanashi 63, "The disguised badger" (Baketa mujina). The tumor that should have been on the right was on the left. The dialogue is missing.
Nagasaki, Kitatakaku-gun, Isahaya: Kōshō 9 9, "The burning rope" (Hinawa no hanashi). The badger was destroyed by a burning rope.

150. The Fake Image of Buddha

One winter young people gathered to work together and talked about catching a fox. It was decided finally that one of them should set out alone to get it. The fellow took the horse from its shed, fastened the load rack onto it, and made his preparations. He went to a place often visited by foxes and pretended to be waiting for somebody. He said aloud to himself, "Well, Granny should be coming along about now." An old woman suddenly appeared. The young man seemed delighted and told her to get onto the horse. He tied the rope around her many times because he said the horse was wild and he wanted to make things safe. When he got home, he had the other young men gather around the horse while he unfastened the ropes. The old woman changed into her real form and ran as a fox into the house. They searched the house from corner to corner, but could not see the fox. The young man who had caught it sat calmly by the hearth smoking. He said to nobody in particular that there were two images of Buddha at his house and that they waved their hands at each other. Another image promptly appeared by the real one and waved its hand. That was what he wanted. He dragged the image that had waved its paw down from the altar and kicked it onto its side. It really was the fox. They made soup of it to eat together. The young man who had caught it said he would taste it first to see if it was poisoned. He ate just a little, but he was seized by a terrible pain. His friends tried to help, but nothing they did was of any use. The frightened young men went in ones and twos. After they were gone the young man, who had been faking illness, ate as much fox soup as he wanted.

Iwate, Isawa-gun

Iwate, Kamihei-gun: Rōō 186, "The fox and the novice" (Kitsune to kozō).
    Shiwa-gun: Shiwa 31, "The fox and the novice" (Kitsune to kozō). See the second example of "Destroying the fox."
    Isawa-gun: Kogane 45, "How a young man fooled a fox" (Wakamono ga kitsune o damashita hanashi). Example. There is more to the story. He found out when the image of Buddha waved its hand.
    Nishiiwai-gun, Hiraizumi: Oshō 97, "Catching a fox with a straw bag" (Tawara de kitsune o totta hanashi).
Fukushima, Iwaki-gun: Iwaki 67, 158, "The novice and the fox" (Kozō to kitsune).
Nagano: Kitaazumi II 83. No title. About Zuitonbō.
Yamanashi, Nishiyatsushiro-gun: Zoku Kai 32, "The fox and smallpox" (Kitsune to hōsō). In Kai they say the story came from Shimabara.
Shimane: Okinoshima 17, "Yamauba" No. 2.
Tokushima: Awa Iyayama 29, "Jizō laughed" (Jizō ga warau).
Fukuoka, Itojima-gun: Fukuoka 114, "Matabei of Fukuma" (Fukuma no Matabei). The fox was destroyed by making it change itself into an old woman. The three images of Jizō turned into four.
Nagasaki, Minamitakaku-gun: TD II 6 15, "The fox that stood his tail up" (Otate no kitsune); Shimabara 60, "Boiling a fox to death" (Kitsune ga nikorosareta hanashi).

151. Admitting Defeat

Once upon a time there was a teahouse on a certain mountain pass in Mimasaka. A man called Kihei and his wife lived there. Late one night a splendidly dressed itinerant samurai stopped there to rest. When they looked at him closely, they could see that he was a disguised fox. The pleated skirt, clothes, the two swords—a big and a little one—all looked real, but he seemed inexperienced. Some hair was still on his face, which came to a point, and his three cornered ears stood up. Kihei was so amused that he could hardly contain himself, but he held back a laugh as he set out a metal basin full of water in front of the samurai and invited him to use it. Presently the fox started to wash. He saw his reflection and realized that his disguise was not complete. With a shout of astonishment, he jumped up and rushed out of the teahouse.

Kihei was on his way home from cutting wood in the hills the next day when he suddenly heard somebody call him. He could not see anyone, but he replied. The voice said, "Wasn't it funny last night, Kihei!" It was the fox that had failed to disguise himself.

Mimasaka (Okayama)

Is this a more pleasant rendition of a story about destroying things?

There is a play on words to the effect that a man should be on his guard, for it may prove to be horse dung.

Iwate: Kunohe 455, "The fox at Bakkurizawa" (Bakkurizawa no kitsune no hanashi). This is told as a true story of the fox at Bakkurizawa in Kokarumai.

A Buddhist priest from Ibonai Terazawa tied a fox onto his horse and brought it back. He intended to roast it. It escaped and called, "The priest from Terazawa is a fool priest, expert at dragging things along and roasting them, *gukwan, gukwan.*"

Kamihei-gun: Tōno 284. No. 193. No title. When a man who forced a fox to eat salt passed the place the next day, a fox called from the mountain, "Salt heshiri, salt heshiri!"

Yamanashi, Nishiyatsushiro-gun: Zoku Kai 45, "Chōemon and the badger" (Chōemon to mujina).

Okayama: Nihon shū, jō 88, "Foxes laugh" (Kitsune ga warau). Example.

152. Kōkōzaka

This is about putting on a mask to fool an enemy, escaping danger and gaining fortune.

It could be called a variant of "The mirror from Matsuyama."

Iwate, Kamihei-gun: Rōō 230, "The girl who put on a demon mask" (Oni no kamen o kabutta musume).

Nagano: Chiisagata 173, "The snake's attack with gold" (Hebi no kane-zeme). A dutiful son went to buy both medicine for his sick father and also a badger mask. He met a snake on his way home. When the snake was about to swallow him, he put on the mask and frightened it. In a dialogue with it about what they feared the most, he said he feared gold, and later got some.

This has some connection with the story about the badger and the actor.

Tokushima: Awa Iyayama 58, "The mask of the tengu's nose" (Tengu-bana no men).

Fukuoka, Ukiwa-gun: Fukuoka 150, "The dutiful maid" (Kōkō naru kahi no hanashi). A maid worshipped a mask that looked like her father's face. Someone exchanged it for a demon mask. This frightened her, and she went home. On the way she put on the mask to warm herself at a fire built by bandits. They were frightened and ran off, leaving their money.

This was probably spread by a writer.

There is a story like this about a stupid person in *Tsugaru mugashiko shū*. It is about the success of a stupid person. There are a number of tales about the success of stupid people in Japan.

Kagoshima: Koshiki 174, "Surprised gamblers" (Bakuchi odorokashi).

Further reference:

Nihon dōwa shū 303, "Noodles and the demon mask" (Sōmen to oni men). It is not clear where the story is from.

153. Comparing Disguises

Once there was a bad fox named Osan at Enami and a badger every bit as bad in Sanuki on Shikoku. The two met one time and decided to have a contest to see which was the more clever at disguises. To begin with, the badger put grass onto his head and changed into a lovely bride and then into a footman. Osan said, "My turn now. A feudal procession will pass along the highway through Masubara day after tomorrow. Just have a look." The badger agreed and they parted. The badger went on that day to the highway to see, and he was filled with admiration. He went up to the feudal lord's sedan chair and said, "Well done, well done!" The accompanying samurai cut him down. The procession was real and Osan had known three days before that it would pass there. The badger was fooled.

Hiroshima

Fukushima, Iwaki-gun: Iwaki 62, 155, "Comparing disguises" (Bake kurabe).

Niigata, Minamikanbara-gun: (no source). A fox looked at a real feudal procession and exclaimed, "You're clever, little badger!" It was killed.

A story of the badger's revenge. Another tale is that Dankurō Fox of Sekiyahama fooled Sankichi Fox of Sado.

Yamanashi, Nishiyatsushiro-gun: Kai 27, "Kozaemon and the fox" (Kozaemon to kitsune). It is about seven and eight disguises, the same as one about Shibaemon Badger of Awaji. Zoku Kai 42, "The fox and the badger" (Kitsune to mujina). They disguised themselves as dead for each other. One disguised himself as a hunter and then as a charcoal-maker and went to town to sell things. The badger was really killed.

Osaka, Sennan-gun: Kōshō 10 31, "Biyakake Badger and Kojirō Fox" (Biyakake no tanuki to Kojirō Gitsune).

Hiroshima: Aki 158, "Osan Fox of Enami" (Enami no Osan Gitsune). Example.

Shimane: TD III 11 44, "The rain of gold coins" (Ōban koban no ame). The fox leader was called Yazaemon in the story about Niemon of Izumo. When the feudal procession passed, he called, "You're clever, Niemon!" It is like the story of Shibaemon of Awaji.

Ehime, Matsuyama: Chihō.* Kompei Fox of Ebara, Katsumata Badger under the tree with eight trunks.

Kumamoto, Yatsushiro-gun: Jinbun I 1 138, "Fooling a fox" (Kitsune o taburakasu hanashi). Hikoshichi fooled a fox. It said, "You did fine, Hikoshichi," when it saw a feudal procession. It ends with the saying, "Don't be fooled by Hikoshichi's manjū."

Tamana-gun: MK I 2 36, "The shrike and the fox" (Mozu to kitsune). The story is close to one about tail-fishing, but new in the way it is told. It is close to "Sky watcher and earth watcher."

Kuma-gun: MK I 5 37, "Comparing disguises" (Bake kurabe). Hikoshichi of Yatsushiro became friendly with a fox. They compared disguises. He showed the fox a feudal procession and it was seized. In the first part there is talk about stone fertilizer lasting three years.

Nagasaki, Ikinoshima: Dai-ichi 79, "The badger and the monkey" (Tanuki to saru). The monkey discovered the badger's tail. The badger pretended to be so humiliated that it died, then it stole the monkey's fish on its way back from work. Then there is a tail-fishing episode.

Two stories have obviously been joined.

This story is also told about Genpanojō of Kikyōgahara, Otama of Yokotegasaki, and Ochio Fox of Akagiyama.

It must be in rather recent years that this kind of tale became a fox and badger story.

Further reference:
Nihon mukashibanashi shū, jō 82, "The story of Shibaemon Badger of Awaji."

154. The Magic Hood with Eight Disguises

Long ago there was a fox called Osumi Fox at an Inari Shrine at the edge of a certain pond who was very clever at disguises. Her skin she used for disguising herself was stolen by a human, however, and after that she was more often than not fooled by humans.

Once a yamabushi showed up and claimed to be Inari Daimyōjin of Kyoto. He fooled the fox by saying that he could restore the magic power of a skin for disguises that had been defiled by a human. She was delighted and brought out her skin. He took it and ran off.

The yamabushi was a good friend of the village head, so one day Osumi Fox borrowed the magic skin of a badger and went to call upon the yamabushi disguised as the village head. She asked him to show her the thing called a fox's disguise skin. He could not refuse the village head and brought it out. The village head fox said she would try it on, and put it across her shoulders. Then she said thanks and took it home. The humiliated yamabushi could do nothing about it.

But he went to the fox again and said he was the real Inari Daimyōjin and offered to pray with his golden staff over magic skins that had been defiled by human hands. He fooled her for a second time and went off with the disguise skin. After that Osumi Fox could only go around like a dog, stealing things to eat.

Nagasaki, Ikinoshima

Noto (Ishikawa): Ishikawa 984. No title.

Nagano, Shimoina-gun: Fukihara No. 3 39, "Hachiroten." A story about fooling a wild fox. The principal character is a sieve maker. The fox's treasure was called Shichiroten [shichi = seven], one less than the hachiroten [hachi = eight] used by the sieve-maker, and the sieve-maker was thus able to trick the fox into trading.

Tottori: Inpaku dōwa 11, "The seven disguises" (Nanabake). A yamabushi named Ryōsokuin rolled up a treasure of seven disguises belonging to a fox and took it away. He bought a hood of eight disguises at Yonego.

Hiroshima, Hiroshima City: Aki 158, "Osan Fox of Enami" Nos. 2 and 3 (Enami no Osan Gitsune). Both stories contain an episode about Osan Fox of Enami and how she received a mask from a Noh actor.

Nagasaki: Shimabara 49, 55, "The fox at Himi Pass" (Himi tōge no kitsune). A seven disguise roll and an eight disguise roll are traded. It follows the plot of the Watanabe Tsuna story, in which a fox disguised as a wet nurse is changed back to its own form. Is this an addition?

"Jirōbei Fox of Nagasaki" (Nagasaki no Jirōbei Gitsune).

Ikinoshima: (Old) Iki 75, 204, 167, "Karatsu Kanne," "Osami Fox" (Osami Gitsune). Example. "The invisible cloak" (Takara mino). Could this be a variation? See also entry for "The invisible cloak and hat."

155. Exchanging Treasures

Long ago a child put a lunch into a wooden box and took it with him to the mountains. A tengu was there, so the child decided to try fooling it. After the child had finished eating, he put his lunch box to his eye. He jumped around and said, "I can see Kyoto! Oh, I can see the pagoda!" The tengu was envious and wanted that box. That seemed to make the boy enjoy it even more, and he would not lend it to the tengu. Finally, the tengu said, "I'll lend you my cloak and hat if you will please let me see it." That was what the boy wanted. He pretended to feel reluctant as he handed the box to the tengu. It looked as hard as it could, but it could not see a thing. When the tengu looked around for the boy, he had already put on the cloak and hat and was invisible. He could not tell where he had gone. The boy went home, and since his mother could not see him, he went confidently to the cake store. He stole cakes to eat. His mischief got worse and worse to the consternation of the villagers.

He put his cloak and hat into a drawer of his mother's chest, but she thought they were filthy old things and burned them up. When the boy found out, he went to the river naked, got himself wet all over and then rolled in the ashes until his body was covered with them. His mother could no longer see him. He ran out to the wine shop and drank as much as he wanted, but the ashes came off around his mouth. Everybody said there was a ghost mouth drinking the wine and started to chase him. Along the way, he had to urinate, and then that place became visible. There was excitement everywhere and everyone chased him. A samurai came along swinging his sword this way and that. The boy was forced to jump off the bridge into the river. Then the ashes all came off and the boy became visible.

Nagano, Kamiina-gun

Iwate, Kamihei-gun: Rōō 81, 210, "The tengu's little fan" (Tengu no ko ōgi). The principal character is a gambler who traded the fan for his dice. The latter part is an amusing tale of making a nose grow high and shrink. It ends with his success in the world.

"The priest and the fox" (Oshō to kitsune). The priest traded his old hood for the fox's magic towel. He put it on his head and teased the young men in the village.

Yamagata, Higshitagawa-gun: MK I 11 33, "The Life Needle and the Death Needle" (Ikibari shinibari). The principal character is a lazy man who got a Life Needle and a Death Needle from a kappa. He tried the Death Needle on the Kappa and ran away. It ends with the clause, "...and that was last night's dream."

Tales about danger are often turned into humorous ones.

Fukushima, Iwaki: Iwaki 60, 155, "The invisible straw cloak of the tengu" (Tengu no kakure mino).

Nishishirakawa-gun: Nihon zenkoku 128, "The treasure of the fox" (Kitsune no takaramono). Isokichi of Futagozuka-mura traded his three-colored hood for the fox pearls of Doemon Fox of Sekiwaku-mura.

Niigata, Minamikanbara-gun: Dai-ichi 49, "The invisible straw cloak and hat" (Kakure mino gasa). A drunkard traded a persimmon seed for an invisible straw cloak and hat of a tengu.

Nagano, Kamiina-gun: Dai-ichi 54, "The tengu's invisible straw cloak and hat" (Tengu no kakure mino gasa). Example. Substituting a cake store owner for the wine merchant and a mother for the wife are good examples of changes to make children's tales. And there is still a wine merchant at the end.

Shimoina-gun: Fukihara No. 3 39. Refer to "Hachiroten."

Saitama, Kumagaya: Chiho.* An old fox turned 999 men into priests. The 1000th was already a priest. He traded a seven-colored umbrella for sixteen hoods.

Hyōgo, Kanzaki-gun: Dai-ichi 67, "The gambler and the tengu" (Baku-chiuchi to tengu).

Shimane, Hinokawa-gun, Hirata: TD II 10 19, "Tarōbei Fox and Priest

Sōshin" (Tarōbei Gitsune to Sōshin Oshō). There is a story in *Nishiizumo zappitsu* about a priest called Kanshin at Yakushiji, who traded an old hood for a pearl with Tarōbei Fox of Iiyama.

Tottori, Seihaku-gun: Inpaku dōwa 11, "The seven disguises" (Nana-bake). Jūnai Fox of Tokamiyama near Yonago traded his seven-disguise treasure with the priest at Ryōsokuin for an old hood the priest claimed had eight disguises. The fox got his treasure back, but he did not know the priest had taken away its magic power. He tried to trick a horse-dealer but his true form was visible, and the horse dealer hit his rear end with a burning hoe and badly burned him. That is why the river at the foot of Tokamiyama is called Shiriyakigawa [burnt-rump river].

There must be some reason why so many folk tales of this sort have been half changed to legends.

Tokushima: Awa Iyayama 110, "The tengu's invisible straw hat and cloak" (Tengu no kakure gasa to kakure mino). It is a Hikoichi story.

Fukuoka, Chikujō-gun: Fukuoka 230, "The young man from the country" (Inaka no wakamono). A chap whose father had turned him out of home because he told lies got a load of sieves and went around selling them. He traded to get the tengu's fan that made noses high or low. (Nothing about an invisible cloak.) The story then goes into a dialogue about what people are the most frightened of, and someone said he was frightened of noses getting high or low. The young man made his own nose high, but it was run over by a cart and he died.

Kumamoto Kuma-gun: MK I 3 43, "The invisible cloak" (Kakure mino). Four Hikoichi stories. In the first there is a fragment of "Blundering Sōbee" in the usual form. In "The robe that hid one," there is a dialogue about what is the most scary, stone fertilizer good for three years and standing a corpse by a door. It also has a part where he traded his sieve for an invisible robe of a tenjin [deity]. The part about ashes and the wine merchant are in the usual form. In "The invisible cloak of the fox," the fox and Hikoichi tried on each other's cloaks. Hikoichi ran away with the fox's cloak and went to a wine shop. He was discovered because his feet stuck out from the cloak. It was burned. Where the fox runs home crying is amusing.

Nagasaki, Minamitakaku-gun: TD II 10 32, "Jūdendon of Jūdenkiba and the fox at Himi Pass" (Jūdenkiba no Jūdendon to Himi tōge no kitsune); Shimabara 49, "The seven mask roll" (Nana men kuri).

156. The Invisible Straw Cloak and Hat

This is in the group as stories about exchanging treasures. By various clever wiles an invisible cloak is seized from a tengu. He comes to get it back but is refused. Usually there is a passage where good

fortune is gained by asking what is the most scary. Many are changed
into humorous tales. Stories in this group are easily lengthened,
changed, or developed.

Aomori, Hachinobe: MK II 10 15, "The invisible cloak of the tengu"
(Tengu no kakure mino). A man put pepper into a gourd and traded
it to a tengu for an invisible cloak. He made a shambles of a cake
store and a wine shop. When he took a nap, his cloak caught on
fire. He complained of his burns and rubbed ashes all over his
body.
    The last part is not well done. It may be the invention of zatō.
Sannohe-gun: MK II 12 27, "The tengu and the gambler" (Tengu to
bakuchiuchi).
Iwate, Shiwa-gun: Shiwa-shū 138, "The invisible straw cloak and hat"
(Kakure mino to kakure gasa).
    Hienuki-gun: Kōshō 10 10, "The tengu and the gambler" No. 2
(Tengu to bakuchiuchi). There are three stories one with trading
dice for an invisible cloak and hat. A man put them on and carried
off the chōja's daughter and hid her. In another, the hero defeated
a tengu at gambling and made him turn into dice. When he used
the dice to gamble with someone he made a mistake and said, "Oni
ko derō" [demon, come out] instead of "Ni ko derō" [two come
out]. A demon came out and the man he was gambling with ran off
frightened leaving his money behind.
Akita, Hiraga-gun: MK II 8 29, "The invisible straw cloak and hat"
(Kakure mino gasa).
Niigata, Nakakanbara-gun: MK I 9 41, "The invisible straw hat and
cloak" (Kakure gasa to kakure mino).
    Minamikanbara-gun: Dai-ichi 49, "The invisible straw cloak and
hat" (Kakure mino gasa).
Ishikawa: Nomi 1107, "The tengu" (Tengu). About Korōyama at Tori-
goshi-mura. A fragment, nothing in detail.
Nagano, Kitaazumi-gun: Kitaazumi I 185, "Tales about fools" (Baka
banashi).
    Kamiina-gun: Dai-ichi 54, "The invisible straw cloak and hat"
(Kakure mino gasa).
Yamanashi, Nishiyatsushiro-gun: Zoku Kai 398, "The invisible cloak"
(Kakure mino). A tengu saw two fish peddlers gambling at Onna-
zaka, Kuishiki-mura. He joined them and wound up losing his invisible cloak. The rest is the usual form.
Gifu, Hida: Hidabito V 6 6, "The invisible cloak" (Kakure mino). The
cloak was obtained after talking things over with Jizō. The rest is
the usual form.
Osaka, Kitakawachi-gun, Hirakata: Nihon zenkoku 13, "The invisible
cloak and hat" (Kakure mino kakure gasa).
Hyōgo, Kanzaki-gun: Dai-ichi 67, "The gambler and the tengu" (Bakuchiuchi to tengu).
Yamaguchi: Suō Ōshima 86, "The invisible cloak" (Kakure mino). He
went to Momotarō's house and stole the invisible straw cloak. The

old woman burned it and he spread its ashes over his body and set
out as a robber.
     Nothing about trading with a tengu.
Ōita, Hayami-gun: MK II 1 46, "The invisible straw cloak and hat"
     (Kakure mino gasa).
     Nakatsu City: Jinbun I 1 133, "The invisible straw cloak and hat"
     (Kakure mino gasa no hanashi).   A Kichigo story.   He traded for
     something with which to tell fortunes.   He spread ashes over his
     body.   The mother comes into the story.   Bungo kijin 222, "Fooling a
     tengu" (Tengu damashi).
Kumamoto, Kuma-gun: MK I 3 43, "The invisible straw cloak" (Kakure
     mino).   Four tales.
Nagasaki: Shimabara 72, 259, "The tengu's dice" (Tengu no saiko) and
     "The invisible straw cloak and hat" (Kakure mino to kakure gasa).
     The second story contains the last part only, and nothing about
     trading with a tengu.   It is a humorous story. (New) Iki 84, "The
     invisible straw cloak" (Takara mino).
Kagoshima: Koshiki 180, "The invisible straw cloak and hat" (Kakure
     mino gasa).

157. The Bird Fan

     In the Isahaya district it seems that stories about trading trea-
sures, such as the tengu's invisible cloak, are called "tori uchiwa" [bird
fan] stories.

Nagasaki, Kitatakaku-gun, Enoura: MK II 9 28, "The tengu" (Tengu
     san).   The hero is a naughty boy who looked through the hole in a
     one-mon coin and claimed he saw Isahaya and Nagasaki.   He traded
     the coin for a bird fan.
     It is amusing how he would spout nonsense about how he could
     see a tengu to surprise people.
     The ending is a little unusual.   He made the chōja's daughter's
     nose high at the village Jizō festival and then cured it.   He
     received lots of money, but he did not become a son-in-law.
     This story contains an episode in which the tengu discovered
     his disadvantage.   The story seems to be changed.

158. "What Are You the Most Scared of?"

     This is the last part of "The invisible straw hat and cloak."   There
is a dialogue with a demon about what each fears the most, by which
a man gains a fortune cleverly.   Also appears in "Tanokyū."

Aomori, Hachinohe: MK II 10 15, "What are you the most scared of?" (Nani ga ichiban kowai).

Iwate, Kamihei-gun, Shizukuishi-mura: Kikimimi 58, "The treasure gourd" No. 7 (Takara fukube). There are faint traces of the treasure exchanging group, but the central interest is in the line, "What are you the most scared of?" The man said he was afraid of red rice and the creature was afraid of the sound of a gun. The man suddenly shot his gun, and the creature ran away, leaving a magic gourd behind.

Hienuki-gun: Kōshō 10 11, "The tengu and the gambler" (Tengu to bakuchiuchi). The tengu was afraid of squash and the man said he was afraid of mochi. An mochi [mochi covered with sweet bean paste] was thrown onto the man.

Miyagi, Momoo-gun: Kyōdo den 3 121, "The priest and his novice" (Oshō to kozō). The novice claimed he was afraid of mochi stuffed with sweet bean paste. The tengu's nose got caught on a thorn and it hurt. The story is broken, but recognizable.

Saitama, Chichibu-gun, Ōtaki-mura: MK II 3 31, "The revenge of Yakujin" (Yakujin Kami no adauchi). Yakujin is the same as Yakubyō Gami [God of Pestilence].

Yamanashi, Nishiyatsushiro-gun: Zoku Kai 115, "Tanobei." Tanobei was a dutiful son who liked dramas. On his way home from a play he met a python and they had a dialogue. The python hated tobacco juice and Tanobei said he hated money.

After the python came and threw a 1000 ryō box at Tanobei, the villagers destroyed it with tobacco juice.

Higashiyatsushiro-gun: Zoku Kai 120, "Tanukiuemon." The hero was a dutiful son who was an actor. The story contains the part where he puts on masks and also the dialogue with the monster, but he just destroyed the monster with tobacco juice and got no money.

Kanagawa, Tsukui-gun: Zoku Kai 24, "The old man fooled by a fox" (Kitsune ni bakasareta jii sama). Two unusual episodes. There is an exchange of questions with a fox that turned itself into a young girl and carried water to a paddy for an old man. Later the fox takes revenge.

Nagano: Chiisagata 235, "Disliking botamochi" (Botamochi girai). Two children quarrel. One dislikes saikachibara and the other dislikes botamochi.

Gifu, Gujōgun: MK II 6 27, "Tanokyu." An actor and a python ghost meet. Here it is a man on his way home to Tanokyū, making it sound like a place name.

Yoshiki-gun, Kamitakara-mura: Hidabito V 8 21, "Seven disguises, eight disguises" (Nanabake, yabake). Here it is an actor and a fox. He said Tanuki Badger and not Tanokyū. The fox had seven disguises, but the actor changed costumes eight times and called them disguises.

The actor said he was afraid of money, which is reasonable. There is no reason for the fox to say he was afraid of nicotine.

Osaka, Sennan-gun: Kōshō 10 30, "The snake and the actor" (Hebi to yakusha). A badger, a snake, and an actor compare disguises. Two tales may be combined here.

Settsu: Nihon zenkoku 23, "The ghost of the white snake" (Hakuja no sei). There is a dialogue after a comparison of disguises with an actor. One hated snails and the other hated gold. When the man disguised himself as a snail, the python first ran away. Then it came to the actor's house and threw gold coins at him as revenge.

Shimane, Yatsuka-gun, Nonami-mura: MK II 1 33, "The gambler and Sai-no-kami [God of dice]" (Bakuto to Sai-no-kami). It is a fragment, but note Sai-no-kami. This deity also appears in a story about exchanging treasures from Iki. TD III 11 44, "The rain of gold coins" (Ōban koban no ame).

Oki: MK I 9 26, "The old woman and the tengu" (Baba to tengu); Okinoshima 10, "The little gold coins and botamochi" (Koban to botamochi).

Hiroshima, Hiroshima City: Aki 159, "Osan Fox of Enami" No. 4 (Enami no Osan Gitsune). This is about Osan Fox and an eel catcher. She said she was afraid of wild boars. He received ten one-yen bills.

Yamagata-gun: Aki 167, "Hokubei and the fox" (Hokubei to kitsune).

Tokushima, Myōsai-gun: MK I 3 37, "The python" (Uwabami). The python disguised himself as a white-haired old man. The boy put on a white fox mask to scare it. Only the python asked what he was scared of.

Mima-gun: Awa Iyayama 93, "The origin of Setsubun" (Setsubun no okori).

Kumamoto, Kuma-gun, Kume-mura: MK I 5 37, "Fooling the badger" (Tanuki damashi). This is a story of Hikoichi of Yatsushiro.

Ōita, Nakatsu: Jinbun I 1 133, "Fooling a tengu" (Tengu o taburakasu). A Kichigo tale.

Nagasaki: Gotō 237, "The dutiful daughter and the wolf" (Kōkō musume to ōkami). This is close to the "Kōkōzaka." A dialogue between the girl and a wolf that threatened to eat her. The girl was afraid of the puckery juice of persimmons and the wolf was afraid of nicotine.

Are there no wolves on this island?

Kagoshima: Kikai 85, "The gratitude of the kappa" (Kappa no ongaeshi). The man became friendly with a kappa, and it left a fish hanging on the lock of the house every night. That made the man uneasy and he asked what it disliked in a dialogue. It disliked octopus. The man hung some up, and the kappa stopped coming.

Further reference:

Chōsen mintan shū 271. This is about a notorious outlaw and a girl.

159. Tanokyū

This belongs to the same group as "What are you the mot scared of?" Transformations from ghost stories to humorous stories, which can also be seen in the "The invisible straw cloak and hat" group.

In these tales plays on words become more complicated.

Fukushima: Iwaki 63, 156, "Tannkyū."
Niigata, Minamikanbara-gun: Kamuhara 155, "The wit of Tanokiyo" (Tanokiyo no tonchi). In this region the sound "u" is often pronounced as o (Tanokiyo), but this aside, the rendition is far more natural to the ear. Could this be the original version?

In the same book on p. 205 there is a story about destroying a mushroom ghost by a dialogue about what it was the most scared of.
Yamanashi, Nishiyatsushiro-gun: Zoku Kai 115, 120, "Tanobei" and "Tanukiuemon." See entry for "What are you the most scared of?"
Gifu, Gunjō-gun: MK II 6 27, "Tanokyū."
   Yoshiki-gun: Hidabito IV 10 40, "Gold and tobacco embers" (Kin to suigara). A charcoal-maker named Kyūsaku lived at Kude on Hirayu Pass. A man came and said he was afraid of tobacco embers, so he recognized him as a snake.

There is nothing here about the badger of Tano. Perhaps there was formerly, but then fell out of the story. There is also an example where the snake has been made into a fox. See Mukashi-banashi kenkyū II 10 15, section on Hachinohe, Aomori.
Yamaguchi: Suō Ōshima 32, "Tanokyū."
Tokushima: Awa Iyayama 137, "Tanokyūbei."
Kumamoto: Kamimashiki 525, "A certain man and a ghost" (Aru otoko to bakemono). An elementary school pupil who became an actor took the name Tanokyū. He had a dialogue with a ghost at Ōeyama in Tanba. The ghost disliked tobacco juice.
Nagasaki: Shimabara 96, "Tanokyū and the big snake" (Tanokyū to daija). The most common form. (New) Iki 79, "Tanokyū."

Further reference:
Minzoku kaii hen 194.

160. Kashikobuchi
[The Water-spider Story]

One summer a man went fishing at a certain pool in the mountains. Oddly enough, he caught many fish that day and his basket was filled soon. He soaked his feet in the water because the day was hot. A water-spider came darting across the pool. It wrapped its thread around the man's big toe and went away. In a short time, it returned and wrapped its thread around his toe again. The man thought this was strange. He lifted the thread off his toe and wound it around the big willow tree near him. He was astonished presently to hear a big voice from the bottom of the pool calling for a crowd to gather. All the fish in his basket leaped out together and disappeared. Then voices in the pond joined in an "en-yara-sa" as the spider's thread began to be pulled. That thick tree was broken off at its root before his very eyes. Nobody went to fish at that pool after that.

Fukushima, Date-gun

This story is told as a legend in some examples, but it probably was originally a story about destroying something.

Aomori, Hachinohe: MK II 10 16, "The water-spider" No. 2 (Mizugumo). This is handed down as a legend about destroying a water-spider. A beautiful robe was left at the foot of a tree to fool the ghost.
    This seems more like a folk tale than the one above, which is now the usual form.

Iwate: Kunohe 468, "The Spider Spirit in Tōhei Pond" (Tōheibuchi ni wa kumo no nushi). This is a legend about Tōhei Pond at Kawai in Yamagata-mura. Once upon a time when Tōhei was fishing, he heard voices shout together in the pond, and the stump beside him was pulled in. The voices laughed.

Kamihei-gun: Tōno 275 No. 183. No title. When a spider web at Kotorigawa got onto a man's face, he moved it to a willow tree. The tree was pulled off at its roots into the water. What he thought were fish were willow leaves.

Miyagi, Sendai: MK II 10 16, "The water-spider" (Mizugumo); Nihon den 124, "The water-spider" (Mizugumo). The first story. Voices called "Clever, clever!" at the end.

Fukushima, Date-gun: Nihon shū, jō 47, "The water-spider" (Mizugumo). Example.

Yamanashi, Nishiyatsushiro-gun: Kai 123, "The spider and the man fishing for salmon" (Kumo to yamame tsuri); Zoku Kai 124, "Spider Pond" (Kumobuchi). This is a legend about Kumobuchi at Shimoku-ishiki. Voices in the pond said, "Yoi-sho."

Aichi, Hakuri-gun: Aichi 27, "The old pile in the river" (Kawa no naka no furui kui). This is a pond at Higashiasai. A great snake disguised as a spider fastened a thread. It came again disguised as a sea tortoise, but its ear was cut off by a very strong man. After that it lived as a great snake with only one ear.

Tottori: Inpaku min I 4 189, "Yaroku Pond" (Yarokubuchi). It is told as a legend. When somebody in the pond called, "Yariko ee ka" [are you ready?] the man answered, "Ee-wa" [ready]. He was pulled in. The man's name was said to be Yaroku, but that is a later change.

Tokushima: Awa Iyayama 64, "Jūzaemon Falls" (Jūzaemon taki). Two men met the ghost of a water spider.

Kumamoto, Kikuchi-gun: Nihon den 125, 126, "The waterfall that restored strength" (Ikiyoi gaeshi no taki) and "Otoroshigabuchi."

Further reference:
    Takagi Toshio, *Nihon densetsu shū*. At Meguro, Meiji-mura, Kita-uwa-gun, Ehime a hunter saw an earthworm, a frog, and a deer, each eaten by something stronger. He decided to give up hunting and started home. A yamajiji in the top of a tree beside him called, "That's a good idea, hunter!"
    This is something brought from China. It was used in a sermon, but only the moral was changed.
    Koshi no fusa, go 3 (In *Essa sōsho* 6, 109). From Niigata, Minami-uonuma-gun. A web was tied to a man's toe. After he moved it to a willow tree, it was broken off at the root.

161. The Eighth Leg of the Octopus

Once upon a time an octopus appeared right in front of an old woman who was doing her laundry at the beach. Although it did not tell her to cut a leg off, it stuck a big one out toward her. She cut it off promptly and took it home happy to eat it. When she was doing her wash again the next day, the same octopus came out and let her cut off another leg. This went on for seven days. On the eighth day, the old woman set out intending to be sure to get the head, too. The octopus stuck out its last leg and waited. When the old woman started to cut it off, the octopus suddenly danced up to her and wound its remaining leg around her neck and dragged her to the bottom of the sea.

Nagasaki, Minamitakaku-gun

This is in the form of a fable, but it probably was originally a ghost story.

Yamanashi, Nishiyatsushiro-gun: Kai 257, "The octopus and the fisherman" (Tako to ryōshi). He cut off three legs and was drawn in when he tried to get the fourth.
That this story is told in a mountain village is strange.
Aichi, Chita-gun: Aichi 9, "Orinjima." Told as a legend from Orin Island.
The old woman's name was Orin. She was pulled in on the eighth day.
Mie, Shima-gun: Nihon zenkoku 38, "The octopus and the monkey" (Tako to saru). The monkey ate six legs first. The octopus deceived him and said he would give him the other two, but it pulled the monkey into the sea with them.
Fukuoka, Itojima-gun: Chikuzen 40.*
Nagasaki, Minamitakaku-gun: Shimabara 26, "The eighth leg of the octopus" (Tako no ashi no hachihonme). Example. Gotō 238, "The revenge for his father" (Oya no adauchi). The form is changed.

Further reference:
Kōshō bungaku 11. Folk beliefs in Kawachi. If someone gets whooping cough, seven legs of the octopus are drawn on paper and pasted onto the earthen stove. When the sickness is over, the eighth leg is drawn and the picture is floated downstream in a river where the current is good.
Kwansai kobanashi. The tale is preserved. A cat ate seven legs of an octopus under a bridge. There is a play on words: don't eat the hand.
Suō Ōshima. At Jinpeiiwa offshore from Niimiya, Nishikata-mura, they say it was an old man, while at Fusaki, Hijoi-mura they say it was an old woman. But in both versions only two legs were cut off and not eight before they were pulled in.

162. The Secret of the Big Tree

Long ago a feudal lord decided to build a castle. He insisted that the ceiling should be made of camphor wood. There were no big camphor trees around, so he sent his men in all directions to look for one. They heard about one at last on the grounds of the shrine in a certain village. He sent several woodcutters immediately with orders to cut it down.

When they arrived, they found a huge tree which ten or even twenty men could not reach around together. No matter how much they tried to cut it, their axes only bounced back, and their work could not proceed. The head man fell into a doze as he pondered how to cut it down. As he slept, a crowd of little men, as small as children, came out and began to talk together. They said the tree could not be cut in an ordinary way. The only way was to put seaweed into a kettle and boil it. The water should then be poured over the roots of the tree. They thought men fools for not knowing that.

As soon as the man woke up, he had seaweed boiled and the water poured over the roots of the tree. In a single night, a swarm of ants came and gnawed the roots of the tree and left them hollow. The woodcutters then cut the tree without any difficulty and took it to the feudal lord. They were well rewarded.

Yamanashi, Nishiyatsushiro-gun

Iwate, Kamihei-gun: Tōno 130, No. 20. No title. Senoki came in a dream and said to burn the cryptomeria tree and cut it at Ichinogongen, Daita, Kuribayashi-mura.

Kamihei-gun, Shizukuishi: TD III 5 5, "The female deity of Shizukuishi river and the burial mound at Dōjōji" (Shizukuishi no shinnyo to Shizukuishi Dōjōji no zuka) by Tanaka Kita. It is the story of wood chips that stuck back onto the tree, and follows the plot of Chibiki densetsu.

Akita, Senhoku-gun: Ugo 327. The story is given briefly. A man who understood what trees and birds said overheard an argument about a tree. He learned that if salt water were put into the cut on the tree, the chips would not fly back. He also cured the illness of a chōja and succeeded in life.

This belongs to "The listening hood" group, but it says nothing about the ghost.

Nagano: Kitaazumi II 68, 72, "The larch that became the roof beam of Genchōji" (Genchōji no nijibari ni natta karamatsu) and "The curse of the tree on the grounds of Reishōji" (Reishōji no teiboku no tatari).

Yamanashi, Nishiyatsushiro-gun: Kai 244, "Cutting down the camphor tree" (Kusunoki o kiru hanashi). Example.

Tanba (Kyoto): Nihon den 47, "The pine tree that drips" (Shizuku matsu).

Shimane, Mino-gun: Shimane 21, "The miracle of the big cryptomeria tree (Ōsugi no rei-i).

Fukuoka, Miike-gun: Shokoku 85, "Sunrise at Onsendake and sunset at Aso" (Asahi wa Onsendake ni yūhi wa Aso). A man learned from the spirit of a katsura vine in a dream that if he cut the vine, the big tree would fall.

Oita: Bungo den 117, 33, "The maidenhair tree at Hōshinji" (Hōshinji no ginkō) and "Kirikabuyama."

Further reference:

Nanki dozoku shiryō 19. The legend of Yanosuke cryptomeria tree.

Nigun kenbun shiki, maki 3 (In *Nambu sōsho* 9, 187). A story about wood chips flying back onto a tree. A tara tree revealed that chips should be burned and salt should be rubbed into the cut on the tree. It is like a folk tale.

Konjaku monogatari, maki 31, No. 37. A story about Ōmi.

163. The Satori and the Hoop
[A Dialogue with a yamauba]

This early became a source for shingaku [moral tales], but it was probably a folk tale originally.

Once upon a time a man went into the mountains to make charcoal. He gathered wood and was baking his charcoal, but he felt uneasy because he had gone far into the mountains alone. He thought, "I'll be all right unless something scary comes out." Just then he heard a voice from somewhere say, "I'll be all right unless something scary comes out." Then a tengu appeared. The charcoal-maker was very frightened and thought, "What's a good way to get away?" The tengu said, "What's a good way to get away?" He said everything the man thought and the man was completely dazed. Presently the rod by which he guided his ox fell and sent sparks flying at the tengu. The tengu went off, observing that men do things they don't think about.

Hyōgo, Kinosaki-gun, Sanshō-mura

Iwate, Iwate-gun: Kikimimi 103, "Bending the hoop of the basket" (Minowa mage). It is told about Hikotarō of Koakazawa. A yamauba was struck and died when the hoop flew open. Dai-ichi 35, "The yamababa and the cooper" (Yamababa to okeya). The bamboo hoop for the basket was overheated and sent sparks flying. That is why humans cannot be trusted. This is a feminine example.

Kunohe-gun: Kunohe 453, "The ghost bird dote" (Kaichō dote no hanashi). It is a legend about a ghost bird called a "dote," whose upper part was that of an owl and lower part that of a man. He appeared before a young man and said everything he was thinking.

It was so surprised when an alms box became filled with coins that it went off.

This conclusion is different and its meaning is hard to grasp.

Akita, Senhoku-gun: Kikimimi 105, "Making snow shoes" (Kanjiki tsukuri). The ghost was a badger. When he came to the fire, he brought out his big testicles. The man's hands slipped accidentally and when the bamboo flew out and hit them, the badger died.

Niigata, Minamikanbara-gun: Kamuhara 135, "The charcoal-maker and the tengu" (Sumiyaki to tengu).

Nagano, Kitaazumi-gun: Otari 147. No title. Kitaazumi I 89. No title.

Yamanashi, Nishiyatsushiro-gun: Kai 199, "The demon Omoi" (Omoi no mamono). The ghost was called Omoi. Zoku Kai, "Satori, the ghost" (Satori no bakemono). This is about a charcoal-maker and a ghost called Satori. What was not thought was more frightening than what was.

Gifu, Gunjō-gun: MK II 6 26, "The Mountain Deity" (Yama-no-kami ga kita hanashi).

Hyōgo, Kinosaki-gun: MK II 9 37, "The tengu and the charcoal-maker" (Tengu to sumiyaki). Example. This can be considered the old form.

Perhaps it started with the experience of an echo. Thinking and talking to one's self were considered the same.

Kumamoto: Amakusa 171, "The chaps called men do things they don't think about" (Ningen to iu yatsu wa omowanu koto o suru). The men involved are coopers, charcoal-makers, basket makers, or case makers.

Further reference:

Koshi no fusa (In *Essa sōsho* 6 52), Nii, Mikuni-mura, Minamiuonuma-gun. The story of an animal in the mountains called a satori.

164. The Mountain where Old Women were Abandoned

This appears to be an old imported story. There are two ways it is told.

The first is about Kirōkoku, a land of abandoned old people. The wisdom of an old person, hidden and cared for, helps solve problems and they became happy. The problems are a thousand bundles of ash rope, the mare and the three-year old colt, the male and female snake, sending ants through, and the end of the log that is its base.

The second type is where children who take their parents to the mountains to abandon them are moved by the love of their parents and try to live with them again.

There are two reasons for abandoning the parents: one is legal—it is the law of the region or the order of the feudal lord. The other is domestic—a scheme of the wife. Many are told as legends, but in Tōhoku and the southern islands, some versions contain the episode of the old man next door, from which we can see that they were formerly folk tales.

The two types are often confused or combined when told.

Aomori, Hachinohe: MK II 10 11, four stories: "A thousand fathoms of ash rope" (Hai nawa chihiro), another with this title, "The cow and the boat" (Ushi to fune), and "The mountain where old women were abandoned type" (Uba sute yama kei). The first three are the of first type. In the last, the old mother was abandoned because of the slander of the wife. She received one big and one little magic mallet from the Mountain Deity and lived comfortably. The hateful wife tried to imitate her by getting her husband to abandon her. She failed to imitate her and was burned to death.

Tsugaru m 39, "The mountain where the father was abandoned" (Oya sute yama no hanashi). The father had to be abandoned when he was fifty years old according to orders. The children were grateful to him for spilling poppy seeds as a guide for them when going home, and they brought him back and hid him.

Tsugaru k 3. No title. Old men became monkeys; MK II 10 17, "The mountain where the father was abandoned" (Oya sute yama). Brothers go to abandon their father, but they bring him back. This is a very common type.

Iwate, Kamihei-gun: Rōō 96, "Abandoning a mother (Oya sute dan). When her son heard his own son say, "Bring the pole and let's go home," he gave up the idea of abandoning his mother.

Tales like this and others like them seem to be invented.

Kikimimi 60, 459, "The magic mallet" (Uchide no kozuchi). The old woman was abandoned by the bride's scheme. She received a magic mallet from a demon's child and became a woman feudal lord. The bride tried to imitate her, but she was burned to death.

"Where old people were abandoned" (Rōjin suteba); Kamihei 167, "Where old people were abandoned" (Rōjin suteba). Type one. Shiwa-gun: Shiwa-shū 89, "The mountain where old people were abandoned" (Okina sute yama). This combines both types.

Fukushima: Iwaki 68, 158, "The mountain where parents were abandoned" (Oya sute yama).

Niigata, Minamiuonuma-gun: MK I 7 26, "The mountain where old women were abandoned" (Uba sute yama). Type one.

Minamikanbara-gun, Kamuhara 186, 155, "The mountain where old women were abandoned" (Uba sute yama), and Note No. 49. Minamikamabara 120, "The mountain where parents were abandoned" (Oya sute yama). Type two. It is combined with "The trials of the son-on-law."

Sado: Sado shū 96, "The mountains where parents were abandoned" No. 1 (Oya sute yama).

Ishikawa: Kaga 70, "The old man's great achievement" (Toshiyori no tegara).

Nagano, Chiisagata-gun: MK I 1 36, "Abandoning an old woman" (Baba sute no hanashi). Type two. The son carried her on his back into the mountains to abandon her because of the feudal lord's order. He was able to return safely because she broke off branches to show him the way. The feudal lord heard about it and changed his mind. There is nothing about problems to solve.

Shimoina-gun: Mukashibanashi 78, "The mountain where old people were abandoned" (Oba sute yama no hanashi).

Gifu, Gunjō-gun: MK II 6 27, "The mountain where old women were abandoned" (Uba sute yama). A combination of types one and two.

Yamanashi, Nishiyatsushiro-gun: Kai 96, "Abandoning a parent" (Oya sute dan). Type two.

Shizuoka, Tagata-gun, Dohi-mura: Kyōdo ken III 4 51, "The legend at Izu about abandoning parents" (Izu no kirō no densetsu). Parents were abandoned when 62 years old. Type two.

Hyōgo, Hikami-gun: TD X 7 52, "The mountain where old women were abandoned" (Oya sute yama).

Shimane, Oki, Kuroki-mura: MK I 9 25, "Abandoning old people" (Rōjin suteru hanashi). Type one.

Okayama, Okayama City area: Dai-ni 79, "The wisdom of the old man" (Rōjin no chie). Type one; Okayama bun II 6 32, "The rope made with ashes" (Hai de nawa o nau).

Hiroshima: Geibi 98, 115, "The mountain where parents were abandoned" (Oya sute yama) and "What a pity! Will this help, will that help?" (Kimyō kinodoku dōshioka kōshioka); Aki 123, "The mountain where old men were abandoned" (Jiji sute yama).

Kagawa, Mitoyo-gun, Shishijima: MK II 5 12, "Notes on collecting tales on Shishijima, Mitoyo-gun" (Mitoyo-gun, Shishijima mukashibanashi saishū) by Takeda Akira.

Nagasaki: (Old) Iki 110, "Abandoning old men" (Rōjin o suteru hanashi, betsu wa). A dutiful child could not abandon his father. It is like the story in Chiisagata-gun, Nagano, about abandoning an old woman.

Kumamoto, Amakusa: MK I 11 44, "The mountain where old women were abandoned" (Uba sute yama). This is a combination of the two types. A story on the next page is like type two. Kyōdo ken V 3 4, "The legend in Izu about abandoning old people" (Izu no kirō densetsu). Type two.

Kagoshima: Koshiki 106, "The mountain where parents were abandoned" (Oya sute yama). A combination of the two types.

Kikaijima: Kikai 130, "The bride who became a rat" (Nezumi ni natta yome). The mother who had been abandoned prayed to the Mountain Deity. Anything she wanted came out when she struck the ground. Her life became happy. The bride became a rat.

Okinawa: Nantō 116, "Burying old people alive" (Rōjin o ikiume shita hanashi). An old man buried alive at 61 was protected because he could solve problems.

Further reference:
Chōsen mintan shū 39, In Appendix No. 5 a story from Zō hōzōkyō is told which combines the two types.
Yamato monogatari, ge.
[Fujiwara] Toshiyori mumyō shō.
Konjaku monogatari, maki 30, No. 9.
Zoku Karin ryōzai shū, jō 271.
Fusō kojiyo 304 (in Kōbunko).
Kokuten sago, 2 kan, 9 no u.
Zōdan shū 4. About the king of a great country long ago. The law was that a parent reaching the age of 40 had to be buried alive. This

was the country of abandoned old people, later called the country
where they were cared for, but there is no tale.
Clouston II 373, "The unfilial child."

165. A Thousand Bales of Ash Rope

This theme, which belongs to those about son-in-law tasks, is
found mainly in Tōhoku. In other regions it is included in "The mountain where old people were abandoned."

Iwate: Kamihei 167, "The place where old people were abandoned"
(Rōjin suteba).

166. The Wife's Cleverness

A merchant set out to Edo to sell flowers used for dyeing. He put
up at an inn on his way. He wagered with the woman innkeeper on
whether or not the cock on the picture scroll would crow and he lost.
He had to give up his flowers. His wife was so provoked when he
returned that she took double the amount of flowers and set out. She
stopped at the same inn and made the same wager. In the night she
sewed the throat of the cock in the picture so it could not crow. She
won the price of the flowers and went home.

Niigata, Minamikanbara-gun

The central interest here is in getting the value back on the
second trip, but the one who takes revenge is not always the wife.

Iwate, Hienuki-gun: MK I 1 37, "Eating mochi" (Mochi kui). The wager
was over eating one to of mochi. The revenge was by the son.
Niigata, Minamikanbara-gun: Kamuhara 48, "The cock on the picture
scroll" (Niwatori no kakezu). Example.
Yamanashi, Nishiyatsushiro-gun: Kai 125, "The tea merchant and the
old woodcutter" (Ocha uri to kiwari jiji).
Hiroshima: Aki 193, "The cock on the picture scroll" (Niwatori no
kakezu). Its relation to the example is interesting.
Kagoshima: Koshiki 114, "Gambling for the load on the boat," No. 1
(Funani kake).
Ōshima-gun: Shima II 431, "The two brothers" (Kyōdai).
Kikaijima: Kikai 149, "The two brothers" (Kyōdai). Once there
were two brothers who did not get along together well. The
younger had a friend in the neighborhood who was like an older

brother to him. The younger brother killed a wild boar in the hills one day, but he told his friend that he had killed a man by mistake and asked him to cover the fact up. Even though they were like brothers, the friend felt that he was an outsider and did not want to be involved. The older brother was surprised, but went to the mountains immediately. The neighbor could not come around again because he thought he knew the real state of affairs. The two brothers were reconciled and lived together with understanding after that.

This is a borrowing from stories about brothers.

It does not seem to be an importation, but it may have been changed.

One wonders if the story about the bride who made it seem that she was eating a corpse when she was really eating mochi came at a later date. It is found in Tōhoku, too. See *Shima* II 470.

167. The Wife who was a Thief

The wife was a robber chief and every day she ordered her husband to go out and steal. If her husband stole a cow, she would rub oil on its horns and burn them to change their shape and keep the officers from catching them. Her constant orders to her husband to steal made him decide one day to give her some trouble. He went to the graveyard and dug up a corpse and brought it home. His wife stuck it into a box and set it on the porch. Two other thieves came by. Presently, she said she had let something slip her mind and had left a treasure in a box on the porch. She said she would have to hurry to get it and rushed out of the house. At the mention of treasure, the two thieves ran around the house the other way to get there first. One of them swung the box onto his shoulders and started to run. The other happened to see there was a body in the box. He yelled, "It's a man, it's a man!" The one with the box shouted, "I'm running away because it is a man!" And they ran off with all speed.

Kagoshima, Kikaijima

Tales like the one about clever Yasohachi disposing of a corpse probably came from this, too. Also tales about extorting the wine merchant.

Aomori, Hachinohe: MK II 10 19, "The wife who was a thief" (Nusubito nyōbō). A man was sent three times to steal by his mother-in-law. The third time he put powder and rouge on a female corpse he stole and set it up by the door of the wine shop. He extorted money from the owner, who happened to knock it over.
Iwate, Kesen-gun: Kikimimi 132 134, "The bad widow" (Warui yamome)

and "The son-in-law who worked nights" (Yokasugu muko). A lazy man in the first tale was ordered by a widow to get a female corpse and blackmail a wine merchant, as in the Hachinohe version. In the second, a father-in-law schemed to fool a feudal lord.

Niigata, Minamikanbara-gun: Kamuhara 200, Note No. 8. A female thief used a man to steal.

Nagano: Chiisagata 163, "Making money with a dead man" (Shinin de kane mōke). It was a corpse of a girl which the old man found when he started to take a drink in the mountains. The old woman's scheme earned money.

Kagoshima: Shima II 428, "It's a man! It's a man!" (Hito da, hito da). Example.

168. The Thief's Wager

Many of these belong to stories about brothers. See "Gorō's broken bowl." The immoral element is probably old.

Nagasaki: Shimabara shū 116, "The thief who took a 1000-ryō box" (Senryō bako dorobō). This has episodes about millet mochi on a girl's rear end and other amusing ones.

169. The Clever Man

A man went to the clever man for advice on how to dispose of the body of the gentleman of the village who had died suddenly. The clever man stood the body up when some young men were gambling. They thought that somebody had come to spy on them and struck it with a stick and knocked it down. The astonished youths thought they had killed the gentleman of the village. They went to the clever man for advice. This time he took the corpse to the door of the gentleman's house and called, "I'm home now. Open the door." His wife scolded him because it was late at night. He said, "All right, then I'll jump into the well and die." He threw the corpse in and ran away. The wife thought her husband had thrown himself into the well, and she went to the clever man for advice. He told her to heat up the corpse in the steamer and then call the doctor to say her husband was ill with a fever. The doctor came in a hurry. He looked at the eyes of the corpse and said, "It is a pity, but he has already stopped breathing." Then she could have a funeral. The clever man received many gifts of thanks from everyone and made a big profit.

Niigata, Minamikanbara-gun

Aomori, Shimokita-gun, Kuriyama: MK II 10 19, "The wife who was a thief" (Nusubito nyōbō). Kobukuro killed an old woman and used her corpse to get money from a wine merchant. The ending is like "Yakushi in the straw bag." It says definitely here that the horse hide talked.

The story without the deception is like "The old man who swallowed a bird."

Iwate: Kogane 66, "Carrying a corpse around" (Shinin o mochimawatta hanashi).

Kamihei-gun: Rōō 233, "Clever Yasohachi" (Funbetsu Yasohachi); Kikimimi 119, "Bakuro Yasohachi."

Akita, Kakunodate: Dai-ni 84, "The five Tarōsaku" (Gonin Tarōsaku).

Niigata, Minamikanbara-gun: Kamuhara 141, "The clever man" (Chie ari dono). Example. More than half of this is like "Clever Yasohachi."

Hiroshima, Takata-gun: (no source) "Clever Gihei" (Funbetsu Gihei).

Kagoshima: Koshiki 183, "Clever Magozaemon" (Funbetsu Magozaemon).

Further reference:

Chōsen mintan shū 314. Punishing a wife who had a lover.

Mukashibanashi kenkyū II 6 17. In "Yue minkan setsuwa ron," by Aita Yoshi, p. 12.

Huet 10.

170. Yakushi in the Straw Bag

A boy who was a liar and undutiful toward his parents went with his father to the mountains to cut trees. He wanted to go home, so he began to cry and say his stomach hurt. His father told him to go home and go to bed. When he reached home, he told his mother his father had been hurt badly and had died. He told her to hurry and become a nun to say prayers for his soul. She cut her hair and was saying prayers at the family altar when the father returned with a big load of wood on his back. He declared that such an undutiful son should be wrapped in a straw bag and thrown into the river. They promptly made a big straw bag. They put their son into it and set him out under the eaves. A blind masseur came along and stumbled on the bag. The son cried out sharply and asked who it was. The man said he was blind and asked to be forgiven. The son told him that he had been blind, too, but after he got into the bag, he could see. He said the blind man could be cured, too, and told him to get in. He fooled the poor blind man and exchanged places with him. The father came out and lifted the bag to his shoulders. He carried it to the river and threw it in.

After the son hid in the mountains for five or six days, he borrowed a salted fish from a fish vendor and went home. He told his parents that he got the fish from the river and told them to hurry and get some. He forced his parents into a straw bag and threw them into the big river. That was the end.

Tochigi, Haga-gun, Sakagawa-mura

Iwate: Kikimimi 119, "Bakuro Yasohachi." A combination of "The clever man" and "Yakushi in the straw bag."
   Shiwa-gun: Shiwa-shū 65, "Ano Sama."
Akita, Senhoku-gun: MK I 11 25, "The feudal lord and his servant" (Tono sama to geboku). It is close to "The feudal lord who sold peaches."
Fukushima: Iwaki 69, 159, "Yakushi in the straw bag heals eyes" (Tawara Yakushi no me no yōjin).
Tochigi, Haga-gun: Dai-ni 85, "The unfilial son" (Oya fukō musuko no hanashi). Example. Shimotsuke 18, "The boy who lied" (Udotsuki kozō).
Nagano: Chiisagata 239, "Yakushi in the straw bag" (Tawara Yakushi). He called, "Tawara Yakushi heals bad eyes." He fooled a cowherd whose eyes were bad.
   Kitasaku-gun: Otari 148. No title.
Hiroshima, Hiba-gun: Geibi 117, 135, "Yakushi in the straw bag" (Tawara Yakushi). The Hiba item is in a note. "The horse that dropped gold" (Kane hiri uma). This is a story of brothers.
Tokushima: Awa Iyayama 125, "Yakushi in the straw bag" (Tawara Yakushi).
Fukuoka, Itojima-gun: Fukuoka 116, "Matabei of Fukuma" (Fukuma no Matabei). This, too, is such a story.
Kumamoto, Tamana-gun: MK I 2 34, "The horse that dropped coins" (Zenitare uma). The latter part.
Kagoshima: Koshiki 187, "The big lie" (Ōba banashi). The latter part.
   Amami Ōshima: MK II 5 44, "The greedy elder brother" (Yoku fukai ani). This is partly about brothers. It is not likely that a good younger brother would kill his elder brother. It can be considered a later addition.

Further reference:
   Chōsen no monogatari shū by Takahashi Kyō. "Katami yatsu."
   "Kokugai ruikei shiryō" in *Mukashibanashi kenkyū* I 7 6.
   Grimm, "The turnip" and "The little farmer."

171. The Horse that Dropped Coins

A certain horse dealer brought a cow along and offered to sell it because it dropped coins. Somebody thought that would make money and bought it at a high price, but when it did not drop coins after many days, he took it back to the horse dealer. The horse dealer said that it had to be fed coins in order to drop them.

Kishū (Wakayama), Kumano

This is a humorous variation on stories such as "The little golden dog" and "The two brothers." It was originally of "The two brothers" type, but later the one fooled became a chōja. The openings are exaggerated.

Iwate: Esashi 7, "Brothers" (Aru kyōdai no hanashi). After a man had fooled his older brother with a horse that dropped coins, he sold him an ordinary kettle that he said heated itself, and a gourd that he said would heal wounds.

New episodes are invented because of the tale's possibilities.

Kamihei-gun: Kikimimi 487, "The picture of an umbrella" (Kasa no e). Somebody sold a picture scroll at a high price. He said the girl in the picture would open the umbrella she was holding on a rainy day. The buyer complained later. The one who sold it asked if the buyer had given the girl anything to eat. He said he had not. He was told she did not have the strength to open it because she was hungry.

Fukushima: Iwaki 175, "The horse that dropped gold" (Kinhiri uma).

Nagano, Minamiazumi-gun, Meisei-mura, Hitoichi: Reported by Mr. Ariga.

It is a story about brothers.

Wakayama, Higashimuro-gun, Kumano: Dai-ichi 65, "The golden cow" (Kogane no ushi). Example.

Shimane: TD III 9 19, "The horse that dropped gold" (Kin no fun o hiru uma no hanashi).

Hinokawa-gun: Shimane 26, "The cleverness of Niemon" (Niemon no tonchi).

Yamaguchi, Suō Ōshima: (no source). A chicken that laid gold eggs and a kettle that did not need fire are here.

They are poorly connected.

Tokushima: Awa Iyayama 106, "The two brothers" (Ani to otōto).

Fukuoka, Itojima-gun: Fukuoka 115, "Matabei of Fukuma" (Fukuma no Matabei). "If you don't feed it coins, it won't drop coins."

Nagasaki: Shimabara 109, "The horse that dropped gold" (Kin o hiru uma). A man fooled his rich younger brother with bellows supposed to restore an old woman's life and a horse that was supposed to drop coins.

Ōita: TD I 5 18, "The horse that dropped gold" (Kin no fun o hiru uma no hanashi).

This is a Kitchu story about fooling a greedy uncle.

Kumamoto, Tamana-gun: MK I 2 34, "The horse that dropped coins" (Zeni tare uma).

Further reference:

Seisuishō 13, "Tankuro and Takuro."

Tōkaidō meishoki. A story about Hidesato in the part about Mikamiyama.

Huet 9. The kettle that boils alone and the horse that drops gold.

172. The Golden Eggplant

There was a certain king who had a one-year-old son. One day the mother broke wind in the midst of a crowd. This angered the king and he set the mother and child adrift in a dugout boat. The boy learned about everything when he grew bigger. At thirteen he got permission from his mother to go home. He crossed over to their former island. He went in front of the king's gate every day and called, "Does anyone want seed that grows golden eggplant?" The king inquired if such a thing were true. The boy said it was true, but the seed would have to be planted by someone who did not break wind. The king declared he never heard of anyone who did not break wind. The boy asked why he found fault with his mother then. The king reflected and immediately restored the mother and his son. He made the wise boy his successor.

Kagoshima, Ōshima-gun, Kikaijima

Iwate: Shiwa 175, "The flower that grew gold" (Kogane no naru fuki-bana); Shiwa shū 4, "The flower that grew gold" (Kogane no naru fukibana).

Fukushima: Iwaki 79, "The nobleman's wife who yawned" (Akubi o shita okugata no hanashi).

Niigata: Sado 195, "The God of Weaving at Kotachi" (Kotachi no Hata-gami); Sadogashima 122, "The tree that grew gold" (Kin no naru ki); Sado shū 237, "The golden eggplant" (Kin no nasu); MK II 6 35, "The golden eggplant" (Kin no nasu). An aristocratic woman came adrift in a dugout boat.

Hiroshima: Geibi 77, "The feudal lord" (Otono sama).

Nagasaki, Tsushima: Tsuchi no ka XVI 5 13, in "Tsushima Sasuna-mura kenkunki" by Mishina Shōie. (Old) Iki 3, "The dugout boat" (Utsuro bune); Dai-ichi 83, "The woman in the dugout boat" (Utsuro bune no onna).

Kumamoto, Amakusa: Kyōdo ken V 3 27, "The golden melon" (Kogane no uri).

Kagoshima, Kikaijima: Kikai 75, "The golden eggplant" (Kin no nasu). Ōshima-gun: Shima II 468, "The golden eggplant" No. 2, (Kin no nasu). Example. Okierabujima: Okinoerabu 176, "The jewel that grew golden flowers" (Kogane no hana saku tama); TD X 6 11. In "Shima no mokushiroku" by Noma Yoshio. It is a legend.

173. The Child of the Sun

Kagoshima: Kikai 24, "The child of the Sun" (Nichirin no kudashigo); Shima II 487, "The child of the Sun" (Nichirin no kudashigo). This tale is related to "The golden eggplant" group. The boy appeared who called himself Child of the Sun. Upon receiving a mandate from heaven, he became the first diviner and his mother became the first shrine yuta.

It is told as a legend of a priest's family.

174. One Thousand Ryō for a Saying

A man left his wife and mother at home while he went here and there for work. He saved his money and decided to go home after many years. He wanted to take home some good sayings as gifts, so he asked for them from a priest at a temple and received three. One was: "Even if a man pauses, his body should not." Another was: "A small tree rather than a big one." The third was: "A short temper loses." He escaped being buried alive and being struck by lightning by the first two. He reached home safely, but as he started into his house, he saw shadows of his wife and a shaven headed person talking together. He raised his scythe in a flash of temper, but recalled that "a short temper loses." He threw his scythe aside and entered. The person he had thought was a priest was his mother. She had shaved her head to relieve dizziness. The sayings of a priest proved to be the best gifts he could have bought.

Kagawa, Shōdojima

Iwate: Kikimimi 506, "Buying a saying" No. 1 (Hanashi kai). He bought a saying from an old man who sold them; Rōō 182, "Buying a saying" (Hanashi kai).
Hienuki-gun: Dai-ni 42, "Buying a saying" (Hanashi kai).
Shiwa-gun: Shiwa-shū 146, "Buying a saying" (Hanashi kai). He bought two sayings for 100 ryō each. This is combined with "The ghost of treasure."
Fukushima: Iwaki 71, "One thousand ryō for a saying" (Hanashi senryō).
Kōsuke-no-kuni (Gunma): Nihon zenkoku 146, "Buying and selling sayings" (Hanashi uri kai).
Tochigi: Shimotsuke 2, "One saying for 100 ryō" (Hitokuchi hyaku ryō). A charcoal seller went to Edo and with the 300 ryō he earned he bought three sayings. It is something like "Jizō Jōdo."
Fukui, Sakai-gun: MK I 1 32, "Buying a saying" (Hanashi kai). A man who went to Edo to hull rice bought sayings to bring home.
Ishikawa: Kaga 133, "Father's doll" (Oyaji no ningyō).
Nagano: Kitaazumi II 96, "The hunter named Shibuemon" (Ryōshi Shibuemon no hanashi).
Gifu, Yoshiki-gun: Hidabito V 6 6, "One thousand ryō for a saying" (Hanashi senryō).
Yamanashi: Kai 85, "Three pardons" (Mittsu no kanben); Zoku Kai 322, "Buying a saying" (Hanashi kai).
Osaka, Senhoku-gun, Torishi-mura: Izumi 35, "Buying a saying" (Hanashi o kau). A man saw a sign that read "A place where wisdom is sold."
Shimane, Ōchi-gun: MK II 9 31, "One thousand ryō for a saying" (Hanashi senryō). Hikohachi worked at Kōnoike and was always saying something to make the gentleman there laugh. Once he put up a tall sign that read: one kanme for a saying. A man who had earned three kanme came along and inquired, etc.
This is probably a fragment.

Okayama, Mitsu-gun: MK I 8 25, "A saying worth 15 ryō (Jūgo ryō no hanashi); Babasama 38, "Hikohachi." Hikohachi bought a saying that saved his life.

Hiroshima: Aki 184, "Hikohachi sayings" (Hikohachi banashi). Sankichi earned 3000 ryō at Edo. He bought three sayings at 1000 ryō each; Geibi 121, "One thousand ryō for a saying" (Hanashi senryō). A man earned 3 kan of gold for hulling rice for three years in Edo. He bought three of "Hikohachi sayings worth one kanme."

Yamaguchi, Suō Ōshima: Kōshō 11 24, "Buying a saying" (Hanashi o kau).

Kagawa, Shōdojima: Dai-ichi 70, "One thousand ryō for a saying (Hanashi senryō). Example.

Tokushima, Miyoshi-gun: Hokuto 31, App. 6, "The sayings seller" (Hana-shiya); Awa Iyayama 36, "One look for 1000 ryō" (Hitome senryō).

Fukuoka, Kurate-gun: Fukuoka 59. No title.

Nagasaki: (Old) Iki 148, "Hekohachi."

Kagoshima: Koshiki 100, 185, "One thousand ryō for a saying" (Hanashi senryō), and "Buying a prayer" (Nenbutsu kai). The second is some-thing between "A saying for 1000 ryō" and "Rat sutra."

Kikaijima: Kikai 99, "Buying a saying" (Hanashi kai); Shima I 5 88, "The shadow without a head" (Kubi no nai kage); Shima II 482, "Buying a saying" (Kotoba kai); MK I 5 42, "Buying a saying" (Hanashi kai).

Okierabujima: Okinoerabu 73, 80, "A saying for 1000 ryō" (Hanashi senryō). Same title for both.

Further reference:

Iro setsuden 570.

Kikimimi sōshi 476. Both parents and a child each bought a saying for 200 mon from a priest at a temple. They made a thief run away with these.

Clouston II 317, 491, "A king's life saved by a maxim."

Bolte—in his history of folk tales.

175. Two Bolts of White Cloth

A bride declared that Atago Sama, the god on the top of the mountain, rides a white horse. Her mother-in-law said he does not ride a horse. The two argued all day without settling the problem. Finally, they decided to ask Judge Ōoka to settle the matter for them. During the night before he was to give his judgment, both the mother-in-law and the bride went separately with a bolt of white cloth for him and asked that he say what she said was right. On the next day the two went together to him. The bride spoke first. She said, "Now, Ōoka Sama, the god called Atago Sama rides a horse, doesn't he?" Ōoka shook his head as though disagreeing. The mother-in-law thought it was settled her way and said, "He dosen't ride a horse, does he?" Again Ōoka shook his head.

Both women thought he had not kept his word. They asked what the name of the god on the mountain was. He replied, "That is Nitan-no-Shiro Tadatori Kō Sama." [A play on words: "two bolts of white for nothing" and the name of a popular hero.]

Iwate, Kamihei-gun

Iwate, Kamihei-gun: Kikimimi 479, "Atago Sama." Example; Rōō 239, 272, "Two bolts of white cloth for nothing" (Nitan no shiro tadatori) and "The Ise pilgrim and the oil seller" (Ise mairi to abura uri).

Niigata, Minamikanbara-gun: Kamuhara 132, "A stork or a goose" (Tsuru ka gan ka). A priest arbitrated for a mother-in-law and a bride.

Nagano, Shimoina: Mukashibanashi 95, "The pronounciation of higan or hiigan" (Higan to hiigan).

Yamanashi, Nishiyatsushiro-gun: Kai 80, "Exactly 300 rabbits" (Chokkuri san byaku shimeko no usuagi). An old man and an old woman argued. A priest arbitrated cleverly.

Shiga, Takashima-gun: MK I 10 46, "The load called konbu" (Konbu). This was an argument among a son-in-law, a bride, and a mother-in-law.

Nagasaki: Shimabara 184, "Pronouncing fune and funa" (Fune to funa).

Shimane, Yatsuka-gun: MK II 1 33, "The bride and her mother-in-law" (Yome to shūtome). This is a fragment.

Further reference:
Among the legends and folk tales collected by Mr. Ariga there is a story called "Nitan-no-Shiro Tadatori." Is this "Nitan-no-Shiro" a later form? There should be an earlier one.
Seisuishō IV 133.

176. The Child Judge

Iwate: Rōō 243, "How Judge Ōoka observed a just judgment by a child" (Ōoka sama jitsugo shirabe). While Judge Ōoka was perplexed over a judgment, he watched three children playing judge on the sandbar by the river.

Further reference:
Chōsen mintan shū App. 30. In another place in the book, "A dialogue between a gifted child and an itinerant priest."
Taihei kōki 248.

177. The Badger's Nest

Something built a nest in a tree on the path between rice paddies. One man said it was a badger's nest and another said it was a chicken's nest. They decided to ask a wise old man to settle the matter. When one asked, "Isn't it a badger [tanuki] nest?" he said, "It certainly is a tree in the field [ta no ki] nest." When the other asked, "Isn't it a chicken [niwatori] nest?" he answered, "It certainly is a two-winged bird [ni wa tori] nest."

Nagasaki, Iki

Iwaki: Shiwa 68, 85, "The hawk's nest in the china pepper tree" (Sanshō no ki ni taka no su) and "The afuri screen" (Afuri no byōbu). In the second story, a son-in-law paid a New Year visit to his poor father-in-law. He stayed several days. The old man fed him frozen rice and soup, and in the shade of a straw mat that he hung up, he laid out a reed mat for him to sleep on, giving him a wooden pestle for a pillow. He covered him with a mat of woven straw. His mother asked him how things had been when he got home. He told her he ate sumisumi rice with sorisori on it, hung up an afuri screen, gave him kingi pillow and a tantan lined cover with a family crest on it.

There is an example where this has been put into the form of a stepchild story. Originally it belonged to a success story of a son-in-law, such as "Improving the omen." We can find examples of the sort in *Seisuishō*.

There are amusing stories of moyogi quilt, hikiage dishes, and such.

Fukuoka, Kurate-gun: Fukuoka 74, "School children" (Gakkō seito).

Nagasaki: (Old) Iki 156, "A badger's nest or a chicken's nest" (Tanuki no su ka niwatori no su ka). Example. Shimabara 185, "The badger's nest" (Tanuki no su). Arbitrated by a priest. This clever word play appears in other forms. See the play on words karasu no su [crow's nest] and kara su [an empty nest] in *Otari kōhi shū*.

178. The Famous Judge

A father left each of his sons a gourd in his will. They were to chose his heir by them. They quarreled and went to a priest to settle the matter. He told them that the one who had received the first gourd would be the heir. Since the first gourd formed would be the heaviest, they weighed them and found the oldest son had it. Thus he won.

Iwate, Kamihei-gun

Iwate: Kikimimi 55, "The first gourd" (Motonari hyōtan). Example. The same story is in *Shikata banashi* 57.
Tochigi: Shimotsuke 4, "Honest Gorō" (Shōjiki Gorō).
Shiga: Nihon zenkoku 101, "The camphor tree witness" (Shōnin kusunoki).

Further reference:
> *Nihon dōwa shū* 567.
> *Shasekishū* 6, 30-o.
Clouston II 367. Judging the amount of money in a purse that had been dropped. This is related to stories of animal arbitrating over things picked up. Sometimes a monkey is judge.

179. Red Rice and the Child

There was a poor man who lived in a shack he rented from somebody. Because he was poor he ate only red rice, a kind that matures early and is of poor quality. When his child went to play at the landlord's, he was asked what he ate at home. He replied it was red rice. The man declared that for some time his red beans had been disappearing a little at a time, and that was probably the reason. He went to the shack to drive the family out. The father cut his child's stomach open to show his innocence and only coarse red rice came out. The landlord killed himself. From that time nobody grew red rice in that place (Nadasaki-mura, Kojima-gun, Bizen). [The coarse rice—akagome—was miscalled **sekihan**: translator.]

                                                                Okayama

Aomori: Tsugaru k 11. No title; Tsugaru m 94, "Hotoke and the poor girl" (Hotoke Sama to binbō no musume). There was a poor family that never had anything but mixed rice to eat. The child did not know that mixed rice was different from azuki rice. When she went to the main family to play, she was asked what she ate every day. She said azuki (red rice). The head of the family was angry at such extravagance and demanded the money he had loaned them be repaid. The father cut his child's stomach open to show, and only mixed rice came out. He had proved his child's innocence, but he had killed his precious child. The next morning he went weeping to pray to Yakushi, whom he worshipped. He found the image there with its stomach cut open. He thought it strange. When he went home, he looked at his child who he thought was dead. He found her alive and without a scratch on her.
Okayama, Kojima-gun: Kyōdo ken I 7 50, "A legend about red rice" (Akagome ni kansuru densetsu). Example.
Nagasaki: (Old) Iki 37, "Cutting a child's stomach open to show" (Wagako no hara o saite miseta hanashi). Little shrimp came out when the child's stomach was cut.

Further reference:
Shokoku monogatari 130. The origin of Jūsanzuka in Hizen.

180. Improving the Omen

A child was born to a couple who had been childless for many years. The delighted father set out to take the news to his wife's family. On the way he found some things that had been dropped—a robe of a priest (**kesa** and **koromo**) and a rosary (**juzu**). He was afraid this was a bad omen and went to consult a priest.

The priest used the day of the month, the 13th Day of the Eleventh Month, and the names of the objects in a poem which meant the child would live as many years as there were beads on the rosary.

Yamanashi, Nishiyatsushiro-gun

All these types of tales are based upon comic poems. That does not mean that there may not have been a similar type earlier. The stepchild example below from Shizuoka may have been taken from "Sara-sara Yama" as a pattern.

Yamanashi, Nishiyatsushiro-gun: Kai 127, "The omen in the poem" (Engi uta). Example.

Shizuoka: Shizuoka 402, "The stepmother and the stepchild" (Mamahaha to mamako no hanashi). When the stepmother would feed her stepson the tail of the fish, he would be glad and say, "You have made me **atotori** (tail or inheritor)." If she gave him the head, he would say, "You've given me **okashira** (head or head place)." When she gave him the center part, he was still happy, so she was won over.

181. The Zatō's Cleverness

That zatō transmitted folk tales is apparent from the fact that frequently the principal character in revisions of stories is such a man.

Aomori, Hachinohe: MK II 10 19, "The zatō's cleverness" (Zatō no tonchi). Four tales.

Iwate: Shiwa shū 34, "Two sheaves, four sheaves" (Futataba yotaba). They planned to avoid giving the zatō any mochi to eat, but he ate it all.

Esashi-gun: Esashi 30, "How the zatō was connected with success" (Zatō ga shinshō ni kakawatta to iu hanashi). A zatō who fell into a well prayed as he was being pulled up, and the fortunes of the family improved afterwards.

This may be an adaptation by zatō of "The hearth fire on New Year's Eve" or "Kōbō's water."

Niigata, Minamikanbara-gun: Kamuhara 37, "Kamekasu Nurinosuke." While an old couple were planning to make kaimochi (ohagi) for supper, a rokubu came along and spent the night. The couple decided to tie a string to the old man's big toe and when the mochi was ready, the old woman was to pull it to wake him up. The rokubu knew this. He switched the string to his own toe. He got up instead of the old man and ate his fill, then wrapped what was left in his straw cloak. When the rokubu was setting out in the morning, the old man asked where his home was. He replied, "Minonikaimochi Kurumi-no-kori" [in the country of the straw cloak wrapping the mochi].

The humor here is how he made up a proper name from a secret unknown to the questioner.

Ōita: Naori 61, "Stories about zatō" (Zatō banashi). Four tales with comic poems.

182. Stories with Riddle

A cowherd was leading a cow that was illtempered enough to gore a man. He met a zatō. The cowherd said, "Say, Zatō, say, please give way." The blind man asked, "What are you?" "I'm thirty days," answered the cowherd. "Oh, one month [hitotsuki may also mean **man gorer**]," said the blind man. The cowherd said, "Its color is like the lower leaves on greens in October." The blind man said, "Oh, red leaves [the word for red hair]."

Hiroshima, Aki-gun

Hiroshima: MK I 4 46, "The zatō and the cowherd" (Zatō to ushioi).
Okayama: Mitsu 45, "The wise zatō" (Zatō no monoshiri). He guessed who made the fire-box, when and what wood it was made from. Such clever sayings can be made up endlessly afterwards.

183. The Priest and his Novice

It is possible to classify these tales minutely, but there is no point in doing so. We must draw the line somewhere. They seem to have developed from tales about precocious children. They must have started as such, but at present most of them have been changed to jokes and are known as stories about a priest and his novice. The priest furnishes the laughs. There are several stories about stupid novices in the foolish village group.

a   Picking up everything the horse drops: A novice who is told to
     pick up what falls from the horse picks up horse dung. The
     instruction is to step on that sort of thing, so when the priest
     falls, he is stepped on.
b   Kwan-kwan kuta-kuta: Hotoke Sama ate the red beans.
c   The calabash wife: The novice makes fun of the priest who is
     enjoying a calabash on which he has painted a face.
d   The novice gets his name changed: The priest likes to eat mochi or
     drink wine aloe. The novice gets his name changed to the word the
     priest uses when eating or drinking. When the priest uses the word
     again the novice answers and shows up.
e   Standing the pillar up and finding mochi: The novice is sent to a
     beam raising ceremony. While he is gone, the priest toasts mochi
     alone. The novice uses fire tongs to show what went on at the
     ceremony and sets them on the mochi, discovering it hidden in the
     ashes.
f   A slip of the tongue when buying tōfu.
g   Trials for the priest: These are based upon son-in-law trials, but
     have been changed gradually into jokes.
h   Hand signals: The priest falls into the privy and claps his hands.
     The novice accordingly cooks one *to* of rice.
i   Overhearing private matters.
j   Substituting words (busu): Calling sugar poison to fool the novice.
     The boy, knowing that calling it poison is a lie, breaks something
     the priest values then eats as much of the sweet as he wants.
k   A story connected with a comic verse.

Aomori: Tsugaru m 87, 89, 91 b and d: "Amida who ate botamochi"
     (Botamochi o kutta Amida Sama), "The noise of blowing hot mochi"
     (Puppu no hanashi), and "Just the right temperature" (Yoikan no
     hanashi).
     Hachinohe: MK II 11 27, a,b,d,e,g,h: "The priest and his novice"
     (Oshō to kozō).
Iwate, Hienuki-gun: MK I 1 40 b: "The clever novice" (Kozō no tonchi).
     Kamihei-gun: Rōō 163, 185, g,e: "The priest and his servant" (Oshō
     to genan). Both tales with the same title; Kikimimi 518 e: "The
     priest and his novice" (Oshō to kozō), and "Pounding mochi" (Mochi
     tsuki).
     Kunohe-gun: Kunohe 480 h: "The clever novice" (Kozō no tonchi).
     Shiwa-gun: Shiwa a: 68, "The hawk nest in the china pepper tree"
     (Sanshō no ki ni taka no su); d: 69 168, "Toasting mochi" (Mochi
     yaki), and "Warm wine" (Kanzake); e: 112, "Toasting mochi" (Mochi
     yaki); h: 84 "One to and one sho of wine" (Sake itto to issho); k
     113, "The full moon" (Jūgoya no tsuki) and a: 166, "The razor"
     (Kamisori).
Yamagata, Mogami-gun: MK II 4 43 d: "The clever novice" (Tonchi
     kozō).
Miyagi, Momoo-gun: Kyōdo den 3 121 b, d: [not available].
Fukushima, Iwaki: MK I 11 35 d: "The priest and his novice" (Oshō to
     kozō); Iwaki 182 a: "Kwan-kwan kuta-kuta"; b: "Poison ame" (Doku

na ame); d: "Jabbing the mochi in the ashes" (Hai no naka no mochi o tsutsuita hanashi); e: "Fufu Pata"; j: "The razor" (Kamisori).

Niigata, Minamikanbara-gun: Kamuhara 89, 145, c: "The priest and his novice" (Oshō to kozō); and a,h: "The priest and his novice" (Oshō to kozō).

Ishikawa: Kaga 93 b: 93, "The stone image ate it" (Kuta-kuta ishibotoke); j: 97 "Poisonous sake" (Doku na sake); e: 95, "The water for the priest" (Oshō no mizu); k: 98, "The broken moon" (Kataware tsuki); g: 100 "Dōmo Kōmo"; a: 102, "Pick it up right away" (Sukū mon ja); and h: 104, "Boil one *to*" (Itto taki).

Nomi-gun, Shiromine: MK II 6 33 b,k: "The priest and his novice" (Oshō to kozō).

Nagano: Chiisagata e: 196, "One pillar about here" (Kono hen ni hashira ga ippon); j: 198, "The novice who liked ame" (Amename kozō); a: 199, "Whatever falls" (Ochita mono); b: 194, "Kwan-kwan kuta-kuta."

Shimoina-gun: Mukashibanashi b: 5, "The main image and ᵗʰe ohagi" (Honzon to ohagi no mochi); e: 25, "The priest and the ᵗoasted mochi" (Oshō Sama to yaki mochi); d: 35, "The priest who liked sweet wine" (Amazake no suki na oshō san). A substitute for wine; d: 43, "Ikkan, the novice" (Kozō Ikkan no hanashi); j: 46, "The priest at the mountain temple and Chinseitō" (Yamadera no oshō to Chinseitō); k: 128, "The snow covered mochi" (Yuki ni uzumerareta mochi) and 109, "The mochi, the priest, and the three novices" (Mochi to oshō to sannin no kozō). This could also be put into tales of cleverness; a: 130, "The priest, his novice, and horse dung" (Oshō to kozō to maguso).

Yamanashi, Nishiyatsushiro-gun: Kai 175, e: "The novice and mochi" (Kozō to mochi); Zoku Kai 342, g: The bee drum (Hachi taiko).

Tochigi, Haga-gun: Shimotsuke 79, b: "Pata-pata, the novice, and Umauma, the novice" (Pata-pata kozō to Uma-uma kozō); d: "The metal image that ate botamochi" (Botamochi o tabeta kanabutsu); e: "Dotsuki mochi."

Kazusa (Chiba): Nansō 97, e,d: "The novice and the priest" (Kozō to oshō). Three stories.

Aichi, Kitashidara-gun: Dai-ichi 58, g: "The priest and his novice" (Oshō to kozō).

Okayama, Mitsu-gun: MK I 11 41, a: "What falls from the horse" (Uma kara ochita mono).

Shimane: Okinoshima 38, a: "The foolish novice" (Kozō no dōra).

Fukuoka, Itojima: Fukuoka 128, "The priest and his novice" (Oshō to kozō) and 139, "The priest and his novice stealing and eating" (Oshō to kozō nusumi gui). Substituting privy mochi and other filthy episodes not found elsewhere.

Munakata-gun: Fukuoka 130. The same kind of filthy stories. d: 132, "The priest and his novice, wine and mochi" (Oshō to kozō, sake to mochi).

Onga-gun: Fukuoka 131, d: "The priest and his novice, wine and mochi" (Oshō to kozō, sake to mochi).

Kurate-gun: Fukuoka 133, e: "The priest and his novice, wine and mochi" (Oshō to kozō, sake to mochi); 134, b: "The priest and his novice, stealing and eating" (Oshō to kozō nusumi gui); 135, h;

"The priest falling into the privy" (Oshō benjo ni ochita); 136, j: "The novice stealing and eating" (Kozō nusumi gui).

Nagasaki: Shimabara 194, h: "One to one sho" (Itto isshō); 202, c: "Calling the beech tree his bride" (Buna o yome ni suru hanashi); and 198, b: "The sweet wine is Nembutsu" (Amazake wa Nembutsu sama).

Further reference:

Look for names such as Eikan, Gettan, and Fufu, type d. Such names are certainly adapted to fit the locality according to the narrator's plan.

Ujishūi monogatari, No. 12. (In *Nihon zuihitsu taikei*, Vol. XVI)

Nihon dōwa shū 199. No place names.

Ikkyū banashi also has these. *Seisuishō* also has many. See Vol. III 115.

Shasekishū IV 18 o: Three children with different mothers. The priest has many children. VII 34 u: Honey is poison.

Nakata Senpo, *Tojin zasso*. A story of renaming novices. All have difficult Chinese characters.

Nakata Senpo. About the priest and his novice.

Chōsen mintan shū 194, "Poisonous dried persimmons." It is said to be a story found all over the country.

Zōdan shū 2, at the end. (Kagen 2nd year, 1305.) A novice was told that trout was a razor. When he was crossing the river, he said, "See the razor. Don't make a mistake and cut your feet." Before that there is a story about a chicken, the father of the eggplant.

PART TWO

Derived Tales

11. Stories about Destiny

184. Singing Bones

Two merchants set out for work. One earned a lot, but the other had to go home empty handed. The one who had not earned anything killed his companion on the way home. He stole his money and loafed around without working for three years. Then he set out along the road again, and when he passed the spot where he had rested with his companion he heard a fine voice singing from the thicket. That seemed strange because there was nobody around. He investigated and found that it was a skull singing. That was remarkable. He asked it if it would sing any time or anywhere it went. It replied that it would. He decided that was a good way to make money and he took the skull home.

He carried it to a rich man's house and announced that he had a skull that would sing. The master there said that skulls do not sing. Finally they agreed that if the skull did not sing, the man would lose his head, and if it did sing the master would turn over all his property to him. Then the man ordered the skull to sing, but it did not. Even though he struck it and rolled it around, it did not sing. The master became impatient and cut the man's head off. At that moment the skull sang in a fine voice, "It's happened, it's happened. What I thought has happened. At last a stork, a tortoise, and five-needled pine!" With that the skull took revenge for what had happened three years earlier.

Kagoshima, Koshikijima

Iwate, Kamihei-gun: Rōō 335, "Tōhei, the flute player" (Fuefuki
Tōhei). It comes in the last part of "Chōja from a straw."
Fukushima, Futaba-gun: MK II 4 36, "The revenge of the skeleton"
(Gaikotsu no adauchi).
Iwaki-gun: Iwaki 14, "The skull's gratitude" (Sarakobe no ongaeshi).
A woman came to help as a wife for three years in thanks for the
funeral the man held for her.
Niigata, Minamikanbara-gun: MK I 3 29, "From a meadow lane in
spring" (Haru no nomichi kara); Kamuhara 70, "The turtle that
sang" (Uta o utau kame).
Kagoshima: Koshiki 120, "Singing bones" (Utai gaikotsu). Example.
Three tales.
Kikaijima: Kikai 95, 96, "Singing bones" (Utai gaikotsu), and "The
singing bowl" (Utai donburi). The bowl sings and dances in the
second tale. There is nothing about taking revenge however. Shima
II 484, 491, "The revenge of the skull" (Dokuro no adauchi) and
"The skull's gratitude" (Dokuro no ongaeshi). A story of repaying
kindness.
Okierabujima: Okinoerabu 215, "The brothers" (Kyōdai).

185. Stories about Forecasting Fortune

There are three types of stories.
One is about forecasting fortunes to a boy and a girl who are born
on the same night. The girl is forecast a good fortune but not the boy.
This is connected with "Charcoal-maker Chōja."
In the second, a child whose soul is destined to be taken by the
Water Spirit is saved by mochi or some other natural means.
The third, called "The horsefly and the hand ax," or some such
name, is about a child whose fortune is to be killed by a hand ax.
When a horsefly is bothering the child, his father waves it off with his
hand ax, but he accidentally kills his child.
An example of the first is about a chōja who set out on a journey,
leaving his pregnant wife behind. He finished his business and started
home. He was overtaken by night in the mountains and put up at an
Ujigami shrine. He heard the jingle of bells on horses in the night, and
two gods came riding up. They said that in a certain village at a certain chōja's house a child was to be born that night. They invited
Ujigami to go with them to the house. A voice from the interior of the
shrine said that he had a guest at his place that night and could not
go and told them to go on. The bells jingled as the gods left.
The chōja who overheard the conversation was sure that the name
of the village and the chōja were his, and he could not sleep for
worry about the strange things going on. Presently the gods came back
and told Ujigami a boy had been born at the chōja's house, but he had
an unfortunate future of only three bamboo trees. Then they rode off.
While the chōja was feeling downhearted at the poor fortune of his
child, the gods came back once again. They invited Ujigami to go with

them to the outcast's hut on the enbankment by the rice fields, but once more the deity excused himself because of his guest. The chōja waited to hear the results. The gods came back and reported a little girl had been born with many treasures, then rode away.

The chōja hurried home at dawn and found that his wife had given birth to a son the night before. The time was exactly as the gods had said, so he was sure it was his family and he was troubled over his son's fortune of only three bamboo. He decided that the best thing to do was to arrange a marriage for him with the outcast's daughter who had such great treasures. When he went to see, he found that a little girl had indeed been born, so he arranged with the outcast to have the children marry in the future.

The two children grew up and married, but for some reason the girl could not stay with the family. She went to another chōja's home as a bride. After that, her second family became many times richer than before. On the contrary, the former family became so poor that they had difficulty having enough to eat. Finally, they began to make bamboo baskets and went around selling them. One day the son came to the house where his former bride had gone. She came out and recognized him. She paid him with rice and hid gold coins in it. All his poor neighbors heard he had brought rice home and came to borrow some. He handed it out ungrundgingly. Once more, he was in want and went to the chōja's house to sell baskets. He was asked what he had done with the rice he had received and whether there wasn't something in it. He said he had loaned it to neighbors, but had not heard of there being anything in it. The woman decided he certainly was a man without fortune and no longer had anything to do with him.

Yamanashi, Nishiyatsushiro-gun

An example of the second type is the story of a man whose wife became pregnant. He went to make petitions to Jizō. One night when the man was praying at the shrine, another Jizō came and invited the man's Jizō to go along, but he refused because of his guest. The other came back to report that a boy with a span of 18 years had been born and he would be carried off by the Spirit of Katsura River in Kyoto. When the man went home, he found that a baby boy had indeed been born.

Shortly after, the man was given a post to watch the rapids of Katsura River. He suffered silently as his child grew older. There was a great flood in the year the boy was 18. He asked to go to help at the river instead of his father, but the father did not want to let him go. The son slipped away without eating breakfast while his father slept. His parents thought he would surely be taken by the Water Spirit and prepared a funeral for him.

The young man stopped at a mochi shop on his way and offered some to a girl he met there. She ate and ate until she had eaten 100 kan of mochi. Since the boy did not have such money with him he left his umbrella as security and left with the girl. When they reached the bank of the river, she said, "I am the spirit of this place and since you have given me so much mochi, I will extend your life from 18 to 61 years." When his parents, who were preparing for the funeral, saw their son return safely, they were delighted.

Hyōgo, Mitaka-gun

An example of the third type is about a pilgrim who came to a certain village and put up at a little shrine for Yama-no-kami. He woke up in the night. He thought he heard some men talking. It was two Yama-no-kami. One said, "Didn't you go tonight?" The other answered, "No, I couldn't because I have a guest. What was the outcome?" "The mother and child are all right." "How old will he be when he dies?" "Seven. He will be killed by a hand ax." The pilgrim wondered what the talk was about as he listened.

Seven years later the pilgrim came to that village and found that a father, a carpenter, had been working near his child where he slept and tried to drive off a horsefly that was circling its face. He used his hand ax, which slipped and cut the child's head. The village was in great confusion. The pilgrim recalled what he had heard at the Yama-no-kami shrine seven years before and realized what it meant.

Iwate, Iwate-gun

Aomori, Hachinohe: MK II 10 16, "Forecasting fortunes" (Unsadame banashi). All three types are here.
Iwate: Shiwa shū 28, "Uemontarō and Saemontarō" (Uemontarō to Saemontarō). This belongs to the first type. There is a part about receiving a hair from a wolf's eyebrow and using it to perceive the nature of persons, then the story continues as part of the charcoal-maker group.
It starts out naturally, but the tale is drawn out, perhaps because it has been made into a katarimono.
Kamihei-gun: Rōō 59, 1, "The old eel woman" (Unagi baba). This is the second type, a story of the fortune of being caught by something in the water.
"The village of the pheasant's voice!" (Kiji no hito koe no sato). A man who overheard a conversation among Sai-no-kami, Hōki-gami, and Yama-no-kami discovered a spring of wine. There is an episode about hitting wild ducks with little gold coins that is like "Charcoal-maker Chōja," but there is no bride. There is a similar story on p. 59 of the same book.
Iwate-gun: Kikimimi 30, "The talk among the Yama-no-kami" (Yama-no-kami no sōdan). Example. The horsefly flying around the child's face seems significant.
Akita, Kazuno-gun: MK I 3 26, "Determining the fortune of a newborn babe" (Umarego no unsadame). The third type, but there is no horsefly.
Miyagi: Tome, ge 877, "The horsefly and the hand ax" (Abu to chōna). This is a legend about the first village Kannon; Kyōdo den 1 49,

"Kōshin Kannon." The third type. Told as a legend of Kannon at Akausawa, Toyosato-mura.

Fukushima, Iwaki-gun: Iwaki 77, "The fortune forecast by the gods" (Kami sama ni un o sadamareta hanashi). The second type.

Niigata, Minamiuonuma-gun: MK I 10 38, "The fortune of a newborn babe" (Umarego no un). The first type. The story is a little broken up, especially at the first. The emphasis put in the latter half is like the Shintō stories in the Ryūkyū.

Minamikanbara-gun: Kamuhara 158, 212. Note No. 52 as well as the one about the charcoal-maker on p.106 belong to the first type. Note No. 85 belongs to the second type. A kappa came for the hero, but because he gave it a big feast, it spared him.

Ishikawa, Nomi-gun: Minzokugaku II 8 42, "The danger is a horsefly and a chisel" (Mujō wa abu to nomi), and "The danger is water" (Mujō wa mizu); Techō 73, "Forecasting fortunes" (Unsadame banashi). The third type, with the horsefly and hand ax.

Yamanashi, Nishiyatsushiro-gun: Kai 182, 176, "The fortune given from birth" (Umaretsuki no un). Example. "Hōkiemon from Hōki-no-kuni" (Hōki-no-kuni no Hōkiemon sama). This also is the first type. The bride herself overheard Ebisu and Daikoku talking; Zoku Kai 144, "The pilgrim and the fortune of the newborn babe" (Rokubu to ubugo no unmei). This is a mixture of forms.

Chiba, Chōsei-gun: Nansō 101, "Kōjin Sama." The first type.

Unakami-gun: Tōtsubito V 8 31. No title. Here it is bee and a razor.

Nagano, Kamiina-gun: Kyōdo I 3 8, "The tree at the head of the procession" (Otō no ki) by Yanagita Kunio. The third type.

Gifu, Hida: MK II 11 38, "Forecasting fortunes" (Unsadame banashi). Five stories. The first, second, and fifth are the first type and the third and fourth are the third type.

Osaka, Senhoku-gun: Izumi 36, "The horsefly and the hand ax" (Abu to chiyono).

Hyōgo, Mikata-gun: MK II 7 39, "An umbrella as security for 100 kan" (Hyaku kan no kata ni amakasa ichimai). Example. Type two. The connection of this proverb to the tale is hard to understand.

Hikami-gun: TD X 7 51, "Forecasting fortunes," (Unsadame banashi) and "Katarō" (Katarō no hanashi). The first is type one and the second is type two.

Shimane, Ōchi-gun: MK II 12 32, "The determined fortune" (Kimatta un). First type.

Yamaguchi, Suō Ōshima: Dai-ni 53, "Kannon and Jizō come when a child is born" (Ko no umareru toki ni wa Kannon Sama to Jizō Sama ga kuru). A man overheard about a child being born. He went home and found it was true. A fragment.

Tokushima, Miyoshi-gun: MK II 10 38, "Forecasting fortunes" (Unsadame banashi). The second type.

Mima-gun: Awa Iyayama 38, 82, 132, "Forecasting fortunes" (Unsadame banashi), "Tawara Tōda," and "The original mochi wrapped in reeds of the Fifth Month" (Gogatsu no yoshi no maki no yurai). The second tale is type three and the others type two.

Kagawa, Mitoyo-gun, Shishijima: MK II 3 37, "Miidera." The first type. The tale explains the origin of the temple Miidera. It is significant that it is not separated from Lake Ōmi. (Refer to the next story group.)

Kagoshima: Kikai 89, 92, "Forecasting fortunes" (Unsadame banashi). Both with the same title. The first is type one. In the second, which is of the second type, precaution was taken to avoid danger that was overheard. Shima II 424, "Forecasting the fortunes of two" (Futari no unsadame banashi). One would die from a nail that would drop from the ceiling and the other would die from kicking his heel with his toe nail. Friends of the former gathered to pray for his repose when he was about to die, and his life was saved. The other kept going in and out of his house in worry, and finally died.

Amami Ōshima: TD I 8 49, "The God of Fortune" (Unmei no kami).

Koshikijima: Koshiki 120, 163, "Determiing fortune" (Unsadame banashi). One is the first type and the other the second type.

Okinawa: Iro 36, No. 59. No title.

Further reference:
Konjaku monogatari, maki 28. No. 19. A man went to Azuma and stopped at a house where a baby was born.

186. Miidera

A hunter who was caught in an evening shower took refuge in a mountain temple. He overheard the conversation of the gods and learned his son just born had only the worth of three bamboo trees as his fortune. He decided to have him marry the daughter of a neighbor who had been born with a fortune of 1000 sacks of rice. The boy became poor and could only make things of bamboo to sell. He had illness and other troubles until the couple finally separated. His wife went to Ōtsu to find work and became the second wife of a very rich man. Not realizing this, her former husband went to her house to sell winnowing baskets. She bought a basket from him each time he came. The Kannon temple at Ōtsu caught on fire later. There was a lack of water for putting out the fire. The woman brought out her winnowing baskets and helped extinguish the flames. The temple was called Miidera of Ōtsu from that time.

Kagawa, Mitoyo-gun, Shishijima

Chiba, Awa-gun, Tomizaki-mura. No source. Long ago a girl from Miidera was married to a snake. She drank iris wine to rid herself of the snake's child.

In the charcoal-maker group there is a version about building a temple from selling baskets.

The story about the snake mother gives the origin of the temple bell at Miidera. There may have been a group of story tellers there.

Kagawa, Mitoyo-gun, Shishijima: Sanuki SS 102, "Miidera."

12. Ghost Stories

187. The Tiny Hakama

Long ago an old woman lived alone in a hut in the mountains. As she was spinning as usual late one night, a little man came out from somewhere. He was tiny and angular and he wore a little hakama neatly. He said, "You must be lonely, Granny. I'll do a dance for you." He danced, keeping time well with the song as he sang, "Tiny, tiny hakama with a wooden sword at my side. Look, Granny, look!" Then he disappeared. The old woman felt uneasy. When it was daylight, she searched all over the house. Under the porch, she found an old wooden pick which had been used to blacken teeth. She burned it to get rid of it. After that nothing more appeared. It is said that in olden days the old picks used to blacken teeth were gathered together and burned to get rid of them.

Niigata, Sado

Niigata: Sadogashima 132, "The tiny hakama" (Chii-chii hakama). Example.

Bitchū (Okayama): Minzoku I 681, "The little boy" (Chin-chin chiyoboshi).

Ōita, Kitaamabe-gun: MK I 4 30, "The ghost story" No. 1 (Bakemono banashi). The translation by Hearne of "Chii-chii hakama" and the Bitchū tale no doubt came from this.

188. Destroying the Ghost

There were two brothers who hunted with guns. They went into the mountains once, and were walking on opposite sides of a stream in a valley. The older brother heard his brother shooting and the shots continued for some time. The older brother thought it must be a very large animal, but suddenly the shots stopped. He was worried, and crossed the stream hastily. He climbed to where his brother should have been, but when he called, there was no answer. Then he noticed a white-haired woman seated at the foot of a huge tree. She was spinning thread. He thought she looked like a ghost and aimed his gun at her. She did not show fear or run away but only looked at him and grinned. He was sure one shot hit her, but there was no response. He fired till he had only two bullets left, then aimed a shot at the box she was putting her thread in. At that the old woman disappeared. He hurried up to see and found a very old baboon. He found no trace of his brother.

Kōshū (Yamanashi), Nishiyatsushiro-gun

Iwate, Kamihei-gun: Kikimimi 161, "The spinning woman" (Itoomi onna). It is told as an anecdote about two hunters, but it is probably a fragment of a folk tale.

Niigata, Sado: MK I 4 43, "Revenge upon a badger" (Mujina no ada-uchi). A badger disguised as a woman invited a man to visit her on a moonlight night. The man cut her shadow and destroyed the badger.

Fukushima, Date-gun, Datezaki-mura: Shintatsu 54, "The fox's prank" (Kitsune no itazura). A woman from Shikibuzaka said to Sagohei of Kitazawa, "Are they black, Sagohei?" as she showed him her face. The next night he told her they were black and destroyed her with a fire box that was beside him.

Yamanashi, Nishiyatsushiro-gun: Kai 254, "Hihibaba." Example.

Tochigi: Shimotsuke 71, "The badger disguised as a priest" (Bōzu ni baketa tanuki).

Tokushima: Awa Iyayama 48, "The night spider" (Yoru no kumo).

Ōita, Kitaamabe-gun: MK I 4 38, "Two ghost stories" (Bakemono banashi futatsu).

Kagoshima: Koshiki 144, "The spider ghost" (Kumo no bakemono); Kikai 121, "The kasha ghost" (Kasha no bakemono). There was a match at scratching each other's head and grasping each other's legs.

Further reference:
  Shiwa-gun mukashibanashi shū 14, "Bakemono dera." There is a story in Tōhoku, too, about a match at striking heads.
  Rōō yatan 37, "Kumo to aonyūdō." A hunter and a big ghost.

189. The Mochi and White Stones

This is one form of the story of "The ghost in the mountain temple."

Iwate, Kamihei-gun: Tōno 25 No. 28. No title. In the form of a legend about the origin of the road in Hayachinesan.

Niigata, Minamikanbara-gun: Kamuhara 151, "The badger's fright" (Tanuki gyōten). This is tied to the story about the badger and eight mats. It was probably made into a story by mat makers.

Yamanashi, Nishiyatsushiro-gun: Kai 45, "The priest and the badger" (Oshō to tanuki). This is also a story of eight mats. It tells about inviting the badger to come up to the fire, but there is nothing about heating white stones.

Wakayama: Nankii 16, "The chest of the yamauba" (Yamauba no naga-mochi). This is about a yamauba who liked mochi and set out in autumn to beg for it. She was fed stones that had been gathered from the sandbar of the river and heated. According to the legend, mochi cannot be made here at New Year because of her grudge.

Okayama, Kawakami-gun: Okayama bun II 3 39, "A badger" (Tanuki). White stones that look like mochi are left in a row at a charcoal-maker's hut. When they are thrown at a badger that comes in disguise, he runs off.

Further reference:
Azuma mukashi monogatari, jō.

190. The Old Woman's Three Moles

This is a story about foxes that overheard people talking and learned their secret. They tried to used what they heard to trick the people, but failed.

Iwate, Shiwa-gun: Shiwa-shū 21, "Jinokazaemon and Babamatsukō" (Jikokazaemon to Babmatsukō).

Niigata, Minamikanbara-gun: Echigo Sanjo 37, "Foxes" (Kitsune no mukashibanashi).

191. The Spider Web

This belongs to the group about the notions peddler and the badger.

A yamabushi went to a certain village and was refused when he asked for lodging. He went to a vacant temple. An ōnyūdō came out from the main hall in the night and called, "Here, you visitor, I'll let you hear me play my shamisen." He tightened its strings and at the same time the priest's throat ached. Each time this happened he cut the strings with his sword, and his throat was relieved. When the ghost finally started to leave, the priest threw his sword at him and killed him. He tossed the remains into the dirt floor room. When the morning sun shined on them, he found they were a huge old spider.

Iwate, Shiwa-gun

This story must be considered the work of a player of a shamisen or a biwa.

Iwate, Kamihei-gun: Rōō 35, "The spider woman at the mountain temple" (Yamadera no kumo onna). The principal character is a notions peddler. When he put up at an old temple one night, a beautiful woman came out and played the shamisen for him. Each time she plucked the strings, his throat felt gripped.

Shiwa-gun: Shiwa 148, "The yamabushi" (Yamabushi). Example.

Niigata, Minamikanbara-gun: Kamuhara 125, "The spider zatō" (Kumo no zatō). A young man offered to mend a broken string of a zatō's koto, but it wound it onto his finger.

Kagoshima: Shima II 433, "The dead man and the wagering song" No. 2 (Mōja to uta kake). Majamun was always asking somebody to fix the strings on his shamisen. He claimed that when his string broke he was drawn into the after world. An old woman in the neighborhood came and showed him a chicken to chase the ghost away.

This story is older than the zatō ghost. On this island they do not call it a spider ghost.

192. The Notions Peddler and the Badger

This belongs in the same group as "The spider's web," "The mochi and white stones," and the like. The hero is a notions peddler.

Iwate, Kamihei-gun: Rōō 35, "The spider woman" (Kumo onna). At a mountain temple.

Nagano, Shimoina-gun: Mukashibanashi 86, "The badger and the notions peddler" (Tanuki to komamonoya). A woman at a lonely house said she wanted a needle. The notions peddler stuck needles she said she did not like into the straw matting. Each time, she said it hurt her. It is an eight mat story.

Tottori: Inpaku dōwa 45, "The lonely house" (Ikkenya).

193. Failing to Destroy the Fox

Someone who thought he could see through a fox's disguise was fooled, himself.

Iwate: Esashi 125, "The man who was given the view of a mare's rump" (Meuma no shiri o nozokasareta otoko).

Kamihei-gun: Kikimimi 299, 285, 287, "The horse that was loose" (Hanashi uma) and "The magic hood" (Kakure zukin). He was dumbfounded when he discovered the fox's tail. In the other story the fox gave a man a magic treasure. He thought his old woman could not see him when it was on his head, but it did not work. This is adapted from the story about the magic straw cloak and hat. "The running horse" (Kake uma). This and others like it have been changed into anecdotes for new tastes. A samurai who boasted he could not be fooled was resting at a pass when a horse came running past him. When he stood up, his riceball rolled away. The fox ate it and ran off.

Yamagata, Mogami-gun: Toyosato 250, "Cut with a yatsume sword" (Yatsumetō de kirareta no koto).

Fukushima, Iwaki-gun: Iwaki 84, "The liar" (Usotsuki otoko no hanashi).

Niigata, Minamikanbara-gun: Kamuhara 40, "The stubborn fox" (Gōjō na kitsune); Minamikanbara 158, "The fox who became a priest" (Teihatsu gitsune). And the man became a priest with him.

Ishikawa, Kashima-gun, Nanao: Dai-ni 41, "Fooled by a fox" (Kitsune ni damasareta hanashi).

Tochigi, Haga-gun: Shimotsuke 69, "The fox disguised as a girl" (Musume ni baketa kitsune). A man beat a fox disguised as a girl to death and became famous.

Saitama, Chichibu-gun, Ōtaki-mura: MK II 2 31, "Being fooled" (Bakasare banashi). The tale is rather broken up. Is it because of the narrator's invention?

Chichibu-gun Tsukikawa-mura: Nihon den Kazusa 31, 32, "When Yagobei was bewitched" (Bakasare Yagobei). Two tales with the same title.

Kazusa (Chiba): Nihon den Kazusa 35, "When Yagobei was bewitched" (Bakasare Yagobei).

Kyoto, Minamikuwata-gun: Kuchitanba 71, "A fox" (Kitsune no hanashi).

Tottori: Inpaku min I 2 69, "Seventy-five badgers" (Nanajūgo tanuki); Hanashi II 3 103, "The yamabushi" (Yamabushi). About Yasaburō Fox from Suō and Osan Fox.

Kumamoto, Tamana-gun: MK I 2 37, "The fox disguised as a biwa player" (Biwa hōshi ni baketa kitsune). Since it is about a blind biwa player, it should be very entertaining if such a person told it.

Nagasaki: Shimabara 144, "The yamabushi and the badger" (Yamabushi to tanuki); TD II 10 34, "The fox sold as the prostitute of Maruyama" (Kitsune ga Maruyama no jorō ni urareta hanashi).

Iki: Nihon zenkoku 360, "The priest's head" (Bōzu atama).

194. The Hōin and the Fox

The principal characters are usually hōin or yamabushi and the fox takes revenge.

Iwate, Hienuki-gun: MK I 1 38, "Fooled by a fox" (Kitsune ni damasareta hanashi); Kōshō 9 1, "Fooled by a fox" No. 2 (Kitsune ni damasareta hanashi).
Esashi-gun: Esashi 127, "Hōrinbō who fell from a bridge" (Hashi kara ochita Hōrinbō).
Shiwa-gun: Shiwa 33, "The man fooled by a fox" (Kitsune ni damasareta otoko).
Isawa-gun: Kikimimi 290, "The vigil for the dead man" (Shinin no ban). This is told as an anecdote about a man called Santarō, but it has been forced into a folk tale.
Kamihei-gun: Tōno 298 No. 203. No title.
Akita, Senhoku-gun: MK I 10 29, "The old man fooled by a fox" (Kitsune ni damasareta jii san).
Fukushima: Iwaki 65, 157, "The hōin and the fox" (Hōin sama to kitsune).
Niigata, Sado: MK II 5 39, "Fooled by a fox" (Kitsune ni damasareta hanashi). An itinerant merchant threw a stone at a fox that was taking a nap. The sun set suddenly. He was asked by an old woman at a lonely house to look after it while she was away. He saw a ghost. Next, he fell from a cliff. People working in the field laughed at him.
Nagano, Ina: Mukashibanashi 32, 56, 145, 84, "Hōgen and the fox" (Hōgen sama to kitsune); "The medicine peddler and the fox" (Kusuri uri to kitsune); "The shōya and the fox" (Shōya sama to kitsune), and "I can reach the lowest branch" (Ichino eda ni te ga todoku zo).
Yamanashi, Nishiyatsushiro-gun: Zoku Kai 20, "The fox barber" (Kamisori gitsune).
Fukuoka, Kurate-gun: Fukuoka 105, "Mistaking a rokubu for a fox" (Kitsune to rokubu no machigai).
Chikujo-gun: Fukuoka 235, "A superstition" (Meishin no hanashi).
Mii-gun: Hanashi II 3 103, "The yamabushi" (Yamabushi). This tale may be from *Sorori monogatari*.
Nagasaki, Shimabara: TD II 3 49, "The yamabushi and the badger" (Yamabushi to tanuki); Shimabara 144, "The yamabushi and the badger" (Yamabushi to tanuki).

Further reference:
Sorori monogatari, maki I 409.

195. The Feud Between a Man and a Fox or Badger

Many of these are told as brief anecdotes, but they are left in the form of folk tales.

Okayama, Oku-gun: Okayama bun II 3 70, "The badger" (Tanuki). A man cut the grass away from the badger's hole and said, "It's lighter now, isn't it?" In the evening the badger came to the man's house and said, "Sell the door and let good fortune in." When the man did that, he lost everything. The badger came along and said, "It's lighter now, isn't it?"
Tottori, Iwami-gun: Inpaku dōwa 49, "Lazy Tasuke" (Namake Tasuke).

196. Surprised Twice

This ghost story is told often. It is popular because of the way it is told.

A night school teacher was walking along a road by the edge of a rice field late one winter night and noticed a beautiful girl standing by the road with her face turned down at the book she was reading. He wondered whether she was a ghost and spoke to her. She did not answer but raised her face. He took one look at her face and his hair stood on end. He threw his coat over his head and ran home. He sat down hurriedly at his kotatsu. His wife seemed to think it strange and asked him over and over what had happened. When he told her about the frightful face of the woman, his wife wanted to know what kind of face it was. He could not explain. She asked, "Was it this kind of face?" At that she turned toward her husband and there she was, the woman with the terrible face. He took one look and gave a shout. Then he fainted as he tried to hide in the kotatsu. When he awoke the next morning, the sun was shining brightly on him as he lay face down by the dam in the middle of his field.

Yamanashi Nishiyatsushiro-gun

Yamanashi, Nishiyatsushiro-gun: Kai 280, "The terrible face" (Kowai kao). Example; Zoku kai 243, "The ghost covered with eyes" (Medarake no bakemono).
Aichi: Sanshū Yoko 111, "The god that sets fires" (Hi o tsukeru kami sama).
Tottori: Inpaku min 56, "Oton Jorō."
Shimane: Kyōdo ken II 3 44. No title.
Kumamoto: Amakusa 104, "The big feet" (Ōki na ashi).
　　Tamana-gun: MK I 5 35, 36, "The nose that grew long" (Hana no nagaku naru hanashi) and "The face that grew long" (Kao no nagaku naru hanashi).

Kagoshima: TD III 10 101, "The eyeless demon in Monjuroku" (Monjuroku no menashi oni). In "Was it this kind of face?" by Shimazu
Hisamoto.

Further reference:
Chihō sōdan. Uzen, Yonezawa.

197. Two Mouths, an Upper and a Lower

This could be put with stories of conquest, but the main point is
the amusing look of the ghosts, two badgers disguised as one woman.
The one below yawned.

Iwate: Esashi 130, "The badgers disguised as a woman" (Onna ni baketa
mujina).
Tochigi, Haga-gun, Sakagawa-mura: Shimotsuke 72, "The badger's
failure to disguise" (Tanuki no bake sokonae).
Kanagawa, Tsukui-gun: Sōshū 41, "Foxes" (Kitsune).
Kagawa, Takamatsu: Sanshū Taka 40, "Badgers" (Tanuki no hanashi).
The origin of demon mochi in Okinawa. In some stories the demon
is astonished.

Further reference:
Enshu roku 1 1-u.

198. The Cat and the Squash

A bad cat was killed and buried. A squash sprouted from its eye.
This is a ghost story about poison in the squash. A man who realized it
was saved from death.

Aomori, Sannohe-gun: Tekkiri 251, "The unforgiving cat" (Neko no
shūnen). Boatsmen are connected to this story.
Iwate: Kikimimi 349, "A ghost cat." No. 9, "A ghost cat" (Kaibyō no
hanashi). A cat that said things was killed. After it was buried,
people who ate squash were poisoned. When they looked, they saw
that squash had sprouted from its mouth. Rōō 202, "The origin of
squash" (Kabocha no hajimari). The way it is told is so much like a
katarimono that it must be the work of a bosama.
Fukushima: Iwaki 58, 151, "The cat and the squash" (Neko to kabocha).
Niigata, Minamikanbara-gun: MK I 2 23, "The grateful rooster" (Niwatori no ongaeshi). The medicine peddler of Etchū is in it. There is
influence from tales of exaggeration.

Tochigi, Haga-gun: Shimotsuke 65, "The cat disguised as a squash" (Kabocha ni baketa neko).

Shizuoka, Suchi-gun: Shizuoka 331, "The cat's gratitude" (Neko no ongaeshi).1

Hiroshima, Futami-gun: Geibi 194, "The cat ghost" (Neko bake banashi).

Kumamoto, Tamana-gun: MK I 4 27, "The evil spell cast by a cat" (Neko no tatatta hanashi). It is told as a true story at Yanagawa, Chikugo.

Amakusajima: Amakusa min 141, "The cat's curse" (Neko no tatari). A big squash grew from where a cat was buried after it was killed. When the squash was cut open, a snake came out.

Kagoshima, Okierabu: Okinoerabu 98, "The wife's scheme" (Tsuma no hakarai).

Further reference:

In the story about the wife from the Sky World in Minamitakaku-gun, Nagasaki, 1000 red cows were buried and squash was planted over them. The squash grew to the sky. Perhaps squash were formerly melons, or this is a trend toward humorous tales. The tale is widely distributed. The narrator may be a rokubu because one has a good part in it.

199. The Cat's Secret

A man and a cat and a rooster lived together. They were all 42 years old. The cat told the rooster he wanted to kill the man and become master, himself. The rooster was astonished and crowed with all his might to warn his master. The man only said it was a sign of bad luck and abandoned the rooster in the mountain. A passing medicine peddler heard about it. He put the rooster in his basket and took it back. He suddenly beat the cat to death as it slept. The master was angry until the peddler explained why he did it. When the peddler stopped at that house the next year and inquired, the master said a squash had grown from where he had buried the cat. He said they could eat it that night. The peddler thought it strange. He dug around the roots of the squash and found it had sprouted from the cat's mouth. Everyone was astonished.

Niigata, Minamikanbara, Mitsuke-shi

Aomori: Tsugaru k 27. No title. The story is also in Hachinohe; Tekkiri 252. A note.

Iwate, Hienuki-gun: MK I 11 46, "The cat's dance" (Neko no odori); Kōshō 9 6, "The cat's ballad" (Neko no shinnai katari).

Kamihei-gun: Kikimimi 348, "The ghost cat" No. 7 (Kaibyō no hanashi). The cat's jōruri. A tired traveler picked up a stick from a grave and used it as a staff. When he tapped with it, he heard a cat's voice, but to other people it sounded like a jōruri; Tōno 268, No. 174. No title.

Akita, Kazuno-gun: Dai-ichi 43, "The cat that sang" (Uta o utau neko). **Hiraga-gun, Asamai-machi:** TD IX 11 18, "Kisōji's cat" (Kisōji no neko).

Miyagi: Kyōdo den 1 90, "The ghost cat of Yoneoka" (Yoneoka no kaibyō). This is a legend at Hakken Koji, Yoneoka-mura, Tome-gun. A cat sang one verse of "Yoshitsune Azuma kudari" to an old lady.

Niigata, Minamikanbara-gun: MK I 2 23, "The grateful rooster" (Niwa-tori no ongaeshi). Example.

Okayama, Mitsu-gun: MK I 9 32, "The dancing cat" (Odori neko). The original form of "The cat's jōruri." Its contents can at least be recognized. The old man who cooked rice at a temple found the cat dancing and singing, "When shall I get our priest? Ohiyari-ko-ohiyarihiyari!" The cat was overcome later in a dialogue with the priest.

Ōita, Hayami-gun: MK I 12 45, "The cat that said things" (Mono iu neko). The cat said to the salt peddler, "Everyone here has gone to pick tea." The man was surprised and told the people. When they asked the cat if it had said it, the cat denied it. This is probably older than the story about biting the bride to death. If it turns into that, it becomes a story of adventure.

Kumamoto, Tamana-gun: MK I 4 28, "The cat that sang" (Uta o utatta neko).

Nagasaki: Shimabara 174, "The revenge of the three-colored cat" (Mikeneko no fukushū).

Kagoshima, Kikaijima: Shima I 2 24, 25, "The rooster's gratitude" (Niwatori no ongaeshi). This resembles the example above in Nii-gata. "The cat's gratitude" (Neko no ongaeshi). While the old man was away, the cat danced and sang the song of the Eighth Month for the old woman. When she started to tell about it, the cat fastened its teeth into her throat and killed her. The rest is the usual story.

Further reference:

Chihō sōdan. The muro tree in the northeastern part of Fukushima. The cat recited a gidayū for an old woman in this. Turning a bullet aside with a mirror follows.

Hanashi zuihitsu, ge 61. It is told at Dentōji Nagaiya Osaka-mura, Kahoku-gun, Ishikawa and handed down as happening in Shōō (1652-1655). It says that a fox showed the priest a Noh drama as thanks. The cat was supposed to have a role by playing a flute, but it would not do it because the man knew about it beforehand. The fox's old man would not come after that, etc.

200. The Cat's Jōruri

This can be considered as connected with stories of dancing cats.

Akita, Kazuno-gun: Dai-ichi 43, "The cat that sang" (Uta o utau neko).

A cat sang a song for an old woman who was looking after things while the family was away. Her son insisted on knowing who was singing when he came home. The old woman forgot her promise not to tell. Just when she started to say the cat, it leaped onto her and fastened its teeth into her throat and killed her.

Yamanashi, Nishiyatsushiro-gun: Dai-ni 22, "The cat's Chūshingura" (Neko no Chūshingura).

Further reference:

A tale is handed down about Neko-gami shrine at Kamiosakabe-mura, Atetsu, Bitchū [Okayama]. In the night before an old man and an old woman were going to go to a play, the cat did one for them. They were afraid of it and wanted to kill it the next morning. It ran away and went into a cave in the mountains. People took turns watching, but the cat grew bigger and bigger until it could not get out. It died there. It is worshipped as a cat deity. Its image is stroked and asked for cures. There are many cat deities around there. Cat worship is called Neko gedō.

201. The Fish That Ate Things

While men were talking about putting poison into dango to catch fish, an unknown priest came along and asked them not to do it. He ate the dango and disappeared. They caught a big fish. When they cut it open, they found the dango there.

Miyagi, Karita-gun, Shiroishi: Kyodo den 1 167, "The nushi of the pond" (Numa no nushi). Example.

Yamanashi, Nishiyatsushiro-gun: Zoku Kai 122, "The trout king" (Yamame no ō). A trout disguised as a novice was fed millet and fished up later. There is nothing about his asking them not to catch fish. This must have been changed because it does not follow the general pattern of the story.

Futher reference:

Hitotsume kozō sonota, and others.

13. Humorous Stories: Exaggerations

202. An Exaggeration

The seed of an orange a man swallowed sprouted in his stomach and grew out of his head. When the fruit ripened, children came to pick the fruit. They were such a nuisance that he pulled the tree up. It left a big hole into which rain fell and made a pond. Then the children were a nuisance because they came to fish. The man could not endure them any longer and threw himself into the pond and drowned.

Kagoshima, Kikaijima

The tale in *Nihon dōwa shū* 574 resembles this.

Iwate: Shiwa shū 44, 109, "The horse with soft hoofs" (Tago uma) and "The persimmon tree on his head" (Atama no kaki no ki). All these were created by zatō. Kikimimi 512, "The persimmon on his forehead" (Hitai no kaki no ki).
   Isawa-gun: Isawa.* A tree grew on the forehead of Gorō from Asagi. The latter part began to be told in the Meiji era.
Akita: Ugo 316. No title. When a man jumped from a high pagoda onto a furoshiki held by novices, they bumped their heads and fire came out of their eyes. That set a tree beside them on fire. That was the hinoki a pun on [fire and tree]. The tale goes on into catching sparrows in this region. Refer to that.

Nagano: Chiisagata 282, "The pox" (Kasa no byōki). The bird that a man swallowed fluttered around in his stomach and made him feel bad. He asked a bird catcher to get it. He went in and got it, but he left his sedge hat [kasa] inside. That is how pox [kasa] started.

Hyōgo, Kinosaki-gun: MK II 9 35, "Fūraibō." He was carried away by birds and fell onto Ginzan in Ikuno. He bored a hole through to the yard of an umbrella maker in Osaka. While he was delivering a big umbrella to a certain temple, a big wind came up. It blew him to the roof of Zenkōji in Shinano. When he jumped down, fire came from his eyes and set fire to the temple, burning it completely.

Nagasaki: (Old) Iki 171, "Chōja from a straw" (Warashibe chōja). When the blind old woman tasted the miso, it was so salty that she leaped up and regained her sight.

Kagoshima: Kikai 154, "The tree on the head" (Atama no ki). Example. In tales of exaggeration about unhappiness, there is "Unlucky Sanoya" (Sanoya no fuun).

Further reference:
Kyōdo kenkyū II 4 225.
Nihon dōwa hyōgoku shū, ge 562.

At present tales of exaggeration in most places are usually obscene. Formerly they were of a harmless variety. The following are the names by which they are known: *ōguchi*, the term around Takatō, Shinshū; *ōbanashi*, the term only for obscene stories in some regions; *ōmono*, at Yanai, Suō, for those who amuse themselves with obscene language; *ōmono iu*, at Iwami about using obscene words; *ogatari* at Antōjō, Mogami-gun, Yamagata for sex stories told in an abundance in mountain huts, and *haeanasu*, at Ishinomaki for nonsense stories among which are obscene ones.

203. The Cucumbers in the Sky

Aomori, Hachinohe: MK II 10 20, "The cucumbers in the sky" (Tenjō kyūri). Perhaps this is a variation of the story of the wife from the Sky World, but the gourd sprouted in the corner of the hearth and reached the sky. It is cloe to the story about the man and his dog connected with Tanabata. There is evidence that exaggerations have been developed from episodes in a genuine folk tale.

Kagoshima: Koshiki 108, "The Milky Way" (Ama-no-kawa).

204. The Bean Story

A secondary humorous story. It seems to be found especially in the Tōhoku region.

Aomori: Tsugaru k 25. No title; Tsugaru m 61, "The old man who went down a rat hole" (Nezumi ana sa haitta jiisa no hanashi).
Iwate: Kunohe 484, "Sending bean flour flying" (Kinako o tobashita hanashi). A single bean is found (a point of exaggeration of the first type). It is toasted and pounded and is finally put into the old man's loin cloth. It is sent flying when he breaks wind. This is derived from "Jizō Jōdo," but some such are found in hayamonogatari or exaggerations; Shiwa shū 26, "One bean" (Mameko hitotsu). This is close to a hayamonogatari and it is amusing because it is told like one. On 114 of the same book, "The old man's little hakama" (Jii na no kobakama). Also, Esashi-gun mukashibanashi 51, in which the rhythm of the hayamonogatari is lost. Kikimimi sōshi 200, "The bean story" (Mameko banashi) in which "Jizō Jōdo" and "Rat sutra" are combined; also 564, "The old man and the old woman and the bean flour" (Jii baba to kinako). More than half of the Kakunodate tales are similar.
Akita, Senhoku-gun: Ugo 154. No title. It is an amusing sort resembling a hayamonogatari. Ugo 217, A brief outline. This variation is also an exaggeration. A big bean was picked up on the dirt floor and planted. It reached the sky, etc. Dai-ni 70, "The big bean picked up and given to a rat" (Mameko hirotte nezumiko ni keda hanashi).
Niigata: Sado shū 103, "An exaggeration" (Ōbanashi). There is no doubt about this being performed by a zatō.

205. Rat Sutra

A pious old woman went to a temple to learn a sutra. The priest sat before the altar, his eyes closed, but he could not think of a thing. He happened to open his eyes and see a rat come out cautiously above the altar. He intoned, "On-choro-choro [you go cautiously]." The rat crouched when it heard a voice. The priest intoned, "Sora fukudanda [there you crouch]." Then the rat started to run away. The priest said, "Nigeyō tatte nigashiwasendo [Even if you want to, you can't run away]." In order not to forget this precious sutra, the old woman repeated it over and over all the way home. That night a thief broke in and was moving cautiously around in the work room. The old woman had made such an effort that she was talking in her sleep. "There you go cautiously"—The thief hid in the shadow of the vat. She continued, "There you crouch"—He thought he was in real danger for his life and started to run away. Then the voice, "Even if you want to, you can't run away"—At that the thief tore off at full speed. That is why sutras are precious things to know.

Ōita, Hayami-gun

Aomori, Hachinohe: MK II 11 24, "Rat sutra" (Nezumi kyō). Three brothers are taught the sutra.
Akita, Senhoku-gun: MK I 10 13, "Suddenly turning into a novice"

(Niwaka kozō). A lad who had lost his way was asked by a pious old woman if he knew a sutra. He got her to let him stay the night and put words about a rat he was watching into a sutra and chased off a thief.
Yamagata, Higashitagawa-gun: MK I 11 32, "Buying a future life" (Goshō kau hanashi). An old man and old woman learned the sutra. Even the sound of the bell, kenu, is in the phrase "Nanmaida-kenu."
Niigata, Nakakanbara-gun: MK II 2 47, "The old man who bought a future life" (Goshō kai jii san).
Gifu, Yoshiki-gun: Hidabito V 8 20, "Rat sutra" (Nezumi kyō).
Tottori: Inpaku dōwa 79, "Sorori-sorori Namu-Amida." This is chanted as he watched a frog.
Okayama, Mitsu-gun: MK I 7 36, "The sutra and the thief" (Kyōmon to dorobō). A traveler asked to stay over night and offered to teach his host a sutra. He taught him a rat sutra; Mitsu 89, "The sutra and the thief" (Kyōmon to dorobō).
Fukuoka, Kurate-gun: Fukuoka 73, "The merit of the devout old man" (Shinjin no kudoku).
Ōita, Hayami-gun: MK I 12 44, "Rat sutra" (Nezumi kyō). Example. The title is usual in Kyūshū.
Kumamoto, Amakusajima: MK I 11 45, "Rat sutra" (Nezumi kyō).
Ashikita-gun: MK I 9 46, "Rat sutra" (Nezumi kyō). This "Rat sutra" is found all over the country and is usually told by blind narrators. It can be considered the feat of an imposter.

206. The Origin of the Room

An old woman was delighted because she had taken such a nice bride for her son, but after four or five days the bride began to grow pale. Finally, she lost all her energy. This worried the old woman and she asked the reason. The bride said it was because she was trying to keep from breaking wind. When she was told there was no reason for that, she was relieved and let one go. It was such a violent breeze that it blew the old woman up to the ceiling and scraped the skin off her scalp. When her son came home, the old woman talked it over with him. They decided to send the bride back to her village. When the girl got as far as the edge of the village, she saw children milling around trying to reach persimmons on a tree. She broke wind for them and the persimmons showered down and scattered like a flock of sparrows. As she continued on her way, she came to a river where a boat-load of rice was stuck midstream. The boatmen could not budge it. She said, "I can work it loose with a blast when I break wind." The men said they would give her the load of rice if she could. This time she let a terrific one go and got the rice as agreed. The bride took the rice back to the old woman's house and asked to be allowed to stay. The old woman and her son thought she was a great treasure and kept her. They built a special place where she could go to avoid danger when she was about to break wind. This is how heya [a little house in the yard, now a room, or a place to break wind] originated.

Niigata, Minamikanbara-gun

This is one group of stories about breaking wind developed from "The old bamboo cutter," one of the plots of humorous tales.

Aomori: Tsugaru m 116, "The bride who broke wind" (Yome no he no hanashi).
Hachinohe: MK II 11 25, "The bride" (Hanayomego).
Iwate: Rōō 246, "The origin of the room" (Heya no okori). This resembles the Minamikanbara version, but it is arranged better. It could not have been accomplished except by a professional.
	Shiwa-gun: Shiwa shū 92, "The bride who broke wind" (Heppiri yomego). It is told in detail, but the play on words about the origin of the room is not present. Nōmin 10, "The bride who broke wind" (Heppiri yomego no hanashi); Kikimimi 573, "The bride who broke wind" No. 1 (Heppiri yome).
	Kunohe-gun: Kunohe 577, "The bride who broke wind" (Heppiri yome).
Miyagi, Momoo-gun: Kyōdo den 2 120, "The bride who broke wind" (Heppiri yome).
Tochigi: Haga 1 2, "Seven folk tales" No. 3 (Mukashibanashi nanatsu); Shimotsuke 91, "Breaking wind" (Hōhi dan).
Niigata, Minamikanbara-gun: Kamuhara 138, "The girl who broke wind" (Hekkoki anesa). Example. The persimmons and the boatload of rice are both in the old way. On 147 of the same book is another story, "Who is it?" (Dare da).
Nagano, Shimoina-gun: Mukashibanashi 112, "The bride who broke wind" (Hehiri yome). This is only the first half and has nothing about knocking pears down.
Yamanashi: Kai 154, "The bride who broke wind" (Heppiri yome). There is a shout to hurry and close the place the wind comes from.
Okayama, Mitsu-gun: MK I 11 35, 42, "The bride who broke wind" (Hehiri yome). The same title for both and no conclusion about the room.
Hiroshima: Aki 216, 219, "The old woman who broke wind" (Hekoki baba) and "The bride who broke wind" (Hehiri yome). The bride in the first tale was blown to the ceiling. The second tale is the usual one about the bride breaking wind.
Nagasaki: Shimabara 276, "Imitating the cat" (Neko no mane). In the last part. The Sawata stories of Kyūshū end with the part about being blown to the ceiling. A senbei peddler comes along at the end in some stories. There is a play on words hea geta in the district of Morioka.

207. "Who Is It"

An old man was hired by the head of a neighboring village to scare off robbers because it sounded like dare-ka dare-ka [who is it, who is it] when he broke wind. When a robber started into a place one night, he was surprised to hear dare-ka dare-ka, but presently he realized what it was. He put a plug in to stop the noise. He felt quite safe after that and started off with a 100 ryō box, but stumbled on the plug. It broke loose and a huge dare-ka dare-ka dare-ka broke out. The thief became completely unnerved and threw the box away as he ran off. The old man received a big reward.

Hiroshima

Iwate, Waga-gun, Kurosawajiri-machi: Kikimimi 571, "The guard who broke wind" (Heppiri bannin).
Yamanashi: Zoku Kai 369, "The art of breaking wind" (He gei).
Hiroshima: Aki 221, "Who is it" (Dare da). Example.
Mitsuki-gun: Geibi 76. A note. This is found in many places as an anecdote about an old man who broke wind. He is hired to look after things while the family goes to Kyoto to visit temples and the like. It can be considered as starting from "The old bamboo cutter."

208. Stories about Breaking Wind

"The origin of the Room" and "Who is it" are included.
An old man's stomach bloated because he ate mochi made from buckwheat and oats. He went to sleep with a stopper in, but the pressure blew it out. It killed a wild goose for him.

Aomori, Gonohe

Aomori: Tekkiri 242, "The old man who broke wind" (Hetare jiji). Example.
Yamaguchi, Ōshima: Suō Ōshima 81, "A contest in breaking wind" (He kurabe). There is a story about a match in breaking wind. It resembles tales about strong men. The house was twisted with one blast and straightened up with another. An ax was blown off and it struck the other contestant as he was leaving. The story about swallowing the bird was probably an old humorous story.

209. Rokubei Who Had Occult Sight

There once was a jealous husband who had the habit when he came home of saying, "You, there, I saw what went on. So and so came today, didn't he?" And he was usually right. His wife would say the fortune telling sticks were liars. It happened that ten 1000-ryō boxes were stolen from the castle in Sendai. No matter how much the matter was investigated, nothing was learned. A rumor was heard about the fortune teller Rokubei, and a sedan chair was sent to meet him and bring him there. Since there was no help for it, the man took courage and went along. When they stopped at the border of the region, the head samurai had the place cleared and then addressed Rokubei. He said, "Now, Fortune Teller, if you go ahead, you will probably locate the money boxes, but it is not likely that I can keep my head. I have a request to make of you. Let me keep one box and you can have one, but do not tell that I took them. If you do not agree, I'll take your life right here and now." The man turned pale and agreed. He asked, "Then where are the money boxes?" He was told they were behind the moat of the castle. After he reached Sendai, he set up his fortune sticks. He said, "Two boxes were carried off by a great bandit to the west, but the others are buried. Hurry and dig them up." (The night before, he and the samurai had hurriedly dug up the two boxes.) Workmen were called, and, sure enough, the eight boxes were there. The feudal lord was delighted. He gave one of them to Rokubei as a reward, so he went home with two. His wife said, "I did not realize what a skillful man you were." After that they lived together as a happy pair.

Iwate, Kamihei-gun

Iwate, Kamihei-gun: Kikimimi 135, "The fake fortune teller" (Nise hakke). Example. Getting the extra box of money as thanks was probably made up. Rōō 174, "Rokubei who had occult sight" (Mitō-shi Rokubei). It resembles "Famous for scenting" closely. There are such stories of confessions by thieves. In this one there is nothing about guessing the fire.

Tottori, Hino-gun: Inpaku dōwa 37, "The boy who told fortunes" (Hakke no kozō). He was only fooling when he laid out fortune sticks, but he was sent for advice. He escaped into the mountains from the sedan chair sent for him. He overheard the secret of thieves.

Kagoshima: Koshiki 176, "The fake fortune teller" No. 1 (Nise hakke). Nabeya Shichibei found the golden jar that had been stolen from the palace. This is in the same group as "Seven enemies in one stroke." In Japanese tales it frequently goes with "Famous for scenting." This also seems quite old.

210. Famous for Scenting

The sailor called Magojiee was a very poor man. Before he set out to sea, he said to his wife, "I am coming home on the 15th Day of New Year, so set fire to our house and burn it down on that day." When the boat left the harbor and started back, Magojiee climbed onto the roof of his boat and declared, "It smells as though my house was burning up." His captain said that was a silly thing to say. They made a wager. If the house had burned, the captain would give him his house and everything. When the boat reached the shore, Magojiee's wife came weeping false tears and said their house had burned down. The captain's house was taken from him. The fame of this spread. Somebody came from the feudal lord of Satsuma to confer with Magojiee about the sword he had lost in battle. He worried and did not know what to do. He made sweet wine and offered it to the kami. He drank half of it and fell asleep. The priest there came out and said, "Somebody has drunk half of the wine. It's probably a prank of the fox at Shiroyama. He's the one who took the sword, but if I say so, suspicion will fall upon me. I must remain silent about it." The result was the Magojiee could return the sword, but he begged the feudal lord not to ask him to scent things out any more.

Kagoshima, Koshikijima

This can be said to have come from success stories.

Iwate: Shiwa shū 18, "Famous for scenting" (Hanakiki). A man saw his wife hide red bean mochi and wine while he looked on from the roof beam of the stable. He pretended to scent it and became famous. He was asked by the chōja to scent the cause of his daughter's illness. When somebody came to meet him, he told his wife to set fire to their house at about the time he should arrive there so he could have a good excuse to leave. He spent that night praying to Aomori Gongen. In a revelation he learned that the girl's illness was due to a spell cast by a snake and a frog.
That it was not a chance discovery is probably made up. There are stories in the West about scenting out food. Most of them are tied to stories about secret lovers.

Fukui, Sakai-gun: Nanetsu IV 25, "The tengu's multiplication" (Tengu no kakezan). He said he learned how to multiply from a tengu in the mountains. He guessed where his wife hid something and was asked by the feudal lord for help. The way he climbed into the rafters to hide and watch his wife is like "The wife without a mouth."

Hyōgo, Taki-gun: Minzokugaku II 12 34, "Jotarō" (Jotarō no hanashi).

Shimane, Suchi-gun: TD III 1 19, "Smelling fire in a distant country" (Engoku ni kaji o kagu). About Niemon of Izumi. His wife helped him.

Hiroshima, Saeki-gun: Geibi 55, "Rokubei who smelled things" (Hanakiki

Rokubei). An old woman who peddled cotton and a housewife were enjoying eating things she had been cooking. Somebody threw cotton thread into the cow shed stealthily. Later he scented it out for the housewife. He was called Hana-gami [Nose God]. Another tale resembles the one about Niemon of Izumo. The start is like the example, but he was asked by a yardage peddler to scent out where the hair ornament was that the maid had stolen. He overheard a lame fox later. Aki, 135, "Famous for scenting" (Hanakiki). She scented ohagi and became famous.

Tokushima: Awa Iyayama 1, "Famous for using a weather vane" (Kasami no meijin).

Kagoshima: Koshiki 178, "The fake fortune teller" No.2 (Nise hakke). Example.

Okierabu: Okinoerabu 81, "The child who had occult sight" (Mitōshi dōji). The beginning is a little different, but he learned about where the king's treasure was from the talk of a lame monkey and scented it out. That resembles the story in Hiroshima. He performed a feat without planning it. This continues with "The gun shaped like the character for *he.*"

211. The Lucky New Samurai

Hachibei of Uekiya found the corpse of a samurai in the mountains. He changed clothes with it and suddenly turned into a samurai. He was challenged in a contest. he aimed at things at random the night before and hit a thief. When he fell from his horse during the contest, he happened to land upon a pheasant's nest and caught the bird by hand. He fainted when he went to destroy a demon, but the demon ate Hachibei's parched flour and choked to death. When Hachibei came to, he found that he had succeeded very well. He exhibited many feats of courage.

Fukuoka, Kurate-gun

Iwate: Shiwa shū 51, "Itonaga Shōji of Harima-no-kuni" (Harima-no-kuni no Itonaga Shōji). When three young men were going to marry, they were given horses to ride. One cried, "Kowai [I'm afraid]," but his father-in-law thought he was singing while riding and praised him as a fine man.

Niigata, Minamikanbara-gun: Kamuhara 212. Note No. 88. It is close to the Iki story even to the poison medicine.

Tokushima: Awa Iyayama 16, "A piece of rope" (Hitosuji no nawa).

Fukuoka, Kurate-gun: Fukuoka 76, "Hachibei of Uekiyama" (Uekiyama Hachibei). Example. There is a Kitchomu story, too, about destroying a big snake with wheat flour.

Ōita, Hayami-gun: MK I 12 44, "Killing a snake with oat flour" (Mugiko de hebi taiji shita hanashi). A man who was considered a fool destroyed a snake and was promoted to be a samurai.

Nagasaki: (Old) Iki 218, "Kichigorō who sold grey mullet" (Borauri Kichigorō). The feudal lord promoted him step by step because of brave deeds done by chance. Shimabara 91, "The exploit of Sannen Nebōtarō" (Sannen Nebōtarō no tegara). Sannen Nebōtarō escaped to Satsuma and performed an exploit. No part about seeking marriage. It is strange that he went to Satsuma. An example in Chihō sōdan.

Kagoshima, Kawabe-gun, Kushi: (No source). A man went to Kushi-gō and falsely claimed to be Kamakura Gongorō. He performed many brave deeds there by chance and displayed bravery. In Kagoshima they call him Kamakura Gongorō for some reason. The tale is close to "The brave tailor" [Killing seven of the enemy with one stroke].

The tendency to attach all sorts of episodes to amusing tales is probably a device to prolong them, as in "Rat sutra" and "Who is it?" or in the story of how a gambler frightened off thieves by chance. He called himself Kamakura Gongorō and performed many brave deeds by chance. Refer to "The lucky new samurai." He was fooled into buying a mask of Hannya [God of Wisdom], frightened another gambler away, and got possession of his gold, thus becoming a chōja, (Tsugaru mugashiko 35). There are many such stories. "Seven enemies at one stroke" by Grimm belongs to this group. A story of a chance brave deed is also in "The three sons-in-law." Refer to the discussion of Huet and the folk tale in *Mukashibanashi kenkyū* II 6 12.

212. Catching Sparrows

To catch a lot of sparrows, gather fresh camellia leaves early in the morning and scatter them around. Put a little wine dregs on each and leave them. Sparrows will come and eat the dregs. They will get drunk and go to sleep there. In the meantime, the sun will come out and wilt the leaves. They will curl up and wrap around the sparrows. Then sweep them into a straw sack.

Nagasaki, Shimabara Hantō

Akita: Ugo 57, 279. Notations. Making a nose look like a walnut to catch little birds.

Nagasaki: Shimabara 300, "Catching lots of sparrows" (Suzume o takusan toru hanashi). Example. Also, to catch a lot of pigeons, tie a string onto a bean. A pigeon will eat it and the bean will come out in the droppings. Another pigeon will eat it, and so on until you have them all on a string like a rosary.

Ōita: Bungo kijin 82, "Catching sparrows" (Suzume tori). Catching little birds with wine dregs, persimmon leaves, and acorns. On page 87 of the same book it tells how to see a play for nothing. There is also a method of painting a hand and holding it out for sparrows to light upon, but camellia leaves and a dipper painted black may be considered earlier versions.

213. The Lucky Hunter

When the little son of a poor man became seven years old, the father had to give a celebration for putting a loin cloth onto him. He went into the mountains and shot a badger. While it was thrashing around in pain from the bullet, it dug up a lot of wild yams. The man shot a wild duck and it fell into the water. When the man went in after it, his divided skirt filled with fish. He carried everything home on his back and was able to prepare a great celebration.

Fukuoka, Munakata-gun

This story is also in "The aged bridegroom" of the Mikawa flower festival. It may also accompany "The three sons-in-law."

Iwate: Shiwa shū 12, 5, "Seventeen potatoes" (Nagaimo jūnana hon). The son-in-law who married the oldest daughter had good luck. All kinds of things, one after the other, came to hand. "Kōta of Furukawa" (Furukawa no Kōta). He caught a lot of wild ducks at Kitakamigawa and tied them to his loin cloth. They flew off with him and dropped him onto the Daibutsu temple at Nara. When he jumped down, he burrowed into the ground. From there it becomes the story of "Gengorō's trip to the sky." Isawa*; Nihon dōwa 153, "The lucky hunter" (Kofuku na ryōshi). The form is rather broken. It says it is a story from Bingo, but this is doubtful.

Fukushima, Iwaki-gun: Iwaki 74, "A rabbit, wild yams, and chestnuts" (Usagi to yamaimo to kuri).

Miyagi, Momoo-gun: Kyōdo den 3 119, "The foolish son" (Baka musuko).

Tochigi, Haga-gun: Shimotsuke 87, "A group of short tales" No. 6 (Kobanashi shū).

Chiba, Chōsei-gun, Shigehara-machi: Nansō 99, "The lucky hunter" (Ma no yoi ryōshi); Nihon den 209, "The lucky hunter" (Ma no yoi ryōshi); Techō 89, "The lucky hunter" (Mano yoi ryōshi). He got good game one after another. When he took wild ducks alive, they flew off with him to the top of a pagoda. When he jumped down, fire flashed from his eyes and burned the pagoda to the ground.

Gifu, Yoshiki-gun: Hidabito V 6 8, "The lucky hunter" (Ma no yoi ryōshi). This is close to "The persimmon growing from the forehead."

Yamanashi: Zoku Kai 367, "The great catch" (Sesshō ō atari). He held the gun unsteadily as he fired and the bullets scattered like little birds. He shot all thirteen wild ducks. This is like "The he shaped gun."

Aichi, Kitashidara-gun: Aichi 366, "Shinza, the liar" (Usokoki Shinza).

In this it begins with, "Once I..." but in the Hanamatsuri it is "When the old man went as a bridegroom."

Tokushima: Awa Iyayama 113, "The lucky hunter" (Ma no yoi sesshō nin).

Fukuoka, Kurate-gun: Fukuoka 80, "A story ending in a word play" (Otoshi banashi). After he caught wild ducks by hand, they carried him to the pagoda of Tennōji. When he jumped down, his teeth were broken off and he became hanashi [toothless or story].

Yame-gun: Fukuoka 159, "The lucky hunter" (Ma no yoi ryōshi no hanashi).

Munakata-gun: Fukuoka 212, "The hunter and the loin cloth celebration" (Ryōshi to heko iwai). Example.

Ōita, Kitaamabe-gun: MK I 4 40, "When Tōto went hunting" (Tōta san no ryō).

Naori-gun: Naori 115, "The great hunt" (Tairyō); TD I 3 7, "Kitchyomu" (Kitchyomu dan); Jinbun I 1 143, "A story from Awa-no-kuni" (Awa-no-kuni no hanashi); Bungo kijin 187, "The lucky hunter" (Un no yoi ryōshi no hanashi). This is quite close to the Hikoshichi story of Kuma, but there is no part about flying off in the sky.

Kumamoto, Kuma-gun: MK I 2 39, "When Yazaemon caught a spotted eel" (Yazaemon no madara unagi tori), "Lucky Magozaemon" (Shiawase Magozaemon), "The otter" (Kawauso), "The old man who caught birds" (Tori tori jii), and such.

Further reference:

Nihon dōwa hōgyoku shū, ge (1921 ed.) 513. It is called "Gonbei, the wild duck catcher," but the names Awa and Bingo do not appear.

Kenshō kokin shū, chū, maki 9. Note No. 9. In the part about "Watanohara no Yasojima."

214. Gengorō's Trip to the Sky

Gengorō was sent by his mother to buy eggplant shoots. He paid 100 mon for a single plant, the price set by the old man selling it. He told Gengorō that it was worth it even if it was costly because a single plant would bear hundreds and thousands of eggplants. He planted it in his garden and cultivated it carefully. The plant grew taller and taller until he had to look up to see the top. Lovely purple flowers hung like a cloud on it. Then presently the eggplants formed. When the 7th Day of the Seventh Month came, his mother wanted some eggplants to offer for the Tanabata festival. She asked her son to pick some. He leaned a ladder against the eggplant tree and climbed into it. He climbed and climbed until he reached the Sky. A splendid palace was there. He found a white-haired old man in a beautiful room. The man said, "Thanks to you I am enjoying eggplants every day. Since you have come this far, please stay a while." He called his two lovely girls out and they entertained the young man in many ways. He sat back and enjoyed the feast. The old man was Raijin [Thunder God]. In the evening he wore a tiger skin around his loins. When it was time for evening showers, he invited the young man to go along with him to help. The girls on either side urged him, too, so he accepted the job of making rain. He ran along after the old man who beat the drums and the girls who flashed lightning with mirrors. In the lower world the Tanabata festival was being celebrated at the Chinju shrines. When the rain started, there was great confusion. Presently they came over the young man's village. He thought he would have a little sport with his friends. He asked the old man to beat his drums loudly and the girls to flash their mirrors. The young man had a big laugh over the excitement of his friends. He happened to look at the girls. They were working so hard that their clothes came open and exposed their white legs. He stepped off the cloud and fell down, down to the lower world. There he was impaled on a mulberry branch. The girls above lamented his fate but there was nothing they could do for him. The Thunder God saw how they felt and said, "I am sorry for the young man. I'll never let a bolt of thunder fall again around a mulberry tree." That is why people fasten mulberry branches under the eaves of their homes when it thunders.

Iwate, Esashi-gun

Iwate: Rōō 143, "The cooper's trip to the sky" (Okeya no shōten); Kikimimi 474, "Helping Raijin" (Raijin no tetsudai).
   Esashi-gun: Esashi 33, 96, "The young man who climbed to the Sky to be the son-in-law of Raijin" (Tenjō ni nobotte Raijin no muko to narō to shita musuko no hanashi). Example; "A teakettle lid that flew" (Chagama no futa ga tonda to iu hanashi). A lazy young man who worked for Inazusawa Chōja. The first story belongs to the "Hachikoku Yama" group of tales.
Akita, Kazuno-gun: MK I 3 27, "The mischievous boy" (Itazura kozō).
Nagano: Kitaazumi 2 152. No title. The story starts from one about one bean, but it does not go into the Hachikoku Yama theme. The Kakunodate version goes into the bean story.
Tokushima Miyoshi-gun: MK II 9 39, "The flower city" (Hana no miyako). It is like "Sannen Netarō," but it has something of "A trip to the Sky."
Nagasaki, Minamitakaku-gun: Shimabara 113, 46, "Gengorō's trip to the Sky" (Gengorō to ten nobori) and "The wife from the Sky World" (Tennin nyōbō). In the latter story, the wife from the Sky World told her husband to bury 1000 red cows and to plant squash above them that would reach the Sky. He lacked one cow of enough, so he could not quite reach the Sky. His wife pulled him up. After that there is the episode of making it rain and his falling. There is a version about 999 pairs of straw sandals. That is the ending of the story about the wife from the Sky World on Amami Ōshima.
Ōita, Hayami-gun: MK II 1 44, "Gengorō" (Gengorō no hanashi). Once there was a man named Gengorō who climbed to the Sky and became the helper of Thunder God. He was told to follow him and scatter water with bamboo grass. While he went along sprinkling water, he came over his own village. Since sprinkling with the

bamboo grass was slow, he decided to pour it from the jar. He not only poured a lot, he missed his footing and fell from the cloud. His field was flooded and turned into Lake Biwa. Gengorō turned into a fish.

This may have come from the story about the wife from the Sky World. One wonders why the name Gengorō was used. If it is considered the name of the narrator, there might be some influence from Ōmi in the title.

Further reference:
Huet, 180. A story about climbing a bean to the sky.

215. The Shrimp and the Big Bird

Long ago there was a huge bird. Everybody praised him because he was so big. He became proud. He set out on a pleasure trip to various countries. He got tired flying over the sea and settled onto a pile that was sticking up out of the water. A voice said, "Who is that on my whisker?" It came from an Ise shrimp. When the shrimp heard about the big bird, he said, "There is not likely to be anyone as big as I." He set out on a pleasure trip, too. Along the way he got tired and went into a cave to rest. A voice said, "Who is that in my nostril?" When he looked closely, he saw it was the snout of a great fish. It sneezed and blew the shrimp to a cliff. When the shrimp struck the cliff, his back was bent. That is why one should not be proud of himself.

Ehime, Kitauwa-gun

There has been an interest in a story explaining beginnings.

Aomori: Tekkiri 311, "The proud owl" (Ohho no jiman).

Niigata, Minamiuonuma-gun: MK I 10 39, "The stork, the shrimp, and the turtle" (Kōnotori to ebi to kame).

Nagano: Kitaazumi 2 179, "The origin of hachijō" (Hachijō no yurai). They say the hachijō, the long white paper strip tied to the New Year pine, is there because a great bird comes from Tenjiku to catch men.

Yamanashi: Kai 71, "Seeing the world" (Sekai kenbutsu).

Shizuoka: Shizuoka 447, "Why the shrimp's back is bent" (Ebi no koshi ga magatta wake).

Okayama, Mitsu-gun: MK I 9 29, 30, "Why the shrimp's back is bent" (Ebi no koshi ga magatta wake) and "Comparing sizes" (Ōkii kurabe). Two stories with the latter title.

Yamaguchi, Suō Ōshima: Kōshō 8 9, "Why the shrimp's back is bent" (Ebi no koshi no magatta wake).

Tokushima: Awa Iyayama 86, "Why the shrimp's back is curved" (Ebi no koshi wa naze marui).

Ehime, Kitauwa-gun MK II 3 34, "Why the Ise shrimp's back is bent" (Ise ebi no koshi wa naze magatta ka). Example.

Fukuoka, Kiku-gun: Fukuoka 162, "The crow's trip around the world" (Karasu no sekai kaikoku). A crow, a shrimp, and a stingaree.

Ōita, Kitaamabe-gun: MK I 3 41, "The stork, the shrimp, and the whale" (Kōnotori to ebi to kujira).

Nagasaki: Shimabara 126, "The hawk, the shrimp, and the clam" (Taka to ebi to hamaguri).

Kumamoto, Ashikata-gun: MK I 7 47, "The confusion of the catfish" (Namazu sōdō). The reason that the scars are on the sea slug is to help the catfish is probably wrong.

Kagoshima: Koshiki 202, "The greatest in the sea world" (Umi no sekai ichi).

Kyoto, Hieizan: Nihon den 120, "The big frog" (Ōgaeru). The big frog at Mt. Hiei is perhaps because the shrimp is sure to come out, due to the translation, or it may have been blown out of a nostril to explain the conclusion that its back is bent.

Further reference:
Ikkyū banashi, chū 16
Chōsen mintan shū 302. This has some similarity.

216. Matching Strength

There may have been an original form, but now it is only handed down among tales of exaggeration. One example is the following.

A strong man called Daikoku went from Japan to China to match strength with Dairikibō. Dairikibō's wife came out and said her husband was away, but she invited Daikoku to come in and rest. She picked up a six foot square fire box and set it down by him and left the room. Daikoku was astonished at the woman's strength and wondered what was in store for him when Dairikibō returned. He ran off in a hurry. When Dairikibō returned presently he heard the story from his wife. He went outside to look, but could see not trace of Daikoku. He did not intend to let him get away. He called forth a cloud to ride and reached the seashore in a single leap. Daikoku had boarded a boat and was headed for Japan. Dairikibō reached out with a long metal hook and started to pull the boat back, but Daikoku cut it with a file and escaped. He barely managed to reach Japan and begged for help at the temple of a certain village. The priest there told him to climb into the bucket of the well to hide. While he was there, Dairikibō arrived, riding on the wind, and began to look everywhere for him. He looked into the well and saw Daikoku's reflection below in the water. He shouted, "So, you're hiding in a place like that!" He jumped in with a splash. Daikoku promptly leaped out of the bucket. He broke the stone wall into bits and tossed the rocks into the well. Dairikibō could no longer get out. He was so humilated that even now he occasionally gives his body a shake, causing an earthquake. Daikoku was saved by the priest, and he remained and served the temple for the rest of his life as thanks. That is how the present name daikoku [priest's wife] originated.

Iwate, Shiwa-gun

Aomori: Tsugaru k 6. No title. This is about Daikoku of Japan and Doyō of India.

Iwate: Shiwa 42, "Dairikibō who turned into an earthquake" (Jishin ni natta Dairikibō). Example.

Kamihei-gun: Kikimimi 146, "Ikiai of Nambu and Bunpai of Akita" (Nambu no Ikiai to Akita no Bunpai). They both died. It says nothing about fleeing for home. It is changed into an anecdote.

Fukui, Sakai-gun: MK I 1 31, "Koppai and Nyūdō" (Koppai to Nyūdō).

Ishikawa: Kaga 117, "The young challenger" (Nobori no musuko). Somebody came to match strength with the son, but he was so surprised at the old father's strength that he ran home.

Nomi-gun: Nomi 928, "Fujinuki Kinai."

Yamanashi, Nishiyatsushiro-gun: Zoku Kai, 246, 249, "Niō and Gaō" (Niō to Gaō) and "Niō and Aō" (Niō to Aō). In the first, the wife had great strength. In the second, the strength was in answer to prayers. There was no contest.

Tochigi, Haga-gun: Shimotsuke 59, "Kankurō and Doyōtarō" (Kankurō to Doyōtarō).

Shizuoka, Ibara-gun: Shizuoka 448, "Niō of Nishiyamadera" (Nishiyamadera no Niō).

Wakayama: Muro 54, "Osodagawa" (Osodagawa no hanashi). A strong man came from Awa to match strength, but he was chased home. Perhaps the part about being chased belongs to another group.

Fukuoka, Miyako-gun: Fukuoka 206, "Fudōmyōō and Seimen Kongō" (Fudōmyōō to Seimon Kongō). A little invented, perhaps.

Nagasaki: Shimabara 128, "Niō and Gama" (Niō to Gama).

Kagoshima: Kikai 129, "Rikiō" (Rikiō no hanashi).

Okinawa: Irō 81, No. 103. No title.

Further reference:
Shimabara hantō minwa shū 284. "A contest in breaking wind" (Hehiri kurabe).

217. Fooling Each Other

Fukuoka, Miyako-gun: Fukuoka 124, "Kichigo" (Kichigo banashi). Kichigo of Nakatsu and Kichigo of Kokura fool each other.

Nagasaki: Shimabara 222, "A revenge contest" (Adauchi kyōsō). Two tales. This turns into a rakugo, a popular entertainment even now. The one that was fooled tricked the wife of the other man into becoming a nun.

218. Matching Tricks

Once upon a time three robbers called Sankaku of Kyoto, Sankaku of Echigo, and Sankaku of Edo broke into a wealthy man's house. Before they could steal anything, the three were caught by young men working there. They begged to be set free because they had only barely entered and had stolen nothing, but the young men said there was no point in letting them off. The three then said they would like to exhibit some entertaining tricks in order to be set free. The master of the house agreed to that. They borrowed a bamboo pole and set it up in the yard. Sankaku of Kyoto turned into a kite and perched on its tip. Then Sankaku of Echigo turned into a rat, and Sankaku of Edo turned into a bean. The rat picked up the bean and scrambled to the top of the pole with the bean in his mouth. The kite picked up the rat with its beak and flew off somewhere.

Niigata, Minamikanbara-gun

Aomori, Hachinohe: MK II 10 18, "Using magic" (Mahō tsukai).
Iwate: Shiwa shū 146, "The young man who became a horse" (Uma ni natta wakamono).
Niigata, Minamikanbara-gun: Kamuhara 148, "The three robbers" (Sannin dorobō). Example.
Nagasaki: Shimabara 183, "Dōmo Kōmo" (Dōmo to kōmo). Dōmo and Kōmo were two doctors who cut off each other's head and fastened it on. Then they tried pulling heads together. Shimabara 129, "The kite and the rat" (Tonbi to nezumi).
Kagoshima, Kikaijima: Shima II 492, "Tōzai's magic" (Tōzai no mahō). Matching strength. This shows the relationship between stories about matching ages and those about brothers. They are not well developed in Japan. Those told at present are either translations or they are some that began as humorous tales.

Further reference:
Clouston I 413. The Western example in detail. The tale from Kikaijima and others must be regarded as fragments.

219. Dōmo, Kōmo

These may be humorous stories about matching tricks.
This is about two doctors, Dōmo and Kōmo, comparing cures. First they compared drawing out blisters. Next it was ointment to stick heads back on that had been cut off. Finally they matched strength by pulling each other's head. Both heads came off, and that is why we say dōmo, kōmo when nothing can be done about it.

Fukuoka, Chikujō-gun

Iwate, Kamihei-gun: Rōō 113, "The two gamblers" (Futari no bakuchi uchi).
Niigata, Minamiuonuma-gun: MK I 10 39, "Dōmo to Kōmo; Minamikanbara 186, "Dōmo, Kōmo" (Dōmo to Kōmo).
Yamanashi, Nishiyatsushiro-gun: Zoku Kai 362, "Dōmo, Kōmo" (Dōmo to Kōmo).
Fukuoka, Chikujōgun: Fukuoka 228, "Dōmo, Kōmo" (Dōmo to Kōmo). Example.

220. Matching Boasts

When a man famous for boasting came to challenge another, he was so surprised at the son's skill that he withdrew. This comes from stories about matching tricks and matching strength. It may also be considered as exaggeration.

Aomori, Hachinohe: MK II 11 26, "The boaster's child" (Horafuki no ko).
Iwate Shiwa-gun: Shiwa 215, "Matching boasts" (Tempo kurabe).
　Kamihei-gun: Kikimimi 498, "Boasts" (Tempo).
　Esashi-gun: Kikimimi 116, "Eijikotarō." The baby of a famous boaster in Japan was left in its basket to look after things alone. He made such a big boast that the boaster who had come from China to challenge his father gave up and went away. His mother was so afraid of him that she set him adrift in a stream. He took the Life Needle which was at his house and succeeded in life with it.
Fukushima, Iwaki-gun: Iwaki 82, 162, "Matching boasts" (Tempo kurabe).
Akita, Kakunodate: Ugo 121. A note.
Niigata, Minamiuonuma-gun: MK I 10 39, "A boast" (Tempo katari).
　Minamikanbara-gun: Kamuhara 77, "Comparing boasts" (Tempo shiai).
　Sado: Sado shū 178, "The liar" (Uso tsuki). At the end it turns into "Yakushi in the straw bag."
Ishikawa: Kaga 116, "Matching boasts" (Tempo kurabe). Feudal lords of Owari, Nanbu, and Kishū compare boasts.
Fukuoka, Miyako-gun: Fukuoka 123, 124, "The two Kichigo" (Kichigo futari) and "Kichigo" (Kichigo no hanashi). The first half of the first tale is about the son's boast.
　Kurate-gun: Fukuoka 85, "Blundering in a boast" (Taigen no shikujiri). Perhaps it is borrowed from the story about the baby looking after things alone because it is about a father and his child.
　Asakura-gun: Fukuoka 113, "The impudent child" (Daitan naru kodomo). A fragment.
Nagasaki: Shimabara 285, "Ubachibukurin." This is like is like "Hakurakuten." (Old) Iki 182, "Benkei, a famous man killer" (Benkei wa

hitokiri no meijin). It is gradually turned into the form of an anecdote.
Kagoshima: Kikai 153, "Wagering" (Kuchikake). The first part is a
series of back talk. In the latter half, the child boasted so much
that everyone was astonished and ran away. Adding to a song or
adding to back talk is some kind of a contest. Perhaps the word
hanashi began from the sport with words, capping the one heard
with another. Koshiki 187, "A boast" (Ōba banashi).

Further reference:
Susuharai, Rakugo 879. A man with a long sword. His wife came to
meet him.
Kamuhara yatan 102, "Boasts" (Tempō monogatari).
Huet 143.

221. Matching Exaggerations
Also, "The lie's skin"

This is one form of boasting contests. "What will you do with its
hide?" "Put it on that big drum" "What will you put on the other
side?" "I'll use the skin of that lie." This sort of exchange.

Fukushima, Iwaki-gun: Iwaki 85, "The big radish" (Ōki na daikon no
hanashi).
Niigata, Minamikanbara-gun: Kamuhara 157, "The cow's entrails"
(Gyūchō). A house 40 ri square was built, but the ceiling was so
high that five or six holes were left for geese to fly through. They
wanted to put a roof on, but they could not raise it—and the like.
Ishikawa: Kaga 116, "Matching boasts" (Tempo kurabe). They spread a
huge horse hide over a big orange tree to make an enormous drum.
When they beat it with a long radish, it sounded tem-po, tem-po.
This form seems rather good.
Nagano, Shimoina-gun: Mukashibanashi 62, "Proud of his region" (Okuni
jiman). People from Ise, Mino, and Mikawa boasted of big trees,
big cow hides, and the length of sweet potato vines. The man from
Ōtsu said they used big trees and cow hides to make big drums.
They fastened the drums with the long sweet potato vines.
That sweet potato vines were used makes the tale seem very
old.
Hiroshima: Aki 247, "Exaggerations" (Ōke na hanashi). The one on 251
is about three monkeys trying to see which knew the oldest thing.
It is plainly an adaptation from a priest's sermon.
Fukuoka, Chikujō-gun: Fukuoka 221, "The three travelers" (Sannin no
tabibito). In this the drum was made with the hide of a big cat.
Kagoshima: Kikai 136, "The boasts of three men" (Sannin no hora).

222. Matching Long Lives

Okayama: Mitsu 118, "Matching big things" (Ōkii kurabe).
Nagasaki: Shimabara 28, "When the monkeys gathered chestnuts" (Saru no kuri hiroi). Three monkeys saw one chestnut. The one that was the oldest could have it.

223. Lies

These have developed much as exaggerations, turning out to be a dream at the end of an absurd tale. They are probably older than tales with word plays. Climbing the Sky, Urashima, and such also have some with this ending. The following is a good example.

Iwate, Kamihei-gun: Kikimimi 110, "Extracting oil" (Abura tori). This is exactly the same form as "Kōketsu Palace." A man ran into the house of an old woman to escape. He hid in the straw sack above the fire shelf. When the man thought his pursuer had found him and was about to drag him down to be ground up, it proved to be a dream.
This sort of imagination occurs only in Tōhoku.

224. Matching Laziness

Iwate: Shiwa 70, "The lazy men" (Sekkoki otoko). One man thought it was too much of a bother to take his lunch off his shoulder and one thought it was too burdensome to tie his sedge hat under his chin. He kept his mouth open and his chin down to hold the strings.
Iwasa-gun: Kikimimi 497, "The lazy man" (Kabane yami).
Nagano, Shimoina-gun: Mukashibanashi 45, "The lazy men" (Zokunashi otoko). Exactly the same tale as the one in Shiwa.
Yamanashi, Nishiyatsushiro-gun: Zoku Kai 433, "The two lazy men" (Futari no zukunashi).
Fukuoka, Kurume: Fukuoka 156, "Lazy men meeting" (Bushō no deai). The lunch and the strings on the sedge hat.

Further reference:
"Shima no machi" Anei 5 (1776). (In *Kinsei bungei sōsho* 6.) The story is here.

225. The Silence Match

Ishikawa: Kaga 141, "Three pears" (Mittsu no nashi) and "Wanting
pears" (Nashi hoshiya). The one who did not speak until morning
would get the pears. Even when the thief broke in, they kept
silence.

Aichi, Nagoya: Oshō 89, "The silence" (Mugon no waza no hanashi).

Aki (Hiroshima): Nihon zenkoku 270, "The couple that liked mochi"
(Mochizuki no fūfu). A married couple who liked mochi decided
that the one who did not speak would get it.

Further reference:

Chōsen mintan shū 226.
Mukashibanashi kenkyū I 9 17.
Shasekishū IV 1 o. The silent senior priest.
Clouston II 15.

226. A Treasure Match by Two Chōja

These are probably derived tales.

Yamanashi, Nishiyatsushiro-gun: Kai 284, "Comparing treasures" (Takara kurabe). One chōja had seven storehouses crammed with treasure. The poor man had seven sons to show.

Nagasaki, Ikinoshima: Dai-ichi 85, "Yuriwaka Daijin."

Kagoshima, Kikaijima: Shima II 424, "Child treasures" (Kodakara).

227. Matching Stinginess

Yamanashi, Nishiyatsushiro-gun: Kai 246, 172, "Medicine for numbness"
(Shibire no kusuri) and "Food robber" (Meshi nusubito). It says the
fish were food robbers.

Chikugo (Fukuoka), Mii-gun, Miyanojin-mura: Hanashi II 4 97, "The free
medicine" (Tada no kusuri).

228. Squirming through Questions and Answers

This would be a source for rakugo now, but it likely has a history.

Yamanashi, Nishiyatsushiro-gun: Kai 266, "The priest and his novice" (Oshō to kozō). An ignorant priest and his novice. The clever novice vanquished a visiting priest who came to examine his priest. Zoku Kai 311, 315, "The deaf mute dialogue" (Oshi mondō) and "Squirming through questions and answers" (Konyaku mondō).

Nagasaki: Shimabara 207, "Suddenly becoming a priest" (Niwaka oshō). There are two tales. Stories based upon interesting use of words could be compared internationally. They can not be understood without broad knowledge. Some seem to have been made up, but there seems to have been an earlier form.

Further reference:
Mukashibanashi kenkyū I 9 17, China.
Minakata zuihitsu 232-233.
Chōsen mintan shū 228, App. 37.

229. The Sandals Three Feet Long

These stories are told everywhere. Perhaps they were made up by preaching priests.

Ishikawa: Kaga 67, "The old woman who didn't work" (Shigoto sezu baba). The bride dozed while she spun flax. The old woman was so cross when she saw it that she did not notice her skirt was scorching. Tarō and Jirō who were weaving sandals enjoyed watching her. Their attention was distracted and they made sandals three feet long.

Saitama, Kitaadachi-gun: Kawagoe 120, "A whole family of fools" (Ikka no baka zoroi).

Okayama: Okayama rekishi II 2 14, "A family's bad habits" (Kuse o motsu uchi).

Hiroshima: Geibi 208, "Akirebō."

Yamaguchi, Suō Ōshima: Suō Ōshima 92, "An absent-minded old man and an absent-minded old woman." (Ukkari jii to ukkari baba). It only says that the two were staring at each other, but no story develops. This is humor of a sort, but it needs practice to do it well.

Further reference:
Nihon dōwa shū 6, 8, "The absent-minded boy and the absent-minded girl" (Ukkari otoko to ukkari onna). This may be from an old story book. The idea may have been taken from "The yellow sparrow" or "The praying mantis."

In Bungo (Hiroshima), Jinseki-gun they say "sandals without ears."

230. Three Crying Together

An illiterate old woman and an illiterate samurai. A peddler of parching pans comes along and they all weep together.

Okayama: TD VI 8 73, "Three crying together" (Sannin naki); Mitsu 7, "Three crying together" (Sannin naki).

231. The Doctor and the Sedan Chair

There was a doctor who wanted to be able to ride in a sedan chair. When he got his wish, people along the way mistook him for a corpse, a lunatic, and a sick man. He was unable to enjoy it.

Yamanashi, Nishiyatsushiro-gun: Kai 278, "The sedan chair" (Tōmaru kago). A doctor who insisted upon having a sedan chair sent for him, whatever the kind, got a round Chinese one, the kind used to transport criminals. People passing said, "That must be a dangerous criminal they are carrying." From inside, the doctor shouted angrily, "I'm not a criminal." Next, people said he must be insane. He stuck his head out angrily and glared as he shouted, "See how full of spirit I am." People said that he certainly was far gone. They decided to get out of his way while they could. They ran off. The doctor decided to remain silent. He fastened his curtains securely and made no sound. Then he heard people say there must be a dead man there. The doctor decided never again to get into a sedan chair.

This form is found in rakugo, also. It becomes interesting as parts are added.

Further reference:
Tsurezuregusa. The high-priced priest, Horiike.
Zoku kyūō dōwa 1, *jō* (Izumi 76). About a preaching priest and a sedan chair.

232. The Three Derelicts

There were three friends, a man with blear eyes, one with his head covered with scabs, and one covered with lice. The blear-eyed man was always rubbing his eyes, the one with scabs was always scratching his head, and the lousy man was always shrugging his shoulders and twisting his back. They were laughed at. They talked things over and decided to give up their bad traits once and for all. They sat by the fire warming themselves. They could endure matters at first, but gradually it was difficult. The one with lice could not stand it any longer. He said, "Look, over on that mountain the deer are trailing along like this," and he shook his whole body and scratched the places that itched with his clothes. The blear-eyed man said, "That's right, they are. Before they run away, I'll take my bow and aim, and if they start off, I'll draw like this." He repeatedly pretended to draw a bow and each time he pulled his hand across his eyes. The one with scabs scratched his head and said, "You fellows would feel bad if those deer ran away."

Iwate, Kamihei-gun

Aomori: Tsugaru m 32, "Blear-eyes, Scurvy and Louse-bitten" (Mekusare, Gambe, to Shiramitagare no hanashi).

Iwate, kamihei-gun: Kikimimi 490, "Blear-eyes, Scabby, and Louse-bitten" (Mekusare Shirakumo, Shiramitakari). Example.

Fukushima, Iwaki-gun: Iwaki 75, 160, "The three derelicts" (Sannin katawa).

Hiroshima, Takata-gun: Geibi 190, "The three derelicts" No. 1 (Sannin katawa). There are stories about three men, Blear-eyes, Snotty-nose, and Cripple and one about Mechyahichi, Hanahichi, and Dekimonohichi.

Kagawa, Shishijima: Sanuki SS 132, "The three derelicts" (Sannin katawa). These, too, are stories with gestures. Before they became rakugo, they were told with gestures by zatō.

Further reference:
Kyōgen sanbyakuban shū 378. The rakugo seems to be this with some changes.

233. Wagering on Stopping Bad Habits

Nagano, Kamiina-gun: A report by Mr. Ariga. The story about the three men with bad habits comes close to "The three derelicts." There is also one with two men with bad habits.

Ōita: Bungo kijin 123, "Changing heads" (Kubi no torikae). A man's fault was always to say, "There ain't no such thing." He was told all sorts of things to make him say it.

Further reference:

Seisuishō 5 2040, "I'll give you 100 kan for this advice." An example of not using the character for *hi* [fire]. Examples of rakugo where the word drink or worthless is avoided.

234. The Child with a Long Name

A child with a long name fell into a well. He drowned while his name was being called.

Aomori, Hachinohe: MK II 11 27, "The child with a long name" (Nagai na no kodomo).

Iwate: Shiwa shū 113, "The child with a long name" (Nagai namae no kodomo).

Morioka: Kyōdo ken IV 9 54, "A long name" (Nagai namae no hanashi).

Kamihei-gun: Kikimimi 502, "The long name" (Nagai namae). Two stories.

Tōno: Jinbun I 1 153, "Failing by giving a long name" (Nagai na o tsukete shippai shita hanashi).

Yamagata, Higashitagawa-gun: MK I 8 46; 10 35, "The long name" No. 1 (Nagai namae no hanashi). Both with the same title.

Niigata, Minamikanbara-gun: Kamuhara 103, "The child with a long name" (Nagai na no ko).

Toyama: Kyōdo ken IV 5 56, "The long name" (Nagai na). Also in Kaga. Giving a short name to a stepchild at the same time.

Nagano: Kyōdo ken II 4 23, "A man given a long name" (Nagai na tsukerareta hito). A stepmother gave a long name for meanness, but the feudal lord was attracted especially by it and the boy made a success in life.

Minamiazumi-gun, Yamato-mura: Nihon kayō II 461, "Things sung to children by the kotatsu" (Nyūji o kotatsu no atetsutsu utau mono). It is a nursery song.

Shimoina-gun: Mukashibanashi 89, "The long name" (Nagai namae).

Yamanashi, Nishiyatsushiro-gun: Zoku Kai 434, "The long name" (Nagai namae). For some reason, it is about the child of a well digger.

Tochigi, Haga-gun: Shimotsuke 73, "Medetaya, Ureshiya."

Gifu, Yoshiki-gun: Hidabito V 8 21, "The child with a long name" (Nagai na no ko).

Shimane, Ōchi-gun: Dai-ichi 72, "The child with a long name" (Nagai na no ko).

Hiroshima: Aki 234, 235, "The long name" Nos. 1 and 2 (Nagai na). Both are stories about falling into a well. In the second story there were three children named Ureshi, Medetaya, and Arigataya [Joy, Felicitude, Thanks]. This is probably a variation.

Okayama: Mitsu 35, 86, "The child with a long name" Nos. 1 and 2 (Nagai namae no kodomo). Both with the same title.

Fukuoka, Kiku-gun: Fukuoka 176, "Hikikinokosuke."

Nagasaki: Shimabara 303, "The long name" (Nagai namae); (New) Iki 161, "Long name, short life" (Chōmei no tanmei).

Kagoshima: Koshiki 186, "The child with a long name" (Nagai na no ko).

Further reference:
   Tsuchi no iro V 4.
   Nihon dōwa shū 181.
   Shumi no densetsu 392.
   Shasekishū 9 7 *u.* Humorous stories with long names are already found here. However, nothing is said about falling into a well.
   These tales are from monogatari. It would be profitable to compare these words as well as those in stories about breaking wind. People in old days had a better relish for the sound of words.

235. How the Mole Chose a Son-in-Law

Humorous stories from those about taking a son-in-law. They are in the form of animal stories, but they are really stories about cleverness, exaggerations, and skill with words.

Fukushima Iwaki-gun: Iwaki 183, "When the rat became a bride" (Nezumi no yomeiri).
Niigata, Minamikanbara-gun: Kamuhara 20, "The mole's bride" (Mogura no yome san); MK II 1 37, "The mole's bride" (Moguramochi no yome san).
Nagano, Shimoina-gun: Mukashibanashi 42, "When the rat married" (Nezumi yomeiri).
Kazusa (Chiba): Nihon zenkoku 91, "The stone mason" (Ishikiri shokunin). A stone mason goes back to being a stone mason once more.
Yamaguchi, Suō Ōshima: Suō Ōshima 89, "The cat's name" (Neko no na). Naming a cat.
Fukuoka, Miyako-gun: Fukuoka 216, "The white mole" (Shiroi mogura no hanashi). A white mole chose a son-in-law.

Further reference:
   Nihon dōwa no shin kenkyū 340, Nakata Senpo.
   Shasekishū 88 20 *u.* It is exactly the same as the Shimoina-gun story.
   Shingaku meijisen 259. From *Kazai Yōdo* 6.
   Riyōshū. "The song for Jizō mai" (Jizō mai no uta). Iwate prefecture.
   Rakugo zenshū 765.

236. Kahei's Hoe

A farmer named Kahei got angry when a crow called, "Kahei, Kahei!" But he noticed that he had forgotten his hoe. Then the crow called, "Ahō, ahō [fool, fool]."

                                                    Nagano, Shimoina-gun

Niigata, Minamikanbara-gun: MK I 2 24, "Is it a baby?" (Akago da ka). A humorous tale about a pigeon, a crow, and a sparrow.

Ishikawa: Kaga 100, "Dōmo, Kōmo." When the boy was sent to buy soy sauce, the crows called, "Go go kara, kara [empty five-go bottle]." He got angry and threw his bottle at them. He cried, "It holds one sho [ten go]!"

Nagano, Shimoina-gun: Mukashibanashi 21, 31, 45, "When Kahei forgot his hoe" (Kuwa o wasureta Kahei no hanashi). Example. It is a humorous tale but probably very old. "Widow Okyūsa" (Goke no Okyūsa). A conversation between the widow Okyūsa and a frog. "Naked Jūbei" (Hadaka Jūbei). A story about a gambler and a frog.

Yamanashi, Nishiyatsushiro-gun: Kai 11, "Kaemon's rooster" (Kaemon no niwatori). This is a humorous story centered upon the rooster's voice. However, it would be hard to think of such a story if there were not animal stories close to it or one like the closing part of the Urikohime story.

There was a woodcutter who liked to shoot. He used to set his saw down and spend his time going around with his gun. His rooster would call, "Oteppo, oteppo [gun, gun]," and tell on him. His old mother and his wife scolded him, so he chased the rooster around. The rooster got angry and called the old mother, "Baba, baba, baba [Granny, Granny, Granny]," and it called the wife, "Kaen kaka Kaen kaka [Kaen's wife, Kaen's wife]." They all got mad at the rooster and chased it around the house. They caught it and as they strangled it, it cried, "Kobiki [sawyer]," and died.

Tochigi, Haga-gun: Shimotsuke 89, "A group of short tales" No. 11 (Kobanashi shū).

Fukuoka, Munakata-gun: Fukuoka 36, "The salt peddler and the crow" (Shiouri to karasu).

Asakura-gun: Fukuoka 112, "Matching wits" (Chie kurabe). This is about a fish peddler with a crow, a pigeon, and a bulbul. The crow called, "Kao, kao [let's buy, let's buy]." The pigeon called, "Gorok-ko [five or six pieces]." The bulbul called, "Hiirota, hiirota [picked it up, picked it up]," as it flew off.

It is close to stories about dividing things that are picked up or bathing stories.

Nagasaki: Shimabara 282, "Going out to sell greens" (Na o uri ni yuku hanashi). A foolish son-in-law was mocked by a crow. This could be an old children's story.

237. The Uneasy Old Man

Nagano, Kamiina-gun: A report by Mr. Ariga. Ill omens were heard while a man planted sweet potatoes, beans, and long radishes,

Tochigi, Haga-gun: Shimotsuke 8, "The uneasy old man" (Kinikake jii san). He thought he heard somebody say, "Habakari sama [I'm sorry or only leaves]." He took it as a word of caution and gave up planting long radishes. [While planting seeds, words having a cheerful meaning should used.]

14. Humorous Stories: Profitless Imitation

238. Learning Gained on a Journey
Also, "Red dishes and bleeding"

A man makes mistakes in using all the words he learned on a journey. It is about a letter he wrote a doctor. Words vary in each region, but there is a version of this sort everywhere. A man falls from a tree and bleeds in each (Shuwan shu o shiki). It has been a humorous story since the days of *Seisuishō*.

Aomori: MK II 11 28, "Learning gained on a journey" (Tabi gakumon); Tsugaru m 91, "A chinkararin dose of medicine" (Kusuri ippuku chinkararin).
Iwate, Kamihei-gun: Kikimimi 499, "Kyoto and Osaka words" (Kamigata kotoba).
    Shiwa-gun: Shiwa shū 122, "Red trays and red bowls" (Shuzen shuwan).
Niigata, Minamikanbara-gun: Kamuhara 19. Note No. 4.
    Sado: Sado shū 196, "The dango and untokoshyo" (Dango to untokoshyo).
Ishikawa: Kaga 114, "The Ise shrimp and the torii at Inari" (Ise ebi to Inari o torii).
Nagano: Chiisagata 184, "Climbing a persimmon tree on his way to Kyoto" (Kaki no ki e jōkyō). The words for red bowl and shaking salt appear in this.
    Shimoina-gun: Mukashibanashi 66, "A man from the country who

went to Kyoto and Osaka" (Inaka mono ga kamigata e itta hana-shi).

Yamanashi, Nishiyatsushiro-gun: Zoku Kai 415, 418, "The stupid son" (Baka musuko) and "New words" (Atarashii kotoba).

Mie, Iinami-gun: Nihon zenkoku 35, "Taira no rin." The little errand boy strung together all kinds of words people taught him and sang them.

Hyōgo, Hikami-gun: TD X 11 61, "The pilgrimage of the persimmon tree" (Kaki no ki sankei).

Hiroshima: Geibi 133, "The messenger to the doctor" (Isha tsukai); Aki 203, "The foolish son" No. 3 (Oroka musuko).

Tokushima, Mima-gun: MK II 1 32, "The scholar's letter" (Gakusha no fumi); Awa Iyayama 129, "Learning gained on a journey" (Tabi gakumon).

Fukuoka, Kurate-gun: Fukuoka 103, "What the student studied at Kyoto" (Gakusei jōkyō shite benkyōsu). The tale has been made over, but it uses shuwan.

Saga: TD XII 9 21, 22, "A fool" (Fuukemon san). An example of how something in Seisuishō survives to this day.

Ōita: Bungo kijin 171, "Learning gained on a journey" (Dōchū gaku-mon).

Kagoshima: Kikai 151, "Words from Yamato" (Yamato kotoba). Red things in this are hichirimen [red crepe] and not shuzen shuwan [red tray, red bowl]. This is probably newly introduced.

There is a story added to the Hirabayashi story. By this we can see they belong to the Seiganji style. They always have a letter to a doctor in them.

Further reference:
Ryūteiki (In Nihon zuihitsu taisei I 1 783).

239. Blundering Sōbee

An excitable man set out on a pilgrimage to Ise carrying his lunch, his sword at his side, and his sedge hat and straw sandals tied on firm-ly. He noticed people laughing at him as he went along. He discovered that he had a wooden pestle fastened to his side, his lunch was wrap-ped in his wife's petticoat, the hat on his head was a bamboo basket, and his sandals and leggings were on wrong. There was no help for it. He opened his lunch box only to find he had his wife's wooden pillow. He did nothing but blunder when he gave his offering at the shrine and when he went to the mochi shop. He arrived home in a terrible state, only to make the mistake of going into a neighbor's house instead of his own.

Yamanashi, Nishiyatsushiro-gun

Iwate: Shiwa shū 57, "The flustered man from Senhoku-machi" (Sen-hoku-machi no tontegi).

Akita, Hiraga-gun, Asamai-machi: MK II 3 30, "Watahachi." A man crawled into a straw bag and went to sleep. A thief picked it up and went off with it. He shaved the man's head. The man was surprised when he woke up. He said, "Oh, my house has flown off." When he rubbed his head, he said, "No, this isn't me."

Niigata, Minamikanbara-gun: Kamuhara 161, Note No. 59. About blundering Rokubei.

Nagano: Chiisagata 256, "The excitable man" (Awate mono).
Shimoina-gun: Mukashibanashi 23, 98, "Sosō Sōbee" and "Hyokosu-kabō."

Yamanashi, Nishiyatsushiro-gun: Kai 74, "The excitable man" (Awate mono). Example. On page 77 of the same book there is a story in which somebody asks "Did you meet a furoshiki with a striped man on its back?"

This story seems to be a later invention, but it is heard everywhere. It may be the work of zatō.

Hyōgo, Akaho-gun: Techō 86, "Blundering Sōbee" (Sosō Sōbee).

Izumo (Shimane): Mr. Shimizu.

Ōita: Bungo kijin 255, "Excitable Kitchyomu" (Awate Kitchyomu).

Nagasaki: Shimabara 138, "Turning the long head" (Chōzu o mawasu hanashi).

240. A Slip of the Tongue

This could be considered a variation of humorous stories about elegant phrases.

Kazusa (Chiba): Nansō 99, "The greedy woman" (Yokufuka onna). "Where did the old furoshiki with fifty rolling eyes go carrying the striped old man on his back?" This and the like are improvised from memory. The one on 77 of *Kai mukashibanashi shū* is one such.

"The horse with miso on it" and "The horse dengaku."

241. The Man Who Ate Brewer's Grains

These tales have appeared endlessly since *Seisuishō*.

Ishikawa: Kaga 90, "Chōbei and his wife" (Chōbei fūfu). A friend asked a man who ate brewer's grains how much he drank. He said 300 grains. He was laughed at. His wife told him what to say. The next time he said three *go*. He gave himself away by adding that he ate them toasted.

There is an example of a child saying that straw was bedding.

242. Part of the Song Left Over

A walking ballad singer who goes beyond his house because he has not finished. TD I 3 10, "The candle" (Rōsoku no hanashi). Kitchyomu went beyond his house with a candle in his hand in *Bungo no kijin Kitchyomu san monogatari*. In *Tsuyushin karukuchi banashi* 3 somebody told the man his house was there, but he said that if he went in, some of his song would be left over.

These may be made up, but many are stories about principal characters in humorous tales.

243. Tea-Chestnuts-Persimmons

The rhythm of the words is especially admired and the narrator was probably a professional. They gradually became moral tales. The following is such an example.

The helper at the store was sent to sell vinegar, chestnuts, persimmons, and tea. He was a chap who spoke very fast and ran the words together as he went along—sukkurikakicha. Nobody could make out what he was selling. He returned without selling anything. He was told to say each by itself. This time he called, "Vinegar is vinegar, by itself; chestnuts are chestnuts, by themselves; persimmons are..."

Fukushima Iwaki-gun: Iwaki 85, 163, "Tea-chestnuts-persimmons" (Chakurikaki).

Tochigi, Haga-gun: Shimotsuke 75, "The foolish shop boy" (Baka na bantō).

Ishikawa, Nomigun: MK II 8 37, "The stupid boy" (Bokoi kozō).

Etchū (Toyama): TD III 2 81, "Tea-chestnuts-persimmons" (Chakurikaki no hanashi).

Yamanashi, Nishiyatsushiro-gun: Zoku Kai 440, "Tea-chestnuts-persimmons" (Chakurikaki). Tea's tea; chestnuts' chestnuts; persimmons' persimmons; *bunbu*. These are scattered all over the country, adjusted to local dialect, which makes it seem that somebody carried them around.

Nagano: Chiisagata 186, "Tea-chestnuts-persimmons" (Chakurikaki).

Kagawa, Shōdojima: Shōdojima.[*]

Fukuoka, Kurate-gun: Fukuoka 78, "Fast talk and slow talk" (Hayaguchi to osoguchi).

Munakata-gun: Fukuoka 202, "The stupid son" (Baka musuko); TD I 3 7, "Kitchyomu" (Kitchyomu no hanashi): TD I 11 87, "Shuju of Hinatayama" (Hinatayama Shūjū no hanashi) by Nakata Senpo. Twenty-five stories.

244. Sieves and Old Metal

Yamanashi, Nishiyatsushiro-gun: Zoku-Kai 444, "The tea peddler, the sieve peddler, and the old metal man" (Ochauri to furuiya to furuganeya). The tea peddler called, "New tea, new tea!" The sieve peddler called, "Furui, furui [sieves or it's old]." They began to quarrel as they went along. The old metal buyer came along calling, "Furukane, furukane [old metal or it isn't old]." So they finally decided to go along together, using his call, "Old metal, old metal [it isn't old]."

The tale is carried all over the country, revising for dialect.

245. What the Boiling Kettle Said
"Batsu dialogue," "Butsu stories," or "Gutsu stories"

The boiling rice gruel seemed to say the name of the foolish boy. He sat by it all the time and answered it. Before and after that passage there is a part abut going to meet the priest at the temple, about burning his robes to fire the bath, and holding the butt of the wine bottle, and such additions.

Aomori, Hachinohe: MK II 11 28, "Gutsu" (Gutsu no hanashi).
Iwate, Isawa-gun: Kogane 127, "The boy and sushizuke" (Kozō to sushizuke).
Niigata, Minamikanbara-gun: Echigo Sanjo 121, "Gutsubata" (Gutsubata no hanashi).
Ishikawa: Kaga 14, 16, "The two brothers" (Kyōdai futari). Two stories.
Nagano: Kitaazumi 1 193. No title; Kitaazumi 2 148, "Gutsu" (Gutsu no hanashi).
Tochigi, Haga-gun: Shimotsuke 77, "Guzutarō."
Hida (Gifu), Ōno-gun, Niugawa-mura: Utsushibana 85, "The foolish girl" (Hakuchi no musume no ko). Here it is a foolish daughter.
Hiroshima: Aki 201, 153, "The foolish son" No. 2 (Oroka musuko) and "The priest and his novice" (Oshō to kozō).
Tokushima, Myōsai-gun: MK I 3 37, "Guzu."
    Mima-gun, Iyayama: MK II 1 29, "Butsu" (Butsu o hanashi).
Kōchi: TD V 12 74. No title. The first of 12 humorous stories.
Fukuoka, Kurate-gun: Fukuoka 195, "Butsu" (Butsu no hanashi).
    Munakata-gun: Fukuoka 199, "Butsugata" (Butsugata no hanashi).
    Kurume: Fukuoka 200, "Guzu" (Guzu no hanashi).
Nagasaki: Shimabara 141, "Buttsu and Gwatta" (Buttsu to Gwatta); Gotō 255 "Gutsu."
Kagoshima: Kikai 143, "The foolish son" (Baka musuko). His name was Butsugata. In Kishū it is connected to the story of the former life

of the cuckoo. We can also imagine that the kuwan-kuwan in the story of the priest and his novice came from this butsukata.

In the story of the priest and his novice told in the Kohama district of Fukui, the boy's name was Gutsugarari. He heard the sound from the priest as he warmed wine in the night and got up because he thought he had been called. See *Oshō to kozō* 42.

15. Humorous Stories:
Tales of Foolish Villages

246. A Series of Instructions

This is in the same group as the words of the boiling kettle. In the form of "At such a time say this—." The humor of the series of blunders carries it along. Events are a funeral, a celebration, a fire, a blacksmith, and brawling cows and such.

Iwate, Kamihei-gun: Rōō 240, "The foolish son" (Baka musuko). The sequence in this is a little forced, or the memory is faulty; Kiki-mimi 526, 527, 556, "The gilt screen" (Kin no byōbu), "Receiving things" (Momo morai), and "Horned by the cow" (Ushi no tsuno tsuki).
Shiwa-gun: Shiwa shū 144, "The foolish son" (Baka musuko).
Isawa-gun: Isawa.*
Kunohe-gun: Kunohe 472, "The foolish son-in-law" No. 4 (Baka muko).
Miyagi, Momoo-gun: Kyōdo den 2 121, "The foolish son-in-law" (Baka muko).
Nagano: Chiisagata 216, 178, "Getting braced up" (Ire damashi). The bride instructs the son-in-law. He went into the midst of a dog fight and got his cheek torn off.
Is "ire damashi" a local term for "ire jie" [borrowed wisdom]? "Burned up last night" (Yūbe yaita). A father wrote his business on a piece of paper and gave it to his boy before he set out. Somebody came to call and asked where his father was. The boy felt in

his sleeve and said, "Gone [dead]"; Kamiina 1363, "The foolish son-in-law" (Baka naru muko sama).

Yamanashi, Nishiyatsushiro-gun: Kai 93, "The foolish son" (Baka musuko). This in pretty much detail. There probably were many forms.

Tochigi, Haga-gun: Shimotsuke 76, "The foolish boy" (Baka na kozō).

Wakayama, Arita-gun: Kii 3, "The simpleton" (Ahō na otoko). This is a fragment.

Tottori: Inpaku dōwa 79, "The dangerous ohagi" (Ochii hagi no mochi).

Kagawa: Shōdojima.*

Fukuoka, Ukiha-gun: Fukuoka 153, 196, "Selling fish" (Sakana uri) and "The foolish man" (Oroka na hito).

  Kurate-gun: Fukuoka 203, "The foolish son" (Baka musuko).

Ōita, Kitaamabe-gun: MK I 4 40, "The fool" (Baka no hanashi).

Nagasaki: (New) Iki 107, "The Sechihara story" (Sechihara banashi).

Further reference:

Shumi no densetsu 20. This is in great detail.

Mukashibanashi kenkyū I 9 17. Numerous examples from China.

Mukashibanashi kenkyū II 6 12. "Simple John," a translation from Huet.

247. The Foolish Son-in-Law

Among these are old tales and some new ones. For example, throwing coins at ducks on the pond is like the story about Charcoal-maker Chōja.

Aomori: Tsugaru m 58, "Foolish son-in-law stories" (Baka muko no hanashi). Two tales. A signal by pulling a string, the ohagi were ghosts, and testing the bath water with a pickled radish. [In family style meals hot water is poured into the rice bowl at the end of the meal. It is cooled by dipping a slice of pickle into it].

Iwate, Kamihei-gun: Kikimimi 527, 539, 544, "Getting things" (Mono morai), a series of blunders; "Calling upon the father-in-law" (Shutō rei), oral messages; and "Dango," calling them "untoko," and about signals with a string.

  Shiwa-gun: Shiwa 62, 62, 45, 90, 101, 179, 203, 206, 213, "The New Year's Day call" (Gonenshi); "The pillow" (Makura); "Shooting with a bow and arrow" (Yumiya iri); "The three sons-in-law" (Sannin muko); "Something dangerous" (Okai monko). The mochi was a ghost, ending with the conversation between him and his mother, something not found elsewhere. "The greeting" (Aisatsu), signaling with a string; "Settoko," an exclamation [forgetting the word for dango]; "The ornament for the pillar" (Hashira kakushi); "Pickled greens" (Takanazuke), helped by friends.

  Kunohe-gun: Kunohe 472, "The foolish son-in-law," No. 4 (Baka muko).

Yamagata, Shōnai [the plain around Yonezawa]: Hanashi I 7 67, "Yosaku from the mountains" (Yama no Yosaku). It is a tale about a series of blunders handed down as a story about Yosaku of Tachi-yazawa.

Fukushima, Iwaki-gun Iwaki 176, "The foolish son-in-law" (Baka muko o hanashi). Seven tales.

Niigata, Minamikanbara-gun: Kamuhara 194, "The foolish son-in-law" (Baka muko no hanashi). Five tales. Planting a single grain of millet was thought to be a polite deed. I have not heard of another like this.

Ishikawa: Kaga 81, "The foolish son-in-law" (Baka muko dan). Three tales about instructions. Fuitokosa for dango.

Yamanashi, Nishiyatsushiro-gun: Kai 206, "Memorizing a phrase" (Goi no atama). Three tales. Signaling with a string, rice cakes are ghosts, and oral messages.

Nagano, Shimoina-gun: Mukashibanashi 37, 38, 48, 106, 116, 124, "Knotholes and charms for the protection from fire" (Fushi no ana to hibuse no ofuda); "Untokoshō"; "The son-in-law who paid a sick call" (Omimai ni itta muko dono); "The son-in-law who ate pickled radish in the bath" (Ofuro de takuwan o tabeta muko dono).

Chiisagata-gun: Chiisagata 177, 214, 215, "The charm for fire protection" (Hi no yōjin fuda), "Untokoshō," "Cooling the bath water" (Oyu zamashi), putting a piece of radish into it to cool it.

Kitaazumi-gun: Kitaazumi 1 192. No titles. Knothole, pickled radish in bath water, dango. Kitaazumi 2 151, "Foolish son-in-law stories" (Baka muko no hanashi). Four stories. Dango, the father-in-law's illness, etc.

Tochigi, Haga-gun: Shimotsuke 83, "The foolish son-in-law" (Baka muko sama no hanashi). Six tales. Dango, knotholes, imitating his wife and putting his clothes on wrong, the cake box showing its teeth, the manju's insides came out and it died, the jar of sweet wine.

Wakayama, Ito-gun: Kōshō 10 22, "The foolish man" (Baka jii).

Tottori, Yazu-gun: Inpaku min I 1 17, "The foolish son-in-law" (Baka muko). The dangerous ohagi. Inpaku dōwa 79, "The leaping dango" (Tobikoshi dango).

Hiroshima: Aki 195, 196, 198, "The foolish son-in-law" Nos. 1, 2 and 3 (Oroka muko). Carrying oral messages, testing the bath water with a pickled radish, knotholes.

Fukuoka, Miyako-gun: Fukuoka 191, "The foolish son" (Baka musuko). He went to his bride's village and praised buckwheat blossoms with words to praise chrysanthemums. It looks newly invented.

Munakata-gun: Fukuoka 204, "The foolish son-in-law" (Oroka na muko dono). Respect for the knotholes.

Saga, Kishima-gun: Kōshō 10 17, "The foolish man and the manjū" (Baka jii to manjū).

Nagasaki: Shimabara 261, "The foolish son-in-law" (Baka muko bana-shi). Twelve tales.

Kagoshima, Kimotsuki-gun: MK I 8 9, "Shūjū of Hinatayama" (Hinata-yama no Shūjū no hanashi). The story of the leaping dango is told as a Hinatayama tale. An example of it is also in Kitchyomu stories.

Kikaijima: Shima II 431, "The foolish son-in-law" (Baka muko). Blundering in a series of greetings.

These are freely expanded, probably by professionals. Caution should be used in son-in-law tales because originally they were about what appeared to be a foolish man who turned out splendidly. (Shiwa-gun mukashibanashi 44, 90.) The tales that only tell about his stupid deeds are derived tales. These are close to the story of the three brothers.

248. The Son-in-Law's Oral Instructions

The son-in-law who was trained in what to say when going to his father-in-law's house blundered.

Iwate: Kunohe 471, "The foolish son-in-law" No. 3 (Baka muko). The son-in-law asked a man who was fishing along his way to his father-in-law's place what to say. The man said, "Only this many before breakfast [referring to his catch]."
    This tale comes a little nearer to being a story of good luck. A different man caught fish here, but it may have been told earlier as being about the son-in-law.
Fukushima, Iwaki-gun: Iwaki 178, "The foolish son-in-law" (Baka muko no hanashi).
Hida (Gifu), Ōno-gun, Niugawa-mura: Zoku Hida 129, "When the simpleton attended a funeral" (Baka na otoko no sōshiki maeri).

Further reference:
    Densetsu minwa ko 323. The title "The son-in-law who imitated words" appears.
    Kyōgen ki also has one.
    "Praising the cow" and "The man who can remember only one thing" belong to this group.

249. The Son-in-Law on a String

Iwate: Kunohe 470, "The foolish son-in-law" No. 2 (Baka muko). His bride taught him three phrases for responses. The cat and the loincloth.

250. The Dango Son-in-Law

This should have some connection with "Dango Jōdo."

Iwate: Kunohe 469, "The foolish son-in-law" No. 1 (Baka muko).
Miyagi, Moyoyashi-gun: Kyōdo den 2 117, "The foolish son-in-law" (Baka muko).
 Momoo-gun, Jūgahama: Kyōdo den 1 178, "A certain foolish son-in-law" (Aru baka muko).
Osaka, Minamikawachi-gun: MK I 11 38, "Shichikō and the dango" (Shichikō to dango). It is set apart from foolish son-in-law tales.
Fukuoka, Kurate-gun: Fukuoka 193, "A place called Noma" (Noma to iu tokoro no hanashi).
 Yame-gun: Fukuoka 196, "The fool" (Baka no hanashi).
 Kurume: Fukuoka 197, "The manjū" (Manjū no hanashi); Fukuoka 111 "Chienoyama."
Ōita, Hayami-gun: MK II 1 44, "Rice cakes are ghosts" (Mochi wa bakemono).

251. Rice Cakes are Ghosts

The bride told her husband before they went to pay a call upon her father that mochi meant ghost, so he would not eat too much of it. He really thought it was dangerous and did all sorts of foolish things.

Fukushima, Iwaki-gun: Iwaki 179, "The foolish son-in-law" (Baka muko banashi).
Miyagi, Momoo-gun: Kyōdo den 2 122, "The foolish son-in-law and fukude mochi" (Baka muko to fukude mochi).
Ōita, Hayami-gun, Tateishi: MK II 1 44, "Rice cakes are ghosts" (Mochi wa bakemono). It is told in some detail as a story about a foolish son-in-law at Takachiho in Hyūga. The explanation of the wife becomes rather tedious.

252. The Jar and the Little Stone
"The Stone and the Wine Jar"

Once upon a time when a foolish son-in-law went to visit his father-in-law, the old man had rice cakes covered with sweet bean paste made and set out for a treat. The young man could not get over that sweet taste. After the old man had settled down to sleep, the young man took the opportunity to get the bean paste jar out of the cupboard where he had watched it put. He stuck his head into it and ate his fill. Then he could not get his head out. In the meantime he wanted to go to the privy. While he was crouching there, his father-in-law came along. The old man finished without noticing him, but there was no wood chip handy to use. He picked up a little stone and made it do. He tossed it away when he was through with it. The stone landed on the jar on the son-in-law's head and broke it. The two men talked it over and agreed to say nothing about what they had done. Some time later the two of them were invited to a wedding ceremony at the home of a relative. The father-in-law was urged to sing at the banquet. He started off, "At the margin of the lake the stork and the tortoise" [kame may mean tortoise or a jar]. The son-in-law interrupted him angrily, "You wiped yourself with that stone!" Thus the story came out.

Iwate, Kamihei-gun

This story does not seem to be one that came out naturally. It may be the work of a zatō, but it can be recognized as rather old.

Iwate: Shiwa 217, "The stone and the syrup jar" (Ishi to amegame). It resembles the Kamihei tale.
    Kamihei-gun: Kikimimi 537, "The little song" (Kouta). Example.
Fukushima, Iwaki-gun: Iwaki 176, "The foolish son-in-law" (Baka muko no hanashi).
Gifu: Hidabito IV 10 41, "The man who liked tororo" (Tororozuki no otoko). A man who liked tororo stole the mixing bowl. It got stuck on his head. He hid in the privy. Another man came there and picked up a stone. After he had finished, he tossed it away and it broke the bowl. The two agreed to keep things secret. That ends the story. It is not about a man and his father-in-law.
Hiroshima, Yamagata-gun, Nakano-mura: MK I 12 33, "The foolish son" (Baka na musuko). When the one began his song, "The stork and the tortoise..." the other chimed in, "You wiped yourself with a stone."
Nagasaki: Shimabara 286, "Wiping with a stone" (Ishi de shiri o fuita hanashi). This story depends upon the skill with which it is told. It is like rakugo in this respect. It seems to me it is also in some old book, perhaps *Seisuishō*.

253. Tying the Pillow on

A foolish son-in-law went to make a visit at his father-in-law's house and used a pillow for the first time. It kept slipping away. He tied it to his head with his loincloth. He explained why when it was discovered. One version is that it was the custom in his village and another, that it was a charm for catching pheasants.

Fukushima, Iwaki-gun: Iwaki 177, "Tying the pillow on the head" (Atama o makura ni musubitsuketa hanashi).
Miyagi, Momoo-gun: Kyōdo den 3 118, "The foolish son-in-law" (Baka

muko). The first version. A simple form like this was probably the early version.

Gifu: Hidabito IV 2 21, "Good manners" (Tokoro no sahō). The first form. He talked it over with his friends and they all went with him to stay over night. They all tied their pillows onto their heads with their loincloths to show they did it that way, too.

Inaba (Tottori), Yazu-gun, Saji-mura: Inpaku min I 1 38, "The pillow and the loincloth" (Makura to fundoshi). The second form. However, the telling is rather broken up. That the son-in-law finally came out ahead gives it a different feeling.

In Rikuchū there is an example in which it is combined with chasing a pheasant. In the story in *Shiwa-gun mukashibanashi* 177 it is added to the story of the three sons-in-law (Hachinohe).

254. The Three Sons-in-Law

Three daughters married at the same time. The son-in-law that had difficulties showed up splendidly while the other two lost face. This seems to be the origin of stories about foolish sons-in-law.

Aomori, Hachinohe: MK II 11 29, "The three sons-in-law" (Sannin muko).

Iwate: Shiwa 44, 90, 81 "The boy from Nambu" (Nambu kozō) and "The three sons-in-law" (Sannin muko). Two stories with the second title.

Miyagi, Momoo-gun, Kita-mura: Kyōdo den 1 182, 177, "The three sons-in-law" (Sannin muko). Same titles. A young man from town, one from a village, and one from the hills were taken by their brides to visit their father-in-law. The one from the hills brought no gift. In the night he got up and went to attend to his needs. A bow was hanging there, so he shot an arrow. In the morning two storks were found shot in the yard. The father-in-law asked, "Who did this morning's big deed?" The son-in-law answered that he did. The next night he did something filthy on the porch. The father-in-law asked again, "Who did this morning's big deed?" The men from the town and the village both spoke up and said they did. This is related to the tale about the lucky hunter.

In the other story, the bride of the third son-in-law tried hard to throw stones at wild geese. She hit one and hung it by the front door. She told her husband to say he did it. The rest of the story is like the first. The other sons-in-law look foolish in these.

This story proves that in the old form the foolish son-in-law succeeded.

Further reference:
Tabi to densetsu XIII 7 24, Korea. The youngest of three sisters became the bride of a toad. He entered a contest with the other two and won. The explanation is lacking. This, however, is evidence that

the son-in-law tales among humorous stories branched off from stories
about marriages with a deity.

225. The Foolish Bride

Iwate, Kamihei-gun: Kikimimi 555, "Words using the prefix o" (O tsuke
kotoba) and "Nightingale words" (Uguisu kotoba). The first only
shows skill in hayamonogatari.
Fukushima, Iwaki-gun: Iwaki 179, "The foolish bride" (Baka yome no
hanashi).
Nagasaki: Shimabara 275 276, "Words to say when making a call"
(Yosoiki kotoba) and "Imitating the cat" (Neko no mane). A story
about breaking wind is added to the latter.

256. Wanting to Go as a Bride

This is an example of a kind of irony being carried into farming
districts.

Iwate, Kamihei-gun: Kikimimi 561, "Wanting to go as a bride" (Yome ni
yukitai hanashi) and "Warming hands" (Te aburi). In the first story
the woman was refused because she had bad eyes. She said, "Oh,
look, the red ants and the black ants are wrestling on the mountain over there." This story is also in the Mura no hanashi column
of Okunan shinpō. In the second story, when she was refused
because she was still a child, she came out and said, "Oh, how
cold I am this morning. Even if I'm 19, my hands are cold."

257. The Foolish Village

Stories supposedly about Noma, Masuko, Sawada, Kawatsu, Mokujiri, Sechihara, Gokasho, Akiyama, Toyama, and the like are found in
every region.

Miyagi, Tamatsukuri-gun, Onikōbe: Kyōdo den 2 84, "The Onikōbe
story" (Onikōbe mukashibanashi).
Nagano: Kitaazumi 1 192. No title; TD XII 5 39, "The Masuma stories
of fools" (Masuma no baka banashi) by Oshio Takashi. Foolish village tales are called Masuma stories in Takita-mura, Awa-no-kuni.
There is one among them which resembles kunihiki [pulling an
island across].

Hyōgo, Yōfu-gun: Dai-ichi 68, "Yokoo in Ōya" (Ōya no Yokoo banashi).

Tottori, around Tottori City: Inpaku min I 3 130, "Making a bream fish" (Tai o tsukuru). A Sajiya story; Dai-ni 90, "A fool from Yamashiro" (Yamashiro no baka banashi). Eleven stories. A story about a place beyond Iwakuni in Yamaguchi. Most of these make fun of men who know nothing about the sea. Mokujiri stories make fun of people from Mokujiri. One from the foolish village tales tells about throwing away the insides of a wreath shell because they were said to be intestines. He ate the shell.

Yamaguchi, Toyoura-gun, Tsunojima-mura: (No source). Around here the stories about Kichigo of Nakatsu are famous. Zatō brought the story of Sangorō, the charcoal-maker, and such here. The Noma story.

Fukuoka, Kurate-gun: Fukuoka 193, "A place called Noma" (Noma to iu tokoro no hanashi); Dai-ichi 76, "Chikuzen Noma stories" (Chikuzen Noma banashi) by Ono Gokatsu.

Miyako-gun: Fukuoka 221, "The Sashida story" (Sashida banashi) and "The Sechihara story" (Sechihara banashi).

Buzen (Fukuoka), Chikujō-gun, Kii: Kokugakuin XXXI 4 69, "Changes in the region of Miyako-gun in Buzen" (Buzen no kuni Miyako-gun chikei no hensen). It is said to be a story from Sawada-mura, Miyako-gun, Fukuoka. [This item is not clear.]

Nagasaki: (New) Iki 107, "The Sechihara story" (Sechihara banashi). There is no village with that name on the island, but there is one in Kitamatsuura-gun.

Kagoshima: Shima*, "Hinatayama." There is a story about a little man at Hinatayama; Kikai 142, "Hinatayama." Also, a story in Satsuma called "Shūjū of Nittōzan." Shūjū was said to be a small man like Issun Bōshi. It is handed down as being about Tokuda Tahei (Tokuda Takeemon), an eccentric who was a little man.

The origin of this and others should be explained.

Further reference:
Zoku Minakata zuihitsu 188. It is told about Hiraga Gennai.

258. Mochi in the Bathroom

Blundering at an inn. A country jake ate the rice husks and salt set out in the bathroom. They served rice cakes [shaped like soap] for him at the inn. He watched what others did with soap and washed his face with mochi.

This appears more often as a story about a foolish son-in-law and joined with the story about pickled radish.

Hiroshima: Aki 239, "The mistakes of the country jake" (Inaka mono no shippai).

Kyūshū: Bungo kijin 90, "Washing the face with mochi" (Omochi de senmen). A story exactly like the Sawada story.

Further reference:
  Gūishō, fuku 30, 3 82. It is told as an anecdote.
  Seisuishō II 69. A story here about pickled radish and the bath.

259. "Turn the Long Head Around

A foolish man was told to bring a wash basin [chōzu]. He looked for somebody with a long head [chōzu]. He twisted it around [mawase].

Iwate, Kamihei-gun: Kikimimi 501, "Turning the long head around" (Chōzu mawashi). [Bring water for washing hands.]
Tokushima, Mima-gun Iyayama: MK II 1 31, "Ise Daiyū."
Fukuoka, Miyako-gun: Fukuoka 220, "The Sashida story" No. 4 (Sashida banashi). Fukuoka 233, "The bark of the paper mulberry tree (Kōso no kawa no hanashi). There are one or two Noma stories in this collection.

260. Pulling Screens and Tossing Dumplings

Foolish men from a village went on a journey and gave up trying to handle a screen at the inn.

Fukui, Sakai-gun: Nanetsu II 3 28, "The foolish village" (Oroka mura). A story about trying to do like the village head. He said, "I gave up at noodles to hang on the ears and digging up dango."
Nagano, Chiisagata-gun: Osa 119, No. 10, "Foolish son-in-law" (Baka muko). He came home singing, "I wrapped the noodles around my neck once, threw manjū, slammed screens, and then day dawned."
Chiba, Sanbu-gun, Chiyota-mura: (No source). This story is told as happening at Kawazuyu.
Yamaguchi, Yamashiro: Dai-ni 90, "Stories about a fool from Yamashiro" (Yamashiro no baka banashi). Eleven tales.
Fukuoka: Dai-ichi 76, "Chikuzen Noma tales" (Chikuzen Noma banashi) by Ono Aname.

261. Hanging Noodles on the Ears
"Putting noodles around the neck"

Are rumors about foolish villages derived from tales of the three sons-in-law?

Iwate, Kamihei-gun: Kikimimi 552, "Manjū and noodles" (Manjū to sōmen). Tossing dumplings and hanging noodles around the neck are told as a foolish son-in-law tale.

Toyama: TD III 2 81, "Hanging soba on the ears" (Mimikake soba no hanashi). Also, throwing manjū.

Nagano: Chiisagata 212, "Otsukiyaren." This is in the form of a foolish son-in-law tale about pulling screens.

Yamanashi, Nishiyatsushiro-gun: Kai 239, "Hōren-heiyō." A story about a priest and his novice.

Tokushima, Mima-gun, Iyayama: Awa Iyayama 136, "The simpleton" (Oroka banashi).

Nagasaki, Iki-gun: (Old) Iki 20, "The bag to jump into and putting noodles around the neck" (Tobikomi bukuro to kubikake sōmen).

Further reference:

Seisuishō. Raw "Yajirō" and cooked "Yajirō."

262. Shaking Rice

(No source.) They let a man who is dying listen to the sound of rice being shaken. This is told at Inbi, Minamiamabe-gun, Ōita.

263. Not Celebrating New Year

There is a place name of that sort in Nagato (Yamaguchi), Toyo-ura-gun, Yoshimi and around Murotsu in Suō (Yamaguchi). They do not make mochi there at New Year. It is said that it is because of a curse of a cat that was burned to death. When they make mochi, it is full of cat hairs and not fit to eat.

One version is told as a foolish village tale. Somebody came to sell pine boughs for door decorations two or three days after New Year and could not sell them.

Nagasaki, Ikinoshima: (Old) Iki 9 Note No. 4. This is a note about sending a New Year pine to the Dragon Palace.

These may be early forms, but they make good humorous tales.

264. The Pheasant-Crow

A man went along with a pheasant hung at his side for a sample and asked if anyone wanted to buy a crow. When somebody said he wanted to buy one, he brought out a real crow. He said the other was just for display.

Hyōgo, Yabu-gun, Ōya: Dai-ichi 68, "Yokoo from Ōya" (Ōya no Yokoo banashi). A pheasant and a sparrow.

Tottori, the neighborhood of Tottori City: Inpaku min I 4 194, "The crow and the pheasant" (Karasu to kiji). Three stories about a man from Sajiya. Also, the Kichiemon story in *Tabi to densetsu* I 3. A wild duck and a crow, a viper and a harmless snake, the wreath shell, and such.

    Selling a one-eyed cow by pasting a sign, "One-eyed cow for sale," over its eye. Putting urine into a wine bottle and passing it around, saying it was wine. People drank it. Probably these are offshoots of the pheasant-crow story. Or they may be told as true stories.

265. The Zatō's Eggs

A foolish village tale. It is clearly the work of a zatō and something carried around by one.

Aomori, Hachinohe: MK II 11 30, "The foolish village" (Oroka mura). A zatō spent the night at Kogarumai. When he spread out his mosquito net, they said, "The zatō has set up his nest." He forgot his manjū when he left. They said, "The zatō laid an egg and left."

    There is a story, also, in the neighborhood of Itsukaichi in Musashi that calls a manjū a zatō's egg.

266. Herring Roe

There is a foolish village story in which they think herring roe should be thrown into a bamboo thicket to soften it before it is eaten.

Shiga, Takashima-gun, Kenkuma-mura: MK I 10 47, "Thicket roe" (Yabu no ko).

Fukuoka, Ukina-gun: Fukuoka 152, "The herring roe and the man from the country" (Kazu no ko to inakabito).

267. The Mirror at Matsuyama

This tale has been handed down as a humorous one from the start. It has been restored. The interest is in how people did not know what a mirror was.

Iwate, Hienuki-gun: MK I 11 31, "The mirror and the father" (Kagami to oyaji). No part about a nun arbitrating. It has been clearly constructed by a priest, but the principal characters are a man and his dutiful son. There is a part in which they went to town and said foolish things. Perhaps it is an earlier version of the story of the mirror.

Fukushima, Iwaki-gun: Iwaki 76, 161, "The priest judge" (Bōzu saiban).

Niigata, Minamikanbara-gun: Kamuhara 166, "The nun mediator" (Ama san chūsai). A son who loved his dead father bought a mirror because he thought it was an image of his father. This caused a quarrel with his wife. A nun mediated.

Is there another story added to the Matsuyama mirror story?

Gifu, Yoshiki-gun: Hidabito V 6 7, "The nun judge" (Ama saiban). The story of a filial son goes as far as where the feudal lord gave the man a mirror as a reward.

Tokushima: Awa Iyayama 110, "The mirror at Matsuyama" (Matsuyama kagami).

Nagasaki: Shimabara 139, "The mirror and the quarrel between the husband and wife" (Kagami to fūfu genka). It is in the Gokashō story.

Further reference:

Kyōdo kenkyū II 474; III 282.

Rekishi to kokubungaku No. 27. "Kagami wari okina ekotoba."

Zoku Kyūō dōwa, ge (Izumi 84). A man from a land that did not know mirrors.

Nakata Senpo, *Nihon dōwa no shin kenkyū* 350. The tale is in India, China, and Korea. It has been carried to many countries.

Chōsen mintan shū 364. An added tale.

Hokumu sagen. (In *Taikei koki* 262).

Mukashibanashi kenkyū I 9 17. China.

16. Tales about Birds, Beasts, Plants and Trees

268. The Sparrow's Filial Piety

Long ago the sparrow and the woodpecker were sisters. When word came that their mother was sick and about to die, the sparrow was just blackening her teeth. But she flew off to care for her mother. The woodpecker was putting rouge and powder on. She took time to complete her makeup before setting out. She did not reach her mother when she breathed her last. For this reason the sparrow can always live where people are although she does not have a beautiful appearance. She can eat as much as she needs of their grain. Even if the woodpecker has beautiful colors, she must fly around from early morning, tapping on the bark of trees and barely getting three worms a day. When night comes, she goes into the hollow of a tree and cries because her beak hurts.

Aomori, Tsugaru

Aomori, Higashitsugaru-gun: Tsugaru k. No title.
    Minamitsugaru-gun: TD III 2 32, No. 21. No title. Superstitions about animals in Aomori.
    Sannohe-gun, Higashikami-mura, Akahonai: Okunan (See the item below).
    Sannohe-gun, Hachinohe: MK II 12 52, "The filial sparrow" (Suzume kōkō).
    Sannohe-gun, Gonohe: Tekkiri 212, "The death of Shaka" (Oshaka sama no rinjū). Before the part about the sparrow and the wood-

pecker, the cat caught a rat that had gone for medicine and was delayed. The centipede had to put a straw sandal onto each foot. For this reason they did not arrive in time for Buddha's last breath.

Calling it the death of Shaka instead of the mother is a source of confusion.

Iwate: Kunohe 488, "The sparrow and the woodpecker" (Suzume to kitsutsuki).

Kamihei-gun: Kamihei 144, "The woodpecker" (Kitsutsuki).

Waga-gun: Dōbutsu No. 17.*

Akita, Senhoku-gun: Ugo 43. Briefly outlined.

Fukushima, Iwaki-gun: Iwaki 183, "The sparrow and the woodpecker" (Suzume to kitsutsuki).

Niigata, Nakakanbara-gun: Koshiji I 10 45. No title. See Shō hōkoku.

Kitauonuma-gun: Fushi 3 92, "The woodpecker" (Keratsutsuki).

Minamiuonuma-gun: MK I 10 45, "Shaka, the sparrow, and the cat" (Oshaka sama to suzume to neko).

Ishikawa, Kashima-gun: Ishikawa 980, "The sparrow and the swallow" (Suzume to tsubame).

Enuma-gun: Kaga 113, "The sparrow and the first rice of the harvest" (Suzume to ohatsuho). No part about blackening teeth.

Fukui, Sakai-gun: MK I 8 33, "The food provided for living things" (Ikimono no kuidane). At the last hour of Shaka they went to learn what they should eat. The first to arrive was the sparrow. The last was the woodpecker. The story includes the earthworm that must eat dirt and the snake that eats last.

It is confused with a story of filial piety.

Nagano, Kitaazumi-gun: Otari 123, "The grief of the little bird" (Kotori aware banashi); Kitaazumi 2 160, "The woodpecker" (Kitsutsuki).

Chiisagata-gun: Chiisagata 165, "The sparrow and the swallow" (Suzume to tsubame).

Higashichikuma-gun: (No source). A sparrow and a swallow. The sparrow was rewarded for reaching her mother in time, but in her haste, she kicked her mother's head. That is why she must hop on two feet.

Minamiazumi-gun: Minamiazumi nen 156. No title. The reason the swallow and the cat can not be included in the calendar. No part about the filial sparrow. Could the story about Shaka have been the result of combining it with the story of the filial sparrow?

Shimoina-gun: Mukashibanashi 122, "The swallow and the sparrow" (Tsubame to suzume).

Yamanashi, Nishiyatsushiro-gun: Kai 205, "The sparrow, the swallow, the cat, and the earthworm" (Suzume to tsubame to neko to mimizu).

Tokyo, Kitatama-gun: Minzokugaku II 8 35. No title.

Chiba, Awa-gun: Awa 185, "Hirutori Niō" A legend of Niō, Sekidōji, Maru-mura.

Shizuoka: Shizuoka 378, "The sparrow and the swallow" (Suzume to tsubame). Examples are given from Shizuoka City; Shita-gun; Haibara-gun, Omaezaki; Ogasa-gun, Tōtōmi; Iwate-gun, Sakuma; Hamamatsu; and other places.

Gifu, Yoshiki-gun, Kamitakara-mura: Hidabito IV 11 16, "The sparrow
and the woodpecker" (Suzume to kitsutsuki no hanashi).
  Masuda-gun, Asahi-mura and Takanei: Minzokugaku II 4 163, "The
  sparrow and the woodpecker" (Suzume to terasu).
  Kamo-gun: Minzoku II 4 198, "The sparrow and the woodpecker"
  (Suzume to kitsutsuki no hanashi).
Osaka, Sennan-gun: Kōshō 11 31, "The sparrow and the woodpecker"
(Suzume to totsutsuki). The sparrow was the little brother and the
woodpecker was his big sister. The sparrow flew off with his
sleeves still tied back. The white streak on his neck is the trace
of the sleeve ties.
Wakayama, Tanabe (Nishimuro-gun): Kyōdo ken I 4 46. No title.
Shimane, Matsue: Nihon den 256, "The sparrow" (Suzume).
Yamaguchi, Suō Ōshima: Kōshō 11 17, "The sparrow and the swallow"
(Suzume to tsubame).
Kagawa, Mitoyo-gun, Shishijima: MK II 12 47, "The sparrow and the
seagull" (Suzume to kamome).
Fukuoka: Buzen.*
Kumamoto, Tamana-gun: MK I 2 33, "Shaka, the sparrow, and the swallow" (Oshaka san to suzume to tsubame).
  Yatsushiro-gun: Minzokugaku II 7 44, "The sparrow and the swallow" (Suzume to tsubame).
Kagoshima: Kikai 145, "The sparrow and the kingfisher" (Suzume to
kawasemi). The sparrow and the kingfisher were sisters. The sparrow went at the death of her mother with an unfinished white
cloth she was weaving thrown over her shoulders. The kingfisher
wove a beautiful dress and went off looking splendid. It was the
mother's will that the sparrow would live in the tall storehouse
and eat rice. The unfilial kingfisher would have to eat worms. The
reason the sparrow's neck is white is that it is the trace of the
cloth she wore.
  Instead of a kingfisher, sometimes it is told about a woodpecker
  or a thrush.
Amami Ōshima: MK I 9 21, "The filial sparrow" (Suzume kōkō). When
it went to its dying mother, it put thread around its neck.
  This is related to the story of the earthworm that wore a reel.

Further reference:
  Ainu minzoku kenkyū shiryō I 23. A story about a sparrow and a
woodpecker. It says it was at a time when all the birds had one parent. The sparrow sprinkled tatoo water on its head and went off to
the bedside of the dying mother. It could eat grain even if it was
soiled. The woodpecker could only eat worms.

269. The Cuckoo Brothers

  Long ago there was a mother and her two sons. Shortly after the
elder one was born, he became blind. The mother and the younger
brother went every day to hunt for good things to eat to give the

older brother. Then the mother died. From that time the younger brother ate only shells of nuts, the end of roots of grass, and such things. He gave his brother the good parts. The older brother gradually became suspicious. One day he pecked at his brother's throat and killed him. Suddenly his sight was restored. Only things not fit to eat came out of his brother's throat. He saw nothing of the sort of things he had been eating. He was filled with remorse. He clung to the lifeless body and cried, "Nodo tsukkitta, nodo tsukkitta! [I tore his throat, I tore his throat]." His throat was torn and blood scattered everywhere. The gods could not stand to see that. They told him if he called 1008 times every morning, his brother would probably forgive him. From that time the cuckoo has called nodo tsukkitta yo until his throat gets raw.

Saitama, Chichibu

Aomori, Hachinohe: MK II 12 53, "The cuckoo brothers" (Hototogisu to kyōdai).
Gonohe: Tekkiri 313, "The cuckoo who longed for his little brother" (Otōto koishi no hototogisu).
Iwate, Kunohe-gun: Hōgen do 6 17, "Tales about birds, their songs, and dialect" (Tori no otogibanashi to nakigoe to hōgen to) by Tachibana Shōichi. The bad one was the younger brother. He doubted his older brother over wild yams. The spirit of the older brother became a bird. The younger went in search and turned into a cuckoo. He calls, "Atcha tondetta ka kocha tondetta ka [Did you fly that way did you fly this way]?" That is why the cuckoo calls, "Atcha tondeta [He flew that way]." Kunohe 474, "The cuckoo" (Hototogisu).
Iwate-gun, Hiradate: Nihon den 257, "The cuckoo" (Hototogisu).
Kamihei-gun: Tōno 39 No. 53. No title. There were two cuckoo sisters. The younger was suspicious and killed the older over wild yams. She turned into a bird that called, "Ganko, ganko [potatoes, potatoes]." The older sister turned into a bird that called, "Hōcho kaketa ka [Did you use the butcher knife]?"
Kesen-gun: Hōgen do 8 24. In "Bird legends: Cuckoo stories" No. 1 (Tori no densetsu: hototogisu no hanashi) by Matsuda Iwahei. Two sisters and wild yams. The one who was killed was the older. She became a cuckoo. The younger became a cuckoo, too. In the second, the stepdaughter who was abused by her stepmother cried, "Matchya kita kedo [But I went and waited]!"
Iwate-gun: Kikimimi 415, "The two cuckoos" (Kakkodori to hototogisu). These were sisters. The one who tore the other's stomach open was the older one.
Akita: Ugo 81. No title. There are two stories. In one the younger brother was mean. He doubted his older brother over wild yams. The older one cut his own stomach open to show him. The remorseful younger brother turned into a bird that called, "Hōcho kaketa ka [Did you use the butcher knife]?" In the second story the mother-in-law was mean. She hid the butcher knife to annoy the bride. She made her hunt it. She called, "Hōcho dotcha yatta,

hōcho dotcha yatta [Where did you put the butcher knife, where did you put the butcher knife]?" Finally she turned into a bird.

Neither of these stories can be considered as in the old form, the versions changed according to the bird call.

Yamagata, Kitamurayama-gun: MK II 6 42, "The cuckoo brothers" (Hototogisu to kyōdai). In various regions they say wild yams, but here it is a coarser variety called hodo. The older brother suspected his younger brother and cut his stomach open to see.

Miyagi, Momoo-gun: Kyōdo den 3 110, "The cuckoo" (Hototogisu no hanashi). The younger brother resented his older brother about yams and killed him. As a punishment, he turned into a bird that cried, "Boto saketa boto saketa."

Fukushima: Iwaki 86, 164, "Longing for the younger brother" (Otōto koishi).

Niigata, Kitauonuma-gun: Fushi 3 87, "The cuckoo" (Hototogisu).

Minamikanbara-gun: Kamuhara 73, "The cuckoo" (Hototogisu).

Minamiuonuma-gun: MK I 10 37, "The origin of the cuckoo" (Hototogisu no yurai). The older brother was blind. He killed his younger brother and asked a neighbor to look. He became a bird because of his sin. He cried, "Otōto tsukkitta ka [Did I cut my little brother]?" After he cried that 8008 times, he could eat three worms.

Nakakanbara-gun: Koshiji I 7 40. No title. See *Shō hōhoku.*

Etchū (Toyama): Nihon shū, Jō 9, "The cuckoo brothers" (Hototogisu no kyōdai).

Ishikawa: Ishikawa 980, "The cuckoo" (Hototogisu).

Nagano, Kitaazumi-gun: Otari 126, "The cuckoo" (Hototogisu); Kitaazumi 2 158, "The cuckoo" (Hototogisu). The older brother was blind. It does not say wild yams, but he suspected him about food. He killed his younger brother. Because of his sin, he turned into a bird that had to cry, "Honzon kaketa ka, otōto koishi" [Did you set up the altar? I long for my little brother]" 1000 times every day before he could drink water.

The story at Mima-mura is almost the same. It does not say the elder brother was blind or that he could not drink water.

Kitasaku-gun: Kitasaku 212, "The cuckoo" (Hototogisu no hanashi).

Minamiazumi-gun: Dai-ichi 51, "The cuckoo brothers" (Hototogisu to kyōdai). It says that the brothers turned into birds. The older called, "Otōto koishi [I long for my little brother]," but it is a stepchild story.

Shimoina-gun: Mukashibanashi 140, "The cuckoo" (Hototogisu). The elder was shiftless, not blind.

Saitama, Chichibu, Ōtaki-mura: MK II 3 33, "The cuckoo" (Hototogisu no hanashi). Parent and child. Since from the start they are called cuckoos, is it a variation of the story of their former life?

Kanagawa, Tsukui-gun, Uchigō-mura: Sōshū 59, "The cuckoo" (Hototogisu). In this, too, there was suspicion about wild yams and the older killed the younger. He cried, "Oto nodo tsukkicho [I cut my brother's throat]" 1000 times in the day and 1000 times in the night as he lamented his brother's death. He had no time to hunt for food, and his throat split open and bled. The shrike saw that and pitied him. He stuck worms and fish onto trees for him to eat.

Tokyo, Nishitama-gun, Hinohara-mura: (No source).
> Minamitama-gun, Ongata-mura: Kyōdo ken IV 3 34, "The legend about the cuckoo" (Hototogisu ni tsuite no densetsu) by Nakamura Narifumi.

Chiba: Nansō 107, "The cuckoo" (Hototogisu). An unfilial child killed his father because he was suspicious about food. This is one example that does not say it was brother or sisters.

Shizuoka, Kamo-gun: MK I 9 21, "The cuckoo brothers" (Hototogisu to kyōdai). A complicated example.
> Kamo-gun, Mihama: Shizuoka 356, "The cuckoo" (Hototogisu). The younger brother became a shrike and caught worms for him. This story is also found in the same gun, Shimokawatsu; Fuji-gun, Tagonoura; Shizuoka City; and Iwate-gun, Sakuma.

Mikawa (Aichi): Sanshū Yoko 72, "The cuckoo who doubted his little brother" (Otōto o utagatta hototogisu).

Aichi: _Tōtōmi 39, "The cuckoo" (Token).

Gifu, Ōno-gun, Kamieda-mura: Hidabito IV 11 17, "The cuckoo brothers" (Hototogisu kyōdai).
> Matsuda-gun, Takane-mura: Minzokugaku ken II 4 159, "The cuckoo" (Hototogisu).

Osaka, Sennan-gun: MK II 5 41, "The cuckoo brothers" (Hototogisu no kyōdai).

Hyōgo, Kinosaki-gun: MK II 9 36, "The bird that digs wild yams" (Imohori tori). A child who doubted his father and killed him wanted to drink water. It looked as though it was on fire and he couldn't.

Kagawa, Shōdojima: Dai-ichi 70, "The cuckoo brothers" (Hototogisu to kyōdai).

Ehime, Kitauwa-gun, Shimonami-mura: MK II 3 34, "Deshi koshi" It wasn't brothers, but a priest and his novice. The priest doubted his novice and killed him. He turned himself into a bird and cried, "Deshi koshi [I long for my novice]." The deshikoshi is probably an owl.

Ōita, Usa-gun: Dai-ni 9, "The kappo bird" (Kappo dori). The brother's name was Kappo. Bungo hōgen 3 59, "The cuckoo's call" (Hototogisu no nakigoe).

Nagasaki: (Old) Iki 38, "The cuckoo" (Hototogisu no hanashi). They were cuckoo brothers and the older was blind. The younger suffered because of his brother's grudge and went into a well and died. The older brother got so hungry that he called, "Otōto iru ka, otōto iru ka [Brother, are you there; brother, are you there]?"

Tsushima: TD XII 9 12, "The cuckoo brothers" (Hototogisu kyōdai).

Further reference:
> Manyūjinkoku 428._
> Seiban densetsu shū 413. Many are about brothers or sisters turning into birds, and what they had were yams.
> Unkin zuihitsu (In Nihon zuihitsu taisei II 16). A picture of a shrike impaling a worm.
> Moshigusa. The cuckoo was formerly a shrike, and the shrike was a cuckoo.

270. The Shrike and the Cuckoo

After the little brother of the cuckoo was carried off by the shrike, it flew around calling him. That is why when the cuckoo is around, the shrike does not come out. When the cuckoo goes away, the shrike comes out.

Shizuoka, Suchi-gun: Shizuoka 359, 360, "The cuckoo" (Hototogisu). Two selections. In the first story, the little brother of the cuckoo was caught and eaten by the shrike. That is why the cuckoo calls, "Otōto o kaese, kaese [Give me back, give me back my little brother]." When the cuckoo comes out, the shrike doesn't. In the second story, the shrike killed the little brother of the cuckoo. That is why it calls, "Otōto koishi" [I long for my little brother]. In order to make amends for its sin, the shrike catches little birds and worms and leaves them fastened on trees for the older brother cuckoo.
Iwata-gun: Shizuoka 361, "The cuckoo" (Hototogisu). When the shrike killed the little brother, its elder brother turned into a cuckoo and went around looking for him. He called, "Otōto koi, otōto koi [Come, little brother; come, little brother]." For this reason, when it is time for the cuckoo, the shrike does not come out.

271. The Cuckoo who was a Shoemaker

Long ago the cuckoo was a shoemaker and the shrike was a horse leader. The shrike always got the cuckoo to fasten shoes on his horse, but he never paid his bill. That is why the cuckoo calls, "Kutsu no dai wa dōshita ka [What about the shoe bill]?" When it comes time for the cuckoo to appear, the shrike does not show up. He fastens little worms onto twigs and leaves them to make the cuckoo better natured.

Wakayama, Naka-gun

Wakayama, Naka-gun: Kyōdo ken IV 7 27, "The legend about the cuckoo" (Hototogisu no densetsu). Example. Nihon shū, jō 10, "The cuckoo and the shrike" (Hototogisu to mozu).
Kōchi, Hata-gun: TD IV 6 34. No title.

Further reference:
Karin ryōzaishō (in Zoku gunsho ruijū XVII 215). Yagumo goshō, the part about the shrike.
Kenchū mikkan 19. Changing the names of the shrike and cuckoo. The shrike was formerly the shoemaker.

Shunrai kudenshō (in *Zoku Gunsho ruijū* 14).

Zuinōshō (in *Komei rokuin*).

Zatsuwa shū, chū. Long ago the cuckoo was a man called Sauri. He made shoes and sold them. A man called Hototogisu came and took the shoes, but he did not pay for them. They both died and in the after-life they became birds. Sauri became a cuckoo and Hototogisu became a shrike. Since the former shoe bill was not paid yet, the cuckoo would call, "Kutsu o nase, kutsu o nase [What about the shoes, what about the shoes]?"

Kōdanshō 3. About changing names.

Hannichi kanwa (in *Nihon zuihitsu taisei* I 4 319).

In Iyo the cuckoo is called "kotte dori."

272. The Cuckoo and the Stepchild

A stepchild who was abused by the stepmother turned into a cuc-koo. Refer to "The cuckoo brothers."

Iwate, Kesen-gun, Arisu-mura: Hōgen do 8 26, "The cuckoo." No. 2 (Hototogisu). A stepdaughter went to meet her father in town, but returned without meeting him. She was scolded and she cried. She turned into a bird and called, "Mattacha itta kedo, mattcha itta kedo [But I went to town, but I went to town]."

Nagano, Minamiazumi-gun: Dai-ichi 51, "The cuckoo brothers" (Hototo-gisu kyōdai). Brothers turned into birds.

Further reference:

Hashiwa no wakaba 77.

273. The Cuckoo and the Little Kettle

The reason the cuckoo appears so often in literature is because it appears so often in folk art.

Aomori: Tsugaru k 157. No title.

Iwate, Hienuki-gun: Kōshō 11 4, "The butcher knife bird" (Hōcho dori). The stepmother hated the stepchild and hid the butcher knife. The child's soul cried, "Hōcho todeda ka [Did you take the butcher knife]?"

Further reference:

Fukuro sōshi (in *Zoku Gunsho ruijū* 16, 815).

Hashiwa no wakaba 77. Two brothers. The older was the stepchild. The younger baked something in a little kettle and was eating it alone.

The older brother returned, but the younger one went this way and that because he wanted to eat everything alone. His back split open and he died. His spirit turned into a bird and called, "Atcha to deta kotcha to deta hotto saketa [I went that way, I went this way, he split me open]."

274. A Legging on One Leg

Once upon a time there was a father and his son. He called his son Kakkō. One day when the father came home tired from the mountains, he could not see any sign of Kakkō. He was startled. He was starting to take off his leggings, but he rushed off with one still on. He called. "Kakkō, Kakkō!" He searched around in the hills and valleys, but he could not find him. He searched until he fell exhausted and he turned into that kind of bird. This is the reason one leg of the kakkō is black.

Fukuoka, Tsukushi-gun

Fukushima, Iwaki-gun: Iwaki 87, "The legging on one leg" (Katappo kyahan).

Hiroshima, Saeki-gun: Geibi 136, "The legging on one leg" (Kata ashi kyahan).

Yamaguchi, Suō Ōshima: Kōshō 10 35, "Chōkichi" (Chōkichi no hanashi). He cried, "Chōkichi koi, Chōkichi koi [Come, Chōkichi; come, Chōkichi]."

Fukuoka: Buzen.* This Kappō story is added to "The stepchild and the flute."

Miyako-gun: Kyūshū* 1. They say that the kakkō bird had only one black leg. A hunter whose child was lost went off to look for him with only one legging on, and he turned into a bird. This same story is found in Itojima-gun. Also, in Ōita, Higashikunisaki-gun, Raisan.

Tsukushi-gun: "The legging on one leg" (Kataashi kyahan). MK I 922. Example.

Kumamoto, Tamana-gun: MK I 4 29, "The origin of the kappō bird" (Kappō dori no yurai).

Further reference:

At Marugame they say a father who was looking for his two daughters, Otetsu and Okatsu, turned into a bird calling, "Tetcho, Katcho."

At Yuzubara in Tosa they say feathers grow on one leg and not on the other of the gappō bird.

At Mitsuya, Tega-mura, Shusō-gun, Ehime they say the cuckoo calls, "Suppo, kappo." There is nothing strange about the kappō having one black leg since it is an imaginary bird.

Kōbunko 15 948. A quotation from Onkō mokuroku 13.

Kyōdo kenkyū II 161. The story is found among the Ainu.

275. Yoshi, Toku

Two girls called Yoshi and Toku were lost in a flood. The mother grieved so much that she turned into a bird and even now calls, "Yoshi, Toku."

Hiroshima City: Aki 140, "The owl and Yōshichi" (Fukuro to Yōshichi). A boy named Yōshichi was lost. His mother put black tabi on one foot and a white one on the other and went around the fields and hills looking for him. She died and turned into an owl.
Kagawa, Shōdojima: Dai-ichi 69, "The owl and the sisters" (Fukuro to shimai). On Shōdojima they call the owl yoshitoku. The mother of two girls who were lost turned into an owl after she died. She went around looking for them.
Nagasaki: Gotō 230, "Yoshi, Toku." There is also a story called "Yoshi Tokkappo" in Shimogotō, Fukue-mura kyōdo shi. At Arikawa a bird called yoshika dori, a kind of owl, calls, "Yoshika, kashika." (Old) Iki 39, "The kuokkuō bird" (Kuokkuō dori).

276. The Cuckoo and her Child

Nagano: Kitaazumi 2 159, "The cuckoo" (Hototogisu). A mother asked her child to scratch her back for her. Because he refused, she tried to rub it on a cliff. She fell into a mountain stream and died. The child repented and turned into a cuckoo. It flew around calling, "Kakō, kakō [I'll scratch it, I'll scratch it]."
Chiba: Nansō 107, "The cuckoo" (Kurakko dori). While a woman was weeding her field, an eagle carried off her child. She turned into a bird and flew off, just as she was, with one leg of her overalls on. She called, "Kurakko, Kurakko [Kura's child, Kura's child]."
Kyoto, Minamikuwata-gun: Kuchitanba 96. No title. A cuckoo. It resembles the Nagano story.

277. The Cuckoo and the Stepmother

Iwate, Kamihei-gun: Tōno 38, No. 51. No title.
Yamanashi, Nishiyatsushiro-gun: Kai 57, "The cuckoo" (Kakko dori).
Wakayama, Naka-gun: Dozoku I 2 52, "The cuckoo" (Kakko no mintan).
Kumamoto, Tamana-gun: MK I 4 29, "The origin of the Kappon bird" (Kappon dori no yurai).
Nagasaki: Gotō 230, "Takejo, where did Hachi go?" (Tantan Takejo Hachiya doke ita).

278. The Hunter and his Dogs

A woman went looking for her husband, a hunter, who did not
return. They died apart from each other. Their two dogs, Shiroben and
Kuroben, also, turned into birds. They still call, "Shiroben, Kuroben."
This story is distributed widely from Aizu to Buzen.

Fukushima, Aizu: Hanashi II 6 78, "Mona and Kuna birds" (Mona Kuna
dori); Yachō zakki 94. Mentioned. Two children of a hunter went
into the hills to look for their father. They did not return, but
turned into birds that called, "Mona Kuna." The names of the two
boys were Genshichi and Kuroshichi.
Hiroshima, Saeki-gun: Geibi 38, "Abusing a stepchild" (Mamako ijime).
About Totopo. A boy named Totopo was chased away by his stepmother. He went into the mountains. His father went to look for
him until his strength gave out. He turned into a bird that still
calls, "Totopo."
Buzen (Fukuoka), Kokura: Shin zoku Bashō 421. The cuckoo called
"Ryōshi koishi, Kuro koishi [I long for the hunter; I long for
Kuro]."
Ōita, Hida-gun: Bungo den 119, "Harusato Chōja." A legend about
Harusato Chōja in Gowa-mura, Uchino Karikura. The chōja cut a
big tree in the mountains. He died from the spell it cast. His
family was about to die out. One daughter remained. A brave man
called Kasanotarō from Chikugo brought his two dogs, Koguro and
Makkuro, and saved her. He married her.
Shimoge-gun, Yabakei: Kyōdo ken III 6 48, "The hunter bird at
Yabakei" (Yabakei no ryōshi dori). A girl looking for her father
turned into a bird. She called, "Ryoshi koi, Kuro koi [Come,
hunter; come, Kuro]."

279. The Meadowlark and the Debt

The meadowlark loaned the Sun money. The Sun was successful
later and climbed into the Sky. The meadowlark went up to demand
the money. The Sun said he would only pay the original loan. The
meadowlark came circling down, calling, "Ri toru, ri toru [I'll get
interest, I'll get interest]."

Akita, Kakunodate

Aomori, Minamitsugaru-gun, Takedate-mura: TD III 2 32, No. 13. No
title. The meadowlark was a gambler. He lost 800 to the rat in the
ground during the winter. He paid it back, but the rat said he

didn't. He kept on demanding it. That is why the meadowlark does not stay on the ground, but sings in the sky.

Aomori City environs: Yachō IV 3 5. In "Hearthside tales" (Rohen monogatari) by Wada Senzō. Practically the same as the Minami-tsugaru story.

Kitatsugaru: Tsuchi no ka* (see the item below); Techō 90, "The meadowlark's debt" (Hibari no shakkin).

Hachinohe: MK II 12 55, "The meadowlark and the quail" (Hibari to uzura). The quail was poor at first. He went to the owl to borrow money, but its eyes shone so much that he was afraid. Then he went to the meadowlark and borrowed, but he would not return it. The meadowlark called from high in the sky, "Totekaba toteke [You got the money; you got the money]." The quail cried, "Kuru-shotote kuwae [I was hungry and ate with it]." Another story says the meadowlark borrowed millet from the quail and did not return it. When he received the demand, he cried, "Jūgonichi ka hatsuka jōya, jōya [I will in 15 or 20 days]." The angry quail cried, "Tote kuwae [You got it and ate it]."

Iwate, Hienuki-gun: Kōshō II 4, "The meadowlark and the quail" (Hibari to uzura). The meadowlark loaned the money. The quail suffered and said, "Gugutsuu, gugutsuu." The meadowlark cried, "Shichi toru, me toru, ko toru [I'll take the interest, your woman, your child]."

Akita, Senhoku-gun: Ugo 78. No title. Example.

Shizuoka, Fuji-gun: Shizuoka 382, "The meadowlark" (Hibari). The meadowlark was a gambler. He lost constantly. He hoped each day he could gain a little, but he had no luck. Finally he became a bird that called, "Hi ichi bu, hi ichi bu [One bu a day; one bu a day]."

Ibara-gun: Shizuoka 383, "The meadowlark" (Hibari). The meadow-lark cried, "Awa san to kashita, sa sa yokose, sa yokose [I loaned you three *to* of millet; now, give it back; now give it back]."

Shizuoka City: Shizuoka 383, "The meadowlark" (Hibari). The meadowlark was a loan shark formerly. He cries, "Ri o yokose, moto o yokose [Hand over the interest, hand over the principal]."

Gifu: Hida tori 166, "Interpreting the meadowlark's song" (Hibari no nakigoe no honyaku). It cries, "Hi ichi bu, hi ichi bu [One bu a day, one bu a day]."

Wakayama, Hidaka-gun, Yada-mura: Minzokugaku II 10 26, "Animals that make demands" (Saisoku suru dōbutsu no hanashi) by Minakata Kumakusu. The frog borrowed five to of rice from the meadowlark and would not return it. In the spring the meadowlark demanded one koku [10 times as much]. He cried, "Ri ni ri kuta, ri ni ri kuta [Interest on interest, interest on interest]." The frog said, "Go to, go to [five *to*, five *to*]." The meadowlark continues to fly around and cry.

Ōita: Bungo hōgen III 57, "The call of the meadowlark" (Hibari no nakigoe).

Miyazaki: Hyūga II 226. No title. When the meadowlark demanded the millet he loaned, "Kyō yare, kyō yare [Return it today, return it today]," the quail answered, "Tsuku tsuchi yarō."

Further reference:

Ainu minzokugaku kenkyū shiryō I 26. The one who borrowed was the rat and the one who loaned was a kami in the Sky. He sent the meadowlark to demand the return. The rat said he would return it when the oak leaves fell, but they never fell. The meadowlark circles above them.

Tabi to densetsu IV 6 34. The Ainu say the meadowlark borrowed millet from the quail.

280. The Meadowlark Cowherd

Nagano, Kitaazumi-gun: Otari 125, "The meadowlark" (Hibari). The meadowlark was the boy at the chōja's house who was supposed to water the horse. He forgot and the horse died. He said, "I really did give water to the horse." But it does not say what the cry is.

Hiroshima, Aki-gun, Kamikamakarijima: Aki 142, "The former appearance of the meadowlark" (Hibari no zenshin). When the meadowlark was a man, he looked after cows and horses at a certain house. He was turned into a meadowlark as a punishment for not giving water to the cows and horses. He wants water now, but it seems to be burning and he can not drink it. This is a fragment.

281. The Bird Who Wants Water

There once was a mother and her son. She worried so much because he did not obey her that she became ill. She wanted water, but he would not go for it. He took a burning brand from the hearth and held it out to her. When she saw it, she died. The son was so surprised that he turned into a bird, one that wanted water. When he went to drink, the water burned a bright red and there was no way for him to drink it. He could drink a little at a time when it rained to keep alive. That is why he calls. "Fure, fure [rain, rain]." This bird is a kingfisher.

Saitama, Chichibu-gun

Iwate, Iwate-gun: Kikimimi 412, "The bell ringer bird and the hell bird" (Kaneuchi dori to jigoku dori). The first part is the "Nukabuku, Komebuku" story. The stepdaughter brought the final water to her dying mother and grieved for her. She turned into a bird that rings a bell. The real daughter did not come at her mother's last moments. Her throat became sore and she cried she wanted water to drink. She turned into a bird that is red from its throat to its breast and died. She is the hell bird.

Saitama, Chichibu-gun, Ōtaki-mura: MK II 3 33, "Rain, rain" (Fure, fure). Example.

Kanagawa, Tsukui-gun: Sōshū 62, "The bird that wants water" (Mizu koi dori). Some call this bird the horse dealer's wife to explain its origin.

Shizuoka, Abe-gun, Ōkawa-mura: Shizuoka 387, "The bird that begs for water" (Mizu kou dori). Because she only spent time to make up her face during her mother's great illness, she became a bird that can only drink rain water.

Suchi-gun: Shizuoka 388. An unfilial child who disobeys is reborn into a bird that can drink only one drop in a thousand that rains. The same story is in Iwata-gun.

Shita-gun: Shizuoka 388. It is called a biidoro bird. The story is about the blind older brother who doubted his younger brother. His cry is, "Ame fure, ame fure [Fall, rain; fall, rain]."

282. Ten or Eleven Persimmons

A stepmother put ten persimmons into a cupboard and went off somewhere on an errand. When she returned and went to the cupboard, there were ten persimmons there, but she said she had left eleven. She accused her stepchild of eating one. The girl tried to explain, but she would not listen. She insisted there should be eleven and scolded the girl severely. The stepchild could not recall anything of the sort. She repeated ten persimmons until she turned into a bird that cried, "Kaki tō, kaki tō [ten persimmons, ten persimmons]." The stepmother insisted there were eleven until she, too, became a bird and called, "Jūichi, jūichi [eleven, eleven].

Yamanashi, Nishiyatsushiro-gun

Yamanashi, Nishiyatsushiro-gun: Zoku Kai 3, "Ten or eleven persimmons" (Kaki tō to jūichi). Example. Kai 58, "Ten persimmons" (Kaiki ton). A persimmon peddler sold ten to a young girl whose mother was away and said she would pay later. He left ten for her, but when he came later, he demanded payment for eleven. The girl kept saying, "Tō da, tōda [ten, ten]." She turned into a bird with that cry. The peddler turned into a bird that cried, "Ojūichi, ojūichi [eleven, eleven]."

The explanation about the kakiton bird may be a later addition, but the tale is connected to lending and borrowing. The jūichi bird is the broad-billed roller. The cuckoo would be the kakiton. Is it?

Gifu, Yoshiki-gun, Kamitakara-mura: Hidabito IV 11 18, "Goki ton." The story is close to Okiku Sarayashiki. A bowl from a set was hidden and missing when it was time to prepare for a special celebration in the family. The maid who had been a favorite until then worried so much that she turned into a bird that cried, "Goki ton, goki ton [ten bowls, ten bowls]." This version seems older, but it is not about a mother and child.

Gunma, Agatsuma-gun, Kuni-mura: Jōmo III 7 19. A note. A mother lost her child who was eleven years old. She turned into a bird and cried, "Jūichi, jūichi [eleven, eleven]." Now that is the real name of a bird.

283. The Unfilial Kite

Once upon a time there was a mother kite and her son. No matter what the mother said, he would do the opposite. She thought she must do something to reform him. When it was time for her to die, she called her son to her and asked that he hold her funeral when it rained. The son became very sad and decided that although he had disobeyed his mother when she was alive, he would now do as she wished. He held the service when it rained. Now when it rains, he recalls his mother and he cries, "Piiyoro, piiyoro."

Shimane, Yatsuka-gun

There are also stories about a frog and a pigeon as well as the kite. The mother asks to be buried in the sandbar of the river.

Fukushima, Iwaki-gun: Iwaki 88, 166, "The unfilial kite" (Oya fukō na tonbi no hanashi).

Ishikawa: Ishikawa 980, "The unfilial pigeon" (Hato no fukō).
    Kashima-gun, Nanao: Dai-ni 9, "Tetepoppo." This is a story about a wild pigeon.

Nagano: Chiisagta 178, "Honest once in his life" (Isshō ichido shōjiki). A story about a father and son.

Chiba: Nansō 106, "The tree frog" (Amagaeru).

Shizuoka, Ogasa-gun: Shizuoka 377, "The kite" (Tobi).
    Hamana-gun: Shizuoka 378, "The kite" (tobi).
    Iwata-gun: Tōtōmi 41. The corpse of the kite's mother was in the sea and he could not get it. He cried, "Uminhiyō, uminhiyō [Sea, dry up: sea, dry up]."

Kyoto, Kitakuwata-gun: Kuchitanba 94. No title.

Hyōgo, Kinosaki-gun: Dai-ichi 66, "The filial kite" (Tobi o kōkō).

Shimane, Yatsuka-gun: MK II 1 33, "The unfilial kite" (Tobi fukō) Example.

Ōita, Hida-gun, Karita: Kōshō 11 32, "The unfilial child type of story" (Konshi ifu kei no hanashi) by Miyatake Shōsō; Bungo den 114, "The girl who turned to stone" (Ishi ni natta musume). A legend about a stone at Takata-machi. It might also be considered an amanojaku tale.

Kumamoto, Tamana-gun: MK I 4 28, "The frog was unfilial" (Kaeru wa oya fukō mono).

Nagasaki, Kitakaku-gun, Isahaya: Kōshō 9 7, "The unfilial tree frog" (Oya fukō na amagaeru).
Kagoshima: Kikai 146, "The filial tree frog" (Amayaku no kōkō). The amayaku is a tree frog.
Okinawa: Nantō 21, "A tree frog" (Amagaku no hanashi).

Further reference:
Minakata zuihitsu 339.
Yūyō zassō zoku shū 4. About the Konshi barrow in Konmei [lake]. It is also noted in *Kodama zoku shū.*
Chōsen mintan shū 55. An unfilial tree frog.
Zoku Hakubutsu shi 9.

284. The Unfilial Tree Frog

In the same group as "The unfilial kite."

Iwate, Iwate-gun: Kikimimi 410, "The blue magpie" (Nagao dori). That it does not tell of the parent's request is an omission.
Okinawa: Nantō 21, 38, "The tree frog" (Amagaku no hanashi) and "The filial tree frog" (Kōkō na amagaku).

285. The Unfilial Pigeon

About the pigeon's cry. He did not take food to his father, and grieved because his father starved to death. He turned into a bird.

Aomori, Sannohe-gun: MK II 12 53, "The unfilial pigeon" (Hato no fukō). The father set out to do spading. The child saw little fish in the stream and gave them the flour he should have taken to his father. He arrived too late, for his father had starved to death. The child turned into a pigeon.
Iwate, Iwate-gun: Kikimimi 407, "The pigeon" (Hato). During the famine year a child played along the way when he was taking flour to his father. He arrived too late, for his father had starved to death. The child turned into a pigeon and called, "Tete kokee [Eat the flour, father]." He calls this 4808 times a day.
Ishikawa, Noto (Kashima-gun): Nihon shū, jō 8, "The pigeon's filial piety" (Hato no kōkō).

286. The Bird Who Begs for Water

Because a boy did not give water to the horse, he turned into a bird and called, "Mizu hoshii, mizu hoshii [I want water, I want water]."

Yamanashi, Nishiyatsushiro-gun: Zoku Kai 5, "The bird who begs for water" (Mizugoi dori). The wife of a horse dealer did not water the horses, and she turned into this kind of bird. It does not say the horse died.
Gifu, Yoshiki-gun: Hidabito IV 11 18, "The bird who begs for water" (Mizugoi dori).

287. The Pigeon and his Parent

The same group as "The Unfilial Kite."

Iwate: Kunohe 476, "The unfilial frog" (Oya fukō na kaeru). This is an unfilial frog instead of a pigeon. When his parent died, he did something according to his parent's request for the first time by making the grave in the sandbar of the river. When it rains, he worries and cries for fear the grave will wash away.
Akita, Senhoku-gun: Ugo 72. A brief outline of the story. While the husband was working on the far side of the river, a great flood came. He could not return. His wife turned into a bird and called before rainfall, "Dede cho koi, dede cho koi [Husband, come today; husband, come today]."
Osaka, Kitakawachi-gun: Kinki I 1 55, "The unfilial cuckoo" (Kakkō fukō). A father asked his son to scratch his back, but his son did not want to. He scratched it with his feet. After his father died, he turned into a bird and cried, "Ima nara kakō, ima nara kakō [Now, I'll scratch it; now, I'll scratch it]." This bird lives on fruit growing on cliffs.
Hyōgo, Kinosaki-gun: MK II 9 36, "The potato-digger bird" (Imohori dori). The potato-digger bird was suspicious of his father and split his stomach open to see what he ate. Since he turned into a bird that calls, "Waō, waō," he may be a blue pigeon.
Kumamoto, Aso-gun: Minzokugaku IV 7 43, "The chochumi bird" (Chochumi dori). A child named Chochumi disobeyed his father and did not water the cow. He died and turned into a chochumi bird. When it flies up from the river, it cries, "Ki-ki-ki-ki-ki," and when it descends, it makes a sound like the river, "Gōwa, gōwa." It is always beside the river and calls at the time wild magnolias bloom. This may have been combined with the story of the amanojaku that buried a cow in the bank of the stream and worried when it rained for fear it would wash away. Or it may have formerly been about a bird that begged for water.

Further reference:
At Gokashō in Higo they say the bird that wants water was formerly an unfilial child.

288. The Owl Dyer

Long ago the crow was a dyer. In those days the kite was pure white, a splendid bird, but he was in danger because he could be seen so easily by men. He went to the crow dyer and asked to have his feathers dyed. The kite got angry when it was finished. He complained, "See what a dirty color you dyed my feathers." He would not pay the bill. Even now, when the crow meets the kite, he shouts angrily at him to pay the bill.

Nagasaki, Ikinoshima

Aomori, Hachinohe: MK II 12 55, "The owl dyer" (Fukurō konya).
Sannohe-gun, Hashikami-mura, Akahonai: Okunan.* See the item below.
Sannohe-gun, Gonohe: Tekkiri 311, "The owl dyer" (Ōho no konya). The owl was the dyer. The eagle, the pheasant and his wife, the woodpecker, the sparrow, the pigeon, and others are explained in detail. Finally, the crow came and asked to be dyed the very best color. The owl thought that was mean and dyed him black. That is why the crow picks on the owl if it comes out in the daytime.
Iwate: Kunohe 483, "The owl and the crow" (Fukurō to karasu).
Hienuki-gun: Kōshō 11 4, "The kite and the crow" (Tobi to karasu). The kite was the dyer. The crow came and asked to be dyed to look better than anybody else. The kite dyed him coal black. When the crow came to see, he did not like it. That is the reason they are not friends.
Iwate-gun, Tairadate: Nihon den 255, "The owl and the crow" (Fukurō to karasu).
Waga-gun: Dōbutsu 17.* A kite dyer. The crow came and asked that his coat be dyed the best color in the world. He didn't like the black it was dyed and asked that it be dyed once more to his former white. He is forever chasing the kite and calling, "Kingorō, the kite, fooled me, kaa."
Iwate-gun: Kikimimi 417, "The crow and the kite" (Karasu to tobi). The kite was the dyer. He was so busy that he finally dyed the crow dark blue all over to get it done.
Akita, Senhoku-gun: Ugo 77. This mentions the owl dyer.
Fukushima, Iwaki-gun: Iwaki 184, "Why the crow is black" (Karasu no kuroi wake).
Nagano, Kitaazumi-gun: MK II 10 19, "The owl dyer" (Fukurō konya). The owl comes out only at night because he is afraid of the crow.

Otari 124, "The owl and the crow" (Fukurō to karasu). The story is the same as the above.

Shizuoka, Abe-gun: Shizuoka 384. No title. In the section about birds. The crow was a dandy. He was so fussy about the color of his clothes that he finally decided he wanted them dyed with all the colors. That is why he was dyed black.

Gifu, Yoshiki-gun, Kamitakara-mura: Hidabito IV 11 16, "The owl dyer" (Fukurō konya). The crow was angry because he said there was a mistake in the dying.

Kyoto, Minamikuwata-gun: Kuchitanba 95. No title. An owl dyer.

Nagasaki: (New) Iki 115, "The kite who does not pay his dyer bill!" (Some dai o harawanu tobi). Example. In this the crow was the dyer.

Further reference:
Tōtōmi dōshiyō shū 40, "Crow, crow, Kanzaburō! Don't forget the kindness of the dyer." [A poem.]

289. The Reed Thrush and the Straw Sandal

Before the reed thrush was a bird, it was the sandal porter at Dogyōji. He was scolded for losing one high clog and even now goes around looking for it. He turned into a bird that calls, "Dogyōji, Dogyōji, are you going to take my head for one high clog? If you're going to cut it off, cut it off!"

Iwate

Iwate: Kunohe 474, "The meadowlark, the quail, and the reed thrush" (Hibari to uzura to yoshikiri). A quail borrowed sandals from the lark and lost one. The reed thrush helped him. The lark attacked the quail, but it hid in the grass. The reed thrush called the lark mean. It said, "Gya-gyaji, gya-gyaji, what's a single straw sandal!" **Hienuki-gun:** Dōbutsu 17.* When the man lost one of his master's sandals, the priest told him to look in the reeds. He cried, "The priest at Tongyōji told me." In this the original form is reflected in the name of the temple. Kōshō 11 3, "The reed thrush" (Yoshikiri). Example.
Kamihei-gun: Kamihei 153, "The reed thrush" (Yoshikiri dori). The maid at the inn lost the sandals of a samurai. He slashed her and she ran to the stream to wash her cuts. In another tale a lewd girl got her seat cut by reeds. She cried, "Shiri kitta [my seat's cut]!" Is the girl in the first story an influence from the latter one?

Akita, Senhoku-gun: Ugo 23. Mentioned. Karagarasu was a servant at Jōkōji. He was chased out because he lost one of the sandals of the priest. He still hates that priest and calls, "Jōkōji, Jōkōji, keekeyashi keekeyashi." Perhaps this song was longer formerly and said something about sandals.

Further reference:
Ainu minzoku kenkyū shiryō I 19.

290. The Wren, King of Birds

Long ago many kinds of birds gathered together and were enjoying a drinking bout when a wren came along and asked to join them. The hawks made fun of him. They said that if he wanted to join them, he should go and take a wild boar. If he got one, he could join them. The wren promptly flew off into the ear of a wild boar that was sleeping in a thicket. The startled boar jumped up and rushed off. The wren hopped around in its ear and hurt it so much that it circled around madly and finally struck its head on the corner of a cliff and died. With that, the wren went back with a great swagger and joined the drinking bout. The bald eagle felt he should not be outdone. He flew off and found two wild boar running together. He clutched them both at the same time, one with his left talons and one with his right. The boar ran off in different directions, splitting the greedy hawk into two.

Harima (Hyōgo)

Examples of this tale are found in many regions. It belongs to stories about gatherings in society.

Iwate, Kamihei-gun: Kikimimi 420, "The wren" (Misosazai). The same story is in Minzoku I 790 and Jinbun I 1 154.
Kanagawa, Tsukui-gun, Uchigōmura: Sōshū 61, "The wren" (Misosazai).
Aichi, Kitashidara-gun: TD II 1 22, "The wren" (Chyonnosuzume).
Gifu: Minzokugaku II 936. No title.
Osaka, Sennan-gun: Kōshō 10 28, "The wren's feather" (Misosazai no hane).
Harima (Hyōgo): Nihon shū, jō 14, "The wren counted among the hawks" (Misosazai mo taka nakama). Example.
Wakayama: Kii 8, "The hawk and the wren" (Taka to misosazai). A story about the wren who perched on a branch and saved a hawk caught in a crevice. And how the hawk tried to imitate the wren that got into the ear of the wild boar.
There are many other stories about the exploits of this bird.
Tokushima: Awa Iyayama 124, 134, "The wren and the hawks" (Misosazai to taka) and "The wren, king of birds" (Misosazai wa tori no ō).

Further reference:
Huet 15, "The wren and the goose."

291. When the Earthworm and the Snake Traded Eyes

Long ago the earthworm had eyes, but a poor voice. The frog had no eyes, but a good voice. One day the frog asked the earthworm to trade his eyes. The earthworm asked how to do it. The frog said that it would be best to ask the Moon to trade them. The Moon agreed quickly enough, but because the frog had made such an unreasonable request, he deliberately put the frog's eyes on his back.

Fukui, Sakai-gun

Iwate: Kunohe 480, "The snake and the earthworm" (Hebi to mimizu). The earthworm is called singing maid, and so forth.

Fukui, Sakai-gun: MK I 1 32, "The earthworm's eyes" (Mimizu no me). Example.

Nagano, Shimoina-gun: Mukashibanashi 112, "The snake and the earthworm" (Hebi to mimizu). It is said that since it did not use its eyes, it would prefer to have a good voice. The last part of the story is missing. Is it a story about origins?

Tochigi, Shimotsuga-gun: Haga I 2. The fifth of seven tales.

Saitama, Kitakatsushika-gun: Satte 21, "The mole cricket" (Kera).

Tokyo, Kitatama-gun, Hōya: Minzokugaku II 8 35, "The snake and the earthworm" (Hebi to mimizu no hanashi).

Kanagawa, Tsukui-gun: Sōshū 65, "The earthworm" (Mimizu).

Shizuoka, Ibara-gun, Fujikawa-machi: Shizuoka 353, "The snake and the earthworm" (Hebi to mimizu). As thanks, a snake caught a frog for the earthworm and took revenge for it.

Gifu: Minzokugaku II 12 38, "The snake and the earthworm" (Hebi to mimizu).

Hiroshima: Aki 103, "The exchange between the snake and the earthworm" (Hebi to mimizu no kaegoto).

Ōita: Buzen.*

Nagasaki, Minamitakaku-gun: Shimabara 21, "The earthworm and the mole" (Mimizu to mogura). Here it is a mole instead of a snake.

292. The Earthworm that Wears a Reel

There were two girls of the same age living as neighbors in a certain village and both of them were skillful weavers. When the village market day approached, they raced as they wove dresses to wear to it. The thread of one was coarse and rough, but she finished sewing her dress. The other wove carefully and she could not finish by the time the market day came. The one who had finished weaving put on her dress and set out for the market happy. The other could not think what to do. She put the reel on her neck and climbed into a jar and asked her husband to carry it on his shoulder. The two girls met in the midst of the crowd and began to make fun of each other. The husband threw the jar down, and that tossed his naked wife onto the ground. She was so ashamed that she burrowed into the dirt. She turned into the earthworm we see today with a white ring around its neck.

Nagasaki, Iki

Aomori, Hachinohe: MK II 12 56, "The earthworm that wears a reel" (Kasekake mimizu).
Iwate, Hienuki-gun: Kōshō 9 2, "The ground cherry and mawappu" (Hōzuki to mawappu). This is a humorous story. The mother told the girls to weave summer dresses in time for the summer festival. One turned into a ground cherry that always keeps its body hidden, but the other's seat sticks out.
Akita, Kazuno-gun: MK I 3 27, "The ground cherry and mawachibu" (Hōzuki to mawachibu). The same story as the one in Hienuki-gun.
Ōita: Naori 86, "The earthworm and the frog" (Mimizu to hiki).
Nagasaki: (Old) Iki 128, "The earthworm that wears a reel on its neck" (Kubi ni kase o kaketa mimizu). This is in a complete form. Perhaps it was changed on the island.

Further reference:
In the story about the filial sparrow on Amami Ōshima, Kagoshima, the sparrow put a reel onto its neck and flew off. Animal tales are often changed into humorous stories, but with old parts left in them.

293. The Kindness of the Bracken
or The Bracken and the Snake

While the snake was taking a nap, a thatching reed sprouted and pierced its body. The bracken lifted the snake from below with its soft hands and freed it from the reed. When people see the snake, they ask it if it has forgotten the kindness of the bracken.

Iwate, Kamihei-gun: Kikimimi 203, "The snake, the reed, and the bracken" (Hebi to chigaya to warabi).
Kazusa (Chiba): Nihon den Kazusa 197, "The viper and the bracken" (Mamushi to sawarabi). When the viper was ill, the bracken lifted it up with its hands. When people meet it, they ask, "Viper-maid of the back hills, have you forgotten the kindness of the bracken?"
Kanagawa, Tsukui-gun: Sōshū 64, "The centipede" (Mukade). Here it is a centipede that was pierced by a reed while it was napping. The bracken lifted it up to rescue it.
Osaka, Sennan-gun, Sugahara: (no source). A slug is added here. The bracken sprouted and destroyed the slime of the slug. The song is, "The pity of the spring bracken, don't forget the bracken." If a man repeats this song three times and spreads the juice of bracken on his hands and feet, a snake will not bite him.

Further reference:
Minakata zuihitsu 399.

294. The Wild Goose and the Tortoise

Once upon a time the tortoise turned to the wild goose and said, "I am tired of being here and I want to go away. Please take me somewhere." The wild goose agreed. He had the tortoise bite the center of a stick. Two wild geese took hold of it, one at each end, and flew up. While they were flying over a certain village, some children thought it funny when they saw the tortoise biting the pole and carried by the geese. They set up a great commotion. The tortoise forgot his instructions and shouted back at them angrily. When he did that, he fell from the stick. The shell of the tortoise has been divided since that time.

Fukushima, Iwaki-gun

Fukushima, Iwaki-gun: Iwaki 89, "The wild goose and the tortoise" (Gan to kame). Example.
Niigata, Minamikanbara-gun: Kamuhara 12, "The stork and the tortoise" (Tsuru to kame).
Fukui, Sakai-gun: MK I 1 30, 32, "The origin of the tortoise shell" (Kame no kō yurai). Even now they say the reply *un* [yes] is like a tortoise. "The frog changed its house" (Kaeru no yadokae).
Nagano: Chiisagata 231, "The wild goose and the tortoise" (Gan to kame). It is in the form of a humorous story. When the children called that it looked like a horseshoe, it answered, "I'm not a horseshoe. I'm a tortoise." Then it fell.
Gifu, Yoshiki-gun, Kamitakara-mura: Hidabito IV 11 18, "The wild goose and the tortoise" (Gan to kame). There are two stories. In the first the two birds were storks. They hung the tortoise from a pole and each carried one end in its beak. Children made fun of them along the way.
Ōita, Usa-gun: Dai-ni 10, "The stork and the tortoise" (Tsuru to kame). It is not a story about origins. The tortoise carried by the storks to Chōshū fell into the river and was killed.
Kumamoto, Yatsushiro-gun: Dai-ichi 78, "The shell of the tortoise" (Kame no kōra). The messengers of the Sun told the tortoise to hold onto a straw with his mouth. When he fell and his shell was split, the messengers from the Sky were surprised. They wrapped him in ivy vines.

Further reference:
Konjaku monogatari, maki 5, No. 24. The tortoise did not believe what the storks told him. He dropped to the earth and his shell was split.

Minzokugaku II 9 545. Mr. Minakata says this is a Hiron legend from Jataka.

295. The Sparrow Wine Dealer

Long ago the sparrow picked grains of rice and left them where water dammed up by the side of a stream. A man found this and the flavor was good. He imitated it and learned to make wine. That is why men at breweries will not hurt sparrows even now.

Gotō, Fukue, etc.

Shimane, Matsue: Nihon den 257, "The sparrow dance" (Suzume odori).

296. The Lizard's Tail

The lizard borrowed man's tail and would not return it. That is why when a man comes near it, he thinks he has come for his tail. He leaves it and runs off.

Ōita: Bunzen.*

297. The Louse and the Flea

This gives the reason fleas are red and for the black spot on the back of the louse. There are all sorts of stories about these origins, and it is even added to a stepmother story.

Yamanashi, Nishiyatsushiro-gun: Kai 295, "The flea and the louse"
(Nomi to shirami). There was a quarrel. The flea fell into the
stream. After that it was afraid of the sound of water.
Kumamoto, Yatsushiro-gun: Dai-ichi 78, "The flea and the louse" (Nomi
to shirami). The flea and the louse went on a pilgrimage to Ise
Shrine. They raced to see who could get there first. The louse
fastened onto a traveler and got there first. The flea was angry
and hit the louse.
Nagasaki: Shimabara 22, "The flea, the louse, and the mosquito" (Nomi
to shirami to ka). The flea and the louse had a big fight. The flea
threw a huge stone onto the back of the louse. It bounced off and
hit the mosquito's legs. The flea strained himself so much that he

turned red. The back of the louse turned black where the stone hit
it. The mosquito, who was a bystander, had his legs bent by the
stone.

298. The Origin of Fleas and Mosquitoes

Aomori: Tsugaru k 10. No title.
Iwate, Hienuki-gun: Kōshō 11 6, "Shutendōji." At the end of the story
of Shutendōji, the head of the demon was cut off. The blood that
spattered turned into fleas, the burned ashes turned into horseflies
and mosquitoes, the joints that did not burn turned into leaches
that suck human blood.

Further reference:
This story may also be among the Ainu.
Yearsley 45.

299. The Origin of Tobacco

A mother who lost her only daughter spent her days weeping at
her grave. One day a strange plant sprouted from the grave. It grew
taller and taller before her eyes. It was not good to eat after boiling
it, roasting it, or steaming it. In the meantime, the leaves dried. She
tried putting them into the end of a bamboo. Then she lighted them
and smoked them. The flavor was beyond description. It was delicious.
No matter what unhappy things happened, it comforted her. That was
tobacco.

Kagoshima, Kikaijima

Kagoshima: Kikai 157, "The origin of tobacco" (Tobako no okori).
Example.

Further reference:
Seiban densetsu shū.
Konjaku monogatari, maki 31, No. 27. The plant of forgetfulness.

300. Why the Jellyfish has No Bones
or "The Monkey's Live Liver"

A jellyfish (or octopus) gave away the plan of a tortoise who was
sent to get live liver and brought the monkey back. The bones were
taken from the jellyfish as punishment.

Aomori, Sannohe-gun: Tekkiri 261, "The bones taken out of the octopus" (Tako no hone nukareta hanashi).

Niigata, Minamikanbara-gun: Kamuhara 32. Note No. 9.

Ishikawa: Kaga 40, "The monkey and the tortoise" (Saru to kame). A monkey told a tortoise to take hold of his tail with his mouth and he would lift him into the tree where his clothes were drying. He told the tortoise to answer "ah" when he was spoken to. The tortoise dropped to the ground when he answered as he was told to do. As revenge, the tortoise offered to take the monkey to the Dragon Palace if he would get onto his back. He pushed him into the sea instead and killed him.

The tale was probably not in its former form.

Fukui, Sakai-gun: MK I 8 33, "The live monkey liver" (Saru no iki gimo). The snake at Kuzuryūgawa gave birth to young and wanted to feed them on live liver. There is no tortoise and monkey in the story. The male snake was the one fooled by the monkey.

It is close to the version in Shasekishū. There is a little dragon.

Wakayama, Ito-gun: Kōshō 9 15, "Why the jellyfish has no bones" (Kurage hone nashi). The one that came for the monkey and the one that did the talking was the jellyfish.

Shimane, Matsue: Nihon den 261, "The jellyfish" (Kurage). The tortoise went to get the monkey and the jellyfish did the talking. It is quite abbreviated.

Yamaguchi: Suō Ōshima 57, "Why the octopus has no bones" (Tako no hone nashi). The illness of the princess. Here it is an octopus.

Kagoshima, Amami Ōshima: MK II 5 43, "Why the jellyfish has no bones" (Kurage hone nashi).

Koshikijima: Koshiki 194, "Why the jellyfish has no bones" (Kurage hone nashi).

Kikaijima: Kikai 147, "Why the octopus has no bones" (Tako hone nashi). The only daughter of the Dragon King was ill and wanted to eat liver of a live monkey. They sent a dog to a far country to find a monkey. He brought one back on his back. An octopus and a globe fish gave it away. As punishment, the bones were taken out of the octopus and those of the globe fish were mixed in order.

Further reference:

Nihon dōwa shū 257.

Shasekishū V 15 o. It is a little dragon. A Buddhist tale.

Enseki zasshi IV.

Nihon dōwa no shin kenkyū 356.

Nihon mukashibanashi shū, jō 4. Is there a trace here of the spirit leaving the body?

Refer to "The monkey and the little dragon," a story of washing a liver and hanging it out to dry.

Sanyo sōdan 3 (in *Kokka daikan* I 34).

In *Tōgoku tsūgan* it was a tortoise and a rabbit. The tortoise was sent to get the rabbit for its liver.

Konjaku monogatari, maki 5, No. 25. The tortoise was deceived by a monkey.

301. The Mole and the Bullfrog

This gives the reason the mole lives in the ground and the frog lays its eggs in the lake.

Kumamoto, Tamana-gun: MK I 1 44, "The Sun, the mole, and the frog" (Nichirin san to mogura to donko). The mole decided to shoot the Sun down because it shone too brightly. It climbed a tree with a bow and arrow. The frog told the Sun about the mole's plan. From that time the mole could only walk underground, and when it comes time for the frog to lay eggs, the water is warm.
Kuma-gun: MK I 8 38, "The mole and the frog" (Mogura to waku-do). The mole ate men. He tried to shoot the Sun down with an arrow because he thought he could eat more if it were dark. The rest of the story is like the Tamana tale.
Kagoshima: Koshiki 200, "The mole and the frog" (Mogura to kaeru).

Further reference:
Seiban densetsu shū. A story about shooting the Sun.

302. The Charcoal, The Straw, and the Bean

One day an old woman put a kettle over her hearth and started to cook broad beans. While she was dozing, one of the beans popped out of the kettle and fell into the hearth. A piece of straw and a piece of charcoal were already there. The three of them talked things over and decided to go on a journey to see the world. They set out and came to a river where there was no bridge. The straw acted as a bridge. The bean crossed safely, but unfortunately there was a spot that was still burning on the charcoal. When it got half way across, the straw caught on fire and the two of them fell into the river. The broad bean started to cry when he saw the two carried away in the current. He cried so hard his jaw became dislocated. A girl came along on her way home from her sewing lesson. She used black thread to mend him because she did not have any white. That is why even now there is a black line on the broad bean's head.

Yamanashi

Yamanashi, Nishiyatsushiro-gun: Zoku Kai 14, "The broad bean, the straw, and the charcoal" (Soramame to wara to sumi). Example.

Shizuoka, Hamana-gun, Hōkawa-mura: Shizuoka 497, "The black line on the broad bean" (Soramame no kuroi suji). The three went on a journey. The broad bean asked a dressmaker to mend him.

Iwata-gun: Shizuoka 496, "The black line on the broad bean" (Soramame no kuroi suji). The trip was by the bean and tōfu. The tōfu trembled as it crossed the bridge, but the bean fell into the river and was hurt. He asked a doctor to sew him up.

Shimane, Ōchi-gun: Dai-ichi 75, "The charcoal, the straw, and the bean" (Sumi to warashibe to mame). The usual form.

Yamaguchi: Suō Ōshima 54, "The charcoal, the straw, and the bean" (Sumi to warashibe to mame). It says this happened when the three were on their way home from the mountains.

Kumamoto, Amakusa-gun: Kyōdo ken V 4 50, "The journey of the charcoal and the straw" (Sumibi wara no ryokō).

Tsushima (Nagasaki): TD XII 8 18, "The charcoal, the straw, and the bean" (Sumi to wara to mame).

Further reference:
Mukashibanashi kenkyū I 10 20. Grimm.

303. The Long Radish, The Carrot, and the Burdock

This is also a story about origins.

Shizuoka, Ogasa-gun: Shizuoka 492. No title. The three went on a pilgrimage to Ise Shrine. The burdock was left behind at the inn. He was surprised and asked the innkeeper. He was told that the others had set out early. A play on *to* [early and gone to seed].

Nagasaki: Shimabara 22, "The long radish, the carrot, and the burdock" (Daikon to ninjin to gobō). The three took a bath together.

304. The Leak-in-an-Old-House

Once upon a time there was an old man and an old woman in a certain place. One day the old woman turned to the old man and asked, "Grandpa, grandpa, what are you scared of the most?" He answered, "I'm most scared of a wolf." The old woman said, "I'm most scared of a buru [a leak in the roof]." It happened that a wolf was standing by the entrance to their house. He was listening. Presently it began to rain. The old woman yelled, "There's that buru. There's that buru." The wolf fled in a hurry. Now it happened that a cow thief was hiding in the rafters. He mistook the wolf for a calf and chased it. Along the way there was a big hole in the road. He fell into it. The wolf thought it was a buru that had fallen. He went to the rabbit's house to tell what had happened. The rabbit went to the hole to see what a buru looked like. As he started down, something below tried to catch onto him. He shouted, "It's a buru! This won't do!" He scrambled back out and ran away.

Kagawa, Takamatsu

Aomori: Tsugaru k 2. No title. Tsugaru m 84, "The leak in a leaky house" (Moriya no mori).
  Hachinohe: MK II 12 57, "The leak-in-an-old-house" (Furuya no mori). The word mori is not clear. They say muri for leak.
  Sannohe-gun: Tekkiri 263, "A leak is more scary than a tondo tiger" (Tondo no tora yori mori ga osoroshii). A bear, not a wolf, overheard them.
Iwate: Shiwa shū 137, "The leak-in-an-old-house" No. 1 (Furuya no mori). There are three stories, those of Tsuchibuchi-mura, Kuriba-yashi-mura, and Tōno-machi.
Miyagi, Kurihara-gun: Kyōdo den 1 177, "How the rabbit's tail came off" (Usagi no shippo ga nuketa hanashi). This does not say it was on a rainy night and muru is not a leak from rain. A tiger came and overheard the talk. The thief fell into the rabbit's house. The tale is broken up. The tiger and the rabbit have no connection with it. And it does not say why the rabbit's tail is short.
  Sendai, the northern area: Kyōdo den 3 111, "The wolf, the leak, and the thief" (Ōkami to muri to dorobō). The thief jumped into a little shrine where the monkey was. When it went out, its tail was taken off completely. It gives the reasons the monkey's tail is short and its face is red.
Fukushima, Iwaki-gun: Iwaki 81, 162, "The thief who was afraid of the dark" (Dorobō ga yami o osoroshigatta hanashi).
Niigata: Minamikanbara 177, "The leak-in-an-old-house" (Furuya no mori); Echigo Sanjo 118, "The leak-in-an-old-house" (Furuya no mori).
Ishikawa: Kaga 129, "A leak is dangerous" (Morizo ga osoroshi).
Nagano: Kamiina 1362, "The monkey's tail" (Saru no o); Mukashibanashi 3, "A leak is more dangerous than a wolf" (Oniōkami yori moruzo osoroshii). A horse dealer and a wolf come to see a thief. At the end the reasons are given for the monkey's short tail and his red face.
Yamanashi, Nishiyatsushiro-gun: Zoku Kai 239, "The leak-in-an-old-house and the man-cave" (Muru to hitoana). The wolf overheard the talk of an old man and an old woman in a mountain hut. The horse thief jumped onto the back of the wolf as it ran away. He rode it into a man-cave on Fuji. There is a conference of the animals and the monkey's adventure. It explains why the monkey's tail is short and what a man-cave is.
Kanagawa, Tsuzuki-gun: MK I 10 45, "The leak-in-an-old-house and animals" (Furuya no mori to dōbutsu). It does not say it was a rainy night and the meaning of muru is forgotten. It is broken in form like the Enuma-gun tale.
Shizuoka, Haibara-gun: Shizuoka 467, "A leak is more dangerous than wolf" (Ōkami yori morozō osoroshii). The horse thief thought that

the wolf was a colt and jumped onto it. He was shaken off into a hole. A monkey came down from a tree overhead to investigate. He felt around with his tail. A story about origins, the reason for the monkey's tail and face. There are five stories all with only the first part.

Tōtōmi (Shizuoka): Tsuchi no iro V 4 9, "It's leaking" (Morozo).

Aichi: Sanshū Yoko 118, "Various charm songs" (Shuju na majinai uta).

Gifu, Hida: Hidabito V 1 60, "It's raining, it's leaking" (Furuzo moruzo).

Osaka, Sennan-gun: MK II 5 41, "The leak-in-an-old-house" (Furuya no morizo). It gives only the first half of the story, to the part where the thief ran away on the wolf. It was not on a rainy night.

Hyōgo, Katō-gun: TD IV 3 35, "A leak is dangerous" (Moro osoroshii).
Kanzaki-gun: Dai-ichi 67, "The leak-in-an-old-house" (Furuya no mori).

Shimane, Yatsuka-gun: Dai-ichi 71, "The leak-in-an-old-house" (Furuya no mori). There is a last part, but the monkey does not appear. Perhaps it is an oversight. It is the old way to say, "Mori dono kori ozokere [afraid of Master Leak]."
Oki, Kuroki-mura: MK I 9 26, "The leak-in-an-old-house" (Furuya no mori). In this it does not say a leak is feared. Could this be the original form?

Hiroshima, Saeki-gun: Aki 169, "The king of beasts" (Kemono no ō). The council of beasts. It continues to where the fox becomes king.

Tokushima: Awa Iyayama 104, "The leak-in-an-old-house" (Furuya no mori).

Kagawa, Takamatsu: Dai-ni 86, "The leak-in-an-old-house" (Furiya no mori). Example.
Mitoyo-gun: MK II 12 44, "The leak-in-an-old-house" (Furuya no mori). She was afraid of purin dono.

Fukuoka, Kurate-gun: Fukuoka 72, "The thief who gave up entering a house" (Nusubito hairu koto o yamu). This is either a fragment or a wrong version.

Ōita, Kitaamabe-gun, Usuki: MK I 10 27. No title. In this there is no tiger-wolf. It only tells that a thief came and was frightened. It seems broken up.

Kumamoto, Ashikata-gun: MK I 7 46, "The tonton tiger" (Tonton tora). No last part about the monkey's tail.
Kuma-gun: MK I 8 39, "The leak-in-an-old-house" (Furuya no mori).
Hōtaku-gun: MK I 9 38, "The leak-in-an-old-house and the tiger-wolf" (Furuya no mori to tora-ōkami).
Aso: Nihon den 254, "The monkey" (Saru).
Amakusa: Kyōdo ken VII 3 43, "The leak-in-an-old-house" (Furue no mori).

Nagasaki: Shimabara 76, "The leak-in-an-old-house" (Furuya no morizō).
Kitatakaku-gun, Asahaya: Kōshō 8 1 "The leak-in-an-old-house" (Furuya no mori).
Minamitakaku-gun: MK I 10 20, "The leak-in-an-old-house" (Furuya no mori).
Minamimatsuura-gun: Gotō 253, "Terrible Matsuhei" (Osoroshii Matsuhei). Matsuhei was more terrible than a tiger or a wolf. He was the thief who lived next door. In the latter part there is the

council of beasts and what happened to the monkey's tail according to the usual pattern. Is this due to a lapse of memory?

Kagoshima, Ōsumi: Nihon zenkoku 353, "Afraid of a leak" (Moru ga kowai); Koshiki 190, "The leak-in-an-old-house" (Furuya no mori).

Further reference:
Nihon zenkoku kokumin dōwa 385.   Korean.
Chōsen mintan shū 277. Dried persimmons are more dangerous than a tiger (It does not say why).
Chōsen mintan shū, Appendix 35.   Reference to an Indian story, "Panchatantra." In this there is no conversation about a leak in the rain. Only about running away.
Shina minzokugaku V 967.   The same kind of story is found in China.
Mukashibanashi kenkyū I 9 19.   A study related to the Chinese tale.

305. Help from Animals

Before tales about repaying kindness, animals helped people without reason. There are parts of tales with this in them, but we have yet to find a tale in which this point was of central interest.

Tochigi, Kawachi-gun: Nihon shū, jō 170, "Suzume-no-miya."

Further reference:
Tōyō kōhi daizen 1019.
Tōgoku ryokōdan. The origin of Suzume-no-miya in Shimotsuke.
Sangoku denki. About the blue heron and the leeks.

306. Animals and People

Iwate, Kamihei-gun: Kikimimi 460, "The man, the snake, and the fox" (Ningen to hebi to kitsune). A fable to show that man is most lacking in gratitude. This is a derived tale about the relationship of man and animals, one that is in contrast to "The leak-in-an-old-house." There is a trace of an old custom in the rescue of the man from prison.

Tochigi, Haga-gun: Dai-ni 19, "The story of the five deer" (Gohiki no shika no hanashi). A story about a man who forgot gratitude. There is a more elaborate description here than in a genuine folk tale. Man becomes the minor character.

Kaga (Ishikawa): Nihon zenkoku 182, "The tortoise that was set free" (Hanashi game). About a man, a tortoise, a fox, and a snake.

Kumamoto, Tamana-gun: MK I 1 45, "The gratitude of the snake and the fox" (Kuchinawa to kitsune no hōon).

Hyūga (Miyazaki): Hyūga I 79. No title. In Miyazaki there is a child's story about overhearing the talk of cows. A man heard from behind an enbankment the secret about the ring in the nose of the cow. Even now the cow will shake its horns at an embankment. There is a story like the one in Hyūga in Okunan shinpō. Cows were lying near each other on a hill and talking to each other. One said, "If man put rings in our noses, we would work obediently."

Kagoshima: Kikai 172, "The kindness of the monkey" (Saru no shinsetsu). A monkey and a man went fishing at night. The man was carrying his child. A crab fastened onto the monkey's paw and the man helped free it. The monkey promptly picked up the child and carried it into the hills. When an eagle was about to attack the child, the monkey chased it off. The man accused the monkey of ingratitude, but it replied that it was afraid the crab would fasten onto the child. There seems to be some mistake in this story.

Further reference:
Tōsakushi. A legend of Shimotakakura-mura, Takakura-mura about Chōjaike. Kyūsaku Chōja overheard talk between cows and horses and became religious. In order to confirm his Way, he made his lovely daughter a peddler of bamboo baskets.

Nihon mukashibanashi shū, jō 23. The monkey's gratitude in "Saru Masamune."

Ashū kiji zatsuwa.

Konjaku monogatari, maki 29, No. 35. After a woman saved a monkey whose paw was caught by a clam, it took her child away and protected it repeatedly.

Chōsen mintan shū, App. 3. "The great flood and mankind." It says that the same kind of story appears in *Rokudōshū kyō* 3, so this may be a translation. There is a story of using a child as a decoy to catch an eagle.

307. The Wolf and the Old Man

Iwate: Shiwa 40, "The old man and the wolf" (Jiina to ōkami). While an old man planted beans in his garden patch on the hillside, he said, "I plant one bean, it becomes a thousand." A mean wolf sat on a rock above and said, "He plants one bean, it becomes one bean." He intended to eat the old man when he took a nap and was waiting there on the rock. That night the old man and his old woman made mochi. The next day they smeared it out on the flat rock. Then the old man pretended to take a nap. The wolf came out and sat on the rock again, but his tail stuck fast. They beat him to death.

This seems to be a broken story about exposing oneself to danger. It can hardly be called an animal story.

308. Animal Races

Long ago a badger and a mudsnail went on a pilgrimage to Ise
Shrine. On the last day of the trip, the mudsnail said to the badger,
"It is not much fun, just walking along like this. Why don't the two of
us race from here to the Grand Shrine of Ise?" The badger agreed.
While he was preparing for the race, the mudsnail lifted the lid of his
shell and fastened onto the tail of the badger. When the badger
reached the torii at Ise, he felt so good, he gave his tail a shake. At
that the snail struck the gate and half of his shell broke off. He fell
to the ground. He looked up at the badger and said, "You're late,
aren't you? I have already arrived and slipped off a sleeve to rest."

Wakayama, Arita-gun

Iwate, Iwate-gun: Kikimimi 264, "The mudsnail and the fox" (Tanishi to
kitsune). There is an exchange of banter through comic songs at
first. It resembles the exchange in "The mudsnail and the wild
yam."
Waga-gun: Kikimimi 280, "The fox and the lion" (Kitsune to shishi).
Fukushima, Iwaki-gun: Iwaki 91, 167, "The animal race" (Dōbutsu
kyōsō).
Shizuoka: Shizuoka 488, "The cat and the signs of the Zodiac" (Neko to
jūnishi).
Gifu, Yoshiki-gun, Kamitakara-mura: Hidabito IV 11 37, "The animal
race" (Dōbutsu kyōsō).
Shiga, Takashima-gun: MK I 10 47, "The Ise pilgrimage of the flea and
the louse" (Nomi to shirami no Ise mairi). The louse rode along on
the straw sandals of the courier.
Osaka, Senhoku-gun: Dai-ni 10, "Why the cat catches rats" (Neko wa
naze nezumi o toru ka).
Wakayama, Arita-gun: Kii 11, "The badger and the mudsnail" (Tanuki
to tanishi). They went on a pilgrimage to Ise. Nihon shū, jō 15,
"The badger and the mudsnail" (Tanuki to tanishi). Example.
Yamaguchi, Suō Ōshima: Kōshō 8 10, "The whale and the sea cucumber" (Kujira to namako). The sea cucumber did not run. It posted
its companions along the way. Kōshō 11 18, "The tiger and the
flea" (Tora to nomi).
Tokushima, Mima-gun: MK II 1 32, "The race between the rabbit and
the crab" (Usagi to kani no kakekurabe).
Fukuoka, Onga-gun: Fukuoka 40, "The race between the fox and the
mudsnail" (Kitsune to tanishi no kyōsō).
Kumamoto, Tamana-gun: MK I 2 35, 36, "The race between the fox and
the tiger" (Kitsune to tora no hashiri kura). It is in the form of
Hakurakuten, in which a Korean tiger comes. A fox was at each ri
along the way. The story about fastening onto the tail is probably
older. "The race between the mudsnail and the fox" (Tanishi to
kitsune no hashiri kura). The usual pattern. He fastened onto the
tail.

Amakusa-gun: Kyōdo ken V 4 43, "The mudsnail and the weasel" (Tanishi to itachi). This has a latter part. It is different in that the weasel rode on the mudsnail. The mudsnail told it to look overhead. When he saw the clouds moving, he thought he was the one that was moving. He was surprised to find himself at the same place when he got off. The mudsnail told him they had made a complete round trip.

Nagasaki: Shimabara 103, "The race between the frog and the dog" (Kaeru to inu no kyōsō); Gotō 261, "The race between the fox and the mudsnail" (Kitsune to tanishi no kakekurabe).

Kagoshima: Kikai 148, "The race between the cat and the crab" (Neko to kani no kakekurabe); Koshiki 201, "The weasel and the frog" (Itachi to donko). Similar to the Amakusa story.

Further reference:

Mukashibanashi kenkyū II 1 9. A Giriak story. "The fox and the abalone."

Kōshi shina. In the example it is a toad and a tiger. There are stories of stationing friends along the way in Africa and in other countries.

Fūken gūki V 287. In a folk tale for children there is a tale about a crab and a monkey that went on a pilgrimage to Kumano.

The pilgrimage to Ise by the badger and the mudsnail is probably in the same group. There is also the story about how the crab won when they made mochi together. Fastening onto the tail or riding on the back seems more like a crab's way than a mudsnail's, but where he says, "I have slipped off a sleeve to rest," is like a mudsnail.

309. The Fox, the Lion, and the Tiger

The three are the Chinese tiger, the Indian lion, and the Japanese fox. They run races. It gives the origin of the lion mask. Refer to "Animal races."

Iwate, Waga-gun: Kikimimi 280, "The fox and the lion" (Kitsune to shishi).

Shizuoka, Shita-gun, Yaitsu: Shizuoka 445, "The fox is not fair" (Kitsune wa zurui). Races by a lion, a tiger, and a fox. In the latter part there is the origin of the lion head mask.

Suchi-gun, Shironishi-mura: Shizuoka 446, "The fox and the lion" (Kitsune to shishi no hanashi). There is no race. The last part gives the origin of the lion head mask like the previous one.

Wakayama, Nishimuro-gun: Muro 91, "The origin of the lion dance" (Shishimai no okori); Kyōdo ken III 8 25, "The origin of the lion dance" (Shishimai no okori). The lion's body broke into three parts. The tiger took the tail and the fox, the head, and they went home. This is the origin of the lion dance.

Hiroshima, Yamagata-gun: MK I 11 47, "The tiger and the fox" (Tora to kitsune). The tiger came from China to match strength with the fox. They raced, but the fox set a companion along the way at each point and won the race. The tiger went home defeated. He handed over an animal that looked like him. That was the cat.

Nagasaki, Tsushima: Nihon zenkoku 365, "The lion head" (Shishi kashira). In this the fox crossed over to China.

310. Animal Feuds

Iwate, Kamihei-gun: Rōō 257, "The wolf and the dog" (Ōkami to inu). The dog was abused by his master. The wolf rescued him and in turn gave him something to do. He wanted to eat chicken and wanted the dog to get him one as thanks. The dog refused. They started to argue. The cat came to help and chased the wolf off. The wolf called demons together in a cave in the mountains to make plans. While they were talking, the cat came, and thought the ears of the demons were rats. It leaped upon them. The demons fled at that.

Niigata, Minamikanbara-gun: Echigo Sanjo 41, "The badger, the monkey, and the otter" (Mujina to saru to kawauso). A badger, a monkey, and an otter went on a pilgrimage to Yahiko. Along the way they picked up a piece of straw matting, a measure of salt, and a quart of beans. The badger was tricky in dividing the things. Refer to "Dividing things that were picked up."

Ishikawa: Kaga 47, "The fox, the rabbit, the monkey, and the otter" (Kitsune, usagi, saru, kawauso). Here it is the rabbit instead of a badger and they set out to sell things instead of to pick things up.

Okayama, Mitsu-gun: MK I 6 42, "The fox and the bear" (Kitsune to kuma no hanashi).

Kagoshima: Kikai 144, "The crow and the cricket" (Karasu to ingira). The cricket was caught by the crow. It praised the crow's voice and asked it to sing, thus escaping.

311. The Monkey and the Shellfish

A story of how the shellfish fastened onto the monkey's paw.

Miyagi, Momoo-gun: Kyōdo den 3 10, "The monkey and the shellfish" (Saru to shihorikai). This is a broken story. Perhaps formerly there was a dialogue. We can imagine this from the way the monkey repeats, "As I look to the hills, the sun is setting. Let me go, shellfish; let me go, shellfish."

312. The Badger's Forecast

The badger became a fortune teller and forecast danger to the monkey.

Tokushima: Awa Iyayama 81, "Destroying the monkey" (Saru taiji).
Nagasaki: (Old) Iki 175, 177, "The badger's forecast" (Tanuki no ura-nai). A man took his dog along and hid in the monkey's house to kill its 12 young. The monkey became suspicious. He met the bad-ger called Sanshōbō and asked him to read his fortune. "The old badger" (Tanuki no onchō). A daughter tried to stop her father from going hunting, but he would not listen to her. On his way home he found his daughter, who had been kidnapped by monkeys, in a little shrine. He hid there to kill the monkeys. The monkeys had the badger read a fortune after they came back. He warned of danger. The badger ran away, but the monkeys were killed by the man.

In examples from Kumano, a rabbit was the fortune teller. Such stories as these got their start from tales about the animal world. In other words, the simple tales of origins were gradually devel-oped into modern romances.

313. Dividing Things that Were Picked Up

Long ago a badger, a monkey, and an otter set out on a pilgrimage to Yahiko. Along the way they picked up a piece of straw matting, a measure of salt, and a quart of beans. They talked of how to divide the things, but could not agree. The clever badger suggested that the monkey should take the matting up into a tall tree in the hills. He could spread it out and enjoy the scenery. The otter could take the measure of salt to a pond where it looked as though there would be fish. He could pour it in to float up the fish. He said he would take the beans that were left and eat them. The other two were off their guard and agreed. The monkey took the straw matting up a tree and spread it out. He was going to sit on it to enjoy the view, but it slipped. He fell from the tree and wrenched his legs. The otter scat-tered the salt on a pond, but when he went in to look for fish, his eyes got red and sore. The monkey and the otter realized that the badger had been unfair. They went to his house to complain. In the meantime, the badger had eaten all the beans. He had fastened the husks into his fur with the help of his wife and pretended to be groan-ing. He said, "We ate those beans and have broken out in boils. Oh, it hurts!" The monkey and the otter were fooled again. They went off saying they were all having trouble and there was nothing to do about it.

Echigo

All kinds of animals pick things up according to the region.

Iwate, Hienuki-gun: MK I 11 30, "The reason the ant's back is slender" (Ari no koshi no hosoi wake). A bee, a spider, and an ant picked up coins. The bee took eight mon [hachi means bee or eight], the spider took nine mon [kumo means spider or nine mon], and the ant started off with what was left, ari kiri [ari means ant, ari kiri means that's that]. The spider tied his thread around the ant's waist to hold him back. Its back has been slender since that time.

Akita, Senhoku-gun: Ugo 141. A bee and an ant.

Yamagata, Higashitagawa-gun: MK I 8 46, "A pilgrimage to Haguro by a spider, an ant, and a bee" (Kubo do ari do haji no Haguro meeri); MK I 12 46, "The monkey and the pheasant" (Saru to kiji no hanashi).

Niigata, Minamikanbara-gun: Echigo Sanjo 41, "The badger, the monkey, and the otter" (Mujina to saru to kawauso). Example.

Ishikawa: Kaga 40, "The monkey and the ant" (Saru to ari). They picked up a sea bream (tai). It turns into a pun: ari ga [the ant] tai [sea bream], that is, arigatai [thankful].

Nagano: Chiisagata 278, "All of it for the ant" (Ari wa aridake). It is the same as the Ina story except that they were on their way to Zenkōji instead of Ise.

Kamiina-gun: Mukashibanashi 76, 141, "Eight mon to the pigeon and four to the shrike" (Hato wa hachi mon shigi shimon) and "The purse and the bee, the spider, and the ant" (Hachi to kumo to ari to saifu).

Yamanashi, Nishiyatsushiro-gun: Kai 152, "All that is left is for the fox" (Ato wa kitsune dono mina mairu). The rabbit, the badger, and the fox who fooled a courier and took his lunch away. There is a part where the fox reads the letter of the courier. Zoku Kai 453, "The bee, the spider, and the ant" (Hachi to kumo to ari).

Gifu, Hida: Hidabito IV 3 39, "The monkey, the wild boar, and the ant" (Saru to inoshishi to ari).

Osaka, Sennan-gun: Kōshō 10 30, "The shrike, the snipe, the pigeon, and the quail" (Mozu to shigi to hato to uzura). The shrike found sixteen mon. The pigeon said he would divide them. For the pigeon, eight mon [ha for hato, pigeon, or hachi for eight]. Four mon for the snipe [shi for four, and shigi, snipe]. To the quail, three mon [u stands for three or uzura, quail]. One to the shrike [mo stands for mozu, shrike, and mon]. The ant does not appear in this tale.

Shimane: Inpaku dōwa 78, "The monkey, the spider, and the ant" (Saru to kumo to ari).

Fukuoka, Kurate-gun: Fukuoka 188, "The fox and the badger match cleverness" (Kitsune to tanuki no chie kurabe). A fox and a badger took mochi from children. In this there is an episode where the fox reads a letter. The message in the letter was probably entertaining.

Chikujō-gun: Fukuoka 237, "The rabbit's cleverness" (Usagi no warujie).

314. Three Mon for the Heron, Eight for the Pigeon

In the same group as dividing things that are picked up. Some animal stories are also changed into humorous stories. Many are euphonious with the pun. Word plays are all new things.

Niigata, Minamikanbra-gun: Dai-ichi 48, "The ant judge" (Ari no chūsai); Kamuhara 146, "The way the ant divided things" (Ari no bunpai).

Yamanashi, Nishiyatsushiro-gun: Kai 152, "What's left is for the fox" (Ato wa kitsune dono mina mairu). There is humor where the fox reads the letter.

315. The Straw Mat and the Soy Beans

The badger took the beans when the beans and the straw mat were divided. He fooled the fox by fastening bean husks onto his body and saying it could be seen that he had smallpox. From that it goes into the story of "Tail fishing." There is a song that says, "Obana Fox is a fox without a tail."

Toyama, Shimoniigawa-gun, Nishifuse-mura: Etchū III 10 1, "The fox at Obana has no tail" (Obana gitsune no o no nai hanashi). There are stories in which it is neither a monkey nor a bear, but a fox. Perhaps because of the words, "A fox without a tail," in the song.

316. The Cat and the Rat

A cat and a rat talked over plans for a feast. The cat ate all the good things that were shut up in a room beyond the main hall. He said there were funerals for men named Uwaname, Nakaname, and Sokoname [eat the top, eat the middle, eat the bottom]. Afterwards, the rat went with the cat to see, and there was nothing left. The rat was angry. The cat said that since he was bad, anyway, he would eat the rat, too. The two animals have been unfriendly ever since.

Iwate, Shiwa-gun

Iwate: Shiwa 35, "The cat and the rat" (Neko to nezumi).

Further reference:
    The second story in Grimm has a story about a friendly cat and
rat.
    Hokuō minwa shū No. 17.

317. The Fox and the Kingfisher

    The fox and the kingfisher planned a feast. The kingfisher fooled a
fish peddler by the way he flew, but in the meantime the fox took the
fish and ate it. The kingfisher persuaded the fox to turn into a pile
while he perched on it. When the former fish peddler came along, he
swung his pole angrily at the kingfisher. It darted away and let the
blow fall on the pile that was the fox. It cried in pain.

Aomori, Gonohe-machi

Aomori: Tekkiri 288, "The fox that imitated a salmon" (Saki no mono-
        mane o shita kitsune). This story is certainly in Kyūshū, too.
        Another which can be considered like it, too, is on Okinawa. "The
        fox and the kingfisher" (Kitsune to kawasemi). About their fooling
        the peddler. See *Mukashibanashi kenkyū* II 12 58. TD XI 12 57,
        "The fox and the kingfisher" (Kitsune to kawasemi). Example.
Hachinohe: MK II 12 58, "The fox and the pheasant" (Kitsune to
kijiko).

318. Tail Fishing

    The otter and the fox decided to exchange invitations to feasts.
The otter started it with an invitation to a fox. He prepared all kinds
of things to eat and waited for the fox. He smiled to himself as he
arrived and sat down to eat. Everything on plates or in bowls and
various dishes was some special kind of fish. The fox ate his fill,
admiring it all. It was the turn of the fox next. He went along the
path by the rice paddy to the river bank early the next morning to
fish, but he could not find a single one. The otter arrived in the evening, but the fox stared motionlessly at the sky and did not reply to
anything the otter said. The otter went home because there was
nothing else to do. The fox went the next morning to apologize. He
said he was sorry, but his turn had fallen to be Sky Watcher. He
invited the otter to come the next evening. The otter went again, but
this time the fox stared fixedly at the ground and did not reply to
anything the otter said. The otter went home because there was
nothing else to do. The next morning the fox went again to apologize.
He said he was sorry, but his turn had fallen to be Earth Watcher. The

otter said that the reason the fox said such things was that he could not catch fish. The fox agreed. The otter then said he would tell the fox how to catch lots of fish. He told the fox to let his tail down into the river on a cold night. Lots of little fish would come and fasten onto it. The fox went home happy. He went to the river that evening after dark and put his tail in as he had been told. The ice formed and rattled, but no fish nibbled. He endured it doggedly until morning in spite of that. In the morning he heard children as they crossed the ice. It would never do to be found. He tried to pull his tail up, but try as he did, he could not budge it. When he gave a desperate try, his tail broke off completely.

Niigata, Minamikanbara-gun

Aomori, Kitatsugaru-gun: Tsugaru k 2. No title.
    Nishitsugaru-gun: MK I 10 21, "Tail fishing" (Shippo no tsuri); Tsugaru m 104, "The otter and the fox" (Kawauso to kitsune); Gonohe.* A story about a fox and an otter with the part about Sky Watcher and Earth Watcher. Another about a fox and a monkey. Tekkiri 265, "The frog and the monkey" (Kaeru to saru).
Iwate: Shiwa shū 85, "The otter and the fox" (Kawauso to kitsune).
    Kamihei-gun: Kamihei 95, "The otter and the fox" (Kawauso to kitsune). Instead of a story about invitations, it is about Sky Watching and Earth Watching. The fox was fooled by the otter and tried to fish with its tail. He was killed by a man who went for water in the morning.
    Iwate-gun: Kikimimi 271, "The otter and the fox" No. 3 (Kawauso to kitsune). The last words of the fox before he was killed by the water carrier are interesting, probably the work of a zatō.
    Esashi-gun: Kikimimi 269, "The otter and the fox" No. 2 (Kawauso to kitsune). In this there is no excuse by the fox. The skin was pulled off his tail and he ran back to the hills.
Akita, Kazuno-gun: MK I 3 27, "The fox and the otter" (Kitsune to kawauso). The otter was invited by the fox and ate lots of beans, which made his bowels loose. In return the otter invited the fox. From there it is the story of tail fishing.
    Senhoku-gun: TD IX 4 48, "The nursery song about an otter" (Kawauso no komori uta). A story about a fox and an otter. The words of the fox are turned into a nursery rhyme. In Tōhoku there are many stories about a fox who got his tail caught and was beaten to death, but there are no stories about losing his tail. This one resembles the Echigo tale. MK I 11 24, "The fox and the otter" (Kitsune to kawauso). The fox was fooled by the otter. Where his tail was cut off becomes a story of how the charcoal-maker killed him. It does not say why his tail became short.
Fukushima, Iwaki-gun: Iwaki 92, 167, "Tail fishing" (Shippo no tsuri).
Niigata, Minamikanbara-gun: Dai-ichi 48, "The fox and the otter" (Kitsune to kawauso); Kamuhara 95, "The fox and the otter" (Kitsune to kawauso). Example. The form is rather well arranged.
Toyama, Toyama City vicinity: MK II 6 29, "The otter and the fox" (Kawauso to kitsune).

Ishikawa, Nomi-gun: MK II 8 36, "The rabbit and the otter" (Usagi to kawauso).

Enuma-gun: Kaga 46, "The fox and the otter" (Kitsune to kawauso). There is a part about their inviting each other, but the memory of the narrator is weak. The fox was killed by children the next morning.

Fukui, Sakai-gun: MK I 8 33, "The otter and the fox" (Kawauso don to kitsune don). The otter told the fox he fished for octopus with his tail to fool him. The fox was pulled in by the octopus. The fox pretended to sleep on the day it was his turn to give the feast. Nihon zenkoku 169, "The monkey's bottom" (Saru no oido).

Nagano, Shimoina-gun: Mukashibanashi 107, "The otter and the fox" (Kawauso to kitsune). The one that did the fooling was the fox and the rabbit was fooled.

Osaka, Sennan-gun: Kōshō 11 30, "The fox without a tail" (O no nai kitsune). A badger did the fooling.

Hyōgo, Kinosaki-gun: MK II 9 36, "The monkey" (Saru).

Tottori, Kedaka-gun: Inpaku min I 4 192, "The monkey's tail" (Saru no o).

Hino-gun: Inpaku mukashi 22, "The rabbit and the fox" (Usagi to kitsune). The one doing the fooling was the fox. He fooled the rabbit. From that time the rabbit's tail was short. Its front legs clawed the ground so hard when he tried to get away that they were worn off.

Shimane, Oki: MK I 7 38, "The old man at Honyashiki and the fox" (Honyashiki no jii san to kitsune). How the old man fooled the fox. There are stories like this among Kichiu stories, too. It is turned into a humorous story. It is the same as the one in *Okinoshima no mukashibanashi to hōgen*.

Hiroshima, Takata-gun: Aki 165, "The novice and the fox" (Kozō to kitsune). Osan Fox was fooled by a novice. It is not like a novice to be going home dangling a big fish.

Yamaguchi, Suō Ōshima: Suō Ōshima 39, "Why the monkey's tail is short" (Saru no shippo wa naze mijikai).

Ōita: Bungo kijin 308, "Getting a fox" (Kitsune tsumami).

Nagasaki: Shimabara 98, 99, "The fox and the otter" (Kitsune to kawauso). It is rather like the tale in Minamikanbara-gun, Echigo. The Sky Watcher and the Earth Watcher. The fox was pulled into the water because of the otter. "Tail fishing" (Shippo no tsuri). Destroying a badger who had disguised himself. The latter part is rather odd.

Further reference:

Huet 11, 14, 160.

Isobo monogatari [Aesop], Iwanami edition, 61. The fox fooled a monkey. He fastened a basket onto his fur and tossed stones into it to make it feel heavy. A similar story about a stork and a fox.

319. The Otter and the Monkey

A story about tail fishing. Probably, stories about a monkey freez-
ing its tail and pulling it until it broke off are only in Japan. Tail
fishing, the fox that fished, and the like are all in the same group.

Aomori: Tsugaru m 103, "The monkey and the otter" (Saru to kawauso);
   Tsugaru k 1. No title.
Niigata, Minamiuonuma-gun: MK I 10 36, "The reason the monkey's tail
   is short" (Saru no shippo no mijikai wake). The central point of
   interest is, "Tail, tail, come out, come out!" It is unusual for the
   bear to be doing the fooling.
Ishikawa: Ishikawa 981, "The monkey and the otter" (Saru to kawauso).
Nagano: Chiisagata 233, "The monkey and the otter" (Saru to kawauso).
   Shimoina-gun: Mukashibanashi 33, 147, "The otter and the monkey"
   (Kawauso to saru) and "The monkey and the crab" (Saru to kani).
Gifu, Yoshiki-gun: Hidabito IV 11 17, "Tail fishing" (Shippo no tsuri).
   The fox fooled the monkey. The monkey's tail was short after
   that. The words of the monkey when he was tugging at his tail—
   "ōdai daimochi ōnyō"—probably made listeners laugh by the way
   they were said.
Wakayama: Kii 9, "The monkey and the badger" (Saru to mujina).
   Nishimuro-gun: Dai-ichi 66, "Why the monkey's face is red" (Saru
   no kao wa naze akai).
Shimane, Matsue: Nihon den 255, "The monkey's tail" (Saru no o). The
   monkey was fooled by the bear.
Tokushima, Mima-gun, Iyayama: MK II 1 28, "Why the monkey hasn't a
   tail" (Saru no o wa naze nai ka). The fox fooled the monkey. No
   part about Sky Watcher and Earth Watcher.
Ehime, Kitauwa-gun: MK II 3 34, "Why the monkey's tail is short"
   (Saru no o wa naze mijikai ka).
Nagasaki, Iki: Dai-ichi 79, "The badger and the monkey" (Tanuki to
   saru).

320. The Monkey, the Crab, and the Persimmon

The monkey met the crab in the mountains and traded a persimmon
seed he had found for the crab's riceball. The crab took the seed home
and planted it. He cultivated it carefully. Every day he said, "Sprout,
sprout, or I'll cut you with my scissors." Then, "Grow big, grow big, or
I'll cut you with my scissors." At last the time came for the fruit to
ripen. The crab brought his sack, intending to pick the fruit, but try
as he did, he could not climb the tree. The monkey came along and
offered to pick the fruit if he wanted him to. He took the sack and
scrambled up the tree. He began to eat the ripe fruit and to toss the
puckery ones at the crab. This exasperated the crab. He called from

below, "Wouldn't it be fun if you filled the sack with ripe fruit and tied it to the end of a dead branch. Then shake it." The monkey thought that sounded good and tried it. The branch broke and the fruit fell to the ground. The crab hurried over and pulled the sack into his hole. The monkey climbed down and went to the hole. He looked in and said, "If you don't give me back the sack of fruit, I'll make a pile in your hole." Then he turned around and pushed his tail toward the hole. The crab grabbed the monkey's seat and would not let go. The pain was too much for the monkey and he begged to be forgiven. He offered to give some of his hair to the crab. That was the origin of yamadachi crab that has hair on its legs. It is also why the monkey's bottom is bare and red.

Fukuoka, Yatsume-gun

Aomori, Sannohe-gun: Tekkiri 265, 264, "When the monkey and the crab made mochi" (Saru kani mochi tsuki) and "The rabbit and the crab" (Usagi to kani). Toward the end of the year, a monkey and a crab pounded mochi at the edge of a cliff. The stone mortar fell over. The monkey followed and pushed it into the river. He was carried away in the current. The crab ate the mochi that had fallen out and had caught on a branch. There is a story about how the rabbit and the crab made mochi. Then the rabbit climbed a peach tree and ate peaches. The crab fooled it and said there was a caterpillar on its back. The rabbit shook itself and dropped a peach in its fright. The crab ate it. This latter version is numerous in Kyūshū. Tsugaru m 23, "The feud between the monkey and the crab" (Saru to kani no adauchi); Tsugaru k 7. No title. No part about the mortar rolling down. It goes directly to the fight.

Iwate, Tōno: Hanashi II 6 51, "Tales concerning mortars" (Usu ni kansuru mintan) by Sasaki Kizen. Kikimimi 256, "The monkey and the crab" No. 2 (Saru to kani). The crab threw mochi onto the monkey's face. When he peeled it off, the skin came with it. That is why the monkey's face is red.

There are some tales in Tōhoku about rolling the mortar downhill. Could this be an abridgement? There is exactly the same tale in this region about a monkey and a frog.

Isawa-gun: Isawa.* There is the story about rolling the stone mortar and the revenge taken by the crab's children.

Akita, Kazuno-gun: Dai-ichi 38, "The monkey and the crab" (Saru to kani).

Fukui, Sakai-gun: MK I 8 34, "Master Crab, Master Crab" (Gan do, gan don). This is close to the usual story of the quarrel between the monkey and the crab. The crab picked up a sea bream. The revenge of the crab's children. It tells why the crab's shell is hollow.

Saitama: Kyōdo K S 111.* At Kanō-mura, Kitaadachi-gun, they say the crab below the tree told the monkey that monkeys long ago could climb down head first, but they no longer could. The monkey tried it, and all the persimmons he had picked fell. The crab picked them up. The monkey was angry and threatened to go that night to steal them. The crab cried.

Hiki-gun, Ogawa-mura: (No source). The crab dug a hole on the slant before he got the monkey to come down head first. The persimmons fell into the hole and the monkey was angry.

Chichibu-gun, Ryokami-mura: (No source). The same story.

Ōsato-gun, Kumagaya vicinity: (No source). The monkey's life was spared, but his tail was cut off.

Kitasaitama-gun, Hiyarigawa-mura: (No source). Among the many who helped was water.

Tokushima: Kyōdo ken I 5 20. No title. This is about the revenge on Monkey Island. The crab's children took millet dango and they were accompanied by a chestnut, scissors, and a grindstone.

Fukuoka: 183, "The monkey and the crab" (Saru to kani no hanashi). In three gun and in Munakata, the mochi was in the top of the tree. In the next three gun, there were persimmons in the tree. The monkey's seat was pinched and he got the worst of the deal. He gave hair from his bottom and asked to be forgiven. There is a part about trading a persimmon seed and a riceball, but they were not things picked up. There is a charm for trees, "Grow, grow, or I'll cut you with my scissors" and the advise, "Set the pieces of mochi on the dead branch and it will look like flowers have bloomed."

There are many of these tales in Fukuoka.

Ōita, Hayami-gun: MK I 10 41, "The crab and the monkey" (Kani to saru). The only difference is that mochi was in the tree instead of persimmons.

Kumamoto, Aso: MK I 6 30, "Why the monkey's tail is short" (Naze saru no o ga mijikai ka). In one version it is about gleaning rice. In the other, there is a council about making mochi and it ends with why the monkey's tail is short.

Amakusa-gun: MK II 1 40, "The monkey and the crab" (Saru to kani).

Nagasaki, Iki: TD IX 4 178, "The feud between the monkey and the crab" (Saru kani kattō no hanashi).

Kagoshima: MK I 6 27, "The monkey and the crab" (Saru to kani). They made mochi together. There is a part about the bend in the pestle. It ends with the monkey losing its tail. It is strange that a cat makes its appearance.

In the example from Takayama, Kimotsuki-gun (MK I 8 8), the tale is the same. There is no part about rolling the mortar down. These are "why stories," the element in "The leak-in-an-old-house."

Further reference

Enseki zasshi IV (in *Nihon zuihitsu taisei* II 10 374). It discusses an illustration in a book of the Hōei Era (1848-1853).

321. The Mochi Race

Once upon a time a monkey and a bullfrog met in the mountains. It happened to be near New Year, and in the village below they had started to make mochi. The monkey said, "Let's get a mortar full of mochi." After they talked it over, the two of them went down the mountain. To begin with, the monkey hid by the back door of the village head. The bullfrog followed and went into the yard. He jumped into the spring with a big splash. The people who were pounding mochi heard the noise and thought the master's little son had fallen into the water. They rushed to the pond, leaving their mochi in the mortar. The monkey took that time to gather the mortar and the mochi into his arms. He went leaping back up the mountain. The bullfrog followed slowly. The monkey proposed that they roll the mortar downhill just as it was with the mochi in it. They would race to catch up with it and whoever got there first could eat the mochi himself. He sent the mortar rolling down into the little valley. The monkey dashed off, but the bullfrog could only move slowly after him. The mochi happened to fall out and get caught on a branch of bush clover by the path. The bullfrog noticed that. He sat down by it promptly and began to eat it. The monkey, who had chased the empty mortar to no purpose, came climbing back disappointed. He discovered the bullfrog and said, "I say, Master Bullfrog, how about us starting to eat it from here?" The bullfrog replied, "What are you talking about? It's my mochi, and I'll eat it from wherever I like."

Echigo, Minamikanbara-gun

Aomori: Tsugaru m 13, "How the bullfrog was crushed" (Hiki no tsubureta hanashi).
Iwate, Kamihei-gun: Kikimimi 255, "When the monkey made mochi" No. 1 (Saru no mochi tsuki).
　　Shiwa-gun: Shiwa 29, 255, "The monkey and the bullfrog" (Saru to gama) and "The monkey thief" (Saru no yatō). At the beginning there is a dialogue that is rather hard to understand, but the detail does not make it any more interesting.
　　Kunohe-gun: Kunohe 487, "The monkey, the rabbit, and the frog" (Saru to usagi to kaeru). It is mainly about how a monkey, a rabbit, and a frog rolled the mortar down and it ends as a "Why story."
Akita, Hiraga-gun: MK II 8 28, "The bullfrog and the monkey" (Bikki to saru). While the bullfrog was eating the mochi, the monkey came up angrily. The bullfrog tore off a piece of hot mochi and threw it at the monkey. It landed on its bottom and that is why it is red.
Yamagata, Kitamurayama-gun: MK II 6 42, "The monkey and the toad" (Saru to gama). The toad hid in the well and imitated a baby's cry. The monkey's face was red after hot mochi was thrown at it. However, the explanation is not well given. The mochi should have cooled by then.

Fukushima, Iwaki-gun: Iwaki 90, "The monkey and the bullfrog" (Saru to hiki).

Shinobu-gun: Shintatsu 100. No title.

Niigata: Echigo Sanjo 114, "The monkey and the bullfrog" (Saru to gama). Example. Minamikanbara 15, "The mochi race of the monkey and the bullfrog" (Saru to hiki no mochi kyōsō).

Nakauonuma-gun: Dai-ichi 46, "The bullfrog and the rabbit" (Gama to usagi).

Ishikawa: Kaga 55, "The rabbit and the frog" (Usagi to kaeru). If one made mochi into little balls with hairy hands, it would not do. The other had warts all over his hands, so neither wanted to make mochi balls. The mochi got caught on a monkey peach tree. That is why even now the rabbit nibbles at this tree.

Nomi-gun: MK II 8 35, "The rabbit, the frog, and the badger" (Usagi to kaeru to tanuki). The badger disguised itself as a girl and stole ears of rice and the three made mochi. The rabbit ate too quickly, so the badger pulled its ears. That is why they are long. The badger beat the frog, and that is why it is covered with lumps.

Nagano, Chiisagata-gun: MK I 1 35, "The bullfrog and the monkey" (Hiki to saru); Chiisagata 232, "The monkey and the bullfrog" (Saru to hiki). There is a part about rolling the mortar down. The words of the bullfrog, "Let's start eating where it hangs down." The monkey's face was red because he was ashamed. A trace of the white mochi remains on the bullfrog's throat.

Kitaazumi-gun: Otari 146. No title. A field cultivated together.

Gifu, Yoshiki-gun: Hidabito IV 3 38; 8 41; 11 17, "The monkey and the frog" (Saru to kaeru). The frog was from the rice paddy, so he brought the rice. The monkey was from the hills, so he brought the mortar and the pestle. They pounded mochi together. The mortar rolled over and away by itself. The monkey was angry and stamped on the frog. That is why its eyes pop out. "The frog and the rabbit" (Kaeru to usagi). Well constructed and brief. "The monkey and the bullfrog" (Saru to gama).

Osaka, Sennan-gun: Dai-ni 11, "The rabbit, the monkey, and the frog" (Usagi to saru to kaeru). The reason the rabbit's forelegs are short.

Hyōgo, Kanzaki-gun: Dai-ichi 66, "The monkey, the bullfrog, and the mochi" (Saru to hiki to mochi). The reason the frog's belly is so big is that he ate so much mochi. The monkey's face is red because he hurried too much.

Taki-gun: Techō 97, "The monkey and the bullfrog" (Saru to hiki).

Hiroshima: Aki 8, "The mochi race of the monkey, the bullfrog, and the rabbit" (Saru to hiki to usagi to no mochi kyōsō).

Izumo (Shimane): Nihon zenkoku 227, "The monkey and the bullfrog" (Saru to gama). There are two forms, one about stealing mochi and the other about cultivating a field together. In the mochi race, there are the monkey, the crab, and a pheasant, too. Exchanging the persimmon seed for the riceball is only in the story of the crab and the monkey.

Fukuoka, Mii-gun: Fukuoka 155, "The race of the rabbit, the monkey, and the tortoise" (Usagi saru oyobi kame no kyōsō). The rabbit and the monkey made the mochi. A turtle came along, but they did not want to divide with him. They carried the mochi up a mountain and hid it. Then they raced. The monkey's bottom was cut off and the rabbit's legs were broken. The tortoise ate the mochi alone. Is this a recently altered tale?

Kumamoto, Amakusa: MK II 1 40, "The monkey and the crab" (Saru to kani). The race between the monkey and the crab. When the crab pinched the monkey's seat, he cried, "Forgive me, forgive me. I'll give you some hair, I'll give you three hairs." That is why there is hair on the crab's legs.

Kagoshima: Koshiki 199, "The monkey, the frog, and the rabbit made mochi" (Saru to kaeru to usagi no mochi tsuki).

322. The Monkey, the Crab, and the Mochi

The monkey and the crab decided to make mochi. They gathered the rice together, but they had no mortar nor pestle. The crab borrowed them from a neighbor. After the mochi was done, the crab went to the neighbor to return the things. While he was gone, the monkey put all the mochi into a bag and climbed with it into a tree and ate it alone. The crab came back and could see nothing of the monkey nor the mochi. He hunted around until he finally saw the monkey up in the persimmon tree in back. The crab said from below, "Give me some." The monkey said, "Climb up," and refused to give any to the crab. It happened that the monkey was sitting on a dead branch. It fell with a crash. The crab grabbed the sack of mochi quickly and dragged it into his hole. This time the monkey begged, "Give me some." The crab answered, "Come here and get it." He would not give him even a little. The angry monkey put something dirty on the crab, but the crab pinched the monkey's bottom. That is why it is red.

Saga, Ogi-gun

Saga, Ogi-gun, Fujitsu-gun, and Kanzaki-gun: MK II 6, 18, 16, 20, "Why the monkey's seat is red" (Saru no shiri wa naze akai). The example is from Ogi-gun on 18. The three have the same title. In the example, a field was cultivated together and has nothing about rolling the mortar down.

Kashima-gun: Kōshō 10 15, "The monkey and the crab made mochi" (Saru to kani no mochi tsuki). When they gleaned, the monkey gave the crab a torn sack. (Connection with the Awabukuro and Kome-bukuro story.) There is no dirty episode.

Further reference:

Nihon dōwa no shin kenkyū 378. At the end, where the monkey was going to do something dirty in the crab's hole, the crab pulled the hairs on his seat. That is why the monkey's seat is red and he has no hair on his bottom. It is the reason for the hair on the crab's legs.

323. The Rice Field the Monkey and the Pheasant Cultivated

The monkey and the pheasant planted a rice field together. The pheasant went to it every day, but when he asked the monkey to go with him, he only made excuses and would not go. When it was time for the harvest, the monkey went for the first time. He took one bundle and the pheasant took one. Then the monkey took one more. The pheasant protested, but the monkey would not listen. The pheasant went home with only one third. After the monkey ate all his, he went to the pheasant's home to take what was there. That the chestnut, the crab, the mortar, and the egg helped the pheasant punish the monkey makes it like "The battle between the monkey and the crab."

Aomori, Hachinohe: MK II 12 58, "The fox and the pheasant" (Kitsune to kiji); Tekkiri 267, "The revenge of the pheasant" (Kiji no ada-uchi).
Iwate: Kunohe 483, 489, "The rabbit and the pheasant" (Usagi to kiji) and "The monkey, the rabbit, and the pheasant" (Saru to usagi to kiji). The pheasant came and ate all the millet in the field that he and the rabbit had cultivated together. The angry rabbit threaten-ed to put him on twelve sticks and broil him. The pheasant was rescued and escaped. One feels sorry for this rabbit. In the other story, the field was made by the monkey, the rabbit, and the pheasant. The monkey was the villian.
Akita, Senhoku-gun: MK I 10 21, "The monkey and the pheasant" (Saru to kiji); Ugo 40. The field was cultivated by the monkey and the pheasant.
Hiraga-gun: MK II 3 30, "The monkey and the pheasant" (Saru to kiji).
Niigata: Minamikanbara 19, "The rat and the weasel" (Nezumi to ita-chi).
Nagano: Chiisagata 236, "The monkey and the pheasant" (Saru to kiji). The monkey and the pheasant went to gather beans. The monkey ate his as they went along, but the pheasant put his into a sack and saved them. The monkey tried to get them in the winter, but the pheasant was protected by an egg, a bee, a crab, cow dung, and a mortar.
Kagoshima: Koshiki 196, "The monkey and the crab made mochi" (Saru to tsugani no mochi tsuki).

324. The Rice Field the Rat and the Weasel Cultivated

The rat and the weasel dug up a grassy place on the sandbar together and planted millet. When it began to grow, the weasel would go by the rat's home to ask it to weed the patch or to fertilize it. Whenever he came, the rat would make excuses and the weasel would go on alone. Finally, the grain ripened to gold. One night the rat slipped into the field secretly and cut the grain. She made mochi for her children and they ate it all up. When the weasel saw the field the next morning, he was astonished. He asked the crow, the kite, and the sparrow about it, but they said they didn't know anything about it. Then he went to the rat's house to tell what had happened. One of the little rats said to its mother, "Last night's millet mochi..." The mother rat was flustered and tried to silence it, but the children began to tease all the more. The weasel caught on and was furious. He said he would pull all the rat's teeth out. He relented, however, and left her two front teeth. That is why the rat has only two front teeth.

Echigo, Minamikanbara-gun

Akita, Kazuno-gun: Dai-ni 12, "The rice field cultivated by the monkey and the pheasant" (Saru do kiji do yoriaida). The monkey made all kinds of excuses and would not work, but when it came to divide the crop, he took two thirds. He said, "One bundle for the monkey, one bundle for the pheasant, and one more for the monkey." The story ends here. No mochi is made.

Niigata: Minamikanbara 19, "The rat and the weasel" (Nezumi to itachi). Example.

Ishikawa: Kaga 54, "The rabbit and the frog" (Usagi to kaeru). The rabbit and the frog made the field together. The rabbit always made excuses and would not go to work. The last part is still very much like the story of the fox and the otter with Sky Watcher and Earth Watcher episodes.

325. The Battle Between the Monkey and the Crab
or "The Crab Story"

Long ago the monkey and the crab went to glean rice and then made mochi together. The monkey thought of a trick to let him eat the mochi alone. He tipped the mortar over after the mochi was done. They had been working on a hill, so the mortar rolled down fast. The monkey chased it quickly, but the crab followed, crying miserably. After the monkey ran ahead to the mortar, the mochi fell out. The crab thought that settled things and he began to eat the mochi. The monkey came back and demanded that the crab divide it with him. The crab asked, "Why don't you eat what is in the mortar?" The monkey replied, "There isn't any in the mortar. Please give me some, even if there is dirt on it." The crab said, "Even if there is dirt on it, the dirt drops off if you toast it, and it tastes good." The monkey's face was red with anger. He shouted, "Well, then, I'm going into the hills and gather a thousand monkeys and we will take revenge on you!" With that, he went off, and the crab was left crying alone. A horse chestnut came along and asked what was the matter. He promised to defend the crab. Then a bee, cow dung, a pestle and mortar came and promised to help. The mortar and pestle climbed into the rafters, the cow dung hid in the corner of the entrance, the bee in a window, the crab in the water bucket, and the horse chestnut hid in the hearth. When the monkey arrived, he said it was cold and he leaned across the hearth to stir the coals. The chestnut popped up and burned the monkey. He went to the kitchen to cool its burns in the water bucket, but the crab pinched him. While he was crying with pain, the bee stung him on his cheek. He started to rush away, but he slipped on the cow dung and fell. Then the mortar and pestle fell on the monkey and crushed him.

Akita, Kazuno-gun

Aomori: Tsugaru m 23, "The revenge of the monkey and the crab" (Saru to kani no adauchi); Tsugaru k 7. No title. It begins with the field they cultivated together, but the monkey was not allowed to eat any. He was angry. While the crab cried, his friends came to rescue him.

Iwate: Shiwa-shū 63, "The monkey's theft at night" (Saru no yatō).
Hienuki-gun: Dai-ni 13, "The pheasant and the monkey" (Kiji to saru).

Akita, Kazuno-gun: Dai-ichi 38, "The monkey and the crab" (Saru to kani). Example. They worked the field together in the first part.

Niigata: Minamikanbara 12, "The monkey and the crab" (Saru to kani). They went to Sarugababa to take revenge. The crab's child took revenge. There is something unusual about the way this is told.
Sado: MK II 4 34, "The crab story" (Kani mukashi). The crab went out to find salt water and he found a persimmon seed. (Nothing unusual about how the tree grew.) The father was killed when the monkey threw persimmons at him. His child went for revenge. He gave millet dango to those who fought for him. These were a chestnut, a bee, a rock on which straw is pounded, a forked stick, a short sword, cow dung, and others.

Ishikawa: Kaga 38, "The monkey and the crab" (Saru to kani).

Nagano:. Chiisagata 236, "The monkey and the pheasant" (Saru to kiji). The monkey and the pheasant picked up beans. Those who helped in the revenge were a bee, a crab, cow dung, a piece of rope, a mortar, etc.

Kōshū (Yamanashi): Nihon dōwa shin ken 300, "The battle between the monkey and the crab" (Saru kani kassen). A little different from the version in *Enseki zasshi*. The works mentioned there have already been noted. The one in *Kogane no uma* is practically the same.

Hiroshima: Geibi 143, "The monkey and the crab" No. 1 (Saru to kani).
Toyota-gun: Aki 3, "The battle between the monkey and the crab" (Saru kani kassen).
Kamo-gun: Aki 6, "The battle over mochi by the monkey and the crab" (Saru kani mochi kassen). These last two tales are different in that there is mochi but no persimmon seed, close to tales of cultivating a field together.

Fukuoka, Miyako-gun: Fukuoka 58, "Oronkoron's revenge for his father" (Oronkoron no oya no katakiuchi). Oronkoron took the best millet dango in Japan with him as he went to Shinoyama in Tanba to take revenge for his father. The enemy was a yamauba. Dialogues are like those in "Momotarō" with a mortar, a cow, and a bee, his companions.

Asakura-gun: Fukuoka 110, "The horse leader's revenge" (Mago no katakiuchi). The last part of the story "The ox-leader and the yamauba" has this kind of revenge. There is a similar tale in *Buzen minwa shū*.

Ōita, Hayami-gun: MK I 12 45, "The crab and the monkey" (Kani to saru).

Kumamoto, Tamana-gun: MK I 1 42, "The monkey and the crab made mochi" (Saru kani mochi tsuki). A monkey fooled by a crab. When the monkey tried to drop something dirty into the crab's hole, his bottom got pinched. That is why it is red.

Nagasaki: Shimabara 101, "The monkey and the crab made mochi" (Saru to kani to mochi tsuki); Gotō 231, "The monkey and the crab" (Saru to kani). The crab hated the monkey in the tree and fooled him. He took the persimmons that were in the bag. In this the crab is mean. The bag is a part left from the story when it was about mochi.

In Kyūshū there are no defenders. There are stories about revenge and of protection. There is no fight in tales about mochi and the monkey and the bullfrog. They only become tales about origins.

Further reference:

Kiryo manroku 185, "Sarugashima." Among the popular songs of Gion in Kyoto, there is one that opens with "Mukashi, mukashi." It continues, "Long ago far back in the mountains...and a tongue-cut sparrow was chased away." In another, "Master Crab, Master Crab, where are you going?" "I'm going to take revenge for my father. A ghost of scissors, a chestnut from Tanba, a stone mortar, and a needle..." From these we can see forms found in Kyoto.

Zukin zasshi (in *Nihon zuihitsu taisei* I 147). In a printing of the Hōei era, an illustration of trading a persimmon seed for toasted mochi can be seen.

Tabi to densetsu IX 4 168. A Mongolian story. The first half is "O Sun, the chain." The she-demon ate the mother. Rescuers came while the four sisters were toasting mochi. They were an egg, a stone handmill, scissors, a needle, and a hog's head. This tale is in Fukuoka as a revenge for the sparrow by Oronkoron.

Chōsen mintan shū 211. An old woman enticed a bad tiger. Charcoal, red pepper, a needle, cow dung, a piece of straw matting and such tortured him. They said nothing and each appeared in turn alone.

326. The Revenge of the Crab

Yamanashi, Nishiyatsushiro-gun: Zoku Kai 219, 224, "The revenge of the crab" (Kani no adauchi) No. 1 and No. 2. There is an exchange of a persimmon seed and a riceball. The mother crab was killed, but a child was born from her shell. It went on revenge. The helpers were a bee, chestnut, a needle, dung, a mortar, and such. The old monkey woman was looking after things at the monkey's house. She gave him bad advice and he plunged into one danger after another. The second tale begins like "Momotarō." A persimmon was picked up along the bank of a river. The old man and old woman made it grow by singing, "Grow, or we will dig you up." The crab appears in the middle of the story.

327. The Sparrow

Long ago the sparrow hatched her young in the hole that was for the handle of the stonemill and left them. While she was away, a demon asked to see the little sparrows. He ate them all. The mother discovered that when she returned. She made corn dango and millet dango and set out to take revenge on the demon. When she met a cow and gave it one dango, it decided to go along with her. She met a bee, a chestnut, and a mortar. She gave each of them a dango, and they decided to fight for her. They found the demon sleeping by the hearth when they arrived at Hell. The chestnut hid in the ashes, the cow dropped dung by the back door, the mortar hid above it, and the bee hid there, too. The chestnut popped with a big noise. The demon woke up in surprise. When he started to run through the back door, he slipped on the cow dung, the bee stung him, and the mortar fell on him. Thus the revenge was carried out.

Hiroshima, Yamagata-gun

Iwate, Kamihei-gun: Rōō 113, "The sparrow's revenge" (Suzume no adauchi). The revenge was upon a yamahaha who took the eggs and ate them. Then she ate the mother. One of the eggs fell from the thicket and hatched. It gleaned rice to make dango when it set out for revenge.
Yamagata Kitamurayama-gun: MK II 11 33, "The monkey and the sparrow" (Saru to suzume).
Tochigi, Haga-gun: Shimotsuke 66, "The monkey, the sparrow, and the crow" (Saru to suzume to karasu). The monkey ate the sparrow's eggs. The crow helped chase the monkey. It ends with a "Why story."
Hiroshima: Aki 11, "The sparrow" (Suzume banashi). Example. It is interesting where the sparrow's nest is made. It may be in the hole for the handle of the mortar or Jizō's ear, or such.
Fukuoka: Buzen.[*]
Kagoshima: Koshiki 192, "The revenge of the colt" (Kouma no adauchi).

328. Kachi-Kachi Yama

Once upon a time an old man and an old woman went to their garden to plant beans. As they planted them, the old woman sang, "If I plant one bean, grow a thousand." The old man sang, "If I plant two beans, grow two thousand." A badger came out and sat on a rock casually. He chanted spitefully, "If you plant one bean, a warped bean; if you plant two, rotten beans." The old woman chased him off and they continued to work as before. The badger came back and sang spitefully again. He kept on coming back no matter how often he was chased away. The old man and the old woman talked over a plan. When they went home for lunch, they made a thick paste like mochi from buckwheat and brought it back with them. They smeared it over the rock on which the badger had sat and started to work again. The badger appeared again, but this time he stuck to the rock. The old man caught him and took him home. He hung him from the beams and said he would make badger soup of him that night. Then he went back to the hills, and the old woman started to pound wheat. The badger asked her to loosen his ropes and offered to help pound the wheat. He killed her with a single blow from the pestle. He disguised himself to look like her and cooked her up. When the old man came back from the hills, he ate what he thought was badger soup. He said, "This is tender and sweet." "Of course," replied the badger, "It's your old woman." With that, he leaped out the window and ran away. The rabbit came by where the old man was weeping alone and offered to help him take revenge. To begin with, he and the badger went to the hills and raced cutting grass. The rabbit set fire to the load the badger was carrying on their way back. He went home badly burned. The rabbit went by his place pretending to be a medicine peddler. He spread red pepper over the badger. This hurt him so much that the rabbit then spread salty bean soup over him. After the badger recovered, the rabbit made a dugout boat and a clay boat for them to go fishing in. The clay boat of the badger sank, and the revenge was complete.

Yamagata, Kitamurayama-gun

This can be said to be a complete version.

Aomori, Hachinohe: MK II 12 58, "Kachi-kachi Yama" Did this story start as an explanation of the trickiness of animals?
   Sannohe-gun, Gonohe: Tekkiri 33, 36, "Kachi-kachi Yama." This is about a bear and a rabbit. It was not for revenge, but just to torment him. "The rabbit at Tandeyama and the badger" (Tandeyama no usagi to tanuki). Close to the former example.
Iwate, Waga-gun: MK I 10 25, "The dugout boat and the clay boat" (Kibune to dorobune). An old man and an old woman cried because the badger ate Urikohime. The rabbit came and said he would take

revenge for them. There are episodes where the rabbit punished the badger when they went to cut grass, in the bamboo thicket, and where cryptomeria grew. The dugout boat and the clay boat are in the usual form.

Kamihei-gun: Kikimimi 306, "The rabbit's revenge" (Usagi no ada-uchi). It starts with the old man planting beans in the usual pattern, but the last is changed in an interesting way.

Iwate-gun, Shizukuishi: Kikimimi 312, "The rabbit and the bear" (Usagi to kuma). It starts from the second part of the story where the rabbit is negotiating with the bear. He made bear soup and went to a neighbor's house to eat it with the children. He fooled the father and made him lose all his teeth. The rabbit was caught and about to be killed, but he fooled the children and escaped. The reason the rabbit's tail became short is like the Gonohe version.

Isawa-gun: Isawa.*

Kunohe-gun: Kunohe 490, "The rabbit" (Usagi no hanashi). The last part of the Kachi-kachi Yama story and why the rabbit's legs are short.

Yamagata, Higashitagawa-gun: MK I 11 33, "The monkey and the rabbit" (Saru to usagi).

Kitamurayama-gun: MK II 6 40, "Kachi-kachi Yama." Example.

Akita, Senhoku-gun: Ugo 26. No title. The version in this region seems close to the one in Tokyo. The crow's telling the old man it was granny soup is like Urikohime.

Fukushima, Iwaki-gun: Iwaki 95, 167, "Kachi-kachi Yama."

Niigata: Minamikanbara 1, "Kachi-kachi Yama." There is nothing about catching a badger in the first part.

Ishikawa, Enuma-gun: Kaga 61, 52, 57, 59, "The rabbit, the monkey, and the otter" (Usagi to saru to kawauso). A story about the rabbit's cleverness. Refer to "Dividing things that were picked up." "The rabbit and the bullfrog" (Usagi to bettō don). After the part about the rabbit and the bullfrog and the mochi, it tells how the rabbit built a straw hut and put the bullfrog into it. He fixed it so he couldn't get out. There is a dialogue about a chin-chin bird and a pon-pon bird. It is rather broken, but the earlier form can be recognized. "The rabbit and badger" (Usagi to tanuki). This is rather like the standard story. "The rabbit and the bear" (Usagi to kuma). This resembles closely the Tōhoku tale about the rabbit tormenting the bear. He made a house, put the bear into it, and burned it to death. He went to a man's house to borrow a kettle and made bear soup. Then he ran into the mountains. No part about the kachi-kachi bird.

Yamanashi, Nishiyatsushiro-gun: Zoku Kai 208, "The rabbit's revenge" (Usagi no adauchi). It is close in form to the Tokyo version.

Gifu: Hidabito V 1 46. A note. Hidabito IX 6 34, "Kachi-kachi Yama." It goes from the badger soup to the revenge of the rabbit in the usual way, but the rabbit's way of fooling is elaborate.

Shizuoka, Ogasa-gun: Shizuoka 460, "Kachi-kachi Yama." The badger ridiculed the way the old man planted beans.

Hiroshima, Toyota-gun: Aki 17, "Granny soup" (Baba jiru); Geibi 21, "The monkey son-in-law" No. 2 (Saru muko iri). The last part of the monkey bridegroom story turns into "Kachi-kachi Yama." The wild boar who became the husband of the youngest daughter was burned to death during talk about a kachi-kachi bird and a bō-bō bird.

Yamaguchi, Suō Ōshima: Kōshō 11 22, "Kachi-kachi Yama." A fox took revenge instead of a rabbit.

Tokushima: Awa Iyayama 30, 36, "Kachi-kachi Yama." Two stories.

Ehime, Kamiukena-gun: Hidabito IX 5 30, "Kachi-kachi Yama." Only the first part and no revenge. A monkey instead of a badger.

    Kitauwa-gun: MK II 3 35, "Kachi-kachi Yama." The part before where the old woman pounded rice is dropped. The revenge begins with the dugout boat and the clay boat followed by the hut in which the bager was burned to death. There is a dialogue about kachi-kachi mountain and a bui-bui bird.

Fukuoka, Kiku-gun: Fukuoka 160, "Kachi-kachi Yama." The story has been revised a little.

Ōita: Naori 51, "Kachi-kachi Yama." There are four stories. A monkey is in the third. A wild boar with only how it was destroyed is in the fourth. The old man next door who fails to imitate is added.

Saga, Kinoshima-gun: Kōshō 11 13, "Kachi-kachi Yama." The old man himself and not the rabbit carried out the revenge. There is only the sport with the boats.

Kumamoto, Hōtaku-gun: MK I 9 37, "Granny raw relish" (Baba namasu). It is quite close to the standard story, but nothing about Kachi-kachi Yama, only the sport with the boats.

    Tamana-gun: MK I 1 43, "The monkey raw relish" (Saru no namasu). Refer to "The monkey raw relish."

    Amakusa-gun: MK I 10 43, "The old man digging in the field" (Tauchi jiji). The monkey is the villian in the first. It goes as far as where he fed granny soup to the old man and fled. The badger was the villain in the other and a fox took revenge.

Nagasaki, Kitatakaku-gun, Isahaya: Kōshō 8 5 "Kachi-kachi Yama."

    Iki: (Old) Iki 45, "The Iki story of Kachi-kachi Yama" (Iki no Kachi-kachi Yama).

    Tsushima, Nii-mura, Chiromo TD XII 8 16, "Kachi-kachi Yama."

Kagoshima: Koshiki 204, "The rabbit and the badger" (Usagi to tanuki). Two stories.

Further reference:

Mukashibanashi to bungaku. "Kachi-kachi Yama."

Mukashibanashi oboegaki. More "Kachi-kachi Yama."

Nihon dōwa shū 226.

Nihon mukashibanashi shū, ge 8. An Ainu example.

Hōgen V 10. Okayama City dialect.

Nihon zenkoku kokumin dōwa (The Chikuzen story). A story about a horse dealer and a yamauba. When the dry wood was broken, she asked, "What is that bug crying kachi kachi?"

Okayama bunka shiryō III 4 (Oku-gun). There is an example of a kachi-kchi bird in the story of the ox leader and the yamauba.

Enseki zasshi (in *Nihon zuihitsu taisei* II 10 104).

329. The Monkey Raw Relish

The badger of Kachi-kachi Yama is a monkey here.

Tokushima, Mima-gun: Awa Iyayama 66, 118, "Kachi-kachi Yama" and "Man and monkey" (Ningen to saru).

Kumamoto, Tamana-gun: MK I 1 43, "The monkey raw relish" (Sarun namasu).

Hōtaku-gun: MK I 9 37, "Granny raw relish" (Baba namasu). This was a badger, not a monkey. It ran off after it said, "There, Grandpa, you ate granny raw relish."

Nagasaki, Tsushima, Nii-mura, Chiromo: TD XII 8 16, "Kachi-kachi Yama." This was a monkey. It ends where the bones are shown under the floor boards. The rabbit did not take revenge on this island.

330. The Rabbit's Wiles

One part of Kachi-kachi Yama.

Gifu, Yoshiki-gun: Hidabito IV 11 18, "The monkey and the toad" (Saru to hiki). The enemy in this was a deer, not a badger. An episode about rolling the mortar down is in the first part. The toad left there. Then the other two went to cut grass. The rabbit burned the deer to death. He fooled its children, borrowed a kettle from them, and ate the deer himself. The second "Kachi-kachi Yama" is in the usual form.

17. Miscellaneous Stories between Folk Tales and Legends

331. Prince Yuriwaka

Yuriwaka was born from a peach and when he was little, he was called Momotarō. He wanted to marry the king's daughter, so he started out as a bath heater. The king told him he would give him the princess as bride if he went along to attack Onigashima, the demon hold. He gave himself the name Yuriwaka and took seven thousand boats to Onigashima (now called Iki). He started back after destroying the demons. He asked for a ride on a sardine boat, but was refused because he was taken for a demon. He managed to reach home finally, but nobody recognized him. Nobody would believe he was the former Yuriwaka. It happened that there was a horse at the king's palace who would let nobody but Yuriwaka ride him. Yuriwaka mounted it and displayed such skill in riding that he proved at last who he was. Then he married the king's daughter.

Iki

Nagasaki: Minzokugaku I 2 71, "Yuriwaka Daijin." Example.

332. A Gift of Thanks from a Woman with a Newborn Babe

A man who was entrusted with the child of a woman in labor was given the gift of great strength. This was inherited by girls through later generations in the family.

Nagasaki: Shimabara 90, "The strong woman" (Onna no tairiki).

Further reference:
The samurai Hiemon of Takijō washed his horse in a river and destroyed a kappa at Kawamoto, Toyota-gun, Aki. He received the gift of strength in return.

Konjaku monogatari, maki 27, No. 43, "Taira-no-Suetake met a woman with a newborn child in Mino-no-kuni. This is like a genuine ghost story. It is an old example.

333. The Human Sacrifice at Nagara Bridge

Kagoshima: Kikai 164, "If the pheasant did not cry" (Kiji mo nakazu ba). When a bridge was being set up on an island, one of four or five women who were looking on suggested that they take a woman with a knot in the tie of her hair as a human sacrifice. When they looked closely, that woman was seen to have such a knot. She was used as the support. Her daughter went as a bride to another island, but she would not speak a word. After a long time, she was to be returned home. A pheasant's cry was heard as she went through the hills on her way back. The girl sang, "The reason the pheasant is killed is that it cries. Because my mother spoke at Nagara Bridge, she was sacrificed." Her husband understood for the first time why his wife had not spoken. He took her back to his home.

Iwate, Hienuki-gun: Kōshō 11 1, "The human sacrifice at Nagara Bridge" (Nagara no hito bashira). This is rather different from the usual form. The wife of an official had a secret lover. She put a patch on her husband's skirt and suggested he be sacrificed because of it. His old mother told her granddaughter not to speak. The girl's song was, "The pheasant sang, 'Keain, keain hototogisu.' My father was the human support in the river's current because of my mother."

Could this be an error that appeared during generations of narrators?

Further reference:
Chōsen mintan shū 54, Keinan, Korea. "A bad wife for three years." This is not about a human sacrifice. A wife did not speak for three years because of her mother's instruction. She spoke for the first time when she heard a pheasant's call.

Chōsen mintan shū, App. 9.   A quotation from a collection of legends about mute wives.

Wakan sansai zue. The original text is on 74.

334. The Mandarin Ducks at Asonuma

Aichi, Nishikasugai-gun: Aichi 318, "The origin of Oshidoridera" (Oshidoridera no yurai). A legend of Shirakibashi, Kasuga-mura, Nishikasugai-gun. Long ago Tōdō, lord of the castle, shot a mandarin
duck with his bow of white wood. A beautiful girl appeared crying
in his dream. When he shot the female the next day, she was
carrying the head of the male duck he had shot. It is an example
of two combined plots. This story appeared very early and is widely distributed, but it can not be called a folk tale. It does not
have the quality of a folk tale.

335. The Silkworm God and the Horse

Nagano, Minamiazumi-gun: Dai-ichi 53, "The silkworm god and the
horse" (Kaeko gami to uma). Long ago the silkworm was a lovely
maid. She lost her mother quite early and her stepmother abused
her. The stepmother tried twice to bury the girl alive in the
stable, but the horse saved her each time. Then she was put into a
boat and floated downstream, but she was rescued and she returned. She was buried again and again in the yard, but rescued. Her
spirit entered a silkworm when she was reborn because of her
suffering.

Yamanashi, Nishiyatsushiro-gun: Kai 161, "The origin of the silkworm"
(Kaiko no okori). There are two tales. We can see that the Shinshū
one is either an abridgment or something has been forgotten. This
kind of story may have been a katarimono, but it could hardly
have sprung up independently from a folk tale. It has been kept
alive among folk tales by some mutual circumstance.

336. Failing to Eat a Mermaid

Kagoshima: Kikai 166, "Nijūsanya Sama." A beggar came to take part
in the gathering for Nijūsanya Sama [Twenty-third Night]. He invited everyone to come to his place for the next gathering. When
they went, they found a splendid house. A baby was being cooked
in the kitchen. (It was actually a mermaid.) Two guests ran away
and only the chief guest stayed to enjoy the feast.

This tale is handed down in Tōhoku as a story about watching
up for Kōshin. It is like the saying that he who eats a mermaid
can enjoy endless youth.

337. The Day on Which Blood Flowed from the Eyes of the Stone Image

A legend of Kōreijima.

Miyagi, Natori-gun, Medeshima-mura: Kyōdo den 1 172, "The jar full of coins" (Zeni no tanto haetta tsubo). A man was told that there would be treasure where dew did not fall at night. He went around as a grass cutter to look for such a place. Someone left a sedge hat on the ground and then took it away. The man dug there and found a jar of coins.

Further reference:
Chōsen mintan shū 61. A legend of Kōho. An old woman at a wine shop was told by a man who traveled around that when the image of the child standing before a grave on the mountainside shed blood from its eyes, she should move to the mountain top. Young men who were full of pranks painted the eyes of the image red in the night secretly. The old woman was the only one who escaped the great flood. See App. 15.

338. Fish That Talk

Miyagi, Tome-gun, Nishikiori-mura, Masabo-no-taki: Kyōdo den 1 177, "Masabō-no-taki." A traveling priest saw two eels at this waterfall. He caught one and put it into his bag and went on. He heard a voice from the pool, "Oh, Masabō! Oh, Masabō! When are you coming back?" The answer came from inside the bag, "Masabō will come back, all right!" The priest took the eel out of the bag in great surprise and set it free. From that time the place name has been written as kurukozu-no-taki, but it is called Masabō-no-taki.

Further reference:
Hitotsume kozō sonota. The story of the fish king that asked to be freed.

339. How the Little Snake Grew

Iwate, Kamihei-gun: Kikimimi 151, "Nue at Hataya" No. 2 (Hataya no Nue). This is an anecdote about a man named Nue.

340. What Happens If a Shark's Bones are Kicked

Shimane, Iwami: TD IX 3 30, "The shark's curse" (Fuka no noroi). A
gentleman of Hamada called Iwai Tomonoshin was a famed marks-
man. He killed a big shark at sea. When he saw the shark's bones
at an inn in Osaka, he kicked them in a fit of anger. They bit
deep into his foot. The poison gradually filled him and he died. A
memorial was set up for him at Hachiman shrine in Hiruko-machi,
Hamada.

341. A Shadow Swallowed by a Shark

Ōita, Kitaamabe-gun: MK I 3 42, "A shadow swallowed by a shark"
(Fuka ni kage o nomareta hanashi). A samurai set out to sea on a
boat, but it came to a standstill. The captain told everyone to
throw his towel into the sea, and the one whose towel sank would
have to be fed to the shark. When that was done, only the towel
of the samurai sank. He was afraid he would be swallowed by the
shark. He took his bow and arrow and shot into the sea. The shark
fled, and the boat moved on. Some time later, the samurai stopped
at a certain port and heard about an unusually large shark that
had washed up onto the beach. He went to look at it and found
that the arrow stuck in its head was none other than his own. He
put his head into the shark's mouth to have a look. Although the
shark was dead, for some reason its mouth closed firmly and killed
the samurai. A shark that swallows a shadow of a man will surely
kill him.

342. The Fish-Stone of Nagasaki

Kagoshima: Kikai 175, "The jewel of the spider" (Kumo no tama). A
man looking for a treasure called a spider jewel agreed to buy a
wretched old house for 1000 ryō. The owner grew greedy. He
cleaned the house thoroughly and refused to sell it at that price.
The buyer came with nets to cover it so no spiders could escape.
He could not find a single one because the house had been cleaned. He refused to buy the house because of that.

Further reference:
   Kikaijima mukashibanashi shū 135, "The fish-stone at Keraji"
(Keraji no uoishi).
   Nihon mukashibanashi shū jō 174, "The fish-stone of Nagasaki"
(Nagasaki no uoishi).

The Fascination of
Folk Tales and Names,
Beginnings and Endings

343. Stories without an End

These are told to protect the narrator when listeners insist upon hearing more. They are called "kirinashi banashi" [stories without an end], "nemutai banashi" [sleepy stories], "nagai hanashi" [long stories], and the like. Stories told just to tease those who like stories are also called such.

Aomori: Tsugaru m 26, "A long story" (Nagai mukashi). The crow and horse chestnut.
    Hachinohe: MK II 12 59, "The story without an end" (Hatenashi banashi). A man said he would give his daughter to whoever told her stories until she said she had enough. A zatō came and told her a story without an end and received her. She substituted a cow along the way, but he did not see. Various things he said to her are amusing.
Iwate: Kamihei 189, "The story without an end" (Kirinashi banashi). Several stories, such as: a man cut the snake with his short sword chokkiri [completely], and it grew out again perot [suddenly]. He cut it chokkiri, it grew out perot, etc. Shiwa 7, "The two-year sesame and the three-year sesame" (Nisai goma to sansai goma). The grandmother of a chōja liked stories, but she gave in at last. The agreement had been to give the narrator a two year old colt

[nisai goma] if he told her enough, but he was given two year old sesame [nisai goma] instead.

Yamagata, Higashitagawa-gun, Karikawa-mura: MK II 7 31, "Sleepy stories" (Nemutai hanashi). One is about what happened on the way to visit Haguro Shrine. A man chased a snake *shii* [shoo], and it glided away *zerot*. He chased it *shii* and it glided away *zerot*, etc. The second setting is also a pilgrimage to Haguro. Bright autumn leaves were on trees along a river bank and many frogs were in it. When a frog croaked *gegu-gegu*, a leaf fell *potat*. A frog croaked *gegu-gegu*, a leaf fell *potat*, etc.

Miyagi, Momoo-gun: Kyōdo den 1 182, "A feudal lord who liked tales" (Hanashi suki na tono sama); Kyōdo den 3 117, "An old woman who liked tales" (Mukashi suki na baba). A feudal lord and an old woman got their fill of tales.

Fukushima, Iwaki-gun: Iwaki 184, "The long story" (Nagai hanashi).

Niigata: Sado shū 200, "The long story" (Nagai hanashi). One story is about a boat loaded with 1000 rats. They jumped onto a bridge one at a time as they said, "Hold onto my tail with your teeth, chii-chii-chii." In the other, a white loin cloth hung down from the sky in clear weather. It still hung there no matter how much it was pulled.

Minamiuonuma-gun: MK I 7 29. One story is about horse chestnuts growing on the bank of a river. The other is about a snake so long that he wrapped himself around Mt. Fuji seven times and a half, and then tried to go home.

Ishikawa: Kaga 132, "The 5000 bushel boat" (Sen goku bune). A 5000 bushel boat packed with frogs.

Nagano, Shimoina-gun: Mukashibanashi 94, 151, "A long scary tale" (Nagakute kowai hanashi) and "The longest story in the world" (Sekai no ichiban nagai hanashi). A story for a feudal lord who liked tales and one about ants that dragged rice one grain at a time.

Gifu, Yoshiki-gun: Hidabito V 6 8, "A tale without an end" (Hatenashi banashi). Four tales with the same title. A chestnut tree on a bank in one. A bride in another taught her husband to say, "The leaves, the stems, and potatoes can be eaten."

Yamaguchi: Nihon zenkoku 275, "The feudal lord who liked tales" (Hanashi suki no tono sama); Nihon den 172, "The feudal lord who liked tales" (Hanashi suki no tono sama). How a feudal lord who liked tales chose a son-in-law.

Tokushima, Mima-gun: MK II 1 31, "A story worth 1000 ryō" (Hanashi senryō). They filled a 1000-bushel boat with fleas and let a few out at a time. Awa Iyayama 135, "The long story" (Nagai hanashi).

Fukuoka, Munakata-gun: Fukuoka 212, "A tale without an end" (Tsuki-nu hanashi). Many frogs gathered at a lake. A big one jumped in *dobon*, then a little one *chibin*.

Ōita: Naori 57, "A story without an end" (Hatenashi banashi). A man sent for a boatload of lice and a boatload of fleas. The lice crawled *zoro-zoro* and the fleas jumped *hot*. The story continued for three days and three nights. The chōja was worn out and took the narrator as his son.

Nagasaki, Iōjima: Minzoku ken No. 19 45. No title.

Kagoshima: Koshiki 210, "The tale about a cormorant" (U no tori banashi).

344. Nonsense Stories

When material for a story is exhausted, stories without a point, fake stories, are told. They make children laugh with tricky words.

Iwate: Kamihei 186, "A sleepy story" (Nemutai banashi). A blind man discovered a fire in the mountain, a dumb man shouted, and a cripple rushed to put it out.

Akita, Kazuno-gun: Kikimimi 578, "The old sword" (Mukashi katana). Mukashi katana may also mean not to tell a story. A wagon was put onto the point of a sword and pulled from there. When asked what it was, the man said it was a mukashi katana. That is why the story can not continued. This makes children give up.

Yamagata, Higashitagawa-gun: MK II 7 31, "A sleepy story (Nemutai banashi). Once there was an old man and an old woman. The old man rested his gun upon a mortar. That's a story without a tempo [point], so it can not be told. The play on words is on teppo [gun] and tempo.

Gunma: Kiryū 175, "Greens and wine" (Na to sake). Four stories. In one, na [greens] without sake [wine], making it nasakenai [miserable]. In another, the board [ita] said ita [it hurts] and the dust [gomi] said gomin nasai [pardon]. Such tales.

Ishikawa: Kaga 108, "Acorns" (Shii no mi). A turnip pulled from both ends lost its leaves. That made it hanashi [without leaves or story]. When a man was looking up to the sky, an acorn fell on his face and he lost his nose, hanashi [no nose or story]. There was a child who would not laugh. When they opened his mouth to see, he had no teeth [hanashi, a story or no teeth].

Kagoshima: Koshiki 209, "A fake story" (Uso banashi).

345. The Story is Stripped off

The story got stripped off; the chōja got bald.

Nagasaki

This is for when one has run out of stories. It is just playing with words.

Iwate: Kikimimi 576, "The trip by three" (Sannin tabi).

Miyagi, Momoo-gun: Kyōdo den 2 118, "The failure of the tengu" (Tengu no shippai). The mukashi put on a mu and the hanashi a ha. The mukashi arrived at Mojiriko and the hanashi arrived at Hantenko. Then they went off to Wakudani.

Toyama, Toyama City environs: MK II 6 29. A note. Jingles that are said when story telling starts. Mukashi flew out from yonder, hanashi flew out of the nose, and long ago they rang a bell, today they hit the bottom of a gourd.

Tottori, Yazu-gun, Saigo-mura: Inpaku min III 2 22. No titles, five stories.

Tokushima: Awa Iyayama 98, "Folk tales" (Mukashibanashi) [This is a difficult jingle to render in English about a monkey's seat, the bird's tail, and saying there is no more].

Nagasaki: Zen Nagasaki 202, "The story is stripped off" (Mukashi ya muketa). Example.

346. A Story Like a Sanbasō

Kumamoto, Hōtaku-gun: MK II 6 22, "A story like a sanbasō" (Hanashi no sanbasō). Once there was an old man and an old woman. The old man went to the mountains to cut grass and the old woman went to the river to do washing. A kappa came out and called, "Let me pull you, Granny!" She thought he said, "Lend me fire." She went for a fire brand and offered it to him, saying, "I'll lend you fire. I'll lend you fire." The kappa came out wearing an ebōshi and called, "Honka, honka."

This was the sign the story was about to start and to get people into the mood. Other examples of this have not been found.

347. Daytime Stories

Stories are not told in the daytime because they say rats will laugh at them.

Iwate: Esashi shi 253, "A common saying" (Rigen). Mentioned. The same in Higashiiwai-gun.

Names, Beginnings and Endings of Folk Tales

[This final section of Yanagita's work is summarized and explained rather than translated because the examples are for the most part presented in *katakana*, their meaning not written in standard Japanese.

The contents, however, contain matters of importance and must be presented. Items in the original text are listed in the same way as up to this point—their geographical distribution and the written source. Their treatment is highly selective and gives a sample rather than a complete survey. Fanny Hagin Mayer.]

The first matter considered is the expression used to indicate the old orally transmitted folk tale. This is the one used by local narrators or their listeners and does not include newly invented terms by scholars, some of which have found their way into more sophisticated use. The term "mukashibanashi" has two elements in it. "Mukashi" establishes the "long ago" of the tale. Sometimes various degrees of past are indicated, just as it may be in English, but the important point is that no certain time is in mind. Formerly "katari" was used for tales or even the ordinary verb "to tell," but when it began to be applied to more pretentious tales or literary works, "hanashi" replaced it when referring to the oral tale. In the northeast, "mukashi-ko" is used even now. The "ko" is an ending given to many nouns. In the southwest there are "ge na banashi," the "ge na" is to establish "so it is said." In other words, the tale is repeated, but the narrator does not vouch for its truth. "Monogatari" or "ohanashikatari" are also still used as the term in some regions.

The next section lists several types of tales which belong to the oral tradition but which are not folk tales in the usual sense. These will be named and described briefly.

"Hayamonogatari" is a type which depends upon a good memory and a quick tongue for telling. It is usually humorous and brief, a sort of practice piece for a young apprentice story teller who is given a chance to try his skill between numbers performed by an experienced narrator.

"Shūku banashi" depends upon a line of a poem to resolve the story. In literary circles this becomes a refined art of quoting classics or matching lines, but the level in the folk tale is more modest. Sometimes a single line can solve a riddle proposed by a chōja. The clever winner may even be rewarded with the hand of the lovely daughter of the chōja.

"Hotoke mai," sometimes called "Jizō mai," is not a dance, as the name might suggest, but a comical song chanted before the door of a home by an itinerant at New Year or a summer festival. There is a bit of bantering with the name Hotoke (Buddha) and the singer is sent along with a donation for his performance.

"Yobanashi" are related at a house where villagers gather for night watches at Kōshin-ko or on Nijūsanya. Offerings of mochi and wine are made and tales are exchanged to pass the time. These are adult tales.

"Toshitori banashi" are told as the family sits up for the New Year. There are a number of genuine folk tales with New Year as central interest and such tales are included.

"Renga banashi" are also tales with an added line of a poem to resolve them. An old example is that of the priest who happened to be holding a piece of mochi he intended to eat alone, but his novice came into the room. The lad exclaimed, "There is no half moon on Fifteenth Night." The priest reluctantly brought out the rest and handed it to the boy. He said, "The other half was hidden by a cloud."

"Kyōka banashi" are comical lines of a poem to cover a blunder, perhaps of a new son-in-law in an outlandish remark while visiting his father-in-law. The bride hurriedly revises it as she repeats it to impress her parents with her husband's cleverness.

"Imoji banashi" are tinker tales. Itinerant tinkers told clever tales as they plied their trade. Their tales tend to be boasts, hence the saying, "Like a tinker's tale" for somebody's bragging.

"Komori banashi" are jingles which include in them references to folk tales, much like counting lines of children who bounce a ball, but no gestures accompany them.

"Usotoki" are tales of an only survivor. There is nobody left to affirm or deny the account of, for example, the cave-in of a fabulously rich vein of gold told by the only survivor.

The third matter discussed is that of leading characters of humorous tales. These stories are "odoke banashi," a number of which are included in the main body of the text. The characters have names which sound amusing to Japanese, such as Hikohachi, Kichigo, Kitchyomu, and the like. Some of the men are numbskulls and others are rascals, their names changing with the region but the contents of tales resembling each other. In some instances the episodes are strung together in a series, but usually they are brief, unrelated events.

Formulas are the last matter presented. The opening formula of the folk tale varies according to region, but it establishes two points. The tale is about long ago and the narrator is only repeating what he has heard and does not vouch for the truth of the tale. This is in marked contrast to the opening of a legend, which usually establishes the place where the event occurred and then relates the circumstances. The closing formulas come in a greater variety of form and meaning. It may be as brief as "ton," a signal that the end has come, or a jingle of several lines which shows some ingenuity and humor. Its purpose is to indicate the end of the tale, that is all there is to it, or that is how the narrator heard it. Besides these, there are those added to state the characters prospered ever after or that they lived in ease or "medetashi, medetashi," which means everything turned out fine. These formulas are not rendered in standard Japanese and their meaning is often obscure. No attempt has been made to render them in English in this translation because the jingle itself would escape.

The other formula is the phrase employed by listeners who chime in as the tale progresses. It is something like the AMEN heard in old time camp meetings which was intended on one hand to encourage the narrator to continue and in the other to express the listener's approval and anticipation of what was to follow. The word is brief, varying as to region, but it is very necessary to the successful rendition of the story.

APPENDED MATERIAL

Bibliography of Sources

Sources are listed first by the abbreviation used to identify them in the text, then by their full name, editor and publication information. The numbers following the abbreviated titles are the story numbers in this book where the works are cited. Items marked with a asterisk were not available to the translator and could not be verified. Information for some was furnished by scholars. Items headed by parentheses are frequently listed without that portion of the title.

Aichi 18, 24, 82, 141, 160, 161, 213, 234
  Aichi-ken densetsu shū, Aichi-ken Kyōikukai, ed. Kyōdo Kenkyūsha: 1937, pp. 397. Legends of Aichi Prefecture.
Aikawa 72
  Aikawa-cho shi, Iwai Hiro, Aikawa, Sado-gun, Niigata. Aikawa-chō Yakuba: 1927, pp. 465. Records about Aikawa.
Aki 1, 3, 8, 14, 18, 19, 28, 30, 33, 40, 42, 48, 51, 57, 58, 59, 67, 69, 105, 106, 107, 124, 133, 134, 139, 140, 153, 158, 164, 166, 174, 206, 207, 221, 224, 245, 247, 275, 291, 304, 318, 321, 325, 327, 328
  Akinokuni mukashibanashi shū, Isogai Isamu. Oka Shoin: 1934, pp. 292. Folk tales of the Hiroshima area.
Akita 67, 114, 128
  Akita gunyū gyotan, Muto Tetsujō. Attic Museum: 1940, pp. 361. Stories of fishing villages in Akita.
Amakusa den 100
  Amakusajima densetsu sanshū, dai isshū, Hamada Ryūichi. Mimeographed by the author: 1931, pp. 36. Twenty variations of yamauba stories found in *Shokoku mintan*.
Amakusa min 1, 107, 163, 196, 198
  Amakusa minzoku shi, Hamada Ryūichi. Kyōdo Kenkyūsha: 1932, pp. 242. Records about Amakusajima.
Ariga 171, 175, 233, 237
  Ariga Kizaemon, privately published *Azuma no minwa*. These tales are scheduled to be included in the volumes of the complete works of Professor Ariga.
Awa den 268
  Awa no densetsu, Hayama Jōtarō. Chiba. Awa Tsūshōsha: 1917, 1937, pp. 492. Legends of Awa (Chiba).
Awa Iyayama 3, 8, 14, 16, 17, 18, 20, 23, 28, 29, 36, 40, 48, 51, 52, 68, 69, 70, 72, 75, 76, 78, 86, 97, 99, 102, 105, 106, 107, 110, 120, 122, 129, 137, 150, 152, 155, 158, 159, 160, 170, 171, 174, 185, 188, 210, 211, 213, 215, 238, 261, 267, 304, 312, 328, 329, 343, 345
  Awa-no-Iyayama mukashibanashi shū, Takeda Akira. Sanseidō: 1943,

pp. 156. A *Zenkoku Kiroku* volume. Now available in a 1973 edition under the title *Tokushimaken Iyayama chihō mukashibanashi shū.* Folk tales of Iyayama.

Baba sama 174
Baba sama no ohanashi, Sakatani Shunsaku. Nagoya. Published by author: 1942, pp. 69. Folk tales told by the author's grandmother.

Shin zoku Bashō 278
Shin Zoku Bashō haikai kenkyū, Komiya Hōryū and others. Iwanami Shoten: 1933, pp. 539. A collection of five studies about the haiku of Bashō.

Bōchō 3, 33
Bōchō bunka Vol. I, No. 2. Yamaguchi: Published by Bōchō Bunka Kenkyūkai: 1937, April. Only two volumes, eight numbers, were published between January, 1937, and October, 1938.

Bungo den 68, 104, 162, 278, 283
Bungo densetsu shū, Ichiba Naojirō. Ōita. Kyōdo Shiseki Densetsu Kenkyūkai: 1931, pp. 130. Legends of Ōita.

Bungo hōgen 269, 279
Bungo hōgen shū No. 3, Ichiba Naojirō, Hatano Sōkai, Kondō Tsuyoi and others. Ōita: 1936. Three numbers were issued from 1933 to 1936.

Bungo min* 106, 296
Bungo minwa shū, Ichiba Naojirō.

Bungo kijin 156, 212, 213, 233, 238, 239, 258, 318
(Bungo no kijin) Kitchyomu san monogatari, Miyamoto Kiyoshi. Ōita. Ōita Minyū Shinbun: 1927, pp. 333. A collection of traditional humorous tales.

Buzen* 48, 105, 111, 268, 274, 291, 296, 327
Buzen minwa shū, Umebayashi Shin'ichi. Fukuoka. Dozoku Gangu Kenkyūkai: 1931.

Chihō* 96, 148, 153, 155, 166, 199
Chihō sōdan.

Chiisagata 1, 3, 17, 18, 20, 28, 30, 33, 36, 37, 42, 43, 48, 72, 79, 100, 107, 117, 139, 146, 152, 158, 167, 170, 183, 202, 238, 239, 243, 246, 247, 268, 283, 294, 313, 319, 321, 325
Chiisgata-gun mintan shū, Koyama Masao. Kyōdo Kenkyūsha: 1933, pp. 314. Tales of Chiisagata-gun, Nagano.

Chikuzen* 107, 161
Chikuzen densetsu shū, Sasaki Jikan. Fukuoka. Kyūshū Dozoku Kenkyūkai. Beginning in 1932, 57 numbers were issued.

Dai-ichi 3, 17, 27, 30, 33, 34, 36, 50, 55, 58, 72, 75, 76, 82, 85, 92, 97, 107, 133, 135, 136, 137, 139, 153, 155, 163, 171, 172, 174, 183, 199, 200, 226, 234, 257, 260, 264, 269, 272, 275, 283, 294, 297, 302, 304, 314, 318, 319, 320, 321, 325, 335
Dai-ichi mukashibanashi gō, Tabi to densetsu, Vol. IV, No. 4, April, 1931. The first number that was devoted entirely to folk tales.

Dai-ni 3, 16, 17, 20, 30, 33, 37, 39, 48, 55, 76, 79, 81, 88, 102, 105, 106, 107, 112, 113, 125, 126, 129, 139, 164, 167, 170, 174, 185, 193, 200, 204, 256, 260, 269, 283, 294, 304, 306, 308, 321, 324
Dai-ni mukashibanashi gō, Tabi to densetsu, Vol. VII, No. 12, December, 1934. The second issue devoted to folk tales.

Densetsu Echigo I: 7, 72; II: 57, 68
    Densetsu no Echigo to Sado, Vol. I, 1923, pp. 280, Nakano Shōgo
    (penname, Jōsui). Niigata. Ginreisha; Vol. II, 1924, pp. 243. Legends
    of Niigata and Sado Island. The title is frequently abbreviated to
    Essa densetsu.
Den Shimoina 97
    Densetsu no Shimoina, Iwasaki Kiyomi. Iida-machi, Shimoina-gun,
    Nagano. Bunseidō Shoten: 1923, pp. 194. This was printed in the
    style of the *Rohen sōsho* series. Legends of Shimoina.
Dōbutsu* 17: 268, 288, 289; 20: 11; 21: 69
    Dōbutsu bungaku, Nos. 17, 20, 21. Hirai Yoneguchi, ed. Publication
    began in June, 1934. No. 53 is listed as August, 1939.
Dozoku 277
    Dozoku to densetsu, Vol. 1, No. 2, Ushijima Gunpei, ed. Bunbudō,
    1918-1919. Only one volume, of four numbers, was published.
Echigo Sanjo 33, 106, 190, 245, 304, 310, 313, 321
    Echigo Sanjo Nangō dan, Toyama Rekirō. Kyōdo Kenkyūsha. 1926,
    pp. 171. Tales of Sanjo Nangō in Niigata. A *Rohen sōsho* volume.
Echigo yashi 57
    Echigo yashi, jō, Odajima Mitsutake. Niigata. Echigo Yashi Kankō-
    kai: 1936, pp. 402. A two volume work with legends and local infor-
    mation about nature in Niigata, originally published as a series of
    shahon from Bunsei (1818) to mid-Tenpū (1830-1834).
Enzoku 106
    Enzoku mondō shū, Attic Museum, ed. Attic Museum: 1939, pp. 231.
    Salt in folklore.
Esashi 14, 39, 55, 57, 75, 76, 80, 81, 100, 122, 136, 139, 140, 171, 181,
    193, 194, 197, 204, 214
    Esashi-gun mukashibanashi, Sasaki Kizen. Kyōdo Kenkyūsha: 1922,
    pp. 167. Folk tales of Esashi-gun, Iwate. A *Rohen sōsho* volume.
Esashi shi 347
    Esashi-gun shi, Iwate-ken Kyōikukai Esashi-gun Bukai, ed. Published
    by the editors: 1925, pp. 465. Records about Esashi-gun.
Etchū 315
    Etchū kyōdo kenkyū, Vol. III, No. 10, Etchū Kyōdo Kenkyūkai.
    Toyama: Chūetsu Kyōdo Kenkyūsha: October 1939. A publication of
    Toyama Shihan Gakkō dealing with folklore in Toyama.
Fugeshi 30, 37
    Fugeshi-gun shi, Fugeshi-gun Yakusho, ed. Kanazawa. Published by
    the editor: 1923, pp. 1324. Records about Fugeshi-gun, Ishikawa.
Fujisawa 135
    Fujisawa shi, Fujisawa-machi Kyōdo Kenkyūkai, ed. Fujisawa-
    machi, Higashiiwai-gun, Iwate. Published by the editor: 1941,
    pp. 305. Records about the town of Fujisawa.
Fukihara 83, 154, 155
    Fukihara, No. 3, Ina Tomi Shōgakkō Kyōdo Kenkyūkai, ed. Ina,
    Kamiina-gun, Nagano. Published by the editor: 1932. The first three
    issues were numbered. Following them, four volumes were listed by
    volume and number from 1932 to 1938.
Fukuoka 1, 3, 8, 20, 28, 33, 36, 39, 40, 42, 48, 50, 65, 97, 105, 109,
    141, 145, 150, 152, 155, 170, 171, 174, 177, 183, 194, 205, 211, 213,

215, 216, 217, 219, 220, 221, 224, 234, 235, 236, 238, 243, 244, 245, 246, 247, 250, 257, 259, 266, 304, 308, 313, 320, 321, 325, 328, 343
Fukuoka-ken mukashibanashi shū. A manuscript. This is now available under the same title, edited by Fukuoka-ken Kyōikukai. Iwasaki Bijitsusha, 1975, pp. 255. Items in the translation are listed by the new page numbers. Folktales of Fukuoka.

Fushi 2: 105; 3: 48, 268, 269
Fushi zappitsu, Sawada Shirōsaku. Osaka. Published by the author. No. 2. 1934 and No. 4 1938. This is a series of booklets covering various parts of Japan and dealing with topics of interest about folklore, legends, and folk tales.

Geibi
(Mukashibanashi no kenkyū) Geibi Sōsho (see below under full title).

Gonohe 318
Gonohe mukashibanashi, Noda Tayoko. A manuscript completed in 1937 or 1938. Refer to *Tekkiri ane sama* below for all but one item. Folk tales of Aomori.

Gotō 1, 69, 105, 124, 158, 161, 245, 275, 277, 304, 308, 325
Gotō minzoku zushi, Kubo Kiyoshi and Hashiura Yasuō. Isseisha: 1934, pp. 577. Folklore of the Gotō Islands.

Haga 206, 291
Haga-gun dozoku kenkyū kaihō, Haga-gun Dozoku Kenkyūkai, ed. Sakawa-mura, Haga-gun, Tochigi. Published by the editors, Vol. I: 1929 -1930; Vol. II: 1931. These are mimeographed reports by the group. The number of pages (folded) vary and some are not numbered.

Hanashi I: 7: 247; II: 3: 194; 4: 227; 6: 278, 320
Hanashi no sekai, collected by Kimura Miki. Published by Adachi Shirōkichi, Vol. I, No. 7, December, 1919, and Vol. II, Nos. 3, 4, and 6, March, April, June, 1920. These numbers vary from 125 to 134 pages. They contain a variety of material from various places in Japan.

Zoku Hida 50, 66, 109, 248
Zoku Hida saihō nisshi, Sawada Shirōsaku. Osaka: Published by the author: 1939, pp. 164. Additional field notes from Hida. This is No. 8 of *Fushi zappitsu*.

Hida den 30
Hida no densetsu to minyō, Takagi Kiyotayū. Takayama. Takayama Nishi Shōgakkō Kenkyūbu: 1933, pp. 93. Legends and folk songs of Hida (Gifu).

Hida fubutsu 27
Hida fubutsuki, Uejima Zen'ichi. Takayama. Hida Mainichi Shinbun: 1929, pp. 352. Customs found in Hida (Gifu).

Hida tori 279
Hida no tori, Kawaguchi Magojirō. Kyōdo Kenkyūsha: 1921, pp. 190. Birds of Hida (Gifu).

Hidabito III: 33, 54; IV: 14, 17, 28, 141, 159, 252, 253, 268, 269, 282, 288, 294, 308, 313, 319, 321, 330; V: 14, 17, 18, 28, 30, 33, 36, 40, 42, 50, 92, 100, 101, 106, 107, 117, 131, 156, 158, 174, 205, 213, 234, 267, 304, 328; VII: 135; IX: 238
Hidabito, Hida Kōkō Minzoku Gakkai. Takayama. Published by Wada Toshihiko. Vol. III: 1935; Vol. IV: 1936; Vol. V: 1937; Vol. VII: 1939;

Vol. IX: 1941. Twelve volumes were issued between 1933 and 1941 on folklore in Hida (Gifu). Items in *Hidabito* were collected by Suzuki Tōzō. They have now been published as *Shyami-shakkiri* (a closing formula), Suzuki Tōzō, Kyōkawa Seiji, ed. Miraisha, Nihon no mukashibanshi, No. 14, 1975.

Higo VI: 72
> *Higo kokushi*, Vol. VI, Morimoto Yoshiharu. Kumamoto: 1885, pp. 209 (folded). Records about Higo. This work appeared originally during Kōhō (1716-1736).

Hōgen IV: 8: 8; 9: 87; V 6: 328
> *Hōgen*, Takatō Takema, ed. Shunyūdō, Vol. IV: 1934; Vol. V: 1935. Eight volumes about dialect issued from 1931 to 1938.

Hōgen do VI: 269; VIII: 269, 272.
> *Hōgen to dozoku*, Tachibana, Shōichi. Morioka. Hōgensha, No. 6, October: 1936; No. 8, February: 1937. Reprted on dialect, a total of 44 numbers.

Hōgen shi, No. 22: 8, 109, 136
> *Hōgen shi*, No. 22, Kokugakuin Daigaku Hōgen Kenkyūkai. Published by the group, September: 1939. This issue was devoted to folk tales of Kitatakaku-gun, Hizen-no-kuni (Nagasaki).

Hokuto 31: 14, 58, 107, 174
> *Hokuto*, Ikeda Shihan Gakkō Kōyūkai. Osaka. Published by the group. No. 31, December: 1930 and appendix pp. 66. Folklore in various places in Japan.

Hyugaga I: 306; II: 279
> *Hyūga no kotoba*, Two Vols., Wakayama Kōzō. Miyazaki. Published by the author. Vol. I: 1930, pp. 213; Vol. II: 1931, pp. 255. A three-volume study of dialect in Miyazaki.

Ichihara 76
> *Ichihara-gun shi*, Ichihara-gun Kyōikukai, ed. Chiba. Ichihara-gun Yakusho: 1916, pp. 1497. Records about Ichihara-gun, Chiba.

Igu 108
> *Igu-gun shi*, Igu-gun Kyōikukai. Igu-gun, Miyagi. Published by the editors: 1926, pp. 734. Records about Igu-gun, Miyagi. Records for each town or village start with a page 1.

(Old) Iki 6, 8, 16, 17, 20, 36, 39, 40, 46, 51, 57, 59, 69, 78, 105, 106, 109, 116, 154, 164, 172, 174, 177, 179, 202, 211, 220, 261, 269, 275, 292, 312, 238
> (Old) *Ikinoshima mukashibanashi shū*, Yamaguchi Asatarō. Kyōdo Kenkyūsha: 1935, pp. 261. Folk tales of Ikinoshima.

(New) Iki 31, 53, 72, 78, 156, 159, 234, 246, 257
> (New) *Ikinoshima mukashibanashi shū*, Yamaguchi Asatarō. Sanseidō: 1943, pp. 184. One of the *Zenkoku kiroku* series. Now available in a 1973 edition under the title *Nagasaki-ken Ikinoshima mukashibanashi shū*.

Inpaku dōwa 110, 125, 154, 155, 192, 205, 209, 246, 247, 313, 318
> *Inpaku dōwa*, Inpaku Shiwakai. Tottori. Yokoyama Shoten: 1925, pp. 103. Folk tales of Inaba and Hōki, now Tottori.

Inpaku min I: 64, 106, 110, 160, 247, 253, 257, 264, 318; III: 58
> *Inpaku mintan*, Tottori Kyōdo Kenkyūkai. Tottori. Published by the group. Vol. I: 1936; Vol. III: 1937. Five volumes on folklore in Tottori published between 1936 and 1938.

Inpaku mukashi 18, 106, 196
   Inpaku mukashibanashi, Inpaku Shiwakai. Tottori. Yokoyama Shoten:
   1931, pp.99. Folk tales of Tottori.
Ina 72
   Ina no densetsu, Iwasaki Kiyomi. Iida. Yamamura Shoin: 1933,
   pp.338. Legends of Ina. These are additional tales gathered after
   Densetsu no Shimoina, listed above.
Inoshishi 59, 111, 141
   Inoshishi shika tanuki, Hayakawa Kōtarō. Kyōdo Kenkyūsha: 1926,
   pp.244. Tales about wild boar, deer, and badgers.
Irō 76, 174, 185, 216
   Irō setsuden, Shimabukuro Seibin, ed. Gakugeisha: 1935, pp.208.
   This work about Okinawa, Miyako Island, appeared first in 1745.
Isawa* 42, 76, 100, 107, 139, 202, 213, 320, 328
   Isawa-gun mukashibanashi shū, Oda Hideo. Published by the author,
   perhaps in 1929. Folktales of Isawa-gun, Iwate. The author was
   imprisoned and all his works were destroyed by order of the court
   during WW II. He died in prison.
Ishikawa 24, 65, 68, 71, 97, 111, 154, 268, 269, 283, 219
   (Ishikawa-ken) *Kashima-gun shi*, Kashima-gun Jichikai, ed. Kashima-gun, Ishikawa. Published by the editors: 1928, Part One,
   pp.1071; Part Two, pp.732. Records about Kashima-gun, Ishikawa.
Iwaki 1, 3, 6, 8, 10, 18, 20, 23, 24, 26, 28, 29, 30, 33, 34, 37, 40, 42,
   48, 58, 63, 66, 67, 69, 74, 76, 80, 86, 97, 98, 100, 103, 105, 106,
   107, 111, 114, 120, 122, 126, 129, 131, 133, 134, 136, 138, 139, 140,
   150, 153, 155, 159, 164, 170, 171, 172, 174, 183, 184, 185, 193, 194,
   198, 213, 220, 221, 232, 235, 243, 247, 248, 251, 252, 253, 255, 267,
   268, 269, 274, 283, 288, 294, 304, 308, 318, 321, 328, 343
   Iwaki mukashibanashi shū, Iwasaki Toshio. Sanseidō: 1942, pp.203. A
   Zenkoku kiroku volume. Now available in a 1974 edition under the
   title *Fukushima-ken Iwaki mukashibanashi shū*.
Iwate 106
   Iwate-gun mukashibanashi shū, Sasaki Kizen. *Shumi no dozoku
   sōsho*, No. 7: 1924, pp.23. Folk tales of Iwate-gun, Iwate, compiled
   and mimeographed by the author.
Izumi 174, 185
   Izumi mukashibanashi shū, Minami Kaname. Osaka: Izumi Kyōdo
   Kenkyūkai: 1939, pp.62. Folk tales of Izumi, Osaka, bound in
   Shokoku mintan.
Jinbun I: 153, 156, 158, 213, 234, 290
   Jinbun, Motoyama Keisen, ed. Jinbun Hakkōsho, Vol. I: 1926. Only
   one number of Volume I was published.
Jinruigaku 128: 136
   Jinruigaku zasshi, Jinrui Gakkai, ed. Tokyo Imperial University, No.
   128 (Vol. XII), November, 1896. An anthropological journal published
   continuously since 1886.
Jōmō III: 282
   Jōmō bunka, Jōmō Bunkakai. Maebashi. Kankodō, Vol. III, No. 7,
   July,1937. Folklore in Gunma. This began in 1936 and has continued
   publication.
Kaga 1, 2, 3, 8, 17, 26, 28, 33, 37, 38, 39, 42, 92, 106, 107 138, 164,

174, 183, 216, 220, 221, 225, 229, 236, 238, 241, 245, 247, 268, 300, 304, 310, 313, 318, 321, 324, 325, 328, 343, 344
(Kaga) *Enuma-gun mukashibanashi shū*, Yamashita Hisao. Ogawa Shoten: 1935, pp. 164. Folk tales of Enuma-gun, Ishikawa.
Kai 10, 15, 17, 20, 30, 40, 42, 50, 52, 61, 65, 72, 76, 91, 94, 97, 100, 106, 107, 110. 111, 117, 118, 120, 130, 141, 142, 153, 160, 161, 162, 163, 164 166, 174, 175, 180, 183, 185, 188, 189, 196, 206, 215, 218, 224, 226, 227, 228, 231, 236, 239, 240, 246, 247, 261, 268, 277, 282, 297, 313, 314, 335
Kai mukashibanashi shū, Dobashi Riki. Kyōdo Kenkyūsha: 1930, pp. 348. Folk tales of Yamanashi.
Zoku Kai 1, 3, 14, 17, 30, 35, 37, 48, 60, 68, 72, 95, 98, 110, 114, 129, 142, 150, 151, 153, 156 158, 159, 160, 163, 174, 183, 185, 194, 196, 201, 207, 213, 216, 219, 224, 234, 238, 243, 244, 282, 286, 302, 304, 313, 326, 328
Zoku Kai mukashibanashi shū, Dobashi Riki. Kyōdo Kenkyūsha: 1936, pp. 473. Additional folk tales of Yamanashi.
Kamihei 54, 55, 61, 63, 73, 96, 121, 123, 129, 136, 147, 164, 268, 289, 318, 344
Kamihei-gun mukashibanashi shū, Sasaki Kizen. Sanseidō: 1943, pp. 203. Folk tales of Kamihei-gun, Iwate, mostly selected from *Kikimimi Sōshi*. A *Zenkoku kiroku* volume. Now available in a 1973 edition under the title *Iwate-ken Kamihei-gun mukashibanashi shū*.
Kamiina 246, 304
Kamiina-gun shi, Karasawa Sadajirō, ed. Kamiina-gun, Nagano: Kamiina-gun Kyōikukai Zōhan: 1921, pp. 1458. A history of Kamiina-gun.
Kamikita* 23
Kamikita-gun densetsu shū. Legends of Kamikita-gun, Aomori.
Kamimashiki 159
Kamimashiki-gun shi, Kamimashiki-gun Chō, ed. Kumamoto. Published by the editor: 1921, pp. 685. Records about Kamimashiki-gun, Kumamoto.
Kamuhara 3, 7, 8, 11, 16, 17, 19, 20, 30, 33, 34, 37, 42, 50, 59, 72, 75, 76, 97, 112, 113, 116, 117, 122, 127, 130, 131, 136, 140, 159, 163, 164, 166, 167, 169, 175, 181, 183, 184, 185, 189, 191, 193, 206, 211, 218, 220, 221, 234, 235, 238, 239, 247, 267, 269, 294, 300, 314, 318
Kamuhara yatan, Fumino Shirakoma (pen name of Iwasaki Ichirō). Genkyūsha: 1932, pp. 227. Folk tales of Minamikanbara-gun, Niigata.
Kawagoe 105, 120, 142, 229
Kawagoe chihō mukashibanashi shū, Suzuki Tōzō. Minkan Denshō no Kai: 1937, pp. 169.
Kii 35, 40, 58, 107, 246, 290, 308, 319
(Kii) *Arita-gun dōwa shū*, Moriguchi Seiichi. Mimeographed by the author: 1916, pp. 99 (folded). Folk tales of Arita-gun, Wakayama.
Kikai 8, 15, 18, 28, 31, 33, 39, 48, 50, 54, 68, 69, 72 81, 92, 93, 94, 98, 99, 105, 108, 109, 113, 118, 158, 164, ·166, 172, 173, 174, 184, 185, 188, 202, 216, 220, 221, 238, 245, 257, 268, 283, 299, 300, 306, 308, 310, 333, 336, 342
Kikaijima mukashibanashi shū, Iwakura ichirō. Sanseidō: 1943, pp. 190. Folk tales of Kikaijima. A *Zenkoku kiroku* voume. Now

available in a 1974 edition under the title *Kagoshima-ken Kikaijima mukashibanashi shū.*

Kikimimi 2, 3, 7, 11, 14, 17, 18, 19, 26, 28, 30, 32, 33, 37, 39, 42, 56, 67, 69, 72, 76, 80, 84, 91, 92, 96, 97, 100, 106, 107, 111, 128, 133, 139, 140, 145, 158, 163, 164, 167, 169, 170, 171, 174, 175, 178, 183, 185, 188, 193, 194, 198, 199, 202, 204, 206, 207, 209, 214, 216, 220, 223, 224, 232, 234, 238, 246, 247, 252 255, 259, 261, 269, 281, 284, 285, 288, 290, 293, 304, 306, 308, 309, 318, 320, 321, 328, 339, 344, 345

Kikimimi sōshi, Sasaki Kizen. Sangensha: 1931, pp. 597. Folk tales of Iwate and bordering districts. Now available in a 1964 edition from Chikuma Shobō.

Kinki I: 287

Kinki minzoku, Ota Matsuo, ed. Kobe. Kinki Minzoku Kankōkai, ed. Vol. I: 1936. A total of three volumes appeared before WW II during 1936 to 1938. It resumed publication after the war.

Kiryū 344

Kiryū Kyōdo shi, Kiryu-machi Yakuba, ed. Kiryu-machi, Yamada-gun, Gunma. Published by the editor: 1911, pp. 54. Folklore in the Kiryū district.

Kitaazumi I: 1: 148, 156, 163, 245, 247, 257; II: 2: 20, 24, 33, 68, 150, 162, 174, 214, 215, 245, 247, 268, 269, 276

Kitaazumi-gun kyōdo shikō, Kōhi densetsu hen, Shinano Kyōikukai Kitaazumi-gun Bukai, ed. Kyōdo Kenkyūsha, Vol. I, No. 1, pp. 216, and Vol. II, No. 2, both in 1930. These two volumes were followed by one more about oral traditions in Kitaazumi-gun, Nagano. Each volume had only one number.

Kitasaku 8, 60, 97, 117, 269

Kitasaku-gun kōhi densetsu shi, Kitasaku-gun Kyōikukai, ed. Nagano. Published by the editors: 1934, pp. 479. Oral traditions of Kitasaku-gun, Nagano.

Kogane 32, 33, 34, 42, 55, 67, 96, 102, 121, 139, 149, 150, 169, 245

(New) *Kogane no uma*, Moriguchi Tari. Jitsugyō no Nihonsha: 1926, pp. 149, New edition, Mikuni Shobō: 1942, pp. 236. Folk tales of Iwate. Pages from the new edition are used in the translation. The new edition was suppressed by the Jōhōkyoku during WW II, but it was the only copy for me to use. It is now available in a 1971 edition published by Miyai Shoten.

Kokugakuin 33: 257

Kokugakuin Zasshi, Kokugakuin Daigaku. Published at the university, Vol. XXXIII, No. 4: 1925. This journal has been published since 1894.

Koshiji I: 268, 269; VI: 33, 134

Koshiji, Kobayashi Zon, the 1st editor. Niigata. Vol. I: 1935; Vol. VI: 1940. Six volumes were published before WW II. Publication resumed after the war. A journal about folklore in Niigata.

Koshiki 3, 5, 6, 8, 10, 12, 16, 17, 18, 21, 26, 27, 31, 33, 36, 51, 53, 54, 55, 67, 68, 69, 70, 72 75, 97, 98, 106, 108, 109, 120, 125, 128, 133, 134, 136, 138, 152, 156, 164, 166, 169, 170, 174, 184, 185, 188, 203, 209, 210, 215, 220, 243, 301, 304, 308, 321, 323, 327, 328, 343, 344.

Koshikijima mukashibanashi shū, Iwakura Ichirō. Sanseidō: 1944, pp. 230. Folk tales of Koshikijima. A *Zenkoku kiroku* volume. Now available in a 1973 edition under the title *Kagoshima-ken Koshiki-jima mukashibanashi shū*.

Kōshō bungaku 8: 34, 42, 105, 107, 215, 304, 308, 328; 9: 33, 140, 149, 194, 199, 283, 292, 300; 10: 30, 33, 40, 42, 48, 76, 107, 147, 153, 156, 158, 247, 290, 313, 322; 11: 30, 106, 107, 110, 161, 174, 268, 273, 279, 283, 288, 289, 298, 308, 318, 328, 333

Kōshō bungaku, Kōshō Bungaku no Kai. Sakai. Edited by Miyamoto Tsuneichi. Nos. 8, 9, 10, 11: 1936. Twelve numbers of oral literture were issued between 1933 and 1936.

Kuchitanba 96, 193, 276, 283, 288

Kuchitanba kōhi shū, Kakita Isoji and Tsuboi Tadahiko, eds. Kyōdo Kenkyūsha: 1925, pp. 193. Oral traditions near Kyoto. A *Rohen sōsho* volume.

Kunohe 3, 27, 34, 106, 107, 148, 151, 160, 163, 183- 204, 206, 246, 247, 249, 250, 268, 269, 287, 288, 289, 291, 321, 323, 328

Kunohe-gun shi, Iwate-ken Kyōikukai Kunohe-gun Bukai, ed., Morioka. Published by the editor: 1936, pp. 616. Records about Kunohe-gun, Iwate.

Kyōdo I: 185

Kyōdo, Shinano Kyōikukai, ed. Nagano. Published by the editor, Vol. I: 1930-1931. Folklore in Nagano. Two volumes were published.

Kyōdo bun 30

Kyōdo bunka. Fukuoka. Kyōdo Bunka Kenkyūkai, Vol. I, No. 3, April: 1928. Local studies in folklore and culture. Publication began in 1927.

Kyōdo den 1: 16, 59, 100, 121, 199, 201, 234, 256, 304, 337, 338, 343; 2: 3, 11, 14, 33, 42, 52, 54, 206, 246, 250, 251, 345; 3: 28, 30, 92, 97, 100, 108, 158, 183, 185, 213, 253, 304, 311, 343

Kyōdo no denshō, Yamamoto Kinjirō, ed. Sendai. Miyagi-ken Kyōikukai, No. 1: 1931, pp. 253; No. 2: 1933, pp. 209; No. 3: 1935, pp. 275. A series of three books on folklore in Miyagi.

Kyōdo ken I: 30, 97, 179, 268, 320; II: 58, 107, 139, 202, 234, 256, 267, 274; III: 40, 164, 267, 278, 309; IV: 133, 234, 269, 271; V: 17, 48, 65, 72, 85, 164, 172, 302, 308; VII: 304

Kyōdo kenkyū, Yanagita Kunio and Takagi Toshio, eds. Vol. I: 1913-1914; Vol. II: 1914-1915; Vol. III: 1915-1916; Vol. 4: 1916-1917; Vol. V: 1931-1932; Vol. VII: 1933-1934. The earliest journal devoted to folklore in Japan.

Kyōdo KS* 320

Kyōdo kenkyū shiryō, Saitama-ken Joshi Shihan Gakkō Kenkyūkai, ed. No. 2: 1931. Four numbers were issued.

Kyūshū* 274

Kyūshū minzokugaku, Vol. I: 1930. Fukuoka. Kyūshū Minzoku Gakkai. One volume, of eight numbers, was published.

Masuda 119

Masuda-gun shi, Gifu-ken Masuda-gun Yakusho, ed. Published by the editor: 1916, pp. 677. Records about Masuda-gun, Gifu.

Mikawa 80

(Mikawa-no-kuni) *Nukata-gun shi*, Aichi-ken Nukata-gun Yakusho, ed. Published by the editor: 1924, pp. 649. Records about Nukata-gun, Aichi.

Minamiazumi nen 107, 268
Minamiazumi-gun nenchūgyōji, Kyōdo chōsa sōsho, dai-ichi hen,
Shinano Kyōikukai Minamiazumi-gun Bukai, ed. Kyōdo Kenkyūsha:
1935, pp. 381. A report on annual festivals and customs in Minami-
azumi-gun, Nagano.
Minamiazumi shi 22, 24
Minamiazumi-gun shi, Nagano-ken Minamiazumi-gun Hensan, ed.
Toyoshina-machi Minamiazumi-gun, Nagano. Minamiazumi Kyōikukai:
1923, pp. 1070. Records about Minamiazumi-gun, Nagano.
Minamikanbara 68, 91, 100, 106, 107, 110, 133, 135, 136, 164, 193,
219, 304, 323, 325, 328
Minamikanbara-gun mukashibanashi shū, Iwakura Ichirō. Sanseidō:
1943, pp. 212. Folk tales of Minamikanbara-gun, Niigata. A *Zenkoku
kiroku* voume. Now available in a 1974 edition under the title *Nii-
gata-ken Minamikanbara-gun mukashibanashi shū*.
Minkan II: 18
Minkan denshō, begun as an organ of Minkan Denshō no Kai. Vol. II,
No. 10, June, 1936; Vol. VII, 1939. Since April, 1949, a journal with
the same title has been published by Minzoku Gakkai.
Minzoku I: 33, 187, 290; II: 268
Minzoku, Yanagita Kunio and Okamura Chiaki, eds. Minzoku
Hakkōjo, Vol. I, No. 6, 1926. Four volumes were published.
Minzoku bun II: 13, 132
Minzoku bunka, Yamaoka Yoshimatsu, ed. Vol. II, No. 7, June, 1941.
Four volumes were published between 1940 and 1943. Resumed
after WW II.
Minzoku ken 19: 343
Minzoku kenkyū, Ichikawa, Chiba. Nihon Minzoku Kenkyūkai, No.
19, May, 1930. Fifty numbers were issued between March 1928 and
1933.
Minzokugaku I: 40; II: 30, 185, 210, 268, 279, 291, 294, 331; IV: 34,
287; V: 30, 33, 37, 106
Minzokugaku, Okamura Chiaki and Koizumi Magane, eds. Through
Vol. II, No. 10, after which it was edited by Koyama Eizō. Minzoku
Gakkai, Vol. I: 1929; Vol. II: 1930; Vol. IV: 1932; and Vol. V: 1933.
Each volume had 12 numbers. A total of five volumes.
Minzokugaku ken II: 26, 268, 269, 290
Minzokugaku kenkyū, Nihon Minzoku Gakkai. Sanseidō. Vol. II: 1936.
This is an ethnological journal which continues publication.
Minzoku sōwa 72, 96
Minzoku sōwa, Tanigawa Iwao. Sakamoto Shoten: 1926, pp. 193.
Studies in folklore.
Mitsu 37, 39, 65, 74, 86, 107, 114, 130, 205, 206, 222, 230, 234
Mitsu-gun mukashibanashi shū, Imamura Katsuomi. Sanseidō: 1943,
pp. 203. Folk tales of Mitsu-gun, Okayama. A *Zenkoku kiroku* vol-
ume. Now available in a 1974 edition under the title *Okayama-ken
Mitsu-gun mukashibanashi shū*.
Mukashibanashi 3, 16, 20, 30, 33, 39, 40, 48, 107, 110, 111, 117, 122,
125, 146, 149, 164, 175, 183, 192, 194, 206, 221, 224, 234, 235, 236,
238, 239, 247, 268, 269, 291, 304, 313, 318, 319, 343
Mukashibanashi, Ina Minzoku Kenkyūkai, Iida, Shinano Kyōdo Shup-

pansha: 1934, pp. 161. Folk tales of the Ina district in Nagano. An Introduction by Iwasaki Kiyomi.

MK I: 1, 2, 3, 5, 10, 11, 12, 14, 15, 16, 17, 18, 19, 20, 21, 26, 27, 28, 30, 33, 34, 35, 36, 37, 39, 40, 41, 42, 48, 50, 57, 58, 59, 60, 72, 74, 75, 76, 81, 86, 88, 92, 93, 97, 98, 99, 100, 103, 105, 106, 107, 109, 110, 111, 114, 115, 117, 118, 123, 125, 126, 129, 132, 133, 134, 136, 137, 138, 139, 140, 143, 153, 155, 156, 158, 164, 166, 170, 171, 174, 175, 183, 184, 185, 187, 188, 193, 194, 196, 197, 198, 199, 205, 211, 213, 214, 215, 216, 219, 220, 225, 228, 233, 236, 244, 246, 247, 250, 252, 267, 268, 269, 274, 277, 283, 288, 291, 292, 294, 301, 302, 304, 306, 308, 309, 310, 313, 318, 319, 320, 321, 323, 325, 328, 329, 341, 343

MK II: 1, 2, 3, 4, 5, 6, 7, 8, 10, 11, 14, 15, 16, 17, 18, 19, 20, 24, 26, 27, 28, 29, 30, 31, 33, 34, 35, 36, 37, 39, 40, 41, 42, 48, 50, 51, 53, 54, 57, 58, 59, 64, 67, 69, 71, 72, 73, 74, 75, 76, 77, 78, 79, 81, 84, 85, 88, 89, 90, 92, 96, 97, 100, 105, 106, 107, 108, 109, 110, 111, 112, 114, 119, 121, 123, 124, 125, 126, 127, 128, 129, 131, 132, 133, 134, 135, 136, 137, 138, 139, 140, 147, 148, 156, 157, 158, 159, 160, 163, 164, 166, 169, 170, 172, 174, 175, 181, 183, 184, 185, 193, 194, 202, 203, 205, 206, 214, 215, 218, 220, 234, 238, 239, 243, 245, 246, 250, 251, 254, 259, 265, 268, 269, 281, 283, 285, 287, 288, 292, 300, 304, 308, 317, 318, 319, 320, 321, 322, 323, 325, 327, 328, 343, 345, 346

Mukashibanashi kenkyū, Vol. I edited by Hagiwara Masanori, Vol. II edited by Seki Keigo. Vol. I: 1935-1936: Vol. II: 1936-1937. A journal devoted to the folk tale. All-Japan in scope.

Geibi 8, 11, 14, 16, 18, 19, 20, 28, 33, 39, 42, 55, 72, 75, 79, 85, 90, 105, 106, 132, 133, 134, 137, 139, 164, 170, 172, 174, 198, 207, 210, 213, 229, 232, 238, 274, 278, 325, 328

(Mukashibanashi no kenkyū) *Geibi sōsho*, Hiroshima Shihan Gakkō Kyōdo Kenkyūshitsu, ed. Hiroshima. Published by the editors: 1939, pp. 232. Field notes on folk tales by students of Hiroshima Normal School. New title: *Geibi mukashibanashi shū*, edited by Muraoka Masao.

Techō 100, 105, 107, 121, 144, 185, 239, 321

(Mukashibanashi saishū) *techō*, Yanagita Kunio and Seki Keigo. Minkan Denshō no Kai, 1936, pp. 24 and 100 tales. A handbook for collecting tales.

MB bun 18, 328

Mukashibanshi to bungaku, Yanagita Kunio. Sōgensha: 1938, pp. 351. A comparative study of selected tales and literary versions.

Mura

Mura no hanashi. See *Okunan shinpō*.

Muro 216, 309

Muro kōhi shū, Saiga Sadajirō. Kyōdo Kenkyūsha: 1927, pp. 232. Oral traditions in Wakayama. A *Rohen sōsho* volume.

Nagakubo 92

Nagakubo ni okeru nenchū gyōji, Koike Atou. Nagata-machi, Chiisagta-gun, Nagano. Published by the author: 1932, pp. 14 (folded). Local folklore.

Nanetsu 4: 210; II: 3: 260

Nanetsu minzoku, Fukui Kyōdo Kenkyūkai. Fukui. No. 4, January

1938; Vol. II, No. 3, June, 1939. Publication under this title ended with Vol. IV, No. 2, 1943.

Nanki 73, 162, 188
Nanki dozoku shiryō, Mori Hikotarō. Minabe-machi, Hidaka-gun, Wakayama. Published by the author: 1924, pp.330. Folklore in Hidaka-gun, Wakayama.

Nansō 183, 185, 213, 240, 269, 276, 283
Nansō no rizoku, Uchida Kunihiko. Ōsetsu Shooku: 1915, pp.166. Village lore in Chiba.

Nantō 30, 51, 69, 72, 75, 107, 164, 283, 284
Nantō setsuwa, Sakima Kōei. Kyōdo Kenkyūsha: 1922, pp.148. Stories about Ginowan village and vicinity on Okinawa. A *Rohen sōsho* volume.

Naori 80, 102, 126, 140, 143, 181, 213, 292, 328, 343
Naori-gun mukashibanashi shū, Suzuki Kiyomi. Sanseidō: 1943, pp.152. Folk Tales of Naori-gun, Ōita. A *Zenkoku kiroku* volume. Now available in a 1973 edition under the title *Ōita-ken Naori-gun mukashibanashi shū*.

Nara 18: 107
Nara, Takeda Jūrō, ed. No. 18: 1922. A journal of folklore.

Nihon den Harima 24
Nihon densetsu sōsho, Harima-no-maki, Fujisawa Morihiko. Nihon Densetsu Kankōkai: 1918, pp.402. Legends of Hyōgo.

Nihon den Kazusa 193, 213, 293
Nihon densetsu sōsho, Kazusa-no-maki, Fujisawa Morihiko. Nihon Densetsu Kankōkai: 1917, pp.379. Legends of Chiba. The two volumes of Fujisawa are part of a series of collection of legends named according to old provices.

Nihon den 3, 20, 27, 28, 39, 57, 72, 105, 110, 113, 160, 162, 215, 268, 269, 288, 300, 304, 319
Nihon densetsu shū, Takagi Toshio. Musashino Shoin: 1913, pp.307. The earliest collection of Japanese legends by a folklorist in Japan.

Nihon dōwa 30, 34, 35, 36, 152, 178, 183, 202, 213, 228, 235, 300, 328, 334, 343
Nihon dōwa shū, Matsumura Takeo. Sekai Dōwa Taikei Kankōkai: 1924, pp.955. This volume of Japanese children's stories is Vol. XVI of *Seki dōwa taikei*, a series of world children's stories.

Nihon dōwa shin ken 267, 300, 322, 325
Nihon dōwa no shin kenkyū, Nakata Senpo. Bunyūsha: 1926, pp.497. A study of selected children's stories.

Nihon kayō 234
Nihon kayō ruijū, ge, Owada Tateki. Hakubunkan: 1898, pp.1016.

Nihon shū, jō 3, 33, 34, 71, 119, 180, 269, 271, 285, 290, 300, 306, 308, 342
Nihon mukashibanashi shū, jō, Yanagita Kunio. Ars: 1930, pp.242. A selection of folk tales made by Yanagita.

Nihon shū, ge 18, 34, 35, 51, 105, 125, 140, 328
Nihon mukashibanashi shū, ge, Kindaichi Kyōsaku, Tanaka Umekichi, Iha Fuyū, and Sayama Yūkichi. Ars: 1929, 248. Folk tales from the Ainu and Okinawa, Korea, and Formosa.

Nihon zenkoku 6, 26, 33, 37, 42, 88, 100, 106, 125, 132, 136, 141,

153, 155, 156, 158, 161, 174, 178, 225, 235, 238, 306, 309, 318, 321,
328, 343
(Nihon zenkoku) *Kokumin dōwa*, Ishii Kendō. Dōbunkan: 1911,
pp. 433. The earliest attempt to collect oral tales for children.
Nishisanuki 66
Nishisanuki mukashibanashi shū, Takeda Akira. Marugame. Kagawa-
ken Marugame Kōjo Kyōdo Kenkyūshitsu, ed. Published by editors:
1941, pp. 120. Folk tales from Kagawa.
Nobechi 8
Nobechi hōgen shū, Nakaichi Kenzō. Sangensha: 1936, pp. 177.
Dialect of the Nobechi district in Kamikita-gun, Aomori.
Nomi 20, 22, 156, 216
Nomi-gun shi, Ishikawa-ken, Nomi-gun Yakuba. Published by editors:
1923, pp. 1621. Records about Nomi-gun, Ishikawa.
Nōmin 206
Nōmin ritan, Sasaki Kizen and Motoyama Keisen. Isseisha: 1934,
pp. 195. Beliefs and tales found in rural communities of Iwate. This
volume contains biographical information about Sasaki.
Noto 57, 142
Noto meiseki shi, Ishikawa-ken Toshokan Kyōkai, ed. Published by
the editors: 1931, pp. 158. This is a modern printing of *Noto-no-
kuni meiseki shi* (1778) attributed to Ota Yorimoto (Michikane) and
other similar works, edited by the association of librarians in Ishi-
kawa.
Ōawa 33
Ōawa no yokogao, Yokoyama Harushige. Tokushima. Tokushima
Nichinichi Shinpōsha: 1934, pp. 703. About Tokushima, Shikoku.
Ōchi 3
Ōchi-gun shi, Moriwaki Ta'ichi. Matsue. Shōbundō: 1937, pp. 1384.
Records of Ōchi-gun, Shimane.
Okayama rekishi II: 11, 229
Okayama rekishi chiri. Okayama. Okayama Rekishi Chiri Gakkai,
Vol. II, No. 2, March, 1935. A publication of the group. Vol. I, No. 1
in November, 1934; Vol. II, No. 3 in May 1935.
Okayama bun II: 21, 34, 85, 164, 189, 195; III: 33, 106, 107, 328.
Okayama-ken bunka shiryō. Okayama. Okayama Bunken Kenkyūkai,
Vol. II: 1929-1939; Vol. III: 1930-1931. A total of three volumes was
published.
Okinoerabu 8, 53, 54, 75, 98, 105, 109, 136, 172, 174, 184, 198, 210
Okinoerabu mukashibanashi, Iwakura Ichirō. Minkan Denshō no Kai:
1943. Available in an edition from Kokan Shoin, 1955, pp. 334.
Pages in this translation are from the later edition. The tales were
collected in May and June of 1936.
Okinoshima 3, 30, 107, 110, 150, 158, 183, 318
Okinoshima mukashibanashi to hōgen, Yokochi Manji and Asada
Yoshirō. Yokoichi-mura, Shikama-gun, Hyōgo: Kyōdo Bunkasha:
1936, pp. 85. Folk tales and dialect of Oki Islands, Shimane.
Okunan* 58, 164, 169
Okunan shinpō, Hachinohe, Aomori. This newspaper published a
column, "Mura no hanashi" (Village Tales) over a period of years.
References within this translation are either explained in the text

or identified with *Mukashibanashi kenkyū*, which made selections from it.

Ono 18
> *Ono-mura nenchū gyōji*, Nakamura Toraichi, ed. Kamiina Shi Hensankai: 1956, pp.49. This is a reproduction of an earlier study of village celebrations at Ono.

Osa 259
> *Osa-mura nenchū gyōji*, Hakoyama Kitarō, ed. Ueda, Nagano: 1935, pp.224. The editor is a folklorist living at Koida, Ueda, Nagano.

Oshō 150, 183, 225, 245
> *Oshō to kozō*, Nakata Senpo. Sakamoto Shoten: 1927, pp.246. Stories about a priest and his novice.

Otari 30, 60, 106, 137, 163, 170, 177, 268, 269, 280, 288, 321
> *Otari kōhi shū*, Koike Naotarō, ed. Kyōdo Kenkyūsha: 1922, pp.219. Legends in the northern tip of Kitaazumi-gun, Nagano. A *Rohen sōsho* volume.

Rōō 17, 18, 20, 30, 38, 39, 42, 54, 55, 57, 59, 60, 62, 65, 69, 70, 72, 86, 88, 89, 91, 96, 98, 106, 116, 119, 130, 136, 140, 141, 149, 150, 152, 155, 164, 169, 174, 175, 176, 183, 184, 185, 188, 191, 192, 198, 206, 209, 214, 219, 246, 310, 327
> *Rōō yatan*, Sasaki Kizen. Kyōdo kenkyūsha: 1927, pp.355. Most of these tales were recited by Haneishi Tanei, an old woman who lived near Sasaki's home in Iwate.

Sado shū 8, 18, 20, 37, 88, 126, 132, 164, 172, 204, 219, 238, 343
> *Sado mukashibanashi shū*, Suzuki Tōzō. Minkan Denshō no Kai: 1939, pp.280. Now available in a 1973 edition from Sanseidō under the title *Niigata-ken Sado mukashibanashi shū*. This is the early collection by Suzuki from Sado Island, Niigata.

Sado 78, 172
> *Sado no mukashibanashi*, Fukurakuan (pen name of Matsuda Yokichi). Mano-mura, Sado-gun, Niigata. Ikeda Shoten: 1937, pp.210. A collection of Sado tales.

Sadogashima 36, 39, 50, 114, 143, 172, 187
> *Sadogashima, mukashibanashi shū*, Suzuki Tōzō. Sanseidō: 1942. pp.191. Folk tales from Sado, mostly those selected from his earlier work. A *Zenkoku kiroku* volume.

Sakurada 72
> Sakurada Katsunori. A folklorist who reported to Yanagita.

Sangaku XIX: 111
> *Sangaku*. Nihon Sangakukai (Japan Alpinist Club), Vol. XIX, No. 3, February, 1925. This publication began in 1906 and continues to the present except for an interruption due to the war.

Sanshū Taka 197
> *Sanshū Takamatsu sōshi*, Miyatake Shōzō. Takamatsu. Published by the author: 1925, pp.178. Folklore in Kagawa.

Sanshū Yoko 196, 269, 304
> *Sanshū Yokoyama banashi*, Hayakawa Kōtarō. Kyōdo Kenkyūsha: 1921, pp.123. Folklore of Yokoyama, Aichi. A *Rohen sōsho* volume.

Sanuki 1*: 72; 8: 137.
> *Sanuki minzoku*, Takeda Akira, ed., Tadotsu, Kagawa. Sanuki Minzoku Kenkyūkai, No. 1, December, 1938: No. 8, not available. Folklore of Kagawa.

Sanuki SS 232
Sanuki Sanagi Shishijima mukashibanashi shū, Takeda Akira. Sansei-dō: 1944, pp. 156. Folk tales of Sanagi and Shishijima Islands of Shikoku. A *Zenkoku kiroku* volume. Now available in a 1973 edition under the title *Kagawa-ken Sanagi Shishijima mukashibanashi shū*.

Satte 291
Satte dōyō shū, Ueno Isamu. Satte-machi, Kitakatsushika-gun, Saitama. Published by the author: 1933, pp. 35. Children's songs and riddles.

Setonaikai 53
Setonaikai tōsho junpō nikki, Attic Museum, ed. Attic Museum: 1940, pp. 349. Notes about islands in the Inland Sea.

Shidara 15: 122
Shidara, Shidara Minzoku Kenkyūkai. Sanrin-mura, Kitashidara-gun, Aichi. Published by the group. No. 15, January, 1937. A journal on local folklore.

Shima I: 6, 9, 44, 92, 111, 172, 174 199; II: 8, 17, 68, 82, 92, 107, 166, 167, 172, 174, 184, 185, 191, 218, 226, 247
Shima, Yanagita Kunio and Hika Shunchō, eds. Published by the editors, Vol. I: 1933; Vol. II: 1934. The first volume had six numbers. The second was a single issue.

Shimabara 6, 7, 8, 11, 12, 14, 16, 18, 19, 25, 27, 28, 30, 32, 38, 65, 72, 107, 125, 145, 147, 150, 154, 155, 156, 161, 175, 177, 183, 199, 206, 216, 217, 218, 220, 222, 228, 234, 237, 247, 252, 255, 291, 297, 303
Shimabara hantō minwa shū, Seki Keigo. Kensetsusha: 1935, pp. 348. The first collection of tales by Seki.

Shimabara shū 50, 51, 55, 56, 97, 105, 106, 159, 168, 171, 193, 194, 211, 214, 215, 216, 218, 239, 245, 266, 304, 308, 318, 325, 332
Shimabara hantō mukashibanashi shū, Seki Keigo. Sanseidō: 1942, pp. 186. Most of the items are from the earlier work. A *Zenkoku kiroku* volume.

Shimane 162, 171
Shimane-ken kōhi densetsu shū, Shimane Kyōikukai, ed. Matsue. Published by he editors: 1927, pp. 342. Legends and oral tales of Shimane. Items from each city and gun begin from a page 1.

Shimane min I: 4: 57
Shimane minzoku, Shimane Minzoku Gakkai. Matsue. Published by the group. Vol. I, No. 4, April, 1939. Folklore in Shimane.

Shimizu 249
Shimizu Hyōzō. The reference to *Izumo no dōwa* by Shimizu is to an unpublished work. He contributed tales to *Kyōdo kenkyū* and *Tabi to densetsu*.

Shimominochi 33, 34, 42, 48, 133
Shimominochi-gun shi, Shimominochi Kyōikukai, ed. Nagano. Published by the editors: 1918, pp. 217. Records of Shimominochi-gun, Nagano.

Shimotsuke 14, 24, 30, 35, 48, 49, 55, 65, 102, 105, 106, 107, 170, 174, 178, 183, 188, 193, 198, 206, 213, 216, 234, 236, 237, 243, 245, 246, 247, 327
Shimotsuke Motegi mukashibanashi shū, Katō Keichi, ed. Sangensha: 1935, pp. 95. Folk tales of Tochigi.

Shintatsu 6, 20, 188, 321
  Shintatsu mintan shū, Kondo Kiichi (One of Yanagita Kunio's pen
  names), Kyōdo kenkyūsha: 1928, pp.207. Tales from Shinobu and
  Date gun in Fukushima. A *Rohen sōsho* volume.
Shinwa* 257
  Shinwa to densetsu. Compiled by Kagoshima Shōgakkō.
Shiwa 1, 10, 18, 34, 42, 51, 57, 69, 88, 92, 100, 115, 136, 147, 172,
  177, 183, 191, 194, 216, 218, 220, 247, 252, 254, 307, 316
  Shiwa-gun mukashibanashi, Sasaki Kizen. Kyōdo Kenkyūsha: 1926,
  pp.238. Folk tales of Shiwa-gun, Iwate. A *Rohen sōsho* volume.
Shiwa shū 3, 8, 16, 17, 30, 33, 34, 37, 39, 42, 50, 54, 62, 72, 76, 80,
  81, 96, 98, 106, 107, 114, 117, 130, 133, 150, 156, 164, 170, 172,
  174, 180, 185, 188, 190, 202, 204, 206, 210, 211, 213, 224, 234, 238,
  239, 246, 253, 304, 318, 325, 343
  Shiwa-gun mukashibanashi shū, Ogasawara Kenkichi. Sanseidō: 1942,
  pp.173. Ogasawara wished to have his tales set down his way. A
  Zenkoku kiroku volume. Now available in a 1973 edition under the
  title *Iwate-ken Shiwa-gun mukashibanashi shū.*
Shizuoka 10, 28, 30, 33, 34, 35, 38, 40, 42, 47, 48, 50, 57, 77, 78, 92,
  107, 140, 180, 198, 215, 216, 268, 269, 270, 279, 281, 283, 291, 302,
  303, 304, 308, 309, 328
  Shizuoka-ken densetsu mukashibanashi shū, Shizuoka-ken Joshi
  Shihan Gakkō Kyōdo Kenkyūkai, ed. Shizuoka. Shizuoka Yajimaya
  Shoten: 1934, pp.512. Folk tales gathered by the group at Shizuoka
  Women's Normal School.
Shōdojima 106, 107, 243, 246
  Shōdojima minzoku shi, Kawano Masao. A manuscript written in late
  Taisho or early Showa. Although several tales were selected, the
  manuscript is now lost.
Shokoku (a bound volume of several works)
  Shokoku mintan. This is a title given a bound volume of several col-
  lections, but it is not a publication.
Shokoku mono 68, 162, 174
  Shokoku monogatari, Suzuki Kanekichi, ed. Osaka. Asahi Shinbunsha:
  1924, pp.315. A selection of tales and legends.
Shumi 96, 234, 246
  Shumi no densetsu, Igarashi Chikara. Nishōdō Shoten: 1913, pp.476.
  A collection of legends and tales.
Sōshū 197, 269, 281, 290, 291, 293
  Sōshū Uchigo-mura banashi, Suzuki Shigemitsu, ed. Kyōdo Kenkyū-
  sha: 1924, pp.165. Folklore of Uchigo-mura, Tsukui-gun, Kanagawa.
  A *Rohen sōsho* volume.
Suō 14, 18, 30, 34, 69, 156, 159, 208, 229, 235, 300, 302, 318
  Suō Ōshima mukashibanashi shū, Miyamoto Tsuneichi. Tachibana-
  machi, Ōshima-gun, Yamaguchi. Ōshima Bunka Kenkyū Renmei:
  1956, pp.119. This is a printing of a manuscript of material gather-
  ed between 1930 and 1940. It escaped bombing because it happened
  to be in the hands of Yanagita. Miyamoto's entire library in his
  home was burned.
Susō 42
  Susō-gun kyōdo ihō, Ehime Kenritsu Susō Kōtō Jogakkō. Susō-gun,

Ehime. Published by the group. Vol. I: July, 1931. Local customs and traditions reported by students.

TD I: 11, 65, 97, 106, 171, 185, 213, 242, 243, 259; II: 14, 27, 30, 81, 150, 155, 194, 290; III: 16, 30, 68, 106, 147, 153, 158, 162, 171, 196, 210, 243, 261, 268, 279; IV: 34, 68, 147, 271, 279, 304; V: 1, 245; VI: 10; VII: 97; IX: 30, 32, 48, 199, 318, 320, 325, 340; X: 6, 14, 17, 30, 33, 50, 72, 92, 164, 172, 185, 237; XI: 128, 317; XII: 3, 30, 67, 128, 139, 238, 257, 269, 302, 329; XIII: 77, 122, 143, 254

Tabi to densetsu, Hagiwara Masanori, ed. Vol. I through XIII, 1928-1941. Published from 1928 to 1944. The volumes featured travel and local customs and tales.

Tabi kyō* 1: 40

Tabi to kyōdo, Vol. 1. This was published by Hokutosha. A total of seven volumes.

Techō. See *Mukashibanashi saishū techō*.

Tekkiri 11, 20, 28, 30, 65, 198, 199, 208, 215, 268, 269, 288, 300, 304, 317, 320, 328

Tekkiri ane sama, Noda Tayoko, Miraisha: 1958, pp. 355. This is the publication of the *Gonohe mukashibanashi* manuscript.

Tome 96, 107, 185

Tome-gun shi, Tome-gun Gunyakusho, ed. Tome-gun, Miyagi. Published by the editor: 1923, Part Two, pp. 1069. Records of Tome-gun.

Tōno 3, 30, 34, 59, 102, 106, 118, 151, 160, 162, 188, 194, 199, 269, 277

Tōno monogatari, Yanagita Kunio. Kyōdo Kenkyūsha: 1935, pp. 434, an enlarged edition. The first printing was by Shūseidō: 1910. Local tradition and customs in the Tōno region, Iwate.

Tōō 39, 45

Tōō ibun, Sasaki Kizen. Sakamoto Shoten: 1926, pp. 178. Folklore of eastern Iwate.

Tōtōmi 269, 283, 288

Tōtōmi dōshiyō shū, Nakamichi Sakuji. Shizuoka. Oka Shoin: 1935, pp. 284. A collection of children's songs and poems in the Tōtōmi region, now a part of Shizuoka and Aichi.

Tōtsubito V 8: 185

Tōtsubito, Shimosa Danwakai Kiroku. Teradai (now Narita), Chiba. Published by the group. Vol. V, No. 8, September, 1939. A journal published by a group of young writers.

Toyosato 76, 148, 193

Toyosato-son shi, Satō Toyoharu, ed. Toyosato-mura, Mogami-gun, Yamagata. Toyosato Yakuba: 1929, pp. 277. Records about the village Toyosato.

Tsuchi iro V: 304, 234; XIII: 73

Tsuchi no iro, Iio Tetsuji, ed. Hamamatsu. Hamamatsu Kodomo Kyōkai, Vol. V, No. 4: 1928; Vol. XIII (No. 67): 1934. Tales and poems gathered by the group.

Tsuchi ka XVI: 279

Tsuchi no ka, Kaga Haruo, ed. Okoshi-machi, Nakajima-gun, Aichi. Dozoku Shumisha, Vol. XVI, No. 5: 1935. Folklore in Aichi. The group was called Dozoku Shumisha in Okoshi.

Tsugaru K 1, 34, 42, 48, 56, 70, 100, 136, 164, 179, 199, 203, 204, 216, 268, 273, 298, 304, 318, 319, 320, 325
Tsugaru kōhi shū, Uchida Kunihiko. Kyōdo Kenkyūsha: 1937, pp. 251. Oral traditions of Tsugaru, Aomori.
Tsugaru M 3, 17, 18, 30, 33, 34, 36, 42, 48, 54, 58, 59, 100, 107, 114, 133, 136, 164, 179, 182, 183, 203, 206, 211, 232, 238 247, 304, 318, 319, 320, 321, 325, 343
Tsugaru no mugashiko shū, Kawai Yūtarō. Aomori. Tōō Nippōsha: 1930, pp. 142. Folk tales of Tsugaru, Aomori.
Ugo 1, 3, 11, 23, 37, 70, 72, 88, 92, 106, 107, 162, 202, 204, 212, 220, 268, 269, 287, 288, 289, 313, 323, 328
(Ugo) *Kakunodate chihō ni okeru chōchū sōmoku no minzokugaku-teki shiryō*, Moto Tetsujō. Attic Museum: 1935, pp. 354. Folklore about birds, insects, plants, and trees in Akita. The title is frequently abbreviated in various ways.
Utsushibana 43, 73, 74, 136, 245
Ustushibana, Sawada Shirōsaku. Osaka. Published by the author: 1941, pp. 126. This was published as No. 10 of *Fushi zappitsu*.
Yachō XIV: 3: 279
Yachō, Vol. XIV, No. 3, March, 1937. A journal devoted to birds that has been in publication since 1934.
Yachō zakki 278
Yachō zakki, Yanagita Kunio, Kōchō Shorin: 1940, pp. 268. One of two volumes on folklore and nature. The other is *Yasō zakki*, dealing with plants.
Yamato 35, 46
Yamato no densetsu, Takada Jūrō. Nara. Yamato Shiseki Kenkyūkai: 1933, pp. 345. Local traditions.
Yambaru 30, 75
Yambaru no dozoku, Shimabukuro Genshichi. Kyōdo Kenkyūsha: 1929, pp. 287. Folklore on Okinawa. A *Rohen sōsho* volume.
Zen Nagasaki 345
(Zen) *Nagasaki kayōshū*, Murata Yoichi, ed. Kōransha: 1931. pp. 454. A collection of traditional songs in Nagasaki.

Reference Index

Numbers refer to the tale groups in which the reference is found.

INDEX TO NON-JAPANESE REFERENCES

Aesop 318
Johannes Bolte und Georg Polivka, *Anmerkungen zu den Kinder-u. Hausmärchen der Brüder Grimm*, Vol. 5. Leipzig: Dieterich, 1913. 48, 170, 174, 211
Chamberlain, B.H., "The language, mythology and geographical nomenclature of Japan viewed in the light of 'An Ainu Grammer' by John Batchelor and a catalogue of books relating to Yezo and the Ainos," *Ainu minzoku kenkyū shiryō* I 31 (Tokyo Imperial University, 1887). 125
Clouston, W.A., *Popular Tales and Fictions, Their Migrations and Transformations*, 2 vols., London and Edinburgh: William Blackwood & Sons, 1887. 98, 164, 174, 178, 218, 225
Huet, Gideon Busken, *Les Contes Populaires*. Paris: E. Flammarion, 1923. 8, 34, 57, 169, 171, 214, 220, 246, 290, 318
Milne, Mrs. Leslie, *Shans at Home, with Two Chapters on Shan History and Literature by Rev. Wilbur Willis Cochrane*. London: John Murray, 1910. 8, 11
Yearsley, McLeod, *The folklore of the Fairy Tale*. London: Watts & Co., 1924. 8, 18, 35, 37, 48, 50, 52, 57, 88, 92, 100,298

Glossary

afuri: A word among others in the tale that are not explained.
Ama Otome: Said to be the deity of Nijūsanya; see Nijūsanya.
amanojaku or amanjaku: A demon with feminine attributes.
ame: Sweet gluten.
an: Sweet bean paste.
anmochi: mochi covered with sweet bean paste; see mochi.
Aomori Gongen: See Gongen.
asanarō or asunarō: A magic plant.
Atago: A deity associated with ancestral worship.
azuki: A small red bean.
Azuki rice: Red beans steamed with glutenous rice for a festive occasion (also called sekihan).

Bashū-no-shū: Worship related to the head of a horse.
Benjo-no-kami: See kami.
Biwa: A lute.
bonboko: See bunbuku.
bosama: See zatō.
botamochi: See ohagi.
bu: One percent or a coin of low denomination.
Buddha: A great Buddhist deity, often referred to as Hotoke or Shaka.
bumbuku: An onomatopoeic term for boiling water written with the character for good fortune.

Chinju: The deity of the locality or the village.
chō: A measurement of 119 yards or 2.45 acres.
chōja: One upon whom unexpected good fortune is bestowed—a man, a woman, a couple, or a family.

Daigongen: A Great Temporary Manifestation of a deity, usually with a place name Fukayama Daigongen, the Great Temporary Manifestation at Fukayama.
Daikoku: A deity of good fortune; also the principal supporting pillar of the roof.
daimyō: A feudal lord.
Daimyōjin: A Great Manifestation.
  Inari Daimyōjin: The Great Manifestation of Inari.
  Nekoza Daimyōjin: The Great Manifestation of a Cat.
  Ohera Daimyōjin: The Great Manifestation in the Ladle.
dango: A small ball made into a cake from glutenous rice flour or other material.
dengaku: Fried tofu with miso on it; see tōfu and miso.
dote: A spectral bird.

Ebisu: A deity of good fortune.
ekisha: A diviner.

Festival of the 5th Day of the Fifth Month: Often called the Iris
   Festival.
Festival of the 7th Day of the Seventh Month: Often called Tanabata.
Fukayama Daigongen: See Daigongen.
Fuku-no-kami: See Kami.
fukude mochi: See mochi.
furoshiki: A cloth used for wrapping things that are carried.

gajimaru: A tropical tree.
gamarijaku: See amanojaku.
gami: See Kami.
ge: The last part of a two or three volume work.
geta: Wooden clogs.
gidayu: A dramatic recital accompanied by music.
gō: A unit of capacity, one tenth of a shō
Gongen: A temporary Manifestation of a deity or a sacred place.
   Aomori Gongen
   Hakusan Gongen
   Hiko-san Gongen
goyō: A highly esteemed variety of pine.
goze: A blind female ballad singer.
gun: An administrative district within a prefecture.

Haguro: The name of a sacred mountain.
Hakama: A loose divided skirt.
Hakusan Gongen: See Gongen.
Hana-no-kami: See Kami.
Hannya: God of wisdom.
Hata-no-kami: See Kami.
Hatsu mizu: First Water drawn at New Year.
Hatsu yume: First Dream of New Year (on the 2nd Night).
hayamonogatari: A brief humorous tale recited rapidly.
hei: A shinto symbol used in purification rites.
Hi-no-kami: See Kami.
Higan: The observance during Equinox.
Hiko-san Gongen: See Gongen.
hōin: See yamabushi.
hōji: A Budldhist memorial service.
hokekyō: A play on words: the cry of the nightingale and the name of
   a sutra.
Hōki-gami: The broom deity usually present at parturition.
hongure: Acorns or testes.
hōsha: A priest like a yamabushi.
hōshi: A general name for a Buddhist priest.
   mekura hōshi: See zatō.
Hotoke: A name used for Buddha or an ancestral spirit.
   Ki-botoke: A piece of a tree worshiped as the image of Buddha.
Hyottoko: A god of luck.

Inari: The field deity.
   Inari Daimyōjin: See Daimyōjin.
Ise: The Grand Shrine of Shinto faith.

Jizō: A Buddhist Bodhisattva that has become identified as a kami. He may be a single Jizō or a group of six or twelve figures.
    Koyasu Jizō: Protector of children.
Jō: The first volume of a two or three volume work.
Jōdo: Paradise.
joruri: A recital about heroes rendered with musical accompaniment.

kachi-kachi: An onomatopoeic term written various ways to refer to the sound of striking flint or burning brush.
kaimochi: See ohagi.
Kami or gami: A deity.
    Benjo-no-kami: Deity of the Privy.
    Fuku-no-kami: Deity of Good Fortune.
    Hana-no-kami: Deity of the Nose.
    Hata-no-kami: Deity of the Loom.
    Hi-no-kami: Deity of the Fire (in the kitchen).
    Hōki-gami: Deity of the Broom.
    Kane-no-kami: Deity of Gold.
    Ki-no-kami: Deity of a Tree.
    Mizu-no-kami: Deity of Water.
    Neko-no-kami: A Cat Deity.
    Sai-no-kami: Deity of the Border or to the approach to a village.
    Sai-no-kami: Deity of Dice.
    Ujigami: The clan deity or tutelary deity.
    Yama-no-kami: Mountain Deity.
kan: A unit of weight; also called kanme.
Kane-no-kami: See Kami.
Kannon: A Buddhist deity usually given feminine attributes; usually enshrined, but one that appears in revelations and dreams.
    Kamoe Kannon: Kannon at Kamoe
    Senju Kannon: Kannon with 1000 hands.
    Kōshin Kannon: Kannon associated with the Kōshin observance; see Kōshin.
kappa: A creature associated with streams.
kasha: A kind of ghost.
katarimono: A story recited to musical accompaniment.
kaya: Thatch (torrera nucifera).
ken: A prefecture.
Ki-no-kami: See Kami.
Kō-jin: See Shin (Jin).
koku: A measurement of capacity, about two bushels.
komekura: A word play on rice storehouse and little blind men.
Kōshin: An observance on the night the two calendar signs of Kanoe (8th calendar sign) and Saru (monkey) coincide. See Nijūsanya.
kotatsu: A frame covered with a quilt set over live coals as a warmer.
Koyase Jizō: See Jizō.
Koyasu son: A deity to protect the birth of a child.
kunotsu: A magic bird.
kyōgen: A comic interlude.

mandara: A picture of Buddhist paradise.

manjū: A steamed bun filled with sweet bean paste.

medetashi: An exclamation to the happy ending of a story.

mihagusa: A kind of plant.

mikankō: A magic cat.

miko: A woman with a special role in folk faith, a shamaness.

miso: fermented bean paste.

Mizu-no-kami: See Kami.

mochi: rice cake which is made by pounding steamed glutenous rice. This rice is used only on festive occasions. Besides steamed and pounded, the glutenous rice is ground into flour to make various cakes.

mon: A coin of low monetary value.

muri: dialect for mori, meaning leak.

namu amida butsu: Words in a Buddhist prayer.

namu toraya: "Hail, Tiger Cat."

nara pears: A wild fruit.

Neko-gami: See Kami.

Nekoza Daimyōjin: See Daimyōjin.

Nijūsanya San: See San.

nishiki ki: uconymus alta.

nushi: A guardian spirit in a tree, rock, pond, or the like.
　　Mizu-no-nushi: Water Spirit.
　　Kumo-no-nushi: Spider Spirit.

o (omote): The upper side of a folded page.

obi: A sash.

ohagi: A dango covered with sweet bean paste served at festivals.

oni-baba: An old she-demon.

Onigashima: A fictitious demon stronghold.

ōnyūdō: A kind of ghost.

oshō: A Buddhist priest.

osōshi: The same as ekisha, a diviner.

Raijin: See Shin (Jin).

rakugo: A comical story usually ending in a word play.

renga: A poem chain.

ri: A measure of distance, about two and a half miles.

rokubu: A mendicant pilgrim.

ryō: A coin of high monetary value.

Ryūgu: Dragon Palace, approached from the sea, a stream, a cave, or a tree.

Ryūjin: See Shin (Jin).

ryūsengan: A magic object.

Sai-no-kami: See Kami.

sake: Rice wine.

samurai: A warrior usually attached to a feudal lord.

san, sama, son: An honorific attached to the name of a shrine or festival to refer the deity at the place or a festival or an object.
　　Atago Sama: A deity associated with ancestral worship.
　　Nichirin San: The Sun.

Nijūsanya San: The deity on the 23rd Night or Kōshin.

Ryūgu San: The deity at the Dragon Palace.

Shōgatsu San: The New Year Deity.

Tanabata San: The deity of the festival of the 7th Day of the Seventh Month.

Tentō San: The Sun.

satori: The name of a ghost.

sembei: A wafer made of rice flour.

Shaka: See Buddha.

shamisen: A three-stringed musical instrument.

Shichi Fukujin: See Shin (Jin).

Shin or Jin: Another reading for the character for kami.

Kōjin: Deity of the kitchen hearth.

Raijin: Thunder deity.

Ryūjin: Dragon Deity, sometimes given feminine attributes.

Shichi Fukujin: A group of seven deities popular at New Year.

Toshitokujin: A New Year Deity.

Yakujin or Yakubō: Deity of Pestilence.

shingaku: A teaching of ethical practices.

shō: A measure of capacity, about one and a half quarts.

Shōgatsu San: See san.

shōgun: Highest ranking civilian official. Official ranks in tales are vague.

shōji: An official representative of the feudal lord.

shōya: The village official answering to the feudal lord.

son: Title of veneration.

sun: A measure of length, about one inch.

Suzume-no-miya: Sparrow Shrine.

tabi: Footwear sewn from cloth.

tabi sō: An itinerant priest.

Tanabata: Vega, the Weaver Star.

tara: A kind of tree.

tengu: A demon that flies.

tenko: A ghost animal.

Tentō San: See San.

to: A measure of capacity ten times greater than a shō.

tōfu: Bean curd.

toragame: A kind of jar.

toranomaki: A magic object.

torii: The gate at the approach to a shrine.

tororo: Grated yam.

Toshitokujin: See Shin (Jin).

tsukigusa: A kind of plant.

u (ura): The underside of a folded page.

Ujigami: See Kami.

Untoko: A little lucky deity.

Yahiko: A sacred mountain.

Yakujin: See Shin (Jin).

Yakushi: A Buddhist deity, a god of healing.

Yama-no-kami: See Kami.

Yamabushi: A priest living in mountains and serving rural areas.

Yamachichi: A malevolent male encountered in mountains; also, yamajii or yamaotoko.

Yamauba: A female, usually malevolent, encountered in mountains; also, yamanba, yamaonna, or yamababa.

yatsumetō: A sword.

yuta: See miko.

zatō: A blind itinerant musician traveling a fixed route and often belonging to a group housed in a temple. Zatō told stories and entertained hosts where they were put up.

An Alphabetical List of
Titles with Tale Numbers

Titles printed in *italics* are those indicated by Yanagita Kunio as being of particular importance.

Alphabetical List of
Japanese Titles to Tale-Types

Titles printed in *italics* are those indicated by Yanagita Kunio as being of particular importance.

Geographical Index

Numbers indicate the tales in which the prefectures are represented.

Maps

OLD PROVINCES OF JAPAN

1 Mutsu
2 Ugo
3 Rikuchū
4 Sado
5 Uzen
6 Rikuzen
7 Echigo
8 Iwashiro
9 Iwaki
10 Noto
11 Etchū
12 Shinano
13 Kōzuke
14 Shimotsuke
15 Hitachi
16 Kaga
17 Hida
18 Kai
19 Musashi
20 Shimōsa
21 Kazusa
22 Awa
23 Sagami
24 Izu
25 Suruga
26 Echizen
27 Mino
28 Owari
29 Mikawa
30 Tōtōmi
31 Wakasa
32 Ōmi

33 Ise
34 Shima
35 Tango
36 Tanba
37 Yamashiro
38 Iga
39 Tajima
40 Harima
41 Settsu
42 Kawachi
43 Izumi
44 Yamato
45 Kii
46 Awaji

47 Inaba
48 Hōki
49 Mimasaka
50 Bizen
51 Bitchū
52 Izumo
53 Bingo
54 Iwami
55 Aki
56 Nagato
57 Suō
58 Iyo
59 Sanuki
60 Awa

61 Tosa
62 Chikuzen
63 Buzen
64 Hizen
65 Chikugo
66 Bungo
67 Higo
68 Hyūga
69 Satsuma
70 Ōsumi
71 Tsushima
72 Iki
73 Oki
74 Ezo

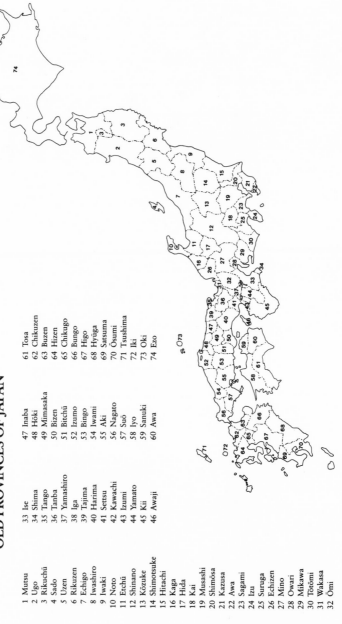

PROVINCES OF MODERN JAPAN

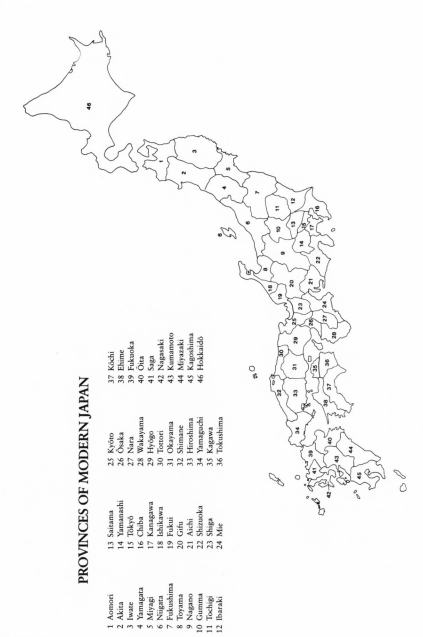

1 Aomori	13 Saitama	25 Kyōto	37 Kōchi
2 Akita	14 Yamanashi	26 Ōsaka	38 Ehime
3 Iwate	15 Tōkyō	27 Nara	39 Fukuoka
4 Yamagata	16 Chiba	28 Wakayama	40 Ōita
5 Miyagi	17 Kanagawa	29 Hyōgo	41 Saga
6 Niigata	18 Ishikawa	30 Tottori	42 Nagasaki
7 Fukushima	19 Fukui	31 Okayama	43 Kumamoto
8 Toyama	20 Gifu	32 Shimane	44 Miyazaki
9 Nagano	21 Aichi	33 Hiroshima	45 Kagoshima
10 Gumma	22 Shizuoka	34 Yamaguchi	46 Hokkaidō
11 Tochigi	23 Shiga	35 Kagawa	
12 Ibaraki	24 Mie	36 Tokushima	